The 1880 Cherokee Nation Census Indian Territory (Oklahoma)

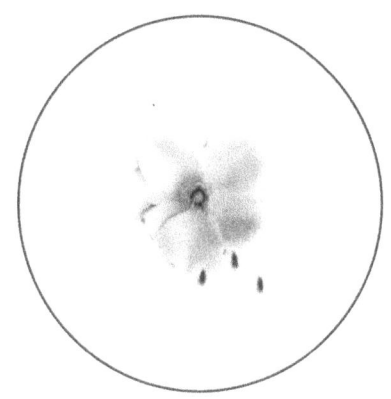

Book One

Transcribed by
Barbara L. Benge

HERITAGE BOOKS
2006

HERITAGE BOOKS
AN IMPRINT OF HERITAGE BOOKS, INC.

Books, CDs, and more—Worldwide

For our listing of thousands of titles see our website
at
www.HeritageBooks.com

Published 2006 by
HERITAGE BOOKS, INC.
Publishing Division
65 East Main Street
Westminster, Maryland 21157-5026

Copyright © 2000 Barbara L. Benge

Other books by the author:
1890 Cherokee Nation Census
CD: 1880 Cherokee Nation Census
CD: 1890 Cherokee Nation Census

All rights reserved. No part of this book may be reproduced or transmitted in any form or by any means, electronic or mechanical, including photocopying, recording or by any information storage and retrieval system without written permission from the author, except for the inclusion of brief quotations in a review.

International Standard Book Number: 978-0-7884-1576-X

Thank You

Rosie Gould, my husbands Aunt, who introduced me to genealogy. Jerry Wright Jordan, Karen Phister, Oleta Benge Kite, Pat Hoffee, Sandi and Forrest Garrett, my support system, always an inspiration, lending a helping hand and a push when I needed it most. My children who endured a messy house and late night dinners while mom was on the computer. Especially to the man in my life who told me I could do it and helped me along the way. A special thanks to C J Adair who when I thought I was finished, made me work even harder, making this project as accurate as possible.

Most of all to my mother and father who raised a child who never new that she couldn't become the President of the United States or a genealogist. To family and friends because that is what genealogy and this book is all about.

The graphic that appears on the cover of this book I designed. The blue circle represents life to the Cherokees. The flower is the Cherokee Rose, three tears fall off its petals, these tears represent my husband's paternal side the Benges, his Maternal great grandmother Eliza Cornsilk, Lowrey, O'Neil nee Thompson, and my Paternal great grandmother Serena Frances Norton.

Cherokee Legends is that during the Trail of Tears in 1839, that for each tear shed during the Removal a Cherokee Rose grew. These roses are spread from North Carolina to Oklahoma in abundance. So many tears shed, so many deaths along the way. It is to those who died and those that survived the harsh struggles they had to endure that I dedicate this book.

Table of Contents

Introduction vii

Canadian 1

Cooweescoowee 41

Delaware 127

Flint 205

Goingsnake 245

Illinois 299

Saline 359

Sequoyah 393

Tahlequah 429

The Orphans 503

Index Explanation 513

Index 515

Introduction

For those researching your Cherokee heritage, you have heard "Check the Dawes". Where do you go from there? Most researchers would like to trace their ancestors beyond 1902. By utilizing the Guion Miller applications, the Dawes applications, Cherokee Nation census cards, and the census rolls, this can be accomplished. The first step is to find out what material is available. Three excellent books that I recommend are James Mooney's Researching Your Cherokee Heritage, Myra Ghormley's Cherokee Connections, and Tony McClure's Cherokee Proud.

You will discover that the first step is to find your ancestor's Dawes roll number. The Dawes has become readily accessible with Ancestry's on line search engine (http://www.ancestry.com) as well as the National Archive's NARA search engine (http://www.nara.gov). The following books by Bob Blankenship include Dawes roll numbers, The Dawes Plus, The Guion Miller Plus, and Cherokee Roots.

One of the pivotal rolls used for eligibility status for enrollment, whether Cherokee, Choctaw, Creek, Chickasaw, Seminole or Freedmen was the 1880 Cherokee Nation census. Once you have obtained your ancestor's census card, you will note that it will have a notation in the census columns if they were on the 1880 or the 1896 (sometimes the 1894 or 1883, as well) census. If they did not appear on the 1880 because they were not old enough, the census card can tell you where the parents were residing during an earlier roll. Some times this is nonspecific or just states Cherokee. Use this as a clue not a fact. This may be referring to where they were on the 1880, 1896 or the 1851 Drennen or 1851 Old Settler's rolls. This is a good way to identify "missing" fathers or mothers that have different surnames.

This book is a transcription of the 1880 Cherokee Nation census, including census card numbers, which were added in 1900. The Dawes Commission used the census card for tribal enrollment. They were sometimes referred to as Field cards. They are available from the National Archives, your local Family History Center and the Oklahoma Historical Society. It is important that you check the correct tribe's census cards. Each tribe had their own census cards, and there were separate cards for the Freedmen of the tribe. Even though a person was Cherokee (or some other tribe) they could be on another tribe's Dawes roll because they were living with that tribe, intermarried or they had ancestors that were members of that tribe. In some cases, members of other tribes were adopted into tribes they were associated with. Shawnees and Delawares can often be found on Cherokee Census cards. Those who appear on Doubtful cards were either transferred to an accepted or to a Rejected card. It is important to then check these census cards as well.

If the person died between 1880 and 1900 the notation will appear under the Census column as "Dead". Researching other census rolls between 1883 to 1896 can clarify the death date further. In some cases a census number is also given and a note added that they are dead, in these cases, they died close to the time of the enrollment in 1900. The actual date of death will often appear on the census card.

Additional remarks have been transcribed from the original roll. When legible, these remarks have been included, along with comments that will help you to locate your ancestors. These remarks usually included the head of the household's occupation and some other notations by the original census takers. Information pertaining to literacy and personal property has not been included, this information is available on the original microfilm. The original notes do not have any special citations, additional information from the census card and my research, is noted by my initials (BLB). This is a transcription and I have tried to transcribe it as accurately as possible any transcription of a hand written original document is open to interpretation, I encourage you to go to the primary source for verification. The original source for this book is the National Archives microfilm 7RA07 roll 2 for the Canadian, Cooweescoowee, Delaware and Flint Districts. Goingsnake, Illinois, Saline, Sequoyah and Tahlequah Districts are on microfilm 7RA07 roll 3. The Orphans were transcribed from microfilm 7RA07 roll 4.

In 1979, James Tyner and Alice Timmons published a version of the 1880 Cherokee Nation Census. This version does not include the census card numbers and contains concurrent numbering not consistent with the actual microfilm. On difficult to read names I have referred to this work to assist in the transcription. On the original microfilm it is possible to see the distinction, in some districts, between family groups with the same surname.

On the original microfilm numbers were often repeated. The Tahlequah District repeats the following numbers: 461 through 560, 701 through 721, again 701 through 723 and at 2281, an entire series was not numbered. Illinois District also repeats 1440 through 1459, Flint repeats 500 through 600. Several districts start with number 2 or repeat number 1. There are a few miscellaneous duplicate numbers through out the districts. Since this numbering system was used on the census cards, they have been transcribed exactly as they appear on the microfilm. Letters have been added to identify duplicate numbers. For the Canadian District, some ages, notes and census card numbers were not transcribed due to the poor condition of the original census.

The names, race, age and sex, have been transcribed as they appear on the original microfilm. In the index, surnames whenever possible, have been corrected. For example, surnames such as Harlan and Harlin, Teehee and Tehee have been unified, to make it easier to search for your families. Look for all possible spellings and misspellings. Compounded names such as Youngwolfe for example, were often listed by part of the name i.e. Wolfe. Rattlinggourd is indexed under Gourd. When known, check both Cherokee and English versions of a name. Tickenseeskee is an excellent example, this family used Catcher or Ketcher, which is the English version of Tickenseeskee.

Terms used to designate race are transcribed as they appear on the original microfilm. Freedmen were descendants of the slaves that had once belonged to the Five Civilized Tribes. Freedmen were eligible to receive an allotment of land that was less than their Indian brethren. In most cases if the Freedmen were mixed blood Indians, they were placed on the Freedmen census cards. This is important to note if you are of African American and Indian heritage. This book uses the abbreviations on the actual microfilm roll with the exception of Delaware Doubtful census cards which uses Del D, in this case I have used DLD so that it will fit into the column.

Abbreviations used under Race Column

A White – Adopted White
A Col – Adopted Colored
A Shaw – Adopted Shawnee
A Del – Adopted Delaware
A Choc – Adopted Choctaw
A Cher – Adopted Cherokee

N Cher – Native Cherokee
N Col – Native Colored

A Chic – Adopted Chickasaw
A Creek – Adopted Creek
A C – Adopted Cherokee

Abbreviations used under Census Column

Del – Delaware census card
DLD – Delaware Doubtful census cards
FD – Freedmen Doubtful census cards
F – Freedmen census cards
D – Cherokee Doubtful census cards
R – Rejected Cherokee census cards

	Name	Race	Age	Sex	Census	Md	Remarks
1	Ashes, Joe	Ncher	43	M	Dead	No	Farmer
2	Ashes, Ridge	Ncher	7	M	7109		
3	Ashes, Jack	Ncher	3	M	Dead		
4	Ashes, Ahkeeloohee	Ncher	43	F	7223		
5	Allen, Midia	Ncher	2	F	5380		
6	Allen, Lizzie	Ncher	9	F	3407		
7	Allen, John	Awhite	38	M	2108	Yes	
8	Allen, Eliza	Ncher	32	F	Dead	Yes	
9	Alton, Sylvester	Awhite	59	M	Dead	Yes	Farmer
10	Alton, Elsie	Ncher	48	F	7035	Yes	
11	Alton, J F	Ncher	15	M	Dead		
12	Alberty, G W	Ncher	33	M	Dead	Yes	
13	Alberty, Eliza	Ncher	31	F	Dead	Yes	
14	Alberty, Elvina	Ncher	13	F	Dead		
15	Alberty, Wm	Ncher	10	M	Dead		
16	Alberty, Eli	Ncher	7	M	5296		
17	Alberty, Emely	Ncher	4	F	Dead		
18	Alberty, James	Ncher	2	M	Dead		
19	Alberty, David	Ncher	3m	M	Dead		
20	Agnew, Walter	Ncher	36	M	2230	Yes	
21	Agnew, Mary E	Ncher	26	F	2230	Yes	
22	Agnew, Laura	Ncher	10	F	5692		
23	Agnew, Ellen	Ncher	8	F	2230		
24	Agnew, John	Ncher	3	M	Dead		
25	Agnew, R M	Ncher	1	M	2256		
26	Allen, V W	Ncher	2	F	9528		
27	Autry, Columbus	Ncher	30	M	Dead	No	Farmer
28	Archer, W M	Awhite	40	M	Dead	No	Farmer
29	Arnold, Susan	Ncher	80	F	Dead		
30	Bertholf, Nancy	Ncher	68	F	Dead	no	
31	Bertholf, J W	Ncher	40	M	Dead	Yes	Farmer
32	Bertholf, W H	Ncher	32	M	7726	Yes	
33	Bertholf, Amada	Ncher	25	F	861		Creek Census
34	Bertholf, Allice	Ncher	3	F	861	No	Creek Census
35	Bertholf, Emma	Ncher	1	F	861	No	Creek Census
36	Bertholf, R R	Ncher	30	M	7139	No	Farmer
37	Bertholf, Ellector	Ncher	45	F	7148	No	
38	Bowden, Frank	Ncher	25	M	2008	No	
39	Bertholf, J R	Ncher	27	M	7318	No	
40	Bertholf, N J	Ncher	23	M	7149	No	
41	Bertholf, Martha	Ncher	18	F	Dead	No	
42	Bertholf, Lilitia	Ncher	16	F	9896	No	

The Canadian District

Name	Race	Age	Sex	Census	Md	Remarks
43 Bertholf, Thomas	Ncher	10	M	4642	No	
44 Bean, Jeff	Ncher	39	M	Dead	Yes	
45 Bean, Susan	Ncher	34	F	2156	Yes	
46 Bean, Russell	Ncher	8	M	7207		
47 Barnett, J W	Awhite	22	M	R626	No	
48 Bigby, John	Ncher	18	M	2359		
49 Barnett, Joel	Ncher	1	M	5294		
50 Buck, James	Ncher	26	M	Dead		
51 Buck, Kahukah	Ncher	20	F	8937		
52 Buck, Etahgurstah	Ncher	2	M	8607		
53 Blackhaw, Nick	Ncher	49	M	Dead	Yes	Farmer
54 Blackhaw, Sarah	Ncher	42	F	Dead	Yes	
55 Bacon, Sarah	Ncher	30	F	Dead		Farmer
56 Bacon, L B	Ncher	3	F	5734		
57 Bacon, B M	Ncher	1	F	4887		
58 Brewer, R M	Ncher	2m	M	Dead		
59 Brewer, R E	Ncher	30	F	4569	no	
60 Beaver, Thomas	Ncher	23	M	7750		
61 Beaver, Nannie	Ncher	5	F	7272		
62 Byrd, Thomas	Ncher	26	M	6939	Yes	Farmer
63 Byrd, Lila	Ncher	25	F	6939	Yes	
64 Blackstone, Peggy	Ncher	7	F	4295		
65 Brown, J C	Ncher	39	M	Dead	Yes	
66 Brown, Bathseba	Ncher	17	F	2166		
67 Brown, Mary	Awhite	30	F	4875	Yes	
68 Brown, Phebe	Ncher	11	F	4872		
69 Brown, Elizabeth	Ncher	8	F	Dead		
70 Brown, Julia	Ncher	5	F	7200		
71 Beavers, C M	Awhite	31	M	4712	Yes	Farmer
72 Beavers, S M	Ncher	28	F	4712	Yes	
73 Beavers, Henry	Ncher	10	M	2111		
74 Beavers, B V	Ncher	8	F	Dead		
75 Beavers, Maud	Ncher	6	F	4663		
76 Brown, E T	Ncher	30	M	Dead	Yes	Farmer
77 Brown, T E	Ncher	29	F	4781	Yes	
78 Brown, Lurader	Ncher	4	F	4782		
79 Barker, Charles	Ncher	28	M	7239	Yes	Farmer
80 Barker, Susie	Ncher	24	F	7239		
81 Barker, Infant	Ncher	6m	M	Dead		
82 Buzzard, Sam	Ncher	21	M	Dead	Yes	
83 Buzzard, Nellie	Ncher	20	F	Dead	Yes	
84 Buzzard, Choowalooka	Ncher	6	M	Dead		

Name	Race	Age	Sex	Census	Md	Remarks
85 Buzzard, Warlaloo	Ncher	4	M	Dead		
86 Brimage, Martha	Ncher	33	F	Dead		
87 Brimage, Nancy	Ncher	4	F	Dead		
88 Brimage, Alex	Awhite	48	M	Dead	Yes	Farmer
89 Brimage, Rebecca	Ncher	21	F	Dead		
90 Bark, Lut	Ncher	32	M	Dead	No	
92 Brimage, J W	Awhite	24	M	Dead		
93 Brimage, Mary	Ncher	29	F	1651	Yes	
94 Brimage, Fred	Ncher	2	M	6614		
95 Brimage, Rachel	Ncher	6m	F	7193		
96 Blackstone, Thomas	Ncher	32	M	Dead		
97 Blackstone, Rosa	Awhite	22	F	1583?		
98 Blackstone, Edward	Ncher	9m	M	1690		
99 Blackstone, E J	Ncher	34	F	7133		
100 Bertholf, Lizzie	Ncher	35	F	1627		
101 Bertholf, John	Ncher	5	M	Dead		
102 Bart, Willie	Ncher	25	M	Dead		
103 Butler, Beau	Ncher	25	M	7185		Farmer
104 Butler, Sockenee	Ncher	45	F	Dead		
105 Butler, Ahlookah	Ncher	18	F	8011		
106 Boggs, Richard	Ncher	20	F	Dead		
107 Benge, Isaac	A Col	27	M	F918	Yes	
108 Benge, Jennie	A Col	25	F	F418		
109 Benge, Charley	A Col	5	M	F420		
110 Blackstone, George	A Col	5	M	2109		
111 Blackstone, Robert	A Col	5	M	6714		
112 Blackstone, R E	A Col	36	M	Dead	Yes	Farmer
113 Blackstone, Sallie	Ncher	24	F	Dead	Yes	
114 Beatie, Quintilla	Ncher	20	F	1841		
115 Beatie, Emiline	Ncher	53	F	1906		
116 Beatie, R W	Ncher	26	M	Dead		
117 Beatie, G W	Ncher	17	M	Dead		
118 Brown, Henry	A Col	30	M	F526	Yes	Farmer
119 Brown, Jane	A Col	28	F	F526		
120 Brown, William	A Col	10	F	F337		
121 Brown, Ribert	A Col	8	M	Dead		
122 Brown, Samuel	A Col	6	M	F528		
123 Brown, Fanney	A Col	3	F	F482		
124 Brown, Mary	A Col	1	F	Dead		
125 Baldridge, George	Ncher	36	M	Dead		
126 Baldridge, James	Ncher	13	M	10266		
127 Baldridge, Nannie	Ncher	7	F	Dead		

Name	Race	Age	Sex	Census	Md	Remarks
128 Barber, Dave	Ncher	45	M	Dead	Yes	Farmer
129 Barber, Eyahner	Ncher	35	F	Dead		
130 Barber, Grapes	Ncher	8	M	7124		
131 Barber, Lucy	Ncher	6	F			No census card number visible (BLB)
132 Barber, Dutch	Ncher	4	F			No census card number visible (BLB)
133 Barber, Tiyanee	Ncher	6m	F	7030		
134 Barber, Oldknife	Ncher	22	M	7223		
135 Blythe, Jackson	Ncher	8	M	7236		
136 Blythe, Billie	Ncher	6	M	Dead		
137 Bray, Charles	Awhite	47	M	1907	Yes	Farmer
138 Bray, Jane C	Ncher	42	F	Dead		
139 Bray, W H	Ncher	11	M	1840		
140 Bray, R R	Ncher	5	M	4857		
141 Bray, Eugene	Ncher	3	M	Dead		
142 Bray, G R	Ncher	1	M	2031		
143 Brewer, O P	Ncher	50	M	Dead	Yes	Farmer
144 Brewer, D A	Ncher	46	F	1622		
145 Brewer, M V	Ncher	22	F	Dead		
146 Brewer, J D	Ncher	20	M	Dead		
147 Brewer, T H	Ncher	16	M	Dead		
148 Brewer, Cherry	Ncher	12	F	1623		
149 Brewer, Oliver Perry	Ncher	9	M	7433		
150 Brewer, John C	Ncher	71	M	Dead		
151 Bracken, Eugene	Awhite	30	M	7008	Yes	Farmer
152 Bracken, CC	Ncher	24	F	7008		
153 Bracken, H S	Ncher	2	M	7018		
154 Bracken, H W	Ncher	2m	M	7008		
155 Barham, Quinn	Ncher	30	F	Dead	Yes	
156 Betts, Chas.	Ncher	___	M	Dead		Admitted A o C Nov 18,1880
157 Betts, Katie	Ncher	32	F	Dead		
158 Betts, Annie	Ncher	12	F	2011		
159 Betts, A A	Ncher	10	F	D1100		
160 Brown, James	Ncher	24	M	1909		
161 Bennett, Mary	Ncher	62	F	5685		Farmer
162 Bracket, J T	Awhite	34	M	3573	Yes	
163 Bracket, Margaret	Ncher	45	F	3573	Yes	
164 Burris, Wm.	Awhite	40	M	Dead	Yes	
165 Burris, Sallie	Ncher	30	F	Dead	Yes	
166 Burris, Bandinot	Ncher	10	M	Dead		
167 Burris, James	Ncher	8	M	1982		
168 Burris, Whit	Ncher	5	M	1983		

Name	Race	Age	Sex	Census	Md	Remarks
169 Burris, Tobe	Ncher	2	M	1984		
170 Burris, James	Awhite	22	M	4672	Yes	
171 Burris, Emma	Ncher	17	F	Dead		
172 Blackstone, P N	Ncher	36	M	7012		Farmer
173 Blackstone, J C	Ncher	33	F	Dead		
174 Blackstone, Fanny	Ncher	9	F	Dead		
175 Blackstone, R E	Ncher	7	M	7033		
176 Blackstone, Louisa	Ncher	5	F	17		
177 Blackstone, D W	Ncher	2	M	7028		
178 Blackstone, Katie	Ncher	4m	F	Dead		
179 Beck, Wm.	Ncher	10	M	2204		
180 Bennett, Simpson	Ncher	41	M	Dead	Yes	Farmer
181 Bennett, Emily	Ncher	39	F	7044		
182 Boyenton, Alice	Ncher	30	F	32		
183 Boyenton, A J	Ncher	1	M	D1326		Dead
184 Buzzard Flopper, Nannie	Ncher		F	10102		This family also uses surname Martin(BLB)
185 Buzzard Flopper, Willie	Ncher		M	7257		
186 Buzzard Flopper, Geo.	Ncher	18	M	Dead		
187 Buzzard Flopper, Jinny	Ncher	7	F	2508		Duplicate of 58 Orphan Roll
188 Blange, Peggy	Ncher	19	F	D1387		Dead, Chickasaw
189 Blanger, Mary	Ncher	4	F	D1388		Chickasaw
190 Burr, George	Ncher	15	M	7367		
191 Bethelhiemer, Louisa	Ncher	16	F	5876		
192 Collins, Robt.	Ncher	24	M	1767	Yes	Farmer
193 Collins, Sis	Ncher	21	F	2150		
194 Collins, Infant	Ncher	2	M	2133		
195 Carry, Eliza	Ncher	23	F	7405		
196 Chisholm, Polly	ACreek	50	F	1389		Creek
197 Chisholm, James	Ncher	27	M	1912		Creek
198 Chisholm, Mary	ACreek	28	F	1912		Creek
199 Chisholm, Ida	Ncher	3	F	1912		Creek
200 Chisholm, John	Ncher	6m	M	D1393		Creek
201 Chisholm, Thomas	Ncher	26	M	Dead	Yes	
202 Chisholm, Martha	ACreek	20	F	D1374		Creek
203 Chisholm, David	Ncher	34	M	D1375		Creek
204 Chisholm, Katie	Ncher	10	F	D1376		Creek
205 Chisholm, Eliza	Ncher	7	F	D1377		Creek
206 Chisholm, Emily	Ncher	4	F	D1378		Creek
207 Chisholm, Jenny	Ncher	24	F	D1379		Creek
208 Coleman, John	Ncher	57	M	2048	Yes	Farmer
209 Coleman, Elizabeth	Awhite	48	F	2048		

Name	Race	Age	Sex	Census	Md	Remarks
210 Coleman, Newton	Ncher	9	M	2049		
211 Coleman, S G	Ncher	5	M	2050		
212 Cloud, Moses	Ncher	4	M	Dead		
213 Crain, Bing F	Awhite	24	M	D1094	Yes	Farmer (or D1099 BLB)
214 Crain, Millie	Ncher	24	F			
215 Cramp, William	Ncher	23	M	D3170		
216 Cramp, Elizabeth	Ncher	25	F	Dead		
217 Cramp, Laura	Ncher	2	F	7237		
218 Cramp, Luie	Ncher	2	F	Dead		
219 Green, Cynthia	Ncher	12	F	D1400		Card 7061
220 Cramp, Luarlahyouka	Ncher	7	F	7238		
221 Cramp, Ahnarwakie	Ncher	5	F	Dead		
222 Cramp, Saliekiney	Ncher	4w	F	7437		
223 Cramp, Peter	Ncher	20	M	Dead		
224 Coon, Kella	Ncher	5	F	9773		
225 Coon, Catcher	Ncher	50	M	Dead		
226 Coon, Cartayah	Ncher	5	F	1769		
227 Campbell, Sam	Ncher	18	M	Dead		Farmer
228 Campbell, Bean	Ncher	20	M	8821		
229 Campbell, Isabell	Ncher	16	F	7039		
230 Campbell, John	Ncher	9	M	7052		
231 Crossland, Richard	Ncher	50	M	Dead		Farmer
232 Crossland, Wm.	Ncher	20	M	1822		
233 Crossland, Horstie	Ncher	8	F	1629		
234 Crossland, James	Ncher	6	M			
235 Crapoe, Jerry	Ncher	27	M	Dead		
236 Crapoe, Bettie	Ncher	19	F	1640		
237 Coleman, John	Ncher	44	M	7440		Farmer
238 Coleman, Nancy	Ncher	50	F	7440		
239 Carlile, S L	Awhite	43	M	1608	Yes	Farmer
240 Carlile, M J	Ncher	40	F	Dead		
241 Carlile, R B	Ncher	6	M	Dead		
242 Carlile, Chas.	Ncher	4	M	7205		
243 Carlile, S N	Ncher	2 1/2	M	5980		
244 Carlile, M L	Ncher	1	F	1069		
245 Carlile, E J	Ncher	24	F	Dead		
246 Carlile, Wm.	Ncher	21	M	1265		
247 Carlile, Ellen	Ncher	19	F	1201		
248 Carlile, Thomas	Ncher	17	M	1190		
249 Chutahkeetah, Ross	Ncher	20	M	7143		
250 Chutahkeetah, Ahkeelahee	Ncher	60	F	Dead		
251 Carey, Samuel	Ncher	55	M	Dead	Yes	

Name	Race	Age	Sex	Census	Md	Remarks
252 Carey, Nellie	Ncher	20	F	Dead		
253 Carey, Ellen	Ncher	11	F	Dead		
254 Carey, L M	Ncher	8	M	Dead		
255 Campbell, Bettie	Ncher	45	F	Dead		
256 Campbell, Alic	Ncher	24	M	1675		
257 Cloud, Rider	Ncher	36	M	Dead		
258 Cloud, Levinia	Ncher	7	F	Dead		
259 Clyne, Ezekial	Ncher	26	M	7344	Yes	Farmer
260 Clyne, Hannah	Awhite	23	F	Dead		
261 Clyne, Beng	Ncher	5	M	6938		
262 Clyne, John	Ncher	1	M	7197		
263 Chinn, John	Awhite	42	M	Dead	Yes	
264 Chinn, J E	Ncher	34	F	Dead		
265 Chinn, Columbus	Ncher	10	M	7320		
266 Chinn, Martha	Ncher	8	F	Dead		
267 Chinn, Katie	Ncher	6	F	Dead		
268 Chinn, John Jr.	Ncher	4	M	7363		
269 Chinn, Jinnie	Ncher	2	F	Dead		
270 Choowalookee, Dan	Ncher	47	M	Dead	Yes	Farmer
271 Choowalookee, Nancy	Ncher	37	F	Dead		
272 Choowalookee, Susan	Ncher	24	F	Dead		
273 Choowalookee, John	Ncher	1	M	2288?		
274 Curry, Jacob	Ncher	18	M	Dead		
275 Conrad, J H	Ncher	55	M	Dead		Farmer
276 Conrad, M T	Ncher	25	M	Dead		
277 Conrad, George	Ncher	23	M	9267		
278 Cloud, James	Ncher	21	M	Dead		
279 Cunningham, M R	Ncher	22	F	4232		
280 Cates, William	Awhite	55	M	Dead		Farmer
281 Crittenden, J W	Ncher	30	M	Dead		
282 Crittenden, Martha	Awhite	28	F	2209		
283 Crittenden, Thomas	Ncher	6	M	Dead		
284 Crittenden, John	Ncher	4	M	7196		
285 Cloud, Chas.	Ncher	2	M	Dead		
286 Cobb, Hornell	Ncher	15	M	4751		
287 Cabin, Sarah	Ncher	91	F	Dead		Farmer
288 Coon, Alic	Ncher	40	M	Dead		
289 Crapoe, Runaway	Ncher	2	M	Dead		
290 Crittenden, Dick	Ncher	20	M	Dead		
291 Chicoowee,	Ncher	27	F	Dead		
292 Choweynka	Ncher	30	F	Dead		Deaf and Dumb
293 Infant	Ncher	1m	F	7997		

The Canadian District

Name	Race	Age	Sex	Census	Md	Remarks
294 Carey, Walker	Ncher	7	M	Dead		
295 Crittenden, Dora	Ncher	11	F	D1401		
296 Duck, Tahnee	Ncher	42	F	7650	Yes	
297 Duck, Ahlu	Ncher	16	F	7656		
298 Duck, Ultesee	Ncher	13	M	Dead		
299 Duck, Chookerwerlusky	Ncher	5	F	7651		
300 Duck, Rachel	Ncher	1	F	7650		
301 Duck, Sarah	Ncher	20	F	7983		
302 Duck, David V	Ncher	1	M	Dead		
303 Duck, Wolf	Ncher	45	M	Dead	Yes	Farmer
304 Downing, Sarah	Ncher	30	F			
305 Downing, Susan	Ncher	29	F	Dead		
306 Downing, Lydia	Ncher	9	F	5315		
307 Downing, Beng	Ncher	5	M	7386		
308 Downing, Peggy	Ncher	3	F	5335		
309 Downing, Chas.	Ncher	1	M	1646		
310 Downing, David	Ncher	33	M	8399		
311 Drunkard, Ellen	Ncher	100	F	Dead		
312 Drunkard, Jenny	Ncher	25	F	Dead		
313 Drunkard, John	Ncher	6	M	7609		Surname Sanders (BLB)
314 Drunkard, Jackson	Ncher	2	M	Dead		
315 Davis, James	Ncher	4	M	6360		
316 Drummer, Nancy	Ncher	7	F	D1402		
317 Davis, J P	Ncher	57	M	Dead	Yes	Farmer
318 Davis,	Ncher	30	F	8008		
319 Dunnagan, R J	Awhite	35	M	7370	Yes	Farmer
320 Dunnagan, G A	Ncher	30	F	7370		
321 Dunnagan, G S	Ncher	3	M	7371		
322 Dunnagan, M L	Ncher	6m	F	Dead		
323 Drew, Lewis	A Col	21	M	Dead	Yes	
324 Drew, John	A Col	2	M	F390		
325 Drew, Henry	A Col	6m	M	Dead		
326 Drew, James	A Col	33	M	F297	Yes	wife on schedule 5, Farmer
327 Drew, Wittie	A Col	4	M	Dead		Children of James Drew &___
328 Drew, Mollie	Ncher	4	F	Dead		
329 Drew, Parlor	A Col	60	M	Dead	Yes	Farmer
330 Drew, Katie	Ncher	55	F	Dead		
331 Drew, Thomas	A Col	22	M	F515		
332 Drew, James	A Col	20	M	F439		
333 Drew, Moses	A Col	18	M	F641		
334 Drew, Ellen	A Col	14	F	F436		
335 Drew, Dick	A Col	12	M	F639		

Name	Race	Age	Sex	Census	Md	Remarks
336 Drew, Henrietta	A Col	6	F	Dead		
337 Drew, Beng	A Col	2	M	F471		
338 Davis, Jug	Ncher	22	M	7995	Yes	Farmer
339 Davis, Nancy	Ncher	23	F	Dead		
340 Davis, Susie	Ncher	3	F	8000		
341 Davis, E J	Ncher	20	F	Dead		
342 Davis, Mary	Ncher	22	F	Dead		
343 Davis, Kile	Ncher	1	M	6718		
344 Davis, George	Ncher	22	M	Dead		
345 Durall, Ann	Ncher	29	F	Dead		
346 Drew, Kate	Ncher	18	F	Dead		
347 Davis, Nancy	Ncher	20	F	7978		
348 Davis, Henry	Ncher	18	M	7980		
349 Drew, John T	Ncher	30	M	1961	Yes	
350 Drew, Mollie	Ncher	23	F	1961		
351 Drew, Nannie	Ncher	2	F	2076		
352 Drew, Charlotte	Ncher	9m	F	2074		
353 Drew, William	Ncher	26	M	6191		Farmer
354 Drunkard, Susie	Ncher	8	F	Dead		
355 Drunkard, Checoonalah	Ncher	3	F	9911		
356 Davis, Thompson	Ncher	2	M			
357 Davis, S T	Ncher	30	M	7173		Samuel Tate Davis (BLB)
358 Davis, Amanda	Ncher	50	F	1610		
359 Davis, J B	Ncher	20	M	5005		
360 Davis, Jeff	Ncher	18	M	Dead		See 1880Coo #882, this is a duplicate census and he is listed on census card 4835 and not dead (BLB)
361 Davis, L D	Ncher	27	M	Dead		Farmer
362 Davis, Jeff	Ncher	24	M	Dead	Yes	Farmer
363 Davis, Takie	Ncher	20	F	Dead		
364 Davis, Warnie	Ncher	3	F	Dead		
365 Davis, S W	Ncher	1	M	7216		
366 Duncan, Samuel	Ncher	22	M	Dead	Yes	Farmer
367 Duncan, Katie	Ncher	19	F	Dead		
368 Duncan, Infant	Ncher	1m	F			
369 Downing, Diana	Ncher	48	F	Dead	Yes	
370 Downing, Bettie	Ncher	20	F	Dead		
371 Downing, Thomas	Ncher	15	M	7261		
372 Delano, C H	Ncher	35	M	7091	Yes	Farmer
373 Delano, Mary	Awhite	25	F	7091		
374 Downing, George	Ncher	48	M	2195	Yes	
375 Davis, D P	Ncher	34	M	Dead		

Name	Race	Age	Sex	Census	Md	Remarks
376 Davis, Nannie	Ncher	7	F	648		
377 Downing, Joe	Ncher	30	M	Dead		
378 Downing, Katie	Ncher	27	F	2180		
379 Downing, Nannie	Ncher	2	F	2178		
380 Downing, Polly	Ncher	26	F	Dead		
381 Duncan, Alex	Ncher	2m	M	Dead		
382 Daniels, Rachel	Ncher	18	F	D1404		
383 Davis, Joe Ross	Ncher	26	M	8001		
384 Daniels, Sally	A Col	14	F	FD1132		
385 Davis, Mary	Awhite	26	F	Dead	Yes	
386 Downing, Walter	Ncher	50	M	Dead		
387 Drew, Rachel	A Col	26	F	F435		
388 Eiffert, J H	Awhite	65	M	2037	Yes	Farmer
389 Eiffert, M A	Ncher	64	F	2037		
390 Earbob, Lone	Ncher	24	M	Dead		Farmer
391 Earbob, Nancy	Ncher	25	F	Dead		
392 Earbob, Mary	Ncher	3	F	Dead		
393 Earbob, Infant	Ncher	1m	F	Dead		
394 Earbob, Aggy	Ncher	17	F	Dead		
395 Elliot, G W	Awhite	45	M	34		
396 Elliot, Louisa	Ncher	10	F	5820?		
397 Elliot, A E	Ncher	31	F	34	Yes	
398 Elliot, W M	Ncher	14	M	Dead		
399 Elliot, G W Jr.	Ncher	12	M	Dead		
400 Elliot, Elizabeth	Ncher	8	F	Dead		
401 Elliot, Ida	Ncher	6	F	2680		
402 Elliot, Mary	Ncher	4	F	34		
403 Elliot, James	Ncher	45	M	Dead	Yes	Farmer
404 Elliot, Jane	Ncher	45	F	Dead		
405 Elliot, William	Ncher	22	M	Dead		
406 Elliot, Mary	Ncher	39	F	2218		
407 Elliot, Robert	Ncher	7	M	2310?		
408 Eldridge, Susie	Ncher	9	F	D1405		
409 Fields, Wm	Ncher	26	M	Dead	Yes	
410 Fields, Minerva	Ncher	36	F	10	Yes	
411 Fields, Chauncy	Ncher	1	M	10		Dead
412 Fodder, Chas or Geo	Ncher	28	M	8962		
413 Fodder, Nancy	Ncher	30	F	Dead		
414 Foreman, Johnson	Ncher	24	M	2011	Yes	Farmer
415 Foreman, Sarah	Ncher	19	F	Dead		
416 Foreman, William	Ncher	1	M	2013		
417 Fields, F T	Ncher	23	M	2093		Farmer

Name	Race	Age	Sex	Census	Md	Remarks
418 Foy, E W	Ncher	8	M	6922		Surname Fooy(BLB)
419 Forl, Betsy	Ncher	31	F			Farmer
420 Foreman, Emma	Ncher	29	F	Dead		
421 Foreman, J C	Ncher	5	M	Dead		
422 Foreman, Charley	Ncher	10	M	Dead		
423 Frazier, Daniel	Ncher	25	M	1631	Yes	Farmer
424 Frazier, Elizabeth	Ncher	23	F	1631		
425 Frazier, John	Ncher	5	M	1618		
426 Frazier, Emma	Ncher	3	F	1619		
427 Frazier, Undine	Ncher	6m	F	1620		
428 Frazier, John	Ncher	5	M	1640		
429 Filmore, Milard	Ncher	35	M	Dead	Yes	Farmer
430 Filmore, Emma	Ncher	28	F	1666		
431 Filmore, J H	Ncher	5	M	Dead		
432 Filmore, Hattie	Ncher	3	F	1666		
433 Filmore, Infant	Ncher	3m	F	7568		
434 Fields, W P	Ncher	50	M	Dead	Yes	
435 Fields, Charlotte	Ncher	45	F	1141		
436 Fields, T J	Ncher	19	M	Dead		
437 Fields, A S	Ncher	15	M	Dead		
438 Fields, W H	Ncher	13	M	Dead		
439 Fields, J R	Ncher	10	M	6225		
440 Fields, James	Ncher	7	M	7152		
441 Fly, Johnson	Ncher	33	M	Dead		
442 Fly, Mary	Ncher	26	F	Dead		
443 Fool, Annie	Ncher	52	F	Dead		
444 Fool, Thomas	Ncher	26	M	Dead		
445 Fool, Jinny	Ncher	16	F	1849		
446 Fool, John	Ncher	13	M	Dead		
447 Fool, William	Ncher	6	M	1850		
448 Fool, Sela	Ncher	30	F	Dead		
449 Fool, Dick		51	M	Dead		
450 Ficlds, Green	Awhite	72	M	Dead	Yes	Farmer
451 Fields, Kittie	Ncher	47	F	1773	Yes	
452 Falling, Ester	Ncher	16	F	7998		
453 Falling, Mary	Ncher	12	F	Dead		
454 Falling, James	Ncher	10	M	Dead		
455 Fields, Squirrel	Ncher	30	M	1222	Yes	Farmer
456 Fields, Betsy	Ncher	35	F	Dead	Yes	
457 Foley, Pat	Awhite	28	M	1770	Yes	Farmer
458 Foley, Adie	Ncher	24	F	1770	Yes	
459 Foley, Katie	Ncher	4	F	1861		

Name	Race	Age	Sex	Census	Md	Remarks
460 Foley, Molly	Ncher	2 1/2	F	7132		
461 Foley, Maggie	Ncher	1	F	1770		
462 Fields, R M	Ncher	24	M	4223		
463 Flying, J P	Ncher	32	M	2172		Farmer
464 Flying, Jennie	Ncher	23	F	Dead		
465 Flying, E N	Ncher	9	F	Dead		
466 Flying, E A	Ncher	6	F	1035		
467 Flying, Davis	Ncher	3	M	7250		
468 Flying, Emma	Ncher	1m	F	Dead		
469 Fields,	Ncher	14	F	7142		
470 Fox, George	Ncher	42	M	Dead	Yes	Farmer
471 Fox, Ellen	Ncher	35	F	Dead		
472 Foreman, Lizzie	Ncher	29	F	Dead		
473 Foreman, Willy	Ncher	9	M	4583		
474 Foreman, M A	Ncher	4	F	4581		
475 Fisher, William	Ncher	9	M	D1406		Creek card 1591 Freedman
476 Fowler, Florence	Ncher	18	F	Dead		
477 Fowler, C C	Ncher	21	M	Dead		
478 Fields, W G	Awhite	33	M	2094	Yes	Farmer
479 Fields, E E	Ncher	26	F	2094		
480 Fields, J A	Ncher	22	M	Dead		
481 Fisher, Akie	Ncher	9	F			Creek Card 63, Creek citizen married Sam Checotah R881
482 Gritts, Franklin	Ncher	43	M	2256	Yes	Farmer
483 Gritts, Johnson	Ncher	19	M			
484 Groves, Sanytah	Ncher	55	M	Dead	Yes	Farmer
485 Groves, Ooloocha	Ncher	39	F	Dead		
486 Groves, Thomas	Ncher	3	M	Dead		
487 Gripenkerl, F	Awhite	50	M	Dead	Yes	Physician
488 Gripenkerl, Mary	Ncher	40	F	2181		
489 Groves, Alic	Ncher	33	M	Dead		
490 Groves, Sally	Ncher	33	F	Dead		
491 Groves, Nancy	Ncher	9	F	Dead		
492 Groves, Annie	Ncher	6	F	Dead		
493 Groves, Johnson	Ncher	2	M	6818		
494 Gray, S W	Ncher	35	M	Dead	Yes	Farmer
495 Gray, E V	Ncher	30	F	Dead		
496 Gray, E W	Ncher	1	M	7137		
497 Girty, Snake	Ncher	50	M	7993	Yes	Farmer
498 Girty, Kalungenstah	Ncher	45	F	Dead		
499 Girty, Jack	Ncher	25	M	Dead		
500 Girty, Ahcooyah	Ncher	12	F	7994		

Name	Race	Age	Sex	Census	Md	Remarks
501 Girty, Daniel R	Ncher	10	M	8006		
502 Girty, Edward	Ncher	6	M	8405		
503 Girty, Jennie	Ncher	1	F	7665		
504 Grass, Jack	Ncher	45	M	Dead	Yes	
505 Grass, Nellie	Ncher	25	F	Dead		
506 Grass, Annie	Ncher	1	F	Dead		
507 Girty, Wilson	Ncher	34	M	8400	Yes	Farmer
508 Girty, Hester	Ncher	41	F	Dead		
509 Girty, William	Ncher	9	M	Dead		
510 Girty, Ella	Ncher	7	F	Dead		
511 Girty, Stud	Ncher	30	M	Dead	Yes	Farmer
512 Girty, Betsy	Ncher	23	F	Dead		
513 Griffin, E J	Ncher	54	F	Dead	Yes	Farmer
514 Griffin, T T	Ncher	21	M	Dead		
515 Griffin, Eliza	Ncher	19	F	7021		
516 Griffin, Felix	Ncher	14	M	Dead		
517 Garrison, B J	Ncher	25	M	Dead		
518 Groves, Isaac	Ncher	31	M	Dead	Yes	Farmer
519 Groves, Eliza	Ncher	22	F	2184		
520 Groves, Louyatah	Ncher	7	M	7999		
521 Groves, Takie	Ncher	4	F	Dead		
522 Groves, Eren	Ncher	2	M	7069		twins
523 Groves, James	Ncher	2	M	7070		
524 Groves,				Dead		
525 Goody, Katie	Ncher	20	F	7143		
526 Girty, Lizzie	Ncher	36	F	Dead		Farmer
527 Gustin, Edward	Awhite	27	M	Dead		
528 Gustin, Malvina	Ncher	23	F	5796		
529 Gustin, S A	Ncher	3	F	Dead		
530 Gustin, H N	Ncher	3	M	Dead		
531 Girty, Jack	Ncher	14	M	Dead		
532 Girty, Sally	Ncher	12	F	Dead		
533 Girty, James	Ncher	10	M	7439		
534 Girty, Thomas	Ncher	8	M	7441		
535 Girty, Oonicuhlurhee	Ncher		F	7439		
536 Griffin, J D	Ncher	27	M	2252		
537 Griffin, Joe	Ncher	4	M	Dead		
538 Griffin, Deliliah	Ncher	3m	M	1955		Enrolled as Lucinda Ragsdale
539 Glass, Fox	A col	38	M	F443	Yes	Farmer
540 Glass, Lucy	A col	30	M	F443	Yes	
541 Glass, Minerva	A col	6m	M	F370		
542 Gilbert, R C	Ncher	33	M	Dead	Yes	

Name	Race	Age	Sex	Census	Md	Remarks
543 Gilbert, Ruth	Ncher	9	M	4381		
544 Gilbert, George	Ncher	1	M	4555		
545 Galcatcher, Tom	Ncher	18	M	Dead		
546 Glass, G W	Ncher	18	M	Dead		
547 Galcatcher, James	Ncher	20	M	Dead		
548 Griffin, Geo	Ncher	30	M	Dead	Yes	Farmer
549 Griffin, Polly	Ncher	25	M	Dead		
550 Griffin, Co???re	Ncher	8	M	Dead		
551 Griffin, Phillips	Ncher	4	M	Dead		
552 Griffin, Enoch	Ncher	1	M	Dead		
553 Glass, Chas	Ncher	10	M	7458		
554 Garland, Tookah	Ncher	23	M	9768		
555 Garland, J N	Ncher	5	M	Dead		
556 Garland, Lewis	Ncher	3	M	Dead		
557 Garland, Lizzie	Ncher	1	M			Daughter of Susan T Garland nee Dawes (BLB)
558 Graves, Thomas	Ncher	28	M	7332	Yes	
559 Graves, Bettie	Ncher	29	M	7332		
560 Girty, Katie	Ncher	23	M	Dead		
561 Grease, Chas	Ncher	19	M	Dead		
562 Gleason, Jno W	Awhite	51	M	7340	Yes	
563 Green, Cynthia	Ncher	12	M	7061		
564 Harmon, Charles	Ncher	36	M	8016		Farmer
565 Harmon, Nancy	Ncher	7	M	Dead		
566 Harmon, Eliza	Ncher	5	M	7283		
567 Harmon, James	Ncher	3	M	1665		
568 Hayes, William	Awhite	41	M	2019?	Yes	
569 Hayes, E J	Ncher	39?	M	Dead		Elvira Jane Hayes nee McClain (BLB)
570 Harris, Susan	Ncher	1	M	6922		
571 Hankins, Jerry	A col	50	M	FD1133		
572 Hicks, Joe	A col	30	M			
573 Hilderbrand, James V	Ncher	30	M	Dead		Farmer
574 Howdershell, A E	Ncher	37	F	Dead		
575 Howdershell, Wm	Ncher	14	M	3920		
576 Howdershell, James	Ncher	11	M	Dead		
577 Howdershell, Nannie	Ncher	6	F	3928		
578 Hilderbrand, S C	Ncher	12	F	D1410		
579 Hysell, Kate	Ncher	23	F	Dead		
580 Hysell, Levi	Ncher	2	M	D1411		Dead
581 Harris, Joe	Ncher	6	M	4600		
582 Harris, John	Ncher	4	M	7208		
583 Harris, Thomas	Ncher	2	M	7209		

Name	Race	Age	Sex	Census	Md	Remarks
584 Harris, Filo	Ncher	30	M	7247		
585 Harris, Ann	Ncher	43	F	7361		
586 Heway, Rachel	Ncher	50	F	Dead		Surname Huey (BLB)
587 Heway, Agnes	Ncher	20	F	2218		Surname Huey (BLB)
588 Hasmer, P Solomon	Ncher	35	M	9766		Farmer
589 Hasmer, M J	Ncher	11	F	Dead		
590 Hasmer, J N	Ncher	6	M	2562		
591 Hasmer, Lizzie	Ncher	4	F	Dead		
592 Harris, James S	Ncher	45	M	2030	Yes	
593 Harris, Pyrena	Awhite	32	F	2030	Yes	
594 Harris, Thomas	Ncher	44	M	Dead		
595 Harris, Martha	Awhite	42	F			
596 Harris, C B	Ncher	20	F	Dead		
597 Harris, Sue	Ncher	12	F	2440		
598 Harris, Minnie	Ncher	10	F	2442		
599 Harris, J E	Ncher	6	F	2333		
600 Harris, Thomas	Ncher	4	M	2334		
601 Harris, D W B	Ncher	2m	M	2335		
602 Hysell, Sarah	Ncher	26	F	2102		
603 Hysell, Wm	Ncher	1	M	D1413		
604 Hammer, James	Ncher	55	M	Dead	Yes	Farmer
605 Hammer, Peggy	Ncher	40	F	Dead		
606 Hammer, Mary	Ncher	11	F	Dead		
607 Hammer, Sooney	Ncher	50	M	?		
608 Harris, Susan	Ncher	65	F	Dead		
609 Harris, Susie	Ncher	18	F	Dead		
610 Harris, Chas	Ncher	35	M	15		
611 Harris, Collins	Ncher	33	M	248		
612 Harris, Angeline	Awhite	21	F	248		
613 Harris, Thomas	Ncher	2 1/2	M	7209		
614 Harman, John	Ncher	23	M	1616		
615 Harman, Alice	Awhite	21	F	D1414		
616 Hedricks, Joe	Ncher	36	M	Dead		Farmer
617 Hedricks, Deliliah	Ncher	35	F	Dead		
618 Hedricks, Samuel	Ncher	11	M	7976		
619 Hedricks, John	Ncher	8	M	Dead		
620 Hedricks, Willie	Ncher	6	M	7248		
621 Hedricks, Moses	Ncher	3	M	Dead		
622 Hedricks, William	Ncher	35	M	1663		
623 Hedricks, Joe Jr.	Ncher	6	M	7249		
624 Hedricks, Geo	Ncher	4	M	Dead		
625 Haryford, James	Awhite	23	M	1671	Yes	

Name	Race	Age	Sex	Census	Md	Remarks
626 Haryford, Sabra	Ncher	20	F	1671		
627 Haryford, Joseph	Ncher	1	M	1670		
628 Hilderbrand, Amanda	Ncher	35	F	Dead		
629 Hilderbrand, Joe	Ncher	10	M	7015		
630 Henry, J D	Ncher	55	M	Dead	Yes	Farmer
631 Henry, Lucy	Ncher	50	F	1290?		
632 Hilderbrand, J M	Ncher	57	F	Dead	Yes	Farmer
633 Hilderbrand, M C	Ncher	51	F	Dead		
634 Hilderbrand, Lizzie	Ncher	12	F	Dead		
635 Harmon, Richard	Ncher	___	M	2291		Admitted AoC Nov 18, 1880 (Daniel Webster Harman BLB)
636 Harmon, Cyntha	Ncher	36	F	2291		
637 Harmon, Emma	Ncher	14	F	Dead		
638 Harmon, Henrietta	Ncher	12	F	2295		
639 Harmon, Jennie	Ncher	10	F	D3182		
640 Harmon, Lenard	Ncher	6	M	259		Laura Davis Holland nee Harman (BLB)
641 Harmon, Elizabeth	Ncher	2	F	2296		
642 Harmon, W D	Ncher	6m	M	Dead		
643 Horn, W M	Ncher	25	M	Dead	Yes	Farmer
644 Horn, Charlotte	Ncher	22	F	Dead		
645 Horn, L R	Ncher	3	M	2264		
646 Horn, E C	Ncher	1 1/2	F	1744		
647 Horn, Infant	Ncher	1m	M	2264		
648 Hilderbrand, Stephen	Ncher	46	M	Dead		Farmer
649 Hilderbrand, John	Ncher	25	M	2288		
650 Hilderbrand, J B	Ncher	23	M	Dead		
651 Hilderbrand, Wm	Ncher	20	M	Dead		
652 Hilderbrand, J B	Ncher	28	M	2276		
653 Hilderbrand, Geo	Ncher	33	M	1666		
654 Hilderbrand, Patsy	Ncher	32	F	Dead		
655 Hilderbrand, Kate	Ncher	9	F	Dead		
656 Hilderbrand, O P	Ncher	7	M	Dead		
657 Hilderbrand, J L	Ncher	5	M	Dead		
658 Hilderbrand, Sarah	Ncher	2	F	Dead		
659 Harris, C J	Ncher	28	M	5893	Yes	Col Johnson Harris (BLB)
660 Harris, Ninnie	Ncher	28	F	Dead		
661 Harris, Buena	Ncher	2	M	7026		
662 Harris, Wm R	Ncher	2m	M	5893		
663 Howland, E J	Awhite	45	M	Dead	Yes	Farmer
664 Howland, S E	Ncher	35	F	1582		
665 Howland, John	Ncher	12	M	7071		
666 Howland, Emma	Ncher	10	F	1617		

Name	Race	Age	Sex	Census	Md	Remarks
667 Howland, M J	Ncher	6	F	73225		
668 Howland, Lutie	Ncher	4	F	Dead		
669 Howland, Samuel	Ncher	1 1/2	M	Dead		
670 Henson, Jeff	A cher	24	M	7451		
671 Horn, Samuel	Ncher	23	M	1917	Yes	
672 Horn, Ellen	Ncher	20	M	Dead		
673 Horn, Annie	Ncher	9m	M	9		
674 Horn, J W	Ncher	34	M	D1415		Dead
675 Hayes, Richard	Ncher	21	M	7021		
676 Hanks, R L	Ncher	40	M	485		Farmer
677 Hilderbrand, C L	Awhite	19	F	Dead		
678 Hilderbrand, Daniel	Ncher	1 1/2	M	1810		
679 Hilderbrand, Lydia	Awhite	23	F	1672		
680 Hilderbrand, Mary	Ncher	4	F	5477		
681 Hilderbrand, Martha	Ncher	6m	F	1668		
682 Hilderbrand, Lizzie	Ncher	37	F	Dead		
683 Hilderbrand, Jennie	Ncher	12	F	D1416		Dead
684 Hilderbrand, Nannie	Ncher	4	F	1863		
685 Hilderbrand, Laura	Ncher	4	F	D1417		
686 Hilderbrand, R M	Ncher	29	M	1672		
687 Hanks, E W	Ncher	39	M	Dead		
688 Hanks, Maggie	Ncher	12	F	1081		
689 Hanks, May	Ncher	8	F	7263		
690 Hanks, Daisy	Ncher	6	F	7349		
691 Hanks, Emma	Ncher	2	F	7409		
692 Hanks, C J	Ncher	8m	M	1269		
693 Hood, Lydia	Awhite	28	F	Dead		Farmer
694 Hood, John	Ncher	21	M	1669		
695 Hood, Ella	Ncher	17	F	Dead		
696 Harris, Daniel	Ncher	40	M	Dead		
697 Harnage, J S	A cher	35	M	Dead		
698 Haley, John	Awhite	40	M	Dead	Yes	Farmer
699 Haley, S A	Ncher	45	F	1679		
700 Handle, Dempy	Ncher	10	M	Dead		
701 Handle, Sally	Ncher	32	F	7982		Farmer
702 Handle, Sophronia	Ncher	4	F	Dead		
703 Handle, Infant	Ncher	6m	F	7982		
704 Henry, Quatie	Ncher	30	F	D1418		
705 Halfbreed, Stand	Ncher	47	M	Dead		Farmer
706 Halfbreed, Nannie	Ncher	8	F	1727		
707 Halfbreed, Lydia	Ncher	5	F	7232		
708 Halfbreed, Bettie	Ncher	30	F	2359		

Name	Race	Age	Sex	Census	Md	Remarks
709 Hair, Joe	Ncher	4	M	Dead		
710 Hair, Martha	Ncher	35	F	Dead		
711 Hair, William	Ncher	12	M	Dead		
712 Hair, Walker	Ncher	10	M	Dead		
713 Hair, Nealy	Ncher	8	M	Dead		
714 Hood, David	Ncher	68	M	Dead	Yes	Farmer
715 Hood, Becca	Awhite	38	F	2014		
716 Hood, Ellis	Ncher	18	M	Dead		
717 Hood, John	Ncher	16	M	Dead		
718 Hood, Sterling	Ncher	13	M	2148		
719 Hood, Mary	Ncher	10	F	2014		
720 Hood, James	Ncher	8	M	Dead		
721 Hood, Lydia	Ncher	8	F	7426		
722 Hood, David Jr.	Ncher	6	M	2153		
723 Hicks, Mary	Ncher	36	F	7984		
724 Hicks, George	Ncher	8	M	7985		
725 Hicks, Ellen	Ncher	5	F	7986		
726 Horn, Robt S	Ncher	50	M	Dead	Yes	
727 Horn, Betsy	Awhite	50	F		Yes	
728 Horn, Lizzie	A cher	17	F	Dead		
729 Hicks, Ella	Ncher	16	F	2711		
730 Hooping, John	Ncher	59	M	Dead		Farmer
731 Hooping, John Selah	Ncher	22	F	Dead		
732 Hayes, J Q	Ncher	1	M	9537		
733 Horsefly,	Ncher	25	M	Dead		
734 Harris, Daisy	Ncher	—	F	15		
735 Horsefly, Lucy	Ncher	2m	F	D1420		
728 Ice, Andy	Ncher	33	M	Dead		
729 Joseph, Eli	Ncher	23	M	Dead	Yes	Farmer, Surname Wilkerson or Chewie (BLB)
730 Joseph, Jenny	Ncher	22	F	Dead		
731 Joseph, Susannah	Ncher	2m	F	7244		
732 Jesse, Annie	Ncher	18	F	D1421		
733 Jesse, Arley	Ncher	6m	F	D1422		
734 Jones, Famous	Ncher	10	M	9269		Surname Whitewater on Dawes (BLB)
735 Jones, Andy	Ncher	27	M	Dead		
736 Jones, C D	Ncher	32	M	6231	Yes	Farmer
737 Jones, Mary	Awhite	34	F	6231	Yes	
738 Jones, William	Ncher	14	M	1122		
739 Jones, Isaac	Ncher	11	M	Dead		
740 Jones, Asa	Ncher	8	M	1131		Asa Ray (BLB)
741 Jones, Nancy	Ncher	5	F	7429		

Name	Race	Age	Sex	Census	Md	Remarks
742 Jones, Rufus	Ncher	6m	M	6231		
743 Jones, Lydia	Ncher	60	F	Dead		
744 Johnson, Mary	Ncher	22	F	2107		
745 Jennings, George	Ncher	22	M	6156		
746 Jordan, J A	A cher	23	M	Dead	Yes	Farmer
747 Jordan, Joe	A cher	19	M	Dead		
748 Jordan, Alic	A cher	43	M	7168	Yes	Farmer
749 Jordan, C	Awhite	27	F	7168		
750 Jordan, R E S	A cher	15	M	7217		
751 Jordan, Mc R	A cher	13	M	Dead		
752 Jordan, A V	A cher	9	M	7027		
753 Jordan, E R	A cher	5	F	7161		
754 Jordan, N C	A cher	3	M	Dead		
755 Jordan, Emma	A cher	2m	F	Dead		
756 Jordan, S A	Awhite	48	F	1874		Widow of Andrew V Jordan (BLB)
757 Jordan, Joe	A cher	20	M	Dead		Farmer
758 Jordan, Vannie	A cher	17	F	2192		
759 Jordan, John	A cher	26	M	4335		
760 Jordan, Amanda	A cher	21	F	Dead		
761 Jordan, Andy V	A cher	2	M	1875		
762 Jordan, Henry	A cher	2m	M	4335		
763 Jordan, John W	A cher	17	M	D1029		
764 Jordan, John W	A cher	36	M	10279		
765 Jordan, Sarah B	Awhite	40	M	Dead		
766 Jordan, R E L	A cher	12	M	10254		
767 Jordan, T J	A cher	10	M	10253		
768 Jordan, J L	A cher	7	M	R887		
769 Jordan, John W	A cher	17	M	10129		
770 Kell, Mary	Ncher	19	F	7016		
771 Kerr, F A	Awhite	68	M	Dead	Yes	
772 Kerr, Louisa	Ncher	60	F	Dead	Yes	
773 Kerr, F A Jr.	Ncher	26	M	1876		
774 Kerr, C C	Ncher	18	M	Dead		
775 Kerr, Frank	Ncher	49	M	1895		
776 Kerr, M E	Ncher	9	F	2053?		
777 Kerr, Neville (Pig)	Ncher	30	M	7164		
778 Kerr, Lucinda	Ncher	29	F	7164		
779 Kerr, J L	Ncher	4	M	7165		
780 Kerr, W W	Ncher	2	M	7169		
781 Kerr, Infant	Ncher	___	M	Dead		
782 Kirk, G W	Awhite	37	M	2273	Yes	Farmer

Name	Race	Age	Sex	Census	Md	Remarks
783 Kirk, Amanda	Ncher	28	F	Dead		
784 Kirk, F M	Ncher	2	M	6559		
785 Kirk, Viola	Ncher	6m	F	2275		
786 Kettle, John	Ncher	45	M	1849	Yes	Farmer
787 Kettle, Nancy	Ncher	30	F	Dead		
788 Kettle, Elsie	Ncher	20	F	7750		
789 Kettle, Lucy	Ncher	18	F	Dead		
790 Kettle, Delilah	Ncher	34	F	Dead		
791 Kouch, Sallie	Ncher	25	F	D1423		
792 Kerr, Bettie	Ncher	24	F	Dead		
791 Lowry, Wm	Ncher	10	M	1896		
792 Lowry, John	Ncher	8	M	1919		
794 Leader, W D	Ncher	23	M	7245	Yes	Farmer
795 Leader, Polly	Ncher	26	F	7245		
795 Leader, Eliza	Ncher	7	F	7350		
796 Leader, Louira	Ncher	3	F	Dead		
797 Leader, C E	Ncher	1	F	Dead		
798 Leader, Ruth	Ncher	5	F	7243?		
799 Larley, Samuel	Ncher	19	M	2837		Creek Card (Surname Lasley BLB)
800 Larley, James	Ncher	17	M	Dead		
801 Love, Nathaniel	Ncher	27	M	Dead	Yes	Farmer
802 Love, Minnie	Awhite	15	F	Dead		
803 Lowry, Charles	Ncher	50	M	Dead	Yes	Farmer
804 Lowry, E M	Ncher	42	F	2034		
805 Lowry, Alice	Ncher	23	F	7096		
806 Lowry, R J	Ncher	16	M	7060		
807 Lowry, P D	Ncher	14	M	Dead		
808 Lester, J T	Awhite	22	M	Dead	Yes	
809 Lester, A C	Ncher	19	F	5		
810 Lynch, J M	Ncher	38	M	Dead		Farmer
811 Lynch, Susan	Ncher	32	F	1105		
812 Lynch, Jesse	Ncher	10	M			
813 Lynch, Ida	Ncher	8	F			
814 Lynch, Johnson	Ncher	4	M	2270		
815 Lynch, Ahelawsene	Ncher	2	M	Dead		
816 Lynch, Lizzie	Ncher	9m	F	Dead		
817 Latta, Felix	Ncher	32	M	7058	Yes	Farmer
818 Latta, Elizabeth	Awhite	18	F	7058		
819 Latta, Gemmina	Ncher	12	F	7219		
820 Latta, Bettie	Ncher	8	F	Dead		
821 Latta, Emily	Ncher	3	F	9833		

Name	Race	Age	Sex	Census	Md	Remarks
822 Lee, Wm	Ncher	32	M	Dead		
823 Lee, Angeline	Ncher	29	F	Dead		
824 Lee, Emma	Ncher	3	F	3895		
825 Lafarer, Nancy	Ncher	13	F	Dead		
826 Langley, Jack	Awhite	24	M	Dead	Yes	Farmer
827 Langley, Lucinda	Ncher	73	F	5120		
828 Langley, Noah	Ncher	18	M	R702		
829 Langley, M J	Ncher	12	F	2252		
830 Langley, T M	Ncher	10	M	Dead		
831 Langley, Lucinda	Ncher	8	F	5252		
832 Langley, Lock	Ncher	6	M	5326		
833 Langley, Thomas	Ncher	4	M	4754		
834 Lee, John	Ncher	28	M	1234	Yes	
835 Lee, Elizabeth	Awhite	33	F	1234		
836 Lee, Rachel	Ncher	8	F	237		
837 Lee, R E	Ncher	3	M	1354		
838 La Barge, D A	Ncher	35	M	F115		Enrollment Refused
839 La Barge, Jennie	Ncher	27	F	Dead		
840 La Barge, M A	Ncher	2	F	Dead	Yes	Farmer
841 Leffew, Beng	Awhite	45	M	Dead	Yes	Farmer
842 Leffew, Katie	Ncher	35	F	Dead		
843 Leffew, Henry	Ncher	5	M	7749		
844 Leffew, Laura	Ncher	2	F	Dead		
845 Leffew, R M	Ncher	2m	M	7199		
846 Leake, Betsy	Ncher	69	F	Dead		
847 Lowry, Henry	Ncher	44	M	Dead		
848 Lowry, Eveline	Awhite	42	F	Dead	Yes	
849 Lowry, Henry Jr.	Ncher	6	M	2085		
850 Lowry, Minnie	Ncher	1	F	4921		
851 Lesenbee, J R	Ncher	8	M	D1425		Left Country 10 or 12 yrs
852 Lowrey, John	Ncher	28	M	4227	Yes	Farmer
853 Lowrcy, Mary	Awhite	22	F	4227	Yes	
854 Lowrey, William	Ncher	1	M	4591		
855 Lowrey, Betty	Ncher	40	F	Dead		
856 Lowrey, George	Ncher	21	M	Dead		
857 Lowrey, H C	Ncher	30	M	12	Yes	
858 Lowrey, Elsie	Ncher	31	F	12		
859 Looney, Alice	Ncher	21	F	29		
860 Looney, William	Ncher	15	M	1761		
861 Looney, Henry	Ncher	8	M	1755		
862 LindseyHarry	Awhite	53	M	2250		Physician
863 LindseyBettie	Ncher	45	F	2250		

Name	Race	Age	Sex	Census	Md	Remarks
864 Lowrey, J M	Ncher	28	M	7229		
865 Lowrey, Susan	Ncher	21	F	7229		
866 Lowrey, Rafail	Ncher	4	M	7014		
867 Lowrey, Anderson	Ncher	3	M	5734		
868 Lowrey, Eliza	Ncher	1	F	7227		
869 Lowrey, James	Ncher	25	M	Dead	Yes	Farmer
870 Lowrey, Clarinda	Ncher	22	F	7553		
871 Lowrey, Lucinda	Ncher	1	F	Dead		
872 Lowrey, Ellis	Ncher	22	M	1936	Yes	
873 Lowrey, Elizabeth	Ncher	24	F	Dead		
874 Lowrey, Johnson	Ncher	1	M	1936		
875 Latta, Allen	A col	70	M	Dead		
876 Latta, M J	Awhite	14	F	10229		
877 Latta, Eliza	Awhite	18	F			
878 Lovejoy, Mary	Ncher	27	F	D1426		
879 Leader, Jim	Ncher	5	M	7300		
880 Laundrum, Jesse	Ncher	20	M	Dead		
881 La Barge, M A	Ncher	2	F	2355		
882 Lourey, George	Ncher	21	M	Dead		Dup of 856
883 Leander, Thomas	Ncher	5	M	7232		
884 Mackay, Louisa	Ncher	56	F	Dead		
885 Mackay, John D	Ncher	30	M	Dead		
886 Mackay, Laura	Ncher	20	F	Dead		
887 Mackay, Lugie	Ncher	15	F	1212		
888 McMaken, W D	Awhite	47	M	Dead	Yes	Farmer
889 McMaken, Savanah	Ncher	32	F	4		
890 McMaken, Jane	Ncher	7	F	4		
891 McMaken, Kinsay	Ncher	4	M	4		
892 McMaken, P C	Ncher	2	M	4		Died since enrolling
891 Martin, David	Awhite	26	M	D1228	Yes	Farmer
892 Martin, Eliza	Ncher	22	F	2228		
893 Miller, Tony	Ncher	12	M	Dead		
894 McDaniel, Robt	Ncher	44	M	Dead	Yes	Farmer
895 McDaniel, Cinderella	Ncher	39	F	7329		
896 McDaniel, David	Ncher	18	M	D1427		Dead
897 Matoy, Betsy	Ncher	50	F	Dead		
898 Matoy, Lucinda	Ncher	12	F	Dead		
899 Matoy, Nancy	Ncher	10	F	Dead		
900 Miller, Geo B	Ncher	6m	M	7203		
901 Miller, Elizabeth	Ncher	19	F	16		
902 Meeker, J T	Awhite	40	M	Dead	Yes	Farmer
903 Meeker, Eveline	Ncher	20	F	2917		

Name	Race	Age	Sex	Census	Md	Remarks
904 Meeker, Henrietta	Ncher	10	F	3753		
905 Meeker, Reese	Ncher	7	M	Dead		
906 Meeker, George	Ncher	2	M	2189		
907 Martin, A L	Ncher	32	M	D1728		Osage citizen, Farmer
908 Martin, Caroline	Ncher	28	F	Dead		
909 Martin, Julia	Ncher	13	F	D1429		Osage citizen
910 Martin, Aggy	Ncher	9	F	D1430		Osage citizen
911 Martin, Ellen	Ncher	2	F	D1431		Osage, now Felix Caton's wife
912 Marrow, J T	Awhite	40	M	7179		
913 Marrow, Nancy	Ncher	44	F	7179		
914 Morgan, Katie	Ncher	57	F	Dead		
915 Munroe, Thos R	Ncher	49	M	Dead	Yes	Farmer
916 Munroe, S L	Awhite	37	F	Dead		
917 Munroe, S C	Ncher	18	F	6393		
918 Munroe, W A	Ncher	15	M	Dead		
919 Munroe, Manerva	Ncher	13	F	6392		
920 Munroe, Ellen B	Ncher	7	F	Dead		
921 Munroe, G A	Ncher	5	F	5865		
922 Munroe, N D	Ncher	2	F	2253		
923 Manning, Worcester	Ncher	35	M	Dead	Yes	Farmer
924 Manning, Tooney	Ncher	34	F	Dead		
925 Morgan, James	Ncher	40	M	7277		
926 Morgan, Josephine	Ncher	21	F	Dead		
927 Morgan, Joshua	Ncher	1	M	Dead		
928 Morgan, Mark	Ncher	30	M	7170	Yes	Farmer
929 Morgan, Cynthia	Ncher	27	F	Dead		
930 Morgan, M J	Ncher	8	F	2047		
931 Morgan, M A	Ncher	5	F	2258		
932 Morgan, Rebecca	Ncher	5	F	4388		
933 Morgan, Elizabeth	Ncher	2	F	7276		
934 Morgan, George	Ncher	6m	M	D1432		Dead
935 Muskrat, James	Ncher	44	M	Dead	Yes	Farmer
936 Muskrat, Susan	Ncher	37	F	Dead		
937 Muskrat, Calhoon	Ncher	20	F	8000		
938 Muskrat, Joe	Ncher	18	M	7074		
939 Muskrat, Sophronia	Ncher	15	F	Dead		
940 Muskrat, Noah	Ncher	13	M	Dead		
941 McLain, James	Ncher	21	M	5028		
942 McLain, Austin	Ncher	19	M	5150		
943 Maker, Marry	Ncher	28	F	Dead	Yes	
944 Maker, William	Ncher	1	M	7301		
945 McLain, William	Ncher	28	M	6508		Farmer

Name	Race	Age	Sex	Census	Md	Remarks
946 McLain, Lizzie	Ncher	24	F	Dead		
947 McLain, Infant	Ncher	1m	M	6508		
948 Marshall, Betty	Ncher	19	F	Dead	Yes	
949 Marshall, C J	Awhite	31	M	Dead		
950 Marshall, Polly	Ncher	2m	F	7410		
951 Moore, Ella	Ncher	8	F	7043		
952 Martin, Dianna	Ncher	27	F	F268		
953 Martin, Wilsley	Ncher	1m	M	F457		
954 Mackey, Chas	A col	45	M	Dead	Yes	
955 Mackey, Rufus	A col	9	M	F460		
956 Mackey, Jenney	A col	16	F	Dead		
957 Mackey, Tony	A col	19	F	Dead		
958 McDaniel, Thomas	Ncher	4	M	1650		
959 Morgan, Thos H	Ncher	2	M	7175		
960 Morgan, Jane	Ncher	35	F	Dead		
961 McDaniel, Johnson	Ncher	19	M	Dead		
962 McDaniel, Claud H	Ncher	22	M	Dead		
963 McClelland, M P	A Cher	42	F	2037		
964 Mink, Nelly	Ncher	20	F	7111		
965 McClure, James	A Cher	53	M	Dead	Yes	Farmer
966 McClure, Rebecca	A Cher	53	F	Dead		
967 McClure, W J	A Cher	33	M	7171		
968 McClure, F D	A Cher	18	M	5672		Should be female (BLB)
969 McClure, C J	A Cher	16	M	2241		
970 McClure, R L	A Cher	14	M	2237		
971 McClure, G L	A Cher	10	M	Dead		
972 McClure, H B	A Cher	24	M	2235	Yes	
973 McClure, S A	Awhite	19	F	2235		
974 Mike, Rachel	Ncher	42	F	Dead		
975 Muskrat, Wilson	Ncher	36	M	7183	Yes	Farmer
976 Muskrat, Choheohee	Ncher	30	F	7183		
977 Muskrat, Lydia	Ncher	8	F	7185		
978 Muskrat, Ahyostah	Ncher	2	F	7182		
979 Murphy, Beng	Ncher	28	M			
980 Mabry, Sarah	Ncher	21	F	2134	Yes	
981 Mabry, S G	Awhite	33	M	2134	Yes	Farmer
982 Mabry, Perly	Ncher	3m	F	Dead		
983 Miller, Jacob	Ncher	35	M	Dead	Yes	
984 Miller, M C	Ncher	23	F	Dead		
985 Miller, Samuel	Ncher	2	M	7294		
986 Maxfield, Octavia	Ncher	22	F	7139		
987 Maxfield, Ida	Ncher	20	F	Dead		

Name	Race	Age	Sex	Census	Md	Remarks
988 Maxfield, Lillie	Ncher	18	F	Dead		
989 McNelty, Jeff	Awhite	21	M	Dead	No	Farmer
990 Miller, John	Ncher	35	M	Dead	Yes	
991 Miller, Mary	Ncher	45	F	7397		
992 Miller, Geo W	Ncher	17	M	D1433		Lives in Coo
993 Miller, A J	Ncher	11	F	7176		
994 Miller, Nancy	Ncher	9	F	Dead		
995 McDaniel, Mary	Awhite	23	F	Dead		
996 McDaniel, S J	Ncher	4	F	2099		
997 McDaniel, Rosie	Ncher	2	F	1339		
998 McDaniel, Alic	Ncher	26	M	Dead		
999 McDaniel, Elizabeth	Ncher	22	F	7230		
1000 McDaniel, Mary	Ncher	2	F	1771		
1001 Murphy, James	Ncher	26	M	Dead	Yes	Farmer
1002 Murphy, S E	Ncher	27	F	Dead	Yes	
1003 Murphy, Emily	Ncher	1	F	7003		
1004 Moore, S F	Awhite	32	M	D1434		
1005 Moore, Abigail	Ncher	30	F	Dead		
1006 Moore, H W	Ncher	2	M	1163		
1007 McPherson, H B	Ncher	46	M	7130		
1008 McPherson, J C	Ncher	9	M	2092		
1009 Mink, Sampson	Ncher	27	M	Dead		
1010 McDaniel, James	Ncher	4	M	D1735		
1011 Manning, Chas	Ncher	29	M	Dead	Yes	
1012 Manning, Peggy	Ncher	29	M	7133		
1013 Merrel, Geo W	Ncher	24	M	D1736		
1014 McSpaniardA	A col	30	M	Dead	No	Farmer
1015 McDaniel, Stephen	Awhite	25	M	7068		
1016 McDaniel, E F	Ncher	24	F	7068		
1017 McCorkle, D W	Ncher	13	M	7438		Farmer
1018 McCorkle, E H	Ncher	9	F	Dead		
1019 Martin, David	Awhite	26	M			Unreadable (BLB)
1020 Manning, Susan	Ncher	18	F	D1437		
1021 McIntosh, T F	Ncher	8	M			Lives close to Checotah on Creek Card 990
1021 Narcony, Nannie	Ncher	32	F	D1439	Yes	
1022 Narcony, David	Ncher	6	M	Dead		
1023 Neal, James	Ncher	48	M	2278	Yes	Farmer
1024 Neal, Polly	Ncher	40	F	2278		
1025 Neal, Samuel	Ncher	4	M	7151		
1026 Neal, Nancy	Ncher	2	F	2287		
1027 Neal, Richard	Ncher	44	M	2277	Yes	Farmer

Name	Race	Age	Sex	Census	Md	Remarks
1028 Neal, M W	Awhite	45	F	Dead		
1029 Neal, Lucy J	Ncher	7	F	7275		
1030 Neal, James	Ncher	5	M	7162		
1031 Nicholson, M H	Awhite	44	F	7290	Yes	Farmer
1032 Nicholson, L A	Ncher	19	F	24		
1033 Nicholson, J B	Ncher	16	M	Dead		
1034 Nicholson, A W	Ncher	13	F	28		
1035 Nicholson, C S	Ncher	10	F	7102		
1036 Nicholson, D W	Ncher	7	M	Dead		
1037 Nicholson, H F	Ncher	5	M	2371		
1038 Nicholson, E V	Ncher	3	F	4109		
1039 Nivens, John C	Ncher	61	F	Dead	Yes	Farmer
1040 Nivens, Delilah	Ncher	56	F	Dead		
1041 Nivens, Josephine	Ncher	25	F			Creek Citizen
1042 Nivens, Ella	Ncher	4	F	Dead		
1043 Nivens, Julia	A choc	32	F	2206		
1044 Nivens, Emma	Ncher	13	F	Dead		
1045 Nivens, Jefferson	Ncher	10	M			
1046 Nivens, Floyd	Ncher	5	M	D2572		Claims Choctaw
1047 Nivens, Infant	Ncher	2	M	Dead		
1048 Nivens, Delilah	Ncher	14	F	4469		
1049 Nivens, Jordan	A col	___?	M	Dead		
1050 Nitts, Ice	Ncher	35	M	Dead		
1051 Nitts, Nakie	Ncher	24	F	D1441		P O Webber's Falls, IT lives with Wilson Girty
1052 Oldfields, Sam	Ncher	14	M	Dead		
1053 Oolaheahtah	Ncher	25	M	Dead		
1054 Owens, Annie	Ncher	20	F	7125		
1055 Owens, Ice	Ncher	38	M	Dead		
1056 Owens, Samuel	Ncher	5	M	1724		
1057 Owens, Lewis	Ncher	30	M	Dead	Yes	
1058 Owens, Nellie	Ncher	25	F	Dead		
1059 Owens, Martin	Ncher	7	M	7669		
1060 Owens, Annie	Ncher	3	F	Dead		
1061 Owens, William (Infant)	Ncher	___	M	Dead		
1062 Philips, William	Ncher	27	M	Dead	Yes	Farmer
1063 Philips, M J	Ncher	25	F	2614		
1064 Philips, Walter	Ncher	7	M	1676		
1065 Philips, Harvey	Ncher	5	M	2606		
1066 Philips, J H	Ncher	3	M	2605		
1067 Philips, Julia	Ncher	1	F	2598		
1068 Philips, W M	Ncher	33	M	Dead	Yes	Farmer

Name	Race	Age	Sex	Census	Md	Remarks
1069 Philips, Rachel	Awhite	37	F	Dead		
1070 Philips, Henry	Ncher	6	M	6968		
1071 Philips, Andrew	Ncher	4	M	470		
1072 Patrick, John	Ncher	19	M	7081		
1073 Petty, J W	Awhite	41	M	D1442		Married out
1074 Petty, J T	Ncher	7	M	7083		
1075 Parris, Susie	Ncher	10	F	D1443		
1076 Payne, William	Ncher	30	M	Dead	Yes	Farmer
1077 Payne, Thomas	Ncher	9	M	Dead		
1078 Payne, Ruth	Ncher	6	F	Dead		
1079 Peaugh, Josephine	Ncher	___	F	Dead		
1080 Peaugh, Mary Jane	Ncher	___	F	2702		
1081 Peck, W B	Awhite	32	M	7279	Yes	Farmer, (Surname Beck BLB)
1082 Peck, M J	Ncher	29	M	7279		Surname Beck (BLB)
1083 Peck, J T	Ncher	11	M	7283		Surname Beck (BLB)
1084 Peck, J C	Ncher	9	M	7280		Surname Beck (BLB)
1085 Peck, E E	Ncher	7	F	7282		Surname Beck (BLB)
1086 Pheasant, Jinnie	Ncher	26	F	Dead		
1087 Pheasant, Thomas	Ncher	9	M	Dead		
1088 Quinton, John	Ncher	21	M	Dead	No	Farmer
1089 Quinton, Hannah	Ncher	19	F	5295		
1090 Quinton, Bettie	Ncher	17	F	5250		
1091 Quinton, Samuel	Ncher	12	M	Dead		
1092 Quinton, Lydia	Ncher	10	F	Dead		
1093 Quinton, Ruth	Ncher	6	F	4936		
1091 Rider, Jessie	A col	30	M	F429		
1092 Rider, Reed	A col	3	M	F428		
1093 Reaves, Lovely	A col	1	M	F1167		
1094 Reaves, L W	Awhite	28	M	Dead	Yes	
1095 Ragsdale, Augeronica	Ncher	26	F	1956		
1096 Ragsdale, Thomas	Ncher	8	M	1955		
1097 Ragsdale, Cynthia	Ncher	6	F	5057		
1098 Riley, Nelson	Ncher	21	M	Dead		
1099 Richey, George	Awhite	35	M	7293	Yes	Farmer
1100 Richey, Mary A	Ncher	55	F	7293		
1101 Roberts, William	Ncher	22	M	5945		Farmer
1102 Roberts, Nancy	Ncher	24	F	Dead		
1103 Robinson, Nancy	Ncher	32	F	2060		
1104 Robinson, John	Awhite	42	M	2060		
1105 Robinson, Lucy	Ncher	11	F	6512		
1106 Robinson, Albert	Ncher	7	M	Dead		
1107 Robinson, Samuel	Ncher	7	M	7354		

Name	Race	Age	Sex	Census	Md	Remarks
1108 Robinson, Chas	Ncher	1	M	7353		
1109 Rat, Absenee	Ncher	30	M	Dead		
1110 Robinson, J H	Awhite	21	M	Dead	Yes	Farmer
1111 Robinson, Catherine	Ncher	23	F	Dead		
1112 Robinson, Dora	Ncher	6m	F	5495		
1113 Riley, Adie	Ncher	17	F	7009	No	
1114 Ross, J T	Ncher	29	M	1093	Yes	Farmer
1115 Ross, Missouri	Awhite	29	F	1093		
1116 Ross, N E	A cher	8	F	5098		
1117 Ross, Lucinda	A cher	8	F	1122		
1118 Ross, Warker	A cher	6	M	1091		
1119 Ross, America	Ncher	4	F	5906		
1120 Ross, Andrew	A cher	69	M	Dead	Yes	Farmer
1121 Ross, Lucinda	A cher	55	F	Dead		
1122 Ross, J G	A cher	17	M	Dead		
1123 Ross, W H	A cher	15	M	996		
1124 Ross, J A	A cher	13	F	Dead		
1125 Ross, R T	A cher	26	M	1607		
1126 Ross, I J	Awhite	25	F	Dead		
1127 Ross, E M	A cher	5	F	1633		
1128 Raymond, Jesse	Ncher	10	M	1698		
1129 Raymond, Ida	Ncher	8	F	2345		
1130 Reynolds, Gideon	Awhite	66	M	Dead	Yes	Farmer
1131 Reynolds, Elsie	Ncher	42	F	Dead		
1132 Reynolds, Polly A	Ncher	32	F	Dead		
1133 Reynolds, William	Ncher	20	M	Dead		
1134 Rowe, Johnson	Ncher	25	M	Dead		
1135 Rowe, Bettie	Ncher	28	F	7995		
1136 Rowe, George	Ncher	4m	M	Dead		
1137 Robinson, G W	Awhite	34	M	Dead		
1138 Robinson, Emma	Ncher	33	F	1962		
1139 Robinson, Mary	Ncher	2	F	7438		
1140 Robinson, Jane	Awhite	39	F	Dead		
1141 Reynolds, W A	Ncher	2	M	1991		
1142 Riley, Carles	Ncher	10	M	Dead		
1143 Reed, Frank	A col	2m	M	F159		
1144 Ratlinggourd	Ncher	40	M	7365	No	Mechanic
1145 Rowe, Peggy	Ncher	23	F	Dead		
1146 Rogers, Sarah	Ncher	70	F	Dead		
1147 Rogers, Chetee	Ncher	26	M	Dead		
1148 Rock, John	Ncher	30	M	7106	Yes	Farmer
1149 Rock, Jinnie	Ncher	30	F	7106		

Name	Race	Age	Sex	Census	Md	Remarks
1150 Rock, Chicayuee	Ncher	7	F	109		
1151 Robins, Louisa	Ncher	26	F	Dead	No	
1152 Robins, B F	Ncher	44	M	Dead	Yes	Farmer
1153 Robins, R C	Awhite	33	F	6297		
1154 Robins, W J	Ncher	9	M	D1444		Dead, left the nation
1155 Robins, M T	Ncher	4	M	2178		
1156 Robins, R B	Ncher	1	M	1732		
1157 Riley, Eliza	Ncher	35	F	2098		
1158 Robinson, E F	Ncher	30	F	7448		
1159 Robinson, J C	Ncher	12	M	7330		
1160 Robinson, M E	Ncher	7	F	7652		
1161 Raven, William	Ncher	5	M	D1445		
1162 Raven, Luther	Ncher	2	M	Dead		
1163 Reece, Chas	Ncher	26	M	7103	Yes	
1164 Reece, Nellie	Ncher	24	F	7048		
1165 Reece, Lewis	Ncher	4	M	2379		
1166 Reece, Nancy	Ncher	2	F	7047		
1167 Riley, Samuel	Ncher	28	M	Dead		
1168 Rider, William	A cher	24	M	4771		
1169 Rider, N J	Ncher	24	F	2158	Yes	Farmer
1170 Rider, Nancy	Ncher	20	F	Dead		
1171 Rider, Laura	Ncher	5	F	2160		
1172 Rowland, Martha	Ncher	21	M	Dead		
1173 Rowland, H W	Ncher	1	M	5*37?		Unreadable (BLB)
1174 Ratley, Jeff	Ncher	18	M	7080	No	
1175 Reed, F B	Awhite	30	M			Unreadable (BLB)
1176 Reed, Josephine	Ncher	22	M	6311		
1177 Reed, A A	Ncher	1	M	33		
1178 Raymond, Hessie	Ncher	10	M	1698		Dup no 1128 as Jessie
1179 Raymond, Ada	Ncher	8	M	2345		Dup no 1129 as Ida
1881 Smith, Hiram	Ncher	30	M	Dead	Yes	Farmer
1882 Smith, Eliza	Ncher	20	F	Dead		
1883 Smith, Ned	Ncher	___	M	2323	No	
1884 Scott, Carrie	Ncher	3	F	D1446		
1885 Steeler, Robert V	Ncher	35	M	5276		
1886 Smart, Henry	Ncher	9	M	7097		
1887 Smart, Clinton	Ncher	3	M	D1447		
1888 Simmons, Tobe	Ncher	23	M	Dead	Yes	
1889 Simmons, Nancy	Ncher	30	F	Dead	Yes	
1890 Schrimsher, Jane	Ncher	35	F	Dead	Yes	
1891 Schrimsher, Susan	Ncher	1	F	2242		
1892 Schrimsher, Edward	Ncher	8	M			Creek card 505

Name	Race	Age	Sex	Census	Md	Remarks
1993 Saltface	Ncher	56	M	Dead	Yes	Farmer
1994 Saltface, Cynthea	Ncher	35	F	Dead		
1195 Saltface, Betsy	Ncher	10	F	Dead		
1196 Saltface, Lizzie	Ncher	6	F	1972		
1197 Sites, Fredric	Awhite	54	M	Dead	Yes	
1198 Sites, Caroline	Ncher	36	F	Dead		
1199 Sites, Alex	Ncher	10	M	2297		
1200 Sites, Delilah	Ncher	8	F	Dead		
1201 Sites, Louisa	Ncher	6	F	4771		
1202 Sites, Fredric	Ncher	3	M	2281		
1203 Sites, F M	Ncher	4	M	Dead		
1204 Simmons, Sarah	Ncher	21	F	Dead		
1205 Simmons, Thomas	Ncher	1	M	1650		Duplicate 958 Can Dist
1206 Smith, McCoy	Ncher	31	M	2202	Yes	Farmer
1207 Smith, J E	Ncher	22	F	2202		
1208 Smith, Edward	Ncher	22	M	2317		
1209 Shepherd, Albert	Awhite	26	M	D157	Yes	
1210 Shepherd, Martha	Ncher	32	F	Dead		
1211 Stout, Abram	Ncher	30	M	1927	Yes	Farmer
1212 Stout, M A	Ncher	27	F	1927		
1213 Stout, F A	Ncher	6	F	Dead		
1214 Stout, N E	Ncher	4	F	1923		
1215 Stout, Anabell	Ncher	2	F	1929		
1216 Stout, Infant	Ncher	1m	M	Dead		
1217 Shepherd, WM	Ncher	39	M	Dead		
1218 Shepherd, Chas H	Ncher	9	M	Dead		
1219 Scoonover,	Awhite	53	M	2346	Yes	
1220 Scoonover, Annie	Ncher	29	F	Dead	Yes	
1221 Scoonover, Lucy	Ncher	1	F	2370		
1222 Scott, F M	Awhite	30	M	Dead	Yes	Farmer
1223 Scott, M E	Ncher	28	F	3352		
1224 Scott, W N	Ncher	6	M	3705		
1225 Scott, C C	Ncher	4	M	6449		
1226 Scott, T A	Ncher	2	M	3378		
1227 Scott, M B	Ncher	6m	M	7067		
1228 Scott, W L	Awhite	28	M	Dead	Yes	Farmer
1229 Scott, Henrietta	Ncher	23	F	7273		
1230 Scott, M J	Ncher	4	M	2357		
1231 Scott, Alfred	Ncher	2	M	7254		
1232 Scott, G W	Awhite	26	M	27	Yes	Farmer
1233 Scott, Stella	Ncher	23	F	Dead		
1234 Scott, Robt L	Ncher	2	M	27		

Name	Race	Age	Sex	Census	Md	Remarks
1235 Scott, V C	Ncher	1m	M	27		
1236 Summerfield, Amos	Ncher	24	M	Dead		
1237 Sevier, J J	Ncher	28	M	6198	Yes	Farmer
1238 Sevier, Maggie	Ncher	22	F	6198		
1239 Sevier, Infant	Ncher	3m	F	6198		
1240 Sevier, John	Ncher	47	M	Dead	Yes	Preacher
1241 Sevier, Arizonia	A cher	18	F	Dead		
1242 Sevier, J A	Ncher	29	M	Dead		Farmer
1243 Sevier, Emma	Ncher	18	F	Dead		
1244 Smith, John	Ncher	31	M	Dead	Yes	Farmer
1245 Smith, L L	Ncher	30	F	7134		
1246 Smith, Louisa	Ncher	6m	F	7134		
1247 Scott, Richard	Ncher	19	M	1082		
1248 Skinnuryah	Ncher	29	M	7222		
1249 Sheppard, Lucy	Ncher	34	F	Dead		Farmer
1250 Sheppard, Fain	Ncher	12	M	Dead		
1251 Sheppard, Eliza	Ncher	10	F	1060		
1252 Sheppard, Linnie	Ncher	9	F	7267		
1253 Sheppard, Rich'd	Ncher	6	M	7087		
1254 Sheppard, Josephine	Ncher	4	F	Dead		
1255 Sheppard, G W	Ncher	23	M	1993		
1256 Sheppard, John	Ncher	21	M	Dead		
1257 Scott, Arley	Ncher	17	F	7005		
1258 Smedley, W M	Awhite	33	M	Dead	Yes	Farmer
1259 Smedley, M J	Ncher	38	F	Dead	Yes	
1260 Smedley, John	Ncher	9	M	5864		
1261 Smedley, Rich'd	Ncher	7	M	5864		
1262 Smedley, William	Ncher	5	M	Dead		
1263 Smedley, Jackson	Ncher	2	M	7010		
1264 Scales, Mack	A col	23	M	Dead	Yes	Farmer
1265 Scales, Lizzie	A col	2	F	Dead		
1266 Silk, Anderson	A col	7	M	F245		
1267 Silk, Squire	A col	5	M	F246		
1268 Silk, John	A col	3	M	F442		
1269 Snow, Daniel	A col	40	M	F164		
1270 Snow, Ruth	A col	32	F	F164		
1271 Snow, Mary	A col	9	F	F624		
1272 Snow, Susie	A col	7	F	Dead		
1273 Snow, Bosie	A col	5	F	F515		
1274 Snow, Henry	A col	3	M	Dead		
1275 Snow, Wilse	A col	2m	F	Dead		
1276 Stephenson, C R	Awhite	40	M	D1449	Yes	In Mexico

Name	Race	Age	Sex	Census	Md	Remarks
1277 Stephenson, Samantha	Ncher	30	F	D1450		In Colorado
1278 Stephenson, J C	Ncher	7	M	D1451		
1279 Stephenson, S E?	Ncher	4	M	D1452		
1280 Sheriff, Fritz	Awhite	50	M	Dead		
1281 Sheriff, Peggy	Ncher	19	F	Dead	Yes	Mechanic
1282 Sheriff, Sophia	Ncher	3	F	Dead		
1283 Sheriff, John	Ncher	2	M	Dead		
1284 Starr, Carworhee	Ncher	6	M	Dead		
1285 Smith, Carty	Ncher	23	M	1819		
1286 Smith, Famous	Ncher	26	M	7156	Yes	Farmer
1287 Smith, M N	Ncher	26	F	Dead		
1288 Smith, Joe V	Ncher	5	M	7157		
1289 Smith, Famous Jr.	Ncher	9m	M	Dead		
1290 Smith, Eliza	Ncher	17	F	6549	No	
1291 Simmons, Martha	Ncher	15	F	1819	No	
1292 Scales, Hannah	A col	37	F	Dead		
1292 Sheppard, Coffee	A col	47	M	F155	Yes	Farmer
1293 Sheppard, M A	A col	54	F	F527		
1294 Sheppard, M E	A col	14	F	F547		
1295 Sheppard, Ednah	A col	11	F	Dead		
1296 Scales, J A	Ncher	48	M	1601	Yes	Farmer
1297 Scales, P J	Ncher	18	M	1601		
1298 Smallwood, Tobacco	Ncher	25	M	Dead	Yes	
1299 Smallwood, Takie	Ncher	25	F	Dead	Yes	
1300 Smallwood, H B	Ncher	1	M	Dead		
1301 Starr, Frost	Ncher	36	M	Dead	Yes	Farmer
1302 Starr, Fanny	Ncher	24	F	1587		
1303 Smallwood, Etehkerstah	Ncher	7	M	1951		
1304 Sunday, Thomas	Ncher	21	M	7237	Yes	
1305 Sunday, Ellen	Ncher	23	F	Dead		
1306 Sunday, Lucy	Ncher	6m	F	Dead		
1307 Starr, James	Ncher	40	M	Dead	Yes	Farmer
1308 Starr, Eliza	Ncher	36	F	7991		
1309 Starr, Luxie or Wm	Ncher	16	M	8010		
1310 Starr, Mulsie	Ncher	12	F	7992		
1311 Starr, Thomas	Ncher	10	M	7990		
1312 Starr, John	Ncher	7	M	Dead		
1313 Starr, Samuel	Ncher	5	M	8013		
1314 Smallwood, William	Ncher	27	M	Dead	Yes	Farmer
1315 Smallwood, Martha	Ncher	22	F	Dead		
1316 Smallwood, Joe V	Ncher	1	M	7192		
1317 Symco, Charley	Ncher	16	M	Dead		

Name	Race	Age	Sex	Census	Md	Remarks
1318 Stansel, Alice	Ncher	9	F	Dead		
1319 Stewart, Wm	Ncher	26	M	2095	Yes	
1320 Stewart, Annie	Ncher	26	F	2095		
1321 Simmons, J C	Ncher	3	M	Dead		
1322 Sanders, Joshua	Ncher	40	M	Dead	no	Farmer
1323 Scoonover, H F	Ncher	1 1/2	M	2349		
1324 Spaniard, George	Ncher	26	M	Dead		
1325 Spaniard, Steve	Ncher	20	M	Dead		
1326 Severe, Thomas	Ncher	14	M	Dead		
1327 Shinn,				Dead		
1328 Starr, Thomas	Ncher	67	M	Dead	Yes	Farmer
1329 Starr, Catherine	Ncher	61	F	Dead		
1330 Starr, Lucinda	Ncher	39	F	7173	No	
1331 Starr, Samuel	Ncher	19	M	Dead		
1332 Starr, Wenonah	Ncher	16	F	2046		
1333 Starr, Lucy	Ncher	6	F	Dead		
1334 Starr, C R	Ncher	32	M	Dead		Farmer
1335 Starr, Calvin	Ncher	7	M	Dead		
1336 Starr, Ellis	Ncher	4	M	1994		
1337 Starr, Tuxie or Wm	Ncher	30	M	Dead	No	
1338 Starr, Chas Mc	Ncher	10	M	Dead		
1339 Starr, M B	Ncher	6	M	Dead		
1340 Starr, Clarissa	Awhite	22	F	Dead	Yes	
1341 Starr, Thomas Jr.	Ncher	24	M	Dead		
1342 Starr, Samuel	Ncher	3	M	1583		
1343 Starr, Henry	Ncher	2m	M	1583		
1344 Starr, Wm	A col	25	M	Dead		
1345 Starr, Rhoda	A col	23	F	F689		
1346 Starr, Vinnie	A col	3	F	F690		
1347 Sakie	Ncher	60	F	Dead		
1348 Shettley, J A	Awhite	38	M	4923	Yes	Farmer
1349 Shettley, E J	Ncher	28	F	Dead		
1350 Simmons, James	Ncher	48	M	Dead		Blacksmith
1351 Simmons, Caroline	Ncher	38	F	Dead		
1352 Simmons, Lewis	Ncher	13	M	1073		
1353 Simmons, J E	Ncher	7	F	1002		
1354 Simmons, Josephine	Ncher	5	F	2132		
1355 Sanders, Jno	Ncher	30	M	Dead	Yes	Farmer
1356 Sanders, N J	Ncher	25	F	7312		
1357 Sanders, E C	Ncher	7	M	1283		
1358 Sanders, Dora	Ncher	2	F	6938		
1359 Sanders, Lillie	Ncher	3m	F	7384		

Name	Race	Age	Sex	Census	Md	Remarks
1360 Sanders, M J	Ncher	?	F	Dead	No	
1361 Spaniard, Jno	Ncher	30	M	Dead	Yes	Farmer
1362 Spaniard, Lizzie	Ncher	25	F	Dead		
1363 Spaniard, Lydia	Ncher	6	F	Dead		
1364 Spaniard, Annie	Ncher	4	F	D1453		
1365 Spaniard, Lucy	Ncher	4m	F	6515		
1366 Splitnose,	Ncher	47	M	Dead	Yes	Farmer
1367 Splitnose, Susan	Ncher	35	F	Dead		
1368 Splitnose, Thomas	Ncher	9	M	7287		
1369 Splitnose, Nancy	Ncher	7	F	1595		
1370 Splitnose, Chas Mc	Ncher	3	M	7285		
1371 Smith, Ellen	Ncher	10	F	7831		
1372 Smith, Thomas	Ncher	8	M	Dead		
1374 Triplett, William	Awhite	59	M	Dead	Yes	Farmer
1375 Triplett, Mary A	Ncher	44	F	7138		
1376 Triplett, Ned	Ncher	9	M	7141		
1377 Trent, Ella	Ncher	38	F	Dead		
1378 Tong, Anderson	Ncher	22	M	Dead	Yes	
1379 Tong, Lydia	Ncher	22	F	7131		
1380 Tong, Elizabeth	Ncher	4m	F	Dead		
1381 Tong, John	Ncher	26	M	8011	Yes	Farmer
1382 Tong, Charlotte	Ncher	25	F	Dead		
1383 Taylor, John	Ncher	9	M	7404		
1384 Toney, Levi	Ncher	20	M	7142	No	
1385 Teequahnahlah, Dick	Ncher	22	M	Dead		
1386 Thompson, Chas Mc	Ncher	30	M	Dead	Yes	Farmer
1387 Thompson, Sarah	Ncher	21	F	Dead	Yes	
1388 Thompson, Annie	Ncher	7	F	Dead		
1389 Trinson, Winnie	Ncher	70	F	Dead	No	Farmer
1390 Thompson, Jno	Ncher	17	M	1772		
1391 Taylor, Richard	Ncher	28	M	Dead	Yes	
1392 Taylor, Sophronia	Ncher	22	F	7170		
1393 Taylor, L H	Ncher	2	M	Dead		
1394 Timberlake, John	Ncher	20	M	10226		
1395 Trent, T C	Awhite	35	M	Dead		
1396 Trent, Eddie	Ncher	7	M	7051		
1397 Tassel, Jackson	Ncher	17	M	Dead		
1398 Tackett, George	Ncher	13	M	Dead		Son of Sarah Tackett (nee Harlan BLB)
1399 Tassel, S A	Ncher	23?	M	Dead		
1400 Taylor, S M	Ncher	62	M	Dead	Yes	
1401 Taylor, J L	Ncher	55	F	1674		

Name	Race	Age	Sex	Census	Md	Remarks
1402 Teenowe, Samuel	Ncher	1	M	Dead		
1403 Teenowe, George	Ncher	25	M	Dead		
1404 Teenowe, Eliza	Ncher	37	F	Dead		
1405 Thompson, Jeff	A col	30	M	Dead	Yes	Farmer
1406 Thompson, Josephine	A col	30	F	Dead		
1407 Turnover, Nancy	Ncher	26	F	Dead		
1408 Turnover, Ellen	Ncher	24	F	2103		
1409 Turnover, Margaret	Ncher	19	F	1632		
1410 Toonyyee,	Ncher	50	M	Dead	Yes	
1411 Toonyyee, Elsie	Ncher	26	F	Dead		
1412 Tunorwee, Sallie	Ncher	35	F	7220		
1413 Teehee, George	Ncher	40	M	Dead	Yes	
1414 Teehee, Katie	Ncher	27	F	2131		
1415 Timson, Susie	Ncher	23	F	Dead		
1416 Triplett, Eugene	Ncher	6	M	5329		
1417 Teehee, Lee	Ncher	14	M	7532		Dup 1434 Seq
1418 Vann, G A	Ncher	3	F	D1454		Enrolled on Chickasaw card D125
1419 Vann, Infant	Ncher	4m	F	D1455		"" D115
1420 Vann, James	Ncher	7	M	D1456		"" D115
1421 Vann, Ellen	Ncher	10	F	D1457		"" D126
1422 Vann, David	Ncher	12	M	D1458		"" D123
1423 Vann, Lotta	A chic	38	F	D1459		"" D115
1424 Vann, W R	Ncher	34	M	26		
1425 Vann, J W						This name scratched out (BLB)
1426 Vestal, J H	Awhite	48	M	1652		
1427 Vestal, E J	Ncher	42	F	Dead		
1428 Vann, Dutch	Ncher	28	M	Dead		
1429 Vann, Elsie	Ncher	20	F	Dead		
1430 Vaught, Joe	Ncher	6m	M	1627?		
1431 Vore, Frank	Ncher	27	M	2292	No	
1432 Vore, I G	Awhite	58	M	Dead	Yes	
1433 Vore, Sallie B	Ncher	50	F	Dead		
1434 Vore, Mary Ellen	Ncher	24	F	3391		
1435 Vore, P I	Ncher	21	M	Dead		
1436 Vore, Sophia J	Ncher	14	F	1600		
1437 Vickory, Eliza	Ncher	60	F	Dead		
1438 Vickory, John	Ncher	24	M	5250		
1439 Vann, James S	Ncher	21	M	D1460		Then switched to 3991? (BLB)
1440 Vann, Annie	Ncher	__?	F	Dead		
1441 Vann, M A	Ncher	17	F	D1461		Dead
1442 Vaught, Wm	Awhite	30	M	R78	Yes	Enrollment Refused
1443 Vaught, Lucy	Ncher	40	F	2028		

Name	Race	Age	Sex	Census	Md	Remarks
1444 Vaught, Sylas	Awhite	27	M	Dead	Yes	
1445 Vaught, Lucinda	Ncher	26	F	1659		
1446 Vann, John or Buster	A col	21	M	Dead		
1447 Vann, Josiah	Ncher	41	M	Dead	Yes	
1448 Vann, Katie	Ncher	38	F	Dead		
1449 Vann, Cahnahyee	Ncher	9	F	Dead		
1450 Vann, A J	Ncher	27	M	1758	Yes	Farmer
1451 Vann, Lizzie	Ncher	23	F	1758		
1452 Vann, W H	Ncher	2	M	2025		
1453 Vann, R P	Ncher	22	M	1066		Farmer
1454 Vann, Coowie	Ncher	20	M	1066		
1455 Vann, Annie	Ncher	6m	F	1066		
1456 Vann, Aggie	Ncher	45	F	Dead		
1457 Vann, John	Ncher	20	M	Dead		
1458 Vann, E P	Ncher	56	F	Dead		
1459 Vann, J E	Ncher	23	F	Dead		
1460 Vann, R F	Ncher	19	M	Dead		
1461 Vann, C E	Ncher	16	M	2345		
1462 Vann, Geo M	Ncher	28	M	1829		
1463 Vann, James	Ncher	9	M	1890		
1464 Vanhoy, A M	Awhite	47	M	1743		
1465 Vann, Martin	A col	65	M	Dead	Yes	Wife on Schedule 3
1470 Wilkins, George	Ncher	4	M	3766		
1471 West, Martha	Ncher	22	F	2268		
1472 Williams, G W	Awhite	38	M	2052	Yes	Farmer
1473 Williams, Nancy	Ncher	49	F	2052	Yes	
1474 Whitewater, Arch	Ncher	21	M	Dead		Farmer
1475 Whitewater, Ruth	Ncher	18	F	Dead		
1476 Watts, Jacob	Ncher	27	M	16	Yes	Farmer
1477 Watts, Amanda	Ncher	26	F	Dead		
1478 Watts, Arch	Ncher	1	M	Dead		
1479 Wicked, Jessie	Ncher	50	M	Dead	Yes	Farmer
1480 Wicked, Nancy	Ncher	48	F	Dead		
1481 White, Fannie	A col	30	F	F907		
1482 White, Lucinda	A col	2	F	F322		
1483 White, Nathan	A col	1m	M	F348		
1484 West, W M	Ncher	45	M	Dead		Farmer
1485 West, C H	Ncher	14	M	7345		
1486 West, E T	Ncher	11	M	7145		
1487 West, R E	Ncher	9	M	2266		
1488 West, F P	Ncher	28	M	Dead	Yes	Farmer
1489 West, N E	Ncher	27	F	1673		

Name	Race	Age	Sex	Census	Md	Remarks
1490 West, J B	Ncher	5	M	6574		
1491 West, R B	Ncher	9m	M	6576		
1492 Wartuck, James	Ncher	48	M	7983	Yes	Farmer
1493 Wartuck, Sam	Ncher	8	M	Dead		
1494 Wartuck, Nancy	Ncher	5	F	7993		
1495 Wartuck, Susannah	Ncher	2	F	7287		
1496 Wartuck, John	Ncher	27	M	Dead	Yes	
1497 Wartuck, Bettie	Ncher	25	F	9297		
1498 Wartuck, Jinnie	Ncher	29	F	8001		
1499 West, J P	Ncher	36	M	Dead	Yes	Farmer
1500 West, Missouri	Awhite	24	F	R111		Enrollment Refused
1501 West, Calvin	Ncher	4	M	2326		
1502 West, James	A cher	1	M	2101		
1503 Wicked, John	Ncher	50	M	Dead	Yes	
1504 Wilkerson, Asa	Ncher	27	M	1058	Yes	Farmer
1505 Wilkerson, Henry	Ncher	5	M	Dead		
1506 Wilkerson, Chas	Ncher	3 1/2	M	Dead		
1507 Wilkerson, Cordelia	Ncher	2	F	6359		
1508 Wilkerson, Robt	Ncher	6m	M	1028		
1509 Wilkerson, Margaret	Ncher	25	M	1058	Yes	
1510 Wicked, Joe	Ncher	26	M	Dead		Farmer
1511 Wicked, Etha	Ncher	20	F	1245		
1512 Wicked, Ella	Ncher	5	F	Dead		
1513 Wilkerson, Nancy	Awhite	60	F	Dead		Farmer
1514 Wilkerson, Whidby	A cher	19	M	Dead		
1515 Wilkerson, L B	A cher	16	F	Dead		
1516 Wilkerson, John	A cher	30	M	Dead		
1517 Watkins, Samuel	Ncher	23	M	2308		
1518 Watkins, Alic	Ncher	19	M	Dead		
1519 Warford, Eli	Ncher	23	M	Dead		
1520 Walkingwolf, Sarah	Ncher	23	F	Dead		
1521 Walkingwolf, Charlotte	Ncher	19	F	Dead		
1522 Walkingwolf, Bettie	Ncher	16	F	Dead		
1523 Whale, Stephen	Ncher	40	M	Dead	Yes	Farmer
1524 Whale, Katie	Ncher	25	F	Dead		
1525 Whale, Deliliah	Ncher	4	F	7110		
1526 Whale, Susan	Ncher	2	F	Dead		
1527 Woodall, Abe	Ncher	47	M	Dead	Yes	Farmer
1528 Woodall, Susan	Ncher	46	F	Dead		
1529 Woodall, T F	Ncher	19	M	1677		
1530 Wilkerson, Aggie	Ncher	24	F	7222		
1531 Wilkerson, Frost	Ncher	5	M	2443		

Name	Race	Age	Sex	Census	Md	Remarks
1532 Woodard, George	Ncher	35	M	7064	Yes	Farmer
1533 Woodard, Darkie	Ncher	30	F	7064		
1534 Woodard, Sarah	Ncher	13	F	7115		
1535 Woodard, Nannie	Ncher	10	F	Dead		
1536 Woodard, John	Ncher	4	M	7066		
1537 Woodard, Annie	Ncher	2	F	7116		
1538 Woodard, Infant	Ncher	1m	F	7064		
1539 Wright, Alice	A col	19	F	Dead		
1540 Wright, Maggie	A col	2	F	Dead		
1541 Wright, Chas	A col	1m	M	F479		
1542 Wolf, Susie	A col	7	F	F531		
1543 Williams, M J	Ncher	9	F	1031		
1544 Wicked, Arva	Awhite	74	F	Dead		
1545 Watts, Rosa	Ncher	14	F	5172		
1546 Wilkerson, James	Ncher	29	M	Dead	Yes	Farmer
1547 Wilkerson, Annie	Ncher	30	F	Dead		
1548 Wilkerson, James	Ncher	7	M	Dead		
1549 Whale, Cinda	Ncher	6	F	8007		
1550 Whitewater, Abigail	Ncher	8	F	Dead		
1551 Watts, Thomas	Ncher	56	M	7098	Yes	Farmer
1552 Watts, Mary	ACreek	45	F	R847		
1553 Watts, Cherokee	Ncher	18	F			Lives at Checotah, IT now Mrs. George Mackey
1554 Watts, Larena	Ncher	11	F	7099		
1555 Watts, Josephine	Ncher	9	F	Dead		
1556 Watts, William	Ncher	4	M	D1052		
1557 Watts, Henrietta	Ncher	2	F			Creek allotment (1659? BLB)
1558 West, Susie	Ncher	5	F	Dead		
1559 West, Margaret	Ncher	17	F	Dead		
1560 West, Sampson	Ncher	28	M	Dead		Farmer
1561 Wells, Samuel	Awhite	23	M	5262		
1562 Wells, Lydia	Ncher	21	F	Dead		
1563 Wells, William	Awhite	50	M	Dead		Farmer
1564 Wells, Ellen	Ncher	4	F	2328		
1565 Wells, Emiline	Ncher	2	F	4374		
1566 Wilson, Laura	Ncher	27	F	Dead		
1567 Wilson, John R	Ncher	7	M	5221		
1568 Wilson, Bell	Ncher	5	F	4486		
1569 Watie, Nancy	Ncher	32	F	Dead	Yes	
1570 Wilkerson, Richard	Ncher	12	M	5164		
1571 Warner, Nancy	Ncher	26	F	D1464		
1572 West, John C	Ncher	38	M	7020		Farmer

Name	Race	Age	Sex	Census	Md	Remarks
1573 West, M E	Ncher	32	F	7020		
1574 West, J H	Ncher	14	M	1645		
1575 West, E C	Ncher	11	M	7160		
1576 West, R F	Ncher	8	M	7159		
1577 West, Laura	Ncher	6	F	7040		
1578 West, T M	Ncher	4	M	Dead		
1579 West, Luellen	Ncher	2	F	2353		
1580 Webber, Chailu	Ncher	20	M	Dead	Yes	
1581 Wilkerson, John	Awhite	33	M	1712	Yes	
1582 Wilkerson, Sarah	Ncher	18	F	1712		
1583 Wilkerson, Asa	Ncher	10	M	Dead		
1584 Wilkerson, N A	Ncher	6	F	Dead		
1585 Wilkerson, James	Ncher	4	M	Dead		
1586 Wilkerson, Lizzie	Ncher	46?	F	Dead		
1587 Wilkerson, Jennie	Ncher	3	F	Dead		
1588 Warner, Mary	Ncher	26?	F	2116		
1589 Whitewater, Mattie	Ncher	8	F	6108		

	Name	Race	Age	Sex	Census	Md	Remarks
1	Allen, David	AWhite	40	M	5787	Yes	Farmer
2	Allen, Mary	NCher	35	F	5787	Yes	
3	Allen, Jos	NCher	7	M	5792	No	
4	Allen, Marriah	NCher	2	F	D866	No	Transferred to census card 10953 (BLB)
5	Adam, William	A Del	45	M	Del306	Yes	Minister
6	Adam, Louisa	A Del	21	F	4647	Yes	Should be listed as White (BLB)
7	Adam, Richard C	A Del	15	M	Del104	No	
8	Adam, Horrace M	A Del	13	M	Del236	No	
9	Adam, Nathan F	A Del	5	M	Del341	No	
10	Adam, Clinton L	A Del	3	M	Dead	No	
11	Adam, Abner G	A Del	6w	M	Del306	No	
12	Anderson, A M	AWhite	46	M	4067	Yes	Farmer
13	Anderson, Rachel	A Del	38	F	Del64	Yes	
14	Anderson, J M	A Del	9	M	Dead	No	
15	Anderson, A J	A Del	7	M	Del34	No	
16	Anderson, C J	A Del	3	F	Del67	No	
17	Anderson, Rachel	A Del	9mo	F	Del69	No	
18	Anderson, Daniel	A Del	25	M	Del71	Yes	Trapper
19	Anderson, Kittie	A Del	24	F	Dead	Yes	
20	Adair, Rebecca	NCher	25	F	2689	Yes	Married to Edward S Adair
21	Ala	NCher	25	F	D1466	No	
22	Ala, Anna	NCher	4	F	D1467	No	Now Mrs Alex Cochran
23	Ala, Squirrel	NCher	2	M	Dead	No	Chickasaw Allottee
24	Ala, Joe	NCher	1	M	D1468	No	Dead, Chickasaw Allottee
25	Abbet, Thomas	AShaw	24	M	D1469	No	Farmer
26	Abbet, Lucy	AShaw	20	F	D1469	No	
27	Adair, Col W P	NCher	50	M	Dead	Yes	Lawyer
28	Adair, S M	NCher	31	F	D1301	Yes	Creek Card
29	Adair, Namie	NCher	15	F		No	Creek Card
30	Adair, Dora Scott	NCher	4	F	662	No	Creek Card
31	Armstrong, Henry	A Del	38	M	Del301	Yes	Merchant
32	Armstrong, L J	A Del	33	F	Dead	No	
33	Armstrong, Albert F	A Del	17	M	Del277	No	
34	Armstrong, Charley Jr	A Del	8	M	Del287	No	
35	Armstrong, Lena	A Del	5	F	Del215	No	
36	Armstrong, Anna	A Del	2	F	Del257	No	
37	Arnold, Josie O	NCher	23	F	4271	No	Teacher
38	Arnold, Jinnie	NCher	2	F	4274	No	
39	Armstrong, Arther	NCher	38	M	Del 76	Yes	Farmer
40	Armstrong, Nancy	A Del	28	F	Dead	Yes	
41	Armstrong, Henry Jr	A Del	11	M	Del75	No	

Name	Race	Age	Sex	Census	Md	Remarks
42 Anderson, Thomas	A Del	40	M	Dead	Yes	Farmer
43 Anderson, Jane	A Del	30	F	Dead	Yes	
44 Anderson, Mary	A Del	40	F	Del87	No	
45 Anderson, Willie Bob	A Del	19	M	Dead	No	
46 Allen, R M	AWhite	42	M	4509	Yes	Farmer
47 Allen, Mary	A Del	28	F	Del248	Yes	
48 Allen, J K	A Del	18	F	Del221	No	
49 Allen, Winnie	A Del	11	F	Dead	No	
50 Allen, R M	A Del	6	M	Del276	No	
51 Allen, Robt J	A Del	3	M	Del212	No	
52 Allen, M A	A Del	2w	F	Del213	No	
53 Armstrong, Charles	A Del	46	F	Dead	Yes	Farmer
54 Armstrong, Mary E	A Del	41	F	Del102	Yes	
55 Armstrong, Carrie V	A Del	23	F	Del125	No	
56 Armstrong, Lillie A	A Del	20	F	Dead	No	
57 Armstrong, Kittie A	A Del	14	F	Del158	No	
58 Armstrong, Mrs Mary	A Del	75	F	Dead	No	
59 Allen, Pink	AWhite	35	M	Dead	Yes	Farmer
60 Allen, Susie	NCher	25	F	4694	Yes	
61 Allen, Henry	NCher	5	M	4494	No	
62 Allen, Beckie	NCher	4	F	4673	No	
63 Allen, Johny	NCher	1	M	4729	No	
64 Alberty, J B	NCher	27	M	Dead	Yes	Farmer
65 Alberty, Wm Jr	NCher	2	M	Dead	Yes	
66 Aldredge, W	AWhite	33	M	Dead	Yes	Farmer
67 Aldredge, Sarah	NCher	26	F	Dead	Yes	
68 Aldredge, Ada	NCher	1	F	5135	No	
69 Aldredge, Ida	NCher	4m	F	Dead	No	
70 Armstrong, Wm	AShaw	45	M	Dead	No	Farmer
71 Armstrong, Katy	AShaw	12	F	Del272	No	
72 Alberty, Susie	NCher	62	F	Dead	No	
73 Alberty, Jake	NCher	26	M	2666	Yes	Farmer
74 Alberty, Anna	NCher	26	F	2666	Yes	
75 Alberty, John	NCher	6	M	2666	No	
76 Alberty, N J	NCher	4	F	Dead	No	
77 Alberty, Josh	NCher	2	M	2696	No	
78 Alberty, G W	NCher	27	M	Dead	No	Farmer
79 Armstrong, Jo	AShaw	29	M	Dead	Yes	Farmer
80 Armstrong, Eliza	AShaw	28	F	Dead	Yes	
81 Armstrong, Louis	AShaw	1	M	Dead	No	
82 Armstrong, Old Susie	AShaw	56	F	Dead	No	
83 Alberty, Jerry	A Col	41	M	F153	Yes	Farmer

Name	Race	Age	Sex	Census	Md	Remarks
84 Alberty, Ruth	A Col	36	F	F153	Yes	
85 Alberty, Louis	A Col	14	F	F157	No	
86 Alberty, Noah	A Col	12	M	F200	No	
87 Alberty, Moses	A Col	10	M	F801	No	
88 Alberty, John	A Col	8	M	Dead	No	
89 Alberty, Carrie	A Col	6	F	Dead	No	
90 Alberty, Josh Jr	A Col	4	M	F202	No	
91 Alberty, Em	A Col	2	F	F204	No	
92 Alberty, Millie	A Col	1	F	F153	No	
93 Alberty, Josh	A Col	31	M	Dead	Yes	Farmer
94 Alberty, Rutha Sr	A Col	35	F	Dead	Yes	
95 Alberty, Easter	A Col	54	F	Dead	No	
96 Alexander, Jim	NCher	30	M	Dead	No	Farmer
97 Alamiatapia	A Del	8	F	Del184	No	
98 Almelonaquah	A Del	5	F	Dead	No	
99 Adams, Sam	AShaw	11	M	4451	No	
100 Attimer, William	A Del	6	M	Dead	No	
101 Attimer, Susie	A Del	2	F	Del312	No	
102 Arlulee, Sallie	NCher	10	F	Dead	No	Lives with Bear Timpson
103 Anderson, Alenor	A Del	18	F	Dead	No	
104 Anderson, James	A Del	15	M	Dead	No	
105 Anderson, Sam	A Del	8	M	Del153	No	
106 Anderson, George	A Del	5	M	Del154	No	
107 Anderson, John	A Del	12	M	Del124	No	
108 Amstid, Louis	A Col	26	M	F1070	No	
109 Amstid, Miss	A Col	18	F	Dead	No	
110 Alberty, E C	NCher	19	M	2757	No	
111 Alberty, Moses	NCher	16	M	5877	No	
112 Alex, Black	A Del	26	M	D23	Yes	Farmer
113 Alex, Tianooquah	A Del	21	F	Dead	No	
114 Adair, Robert	A Col	10	M	F592	No	
115 Adair, Wm	A Col	16	M	F1039	No	
116 Arnold, Harry	A Del	30	M	Del138	Yes	
117 Arnold, Betsy	A Del	30	F	Dead	Yes	
118 Allen, Rufus				Del222	No	
119 Alberty, Jane				Dead	No	
120 Alberty, (child)				FD234	No	
121 Anderson, Matilda		21	F	1854	No	
122 Anderson, Jane		Infant	F	1854	No	
123 Anderson, Josh				1854	No	
124 Ahpamelenowaqua,				Dead	No	Enrolled as Mrs A Drum 861
124a Brown, Charlie	NCher	26	M	6517	No	

Name	Race	Age	Sex	Census	Md	Remarks
125 Beck, William	A Col	10	M	F402	No	
126 Bluejacket, Steve	AShaw	41	M	3458	Yes	
127 Bluejacket, Emily	AShaw	40	F	Dead	Yes	
128 Bluejacket, Eddie	AShaw	15	M	5677	No	
129 Bluejacket, Racy	AShaw	10	F	3510	No	
130 Bluejacket, Reener	AShaw	8	F	3716	No	
131 Bluejacket, Carrie	AShaw	6	F	9578	No	
132 Bluejacket, Tecumpseth	AShaw	1	M	3458	No	
133 Brown, William	NCher	26	M	3370	Yes	Carpenter?
134 Brown, Francis	AShaw	21	F	Dead	Yes	
135 Brown, Richard	AShaw	9m	M	3348	No	
136 Blythe, Jamaina	NCher	47	F	3017	No	
137 Blythe, Ella H	NCher	19	F	3900	No	
138 Blythe, Fannie E	NCher	17	F	3304	No	
139 Beatty, W T	AWhite	45	M	3474	Yes	Mechanic
140 Beatty, Mary E	AShaw	32	F	Dead	Yes	
141 Beatty, Ida	AShaw	15	F	3597	No	
142 Beatty, James	AShaw	10	M	Dead	No	
143 Beatty, Babe	AShaw	3	F	3399	No	
144 Beatty, Morris	AShaw	5m	M	Dead	No	
145 Bible, Louis	NCher	36	M	4401	Yes	Trader
146 Bible, R L	NCher	37	F	Dead	Yes	
147 Bible, Ellen	NCher	11	F	5151	No	
148 Bible, Arther	NCher	8	M	4599	No	
149 Bible, Martha	NCher	5	F	4424	No	
150 Bible, Sidney	NCher	2	F	Dead	No	
151 Beck, Joe	A Col	22	M	Dead	No	
152 Bigknife, James	AShaw	36	M	3988	Yes	
153 Bigknife, Susie	AShaw	28	F	Dead	Yes	
154 Bigknife, Henry	AShaw	12	M	Dead	No	
155 Bigknife, Jane	AShaw	3	F	Dead	No	
156 Bigknife, Reuben	AShaw	10m	M	Dead	No	
157 Brown, John	NCher	60	M	Dead	Yes	Politician
158 Brown, Louis	NCher	4	F	4483	No	
159 Brown, Polly	AWhite	63	F	Dead	No	
160 Brown, Wm	AWhite	24	M	4171	Yes	Farmer
161 Brown, G A	NCher	23	F	Dead	Yes	Georgia Ann McGhee (BLB)
162 Brown, Larkin	NCher	5	M	4129	No	
163 Brown, Morris	NCher	7	M	4142	No	
164 Brown, Addie	NCher	4	F	D1471	No	Dead
165 Brown, Ada	NCher	2	F	4141	No	
166 Barker, Lizzie	A Del	19	F	Del63	Yes	

Name	Race	Age	Sex	Census	Md	Remarks
167 Barker, Loura	A Del	4m	F	Dead	No	
168 Bluejacket, Moris	AShaw	20	M	Dead	Yes	
169 Bluejacket, Sofphy	AShaw	19	F	Dead	Yes	
170 Bluejacket, Price	AShaw	24	M	Dead		
171 Bluejacket, Julia	AShaw	20	F	Dead		
172 Brown, Elizabeth	AWhite	25	F	R272	No	Enrollment Refused, Non citizen Married out
173 Brown, Sarah E	NCher	2	F	4460	No	
174 Barker, Mary	NCher	20	F	4177	Yes	
175 Ball, J L	AWhite	34	M	Dead	Yes	Farmer
176 Ball, M A	NCher	20	F	4577	Yes	
177 Ball, R J	NCher	5	F	Dead	No	
178 Ball, A C	NCher	3	M	Dead	No	
179 Ball, J C	NCher	1	F	Dead	No	
180 Biggfield, Widow	A Del	38	F	Dead	No	
181 Bigfield, Mary	A Del	13	F	Del339	No	
182 Bigfield, George	A Del	15	M	Dead	No	
183 Bigfield, Kate	A Del	9	F	Dead	No	
184 Bird, Sopha	A Col	21	F	Dead	No	
185 Bird, William	A Col	4	M	F950	No	
186 Bird, Henry	A Col	1	F	F1078	No	
187 Brown, Joe	A Del	22	M	Dead	No	Trapper
188 Brown, Polly	A Del	21	F	Dead	No	
189 Bluejacket, Thomas	AShaw	39	M	3492	Yes	Farmer
190 Bluejacket, Josaphine	AWhite	37	F	3492	Yes	
191 Bluejacket, Stephen	AShaw	20	M	Dead	No	
192 Bluejacket, Emma	AShaw	18	F	Dead	No	
193 Bluejacket, William	AShaw	14	M	3821	No	
194 Bluejacket, Sarah	AShaw	12	F	3312	No	
195 Bluejacket, A	AShaw	4	F	3518	No	
196 Bluejacket, Joe	AShaw	2	M	Dead	No	
197 Bluejacket, Doughlass	AShaw	2m	M	Dead	No	
198 Balentine, H	NCher	30	M	2924	Yes	___"Broom? (Bl.B) Maker
199 Balentine, M E	NCher	24	F	2924	Yes	
200 Balentine, S T	NCher	7m	M	Dead	No	
201 Balentine, A H	NCher	57	F	Dead	No	
202 Balentine, J H	NCher	18	M	Dead	No	
203 Bible, Georgia	NCher	18	F	Dead	Yes	Married a man by the name of Bill Sullivan and ____
204 Boot, John	NCher	33	M	Dead	Yes	Farmer
205 Boot, Lizzie	NCher	40	F	3223	Yes	
206 Boot, Wm Joe	NCher	2	M	3213	No	
207 Beck, Rachiel	NCher	50	F	3220	No	

Name	Race	Age	Sex	Census	Md	Remarks
208 Beck, Thomas	NCher	17	M	3286	No	
209 Buzzard, Betsy	NCher	50	F	Dead	No	
210 Buzzard, Lizzie	NCher	30	F	3211	No	
211 Buzzard, Jane	NCher	20	F	3215	No	
212 Bryan, J M	AWhite	71	M	Dead	Yes	Lawyer
213 Bryan, Rebeccah	NCher	67	F	Dead	Yes	
214 Bryan, Joel Jr	NCher	25	M	2732	No	
215 Bennett, Doily	NCher	13	F	Dead	No	Belongs to Bryan Family
216 Bough, Joel	NCher	22	M	3799	No	Teacher
217 Brown, Abbey	A Col	30	F	Dead	No	Cook
218 Buffington, Nan	NCher	44	F	Dead	No	
219 Buffington, Sabra	NCher	18	F	2570	No	
220 Buffington, Covey	NCher	16	M	2797	No	
221 Benge, James	NCher	32	M	3729	Yes	"Nothing"
222 Benge, Ruth	NCher	25	F	Dead	Yes	
223 Benge, Maggie	NCher	10	F	3428	No	
224 Benge, Dora	NCher	6	F	Dead	No	
225 Benge, Joseph	NCher	4	M	5167	No	
226 Benge, Jin Anna	NCher	5m	F	3269	No	
227 Barnett, Charles	AWhite	45	M	Del547	Yes	Stockman
228 Barnett, Mrs C	A Del	40	F	Dead	Yes	
229 Bivins, Catharine	NCher	40	F	Dead	No	
230 Bivins, David	NCher	5	M	4207	No	
231 Bivins, Walter	NCher	2	M	4247	No	
232 Brown, Starr	A Del	21	M	Dead	No	Hunter
233 Bullett, Boston	A Del	30	M	Dead	Yes	Farmer
234 Bullett, Mrs	A Del	18	F	Del194	Yes	
235 Bullett, Henry	A Del	6	M	Del129	No	
236 Bullett, Mary	A Del	9	F	Del203	No	
237 Bullett, Jane	A Del	5m	F	Del201	No	
238 Barnett, Rebecca	A Del	30	F	Dead	No	Seamstress
239 Barnett, Amanda	A Del	18	F	3084	No	Nancy Dority belongs to this family
240 Barnett, Hettie	A Del	6	F	Dead	No	
241 Barnett, Henry	A Del	9	M	5646	No	
242 Bigbuffaloe, Widow	A Del	70	F	Dead	No	
243 Brown, Big Sis	A Del	30	F	Dead	No	Farmer
244 Brown, Sissie	A Del	12	F	Dead	No	
245 Brown, Wm	A Del	13	M	Del194	No	
246 Beaver, Lizzie	A Del	25	F	Del148	No	Farmer
247 Beaver, John	A Del	15	M	Dead	No	
248 Bill, John	A Del	42	M	Dead	Yes	Farmer

Name	Race	Age	Sex	Census	Md	Remarks
249 Bill, Susie	A Del	24	F	Dead	Yes	
250 Bill, Thomas	A Del	13	M	Dead	No	
251 Busby, S T	A White	37	M	R324	Yes	Enrollment Refused, Farmer
252 Busby, Mary	N Cher	27	F	Dead	Yes	
253 Busby, Samuel	N Cher	11	M	5298	No	Sam Spenser on Dawes (BLB)
254 Busby, Thompson	N Cher	5	M	D1472	No	A White child
255 Belzier, Stephen	A Del	22	M	Del308	No	
256 Belzier, Julley	A Del	18	F	Dead	No	
257 Bennett, J H	A White	43	M	4265	Yes	Farmer
258 Bennett, Huldey	A White	30	F	4265	Yes	
259 Bennett, Rockey	A White	2	F	4266	No	
260 Bartles, J H	A White	39	M	4326	Yes	Merchant
261 Bartles, N M	A Del	36	F	10516	Yes	
262 Bartles, Joseph, Jr	A Del	5	M	10519	No	
263 Beaver, Big	A Del	50	M	Dead	Yes	
264 Beaver, Mrs Big	A Del	30	F	Del152	No	
265 Beaver, Jane	A Del	8	F	Del150	No	
266 Beaver, Dick	A Del	4m	M	Dead	No	
267 Buffalo, Thomas	A Del	22	M	Del117	Yes	
268 Buffalo, Lucy	A Del	18	F	Dead	Yes	
269 Buffalo, Willie	A Del	1m	M	Dead	No	
270 Bascom, Henry	A Del	20	M	Del317	Yes	
271 Bascom, Molinda	A Del	22	F	Dead	Yes	
272 Brown, John	A Del	42	M	Del162	Yes	Farmer
273 Brown, Amanda	A Del	16	F	Del167	No	
274 Brown, Choteau	A Del	12	M	Dead	No	
275 Brown, Lillie	A Del	5	F	Del177	No	
276 Blossey, Amanuel	A White	35	M	Dead	Yes	Correct surname Blosser (BLB)
277 Blossey, Lizzie	N Cher	31	F	4304	No	
278 Blossey, Joseph	N Cher	5	M	4308	No	
279 Bibles, George	N Cher	45	M	4414	Yes	
280 Bibles, Hannah	A Shaw	40	F	Dead	Yes	
281 Bibles, Willie	N Cher	19	M	5099	No	
282 Bibles, Mary	N Cher	14	F	Dead	No	
283 Bibles, John	N Cher	12	M	Dead	No	
284 Bear, Willie	N Cher	29	M	4559	No	Farmer
285 Bear, Rachel	N Cher	50	F	Dead	No	
286 Bear, Delila	N Cher	15	F	5356	No	
287 Bullett, George	A Del	20	M	Del325	No	Farmer
288 Bullett, John	A Del	26	M	Del319	No	Trader
289 Brown, Jesse	A Col	47	M	Dead	Yes	Farmer
290 Brown, Lucinda	A Col	28	F	Dead	Yes	

Name	Race	Age	Sex	Census	Md	Remarks
291 Brown, Sarah	A Col	13	F	F1015	No	
292 Brown, Anderson	A Col	10	M	F997	No	
293 Brown, Jesse Jr	A Col	8	M	F1010	No	
294 Brown, Willie	A Col	6	M	F992	No	
295 Brown, Polly	A Col	4	F	F989	No	
296 Brown, L B	A Col	8m	M	Dead	No	
297 Black, James	AWhite	35	M	Dead	No	Farmer
298 Black, Susan	NCher	4	F	D1473	No	
299 Buffington, Mit	A Col	25	F	Dead	No	Three Johnson children belong to this family
300 Bly, Mary	NCher	20	F	Dead	No	
301 Bell, J M	NCher	20	M	5427	Yes	
302 Bell, M C	NCher	18	F	5427	Yes	
303 Bell, Paster	NCher	2w	M	Dead	No	
304 Buffington, Jo	NCher	27	M	Dead	Yes	Farmer
305 Buffington, Susie	NCher	25	F	Dead	Yes	
306 Blanket, Fields	NCher	20	M	3228	No	Hunter
307 Blanket, Sallie	NCher	50	F	Dead	No	
308 Burr, Maggie B	NCher	22	F	2771	Yes	
309 Burr, Walter	NCher	2	M	7581	No	
310 Burr, Wm	NCher	2m	M	2771	No	
311 Blanket, John	NCher	22	M	Dead	Yes	
312 Blanket, Becky	NCher	29	F	Dead	Yes	
313 Bear, Jacob	AShaw	26	M	Dead	Yes	Farmer
314 Bear, Amanda	AShaw	16	F	Dead	Yes	
315 Bear, Wm	AShaw	6	M	Dead	No	
316 Bean, Jo S	NCher	27	M	9956	Yes	Carpenter
317 Bean, Eveline	NCher	23	F	4917	Yes	
318 Bean, A E	NCher	2	F	5525	No	
319 Bean, Esther	NCher	1	F	5636	No	
320 Buster, John	NCher	32	M	4968	Yes	Farmer
321 Buster, Nancy	AWhite	23	F	Dead	Yes	
322 Buster, Lilly	NCher	8	F	Dead	No	
323 Buster, James	NCher	5	M	Dead	No	
324 Buster, Lou	NCher	3	F	4972	No	
325 Buster, Lizzie	NCher	1	F	Dead	No	
326 Beck, John H	NCher	19	M	Dead	No	Teacher
327 Burgess, Wm	A Col	27	M	Dead	Yes	Farmer
328 Burgess, Sarah	A Col	26	F	F671	Yes	
329 Burgess, Anderson Jane	A Col	6	F	Dead	No	
330 Burgess, Mariah	A Col	1	F	F1074	No	
331 Bird, George B	NCher	29	M	Dead	No	

Name	Race	Age	Sex	Census	Md	Remarks
332 Backbone, Jinnie	NCher	60	F	Dead	No	
333 Bear, Henry	NCher	29	M	Dead	No	
334 Bear, Beck	AWhite	28	F	7135	No	On Dawes as Rebbeca Miller Intermarried White (BLB)
335 Bread, Sam'l	NCher	53	M	3545	Yes	Farmer
336 Bread, Mary	AShaw	42	F	3545	Yes	
337 Bread, Gayno	NCher	11	M	Dead	No	
338 Bird, Ed W	AWhite	35	M	5432	Yes	Farmer
339 Bird, Jane	NCher	25	F	5432	Yes	
340 Bird, Henry	NCher	2	M	5473	No	
341 Bird, Daisy D	NCher	2w	F	5432	No	
342 Beef, John	NCher	30	M	Dead	Yes	Farmer
343 Beef, Betsy	NCher	30	F	4364	Yes	
344 Beef, Cahtayoh	NCher	3	F	4212	No	
345 Blackfeather, Charles	AShaw	24	M	Dead	Yes	Fisherman
346 Bigfox, Coffee	AShaw	24	M	Dead	Yes	Hunter
347 Bigfox, Sallie	AShaw	30	F	Dead	Yes	
348 Bluejacket, Florence	AShaw	14	F	4115	No	
349 Blackfeather, Lizzie	AShaw	36	F	Dead	No	Cook
350 Blackfeather, Frank	AShaw	4	M	Dead	No	
351 Blackfeather, Nan	AShaw	11m	F	Dead	No	
352 Blackfeather, Eliza	AShaw	11m	F	Dead	No	
353 Bluejacket, George	AShaw	38	M	Dead	Yes	Mechanic
354 Bluejacket, Eliza	AShaw	28	F	Dead	Yes	
355 Bluejacket, Ida	AShaw	10	F	Dead	No	
356 Bean, Ed	NCher	21	M	4804	No	Farmer
357 Buffington, D W	NCher	28	M	3544	Yes	
358 Buffington, Martha	NCher	27	F	Dead	Yes	
359 Buffington, David	NCher	2	M	9294	No	
360 Buffington, Francis	NCher	1m	F	Dead	No	
361 Baugh, J H	AWhite	55	M	2464	No	Carpenter
362 Baugh, Robert E Lee	NCher	14	M	2548	No	
363 Baugh, John C	NCher	19	M	Dead	No	
364 Bendoura, James	AWhite	33	M	Dead	Yes	Farmer
365 Bendoura, Sarah	NCher	31	F	5121	Yes	
366 Bendoura, John B	NCher	9	M	5119	No	
367 Bendoura, G	NCher	6	M	5124	No	
368 Bendoura, Charles	NCher	2w	M	5121	No	
369 Baldridge, Anna	NCher	80	F	Dead	No	
370 Backbone, Lizzie	NCher	20	F	2459	No	
371 Backbone, Rabbit	NCher	2m	M	Dead	No	
372 Biglegs, Mrs	NCher	50	F	Dead	No	Farmer

Name	Race	Age	Sex	Census	Md	Remarks
373 Biglegs, Ben	NCher	7	M	Dead	No	
374 Biglegs, Dick	NCher	20	M	Dead	No	Fisherman
375 Barney, Charles	AWhite	40	M	5552	Yes	Farmer
376 Barney, Catherine	NCher	40	F	Dead	Yes	
377 Barney, Ruth R	NCher	13	F	5424	No	
378 Barney, Felix	NCher	5	M	5545	No	
379 Bumgarner, J L	NCher	25	M	3381	Yes	
380 Bumgarner, Charlot	NCher	19	F	3381	Yes	
381 Bushyhead, Joe	NCher	30	M	Dead	No	Hunter
382 Blackfox, John	AShaw	25	M	Dead	No	
383 Boudinot, Alex	A Col	35	M	F1089	No	
384 Bushyhead, Smith	NCher	36	M	4795	Yes	Hustler? (or Hostler BLB)
385 Bushyhead, Lizzie	NCher	30	F	Dead	Yes	
386 Bushyhead, George	NCher	12	M	2413	No	
387 Bushyhead, Delilah	NCher	7	F	2398	No	
388 Bushyhead, Nancy	NCher	6	F	Dead	No	
389 Bushyhead, Jake	NCher	1	M	2437	No	
390 Bushyhead, Gillard	NCher	1	M	Dead	No	
391 Beaver, Ellen	NCher	26	F	Dead	No	
392 Beaver, George	NCher	7	M	5301	No	
393 Beaver, Charles	NCher	3	M	Dead	No	
394 Baker, John	AWhite	28	M	5393	Yes	Farmer
395 Baker, Lizzie	NCher	24	F	5393	Yes	
396 Baker, M J	NCher	4	F	Dead	No	
397 Baker, S E	NCher	5m	F	5394	No	
398 Buffington, Susie	NCher	52	F	Dead	No	
399 Beard, John	NCher	23	M	Dead	Yes	Farmer
400 Beard, Anna	NCher	28	F	Dead	Yes	
401 Beard, Lizzie	NCher	4	F	5175	No	
402 Beard, Henry	NCher	2	M	Dead	No	
403 Blythe, N B	NCher	30	M	10394	No	Boatsman
404 Blakney, John	AShaw	15	M	D1474	No	Lives at Carthage, MO
405 Buffaloe, Widow	A Del	48	F	Dead	No	
406 Blackfox, David	NCher	35	M	Dead	Yes	Preacher
407 Blackfox, Nelly	NCher	35	F	8767	Yes	
408 Blackfox, Ned	NCher	10	M	8768	No	
409 Blackfox, Thomas	NCher	3	M	Dead	No	
410 Blackfox, M A	NCher	1m	F	Dead	No	
411 Bill, Louisa	A Del	25	F	Dead	No	These Three Bill Children belong to the Hester Leonard Family
412 Bill, Caroline	A Del	9	F	Dead	No	
413 Bill, Charlie	A Del	1	M	Del386	No	

Cooweescoowee District

Name	Race	Age	Sex	Census	Md	Remarks
414 Black, Amanda	A Del	12	F	Del22	No	
415 Bowls, Susan	A Col	37	F	F1055	Yes	
416 Bowls, Jinnie	A Col	18	F	F855	Yes	
417 Butter, Frank	A Del	13	M	DLD26	No	Not known to the Dels.
418 Butter, Lizzie	A Del	10	F	DLD27	No	Not known to the Dels.
419 Brown, Wm	NCher	21	M	D1475	No	
420 Brown, Joe	A Col	16	M	Dead	No	
421 Brown, Israel	A Col	11	M	F1023	No	
422 Blackbird, Kate	A Col	9	F	9621	No	
423 Blackbird, Lizzie	A Col	12	F	10086	No	On Dawes as Lizzie Trimble (BLB)
424 Belle, Minnie	NCher	27	F	Dead	No	
425 Butler, Lucy	NCher	25	F	Dead	Yes	
426 Brown, Sam	NCher	17	M	D1476	No	
427 Burgess, Wm	A Col	6	M	FD1134	No	
428 Bigjohn, Joseph	A Del	16	M	Dead	No	
429 Brown, Charlie	NCher	26	M	6517	No	
430 Buffalo, Widow	A Del	48	F	Dead	No	
431 Bestquality, Mr	A Del	29	M	Dead	Yes	Farmer
432 Bestquality, Mrs	A Del	34	F	Dead	No	
433 Burgess, Minty	A Col	16		FD1135	No	
434 Booth, Frank	AShaw	19	M	7271	No	
435 Barnett, Joe	AShaw	20	M	Dead	No	
436 Burnett, Andson	AShaw	16		D1477	No	Not known to the Shawnees
437 Burnett, Henry	AShaw	12	M	D2823	No	
438 Bigjohn, James	A Del	19	M	Dead	No	
439 Bibles, James				4945		
440 Buster, William Sr				4908		
441 Ballad, Jno				Dead		
442 Balad, Sabra				Dead		
443 Burgess, Nellie				Dead		
444 Burgess, Sissie				D1478		Creek Allotment
445 Bell, James M				7042		
446 Bell, Watie				Dead		
447 Beef, Jim				5531		On Dawes as Jim Smith (BLB)
448 Burgess, Fannie				Dead		
449 Bryant, Nellie				D1479		
450 Buffaloe, Lincoln	A Del			Del24		
451 Blackwing, John	AShaw			Dead		
452 Byrd, Henry				5473		
453 Burgess, John				5234		
454 Chambers, Mack	NCher	30	M	Dead	No	Farmer

Cooweescoowee District

Name	Race	Age	Sex	Census	Md	Remarks
455 Coody, Sarah	NCher	17	F	3817	No	
456 Coody, Dave	NCher	11	M	Dead	No	
457 Coody, Osie	NCher	8	M	7355	No	
458 Cochran, Tom	NCher	8	M	7310	No	
459 Cridinden, John	NCher	14	M	6969	No	
460 Collens, Wm	A Del	9	M	Dead	No	
461 Collens, George M	A Del	7	M	Del327	No	
462 Coker, Calvin	NCher	29	M	4646	Yes	Farmer
463 Coker, Lizzie	A Del	30	F	Dead	No y	
464 Coker, Charlie	A Del	9	M	Del337	No	
465 Coker, Nancy	A Del	7	F	Del336	No	
466 Coker, Cherokee	A Del	5	F	Dead	No	
467 Coker, Georgia	A Del	3	F	Del334	No	
468 Coker, Emma	A Del	1	F	Del269	No	
467 Connor, Caleb	AWhite	42	M	2979	Yes	Farmer
468 Connor, Lucy	NCher	32	F	2979	Yes	
469 Connor, Joseph	NCher	16	M	3795	No	
470 Connor, Susie	NCher	9	F	10143	No	
471 Connor, Mollie	NCher	6	F	3855	No	
472 Connor, Nancy E	NCher	17	F	74	No	
473 Chamberlain, W C	NCher	28	M	3733	Yes	
474 Chamberlain, L A	NCher	22	F	Dead	Yes	
475 Chamberlain, Flora	NCher	3	F	Dead	No	
476 Chamberlain, Edith	NCher	1	F	Dead	No	
477 Crutchfield, Jo, Jr	NCher	20	M	Dead	No	
478 Coody, E C	NCher	31	M	Dead	Yes	Barber
479 Coody, Nancy	AWhite	22	F	Dead	Yes	
480 Coody, Elizabeth	NCher	5	F	Dead	No	
481 Coody, John H	NCher	1	M	3332	No	
482 Cook, Henry	AWhite	40	M	Dead	Yes	Jobber
483 Cook, Susan	NCher	29	F	3923	No	
484 Cook, Henry A	NCher	12	M	7400	No	
485 Cook, Willie B	NCher	10	M	10877	No	
486 Cook, Isabelle	NCher	8	F	R721	No	
487 Cook, Florence	NCher	3	F	3157	No	
488 Conner, John D	A Del	37	M	Del246	Yes	Hunter
489 Conner, Delilah	A Del	40	F	Dead	Yes	
490 Conner, George	A Del	13	M	Del278	No	
491 Conner, Susan	A Del	10	F	Del326	No	
492 Cullin, Polly	A Del	34	F	Dead	Yes	
493 Cullin, Amanda	A Del	4	F	Del282	No	
494 Childers, D J	NCher	23	M	5220	No	

Name	Race	Age	Sex	Census	Md	Remarks
495 Couch, M W	AWhite	38	M	5397	Yes	Farmer
496 Couch, Vie	NCher	24	F	Dead	Yes	
497 Couch, John F	NCher	14	M	5203	No	
498 Couch, I S F	NCher	11	M	5688	No	
499 Couch, Robert L	NCher	8	M	10173	No	
500 Couch, Nancy V	NCher	5	F	5542	No	
501 Couch, Sam'l	NCher	8m	M	Dead	No	
502 Couch, Sarah	NCher	16	F	5422	No	
503 Couch, Lissa	NCher	14	F	Dead	No	
504 Couch, Polly	NCher	12	F	5484	No	
505 Couch, Kinney	NCher	10	F	Dead	No	
506 Clark, John	AWhite	40	M	3424	Yes	
507 Clark, Nancy	NCher	36	F	Dead	Yes	
508 Clark, Alice	NCher	11	F	3053	No	
509 Clark, Mary	NCher	3	F	2911	No	
510 Clark, Wm	NCher	6m	M	4170	No	
511 Chamberlain, A N	AWhite	59	M	Dead	Yes	Farmer
512 Chamberlain, E D	NCher	61	F	Dead	Yes	
513 Chamberlain, A E	NCher	30	F	4698	No	
514 Chamberlain, A F	NCher	23	M	3642	No	
515 Chamberlain, H E	NCher	20	M	Dead	No	
516 Chamberlain, R L	NCher	15	M	3659	No	
517 Chamberlain, Ned	NCher	25	M	Dead	No	
518 Childers, James	NCher	21	M	Dead	No	Farmer
519 Conor, Anderson	A Del	19	M	Dead	Yes	
520 Combs, Martha J	NCher	15	F	D1480	No	Creek allottee
521 Chaney, James	AWhite	31	M	4393	Yes	Farmer
522 Chaney, Pinkey	NCher	24	F	4393	Yes	
523 Chaney, Charlie	NCher	5	M	4527	No	
524 Chaney, Susie	NCher	3	F	4413	No	
525 Coplin, Jno	A Del	33	M	Del262	Yes	
526 Coplin, Mrs	A Del	23	F	Dead	Yes	
527 Coplin, George	A Del	4	M	Del315	No	
528 Carey, W V	NCher	23	M	Dead	No	Teacher
529 Cochran, Bill	NCher	26	M	6284	Yes	These are Cherokee that have just came in from the Cherokee Nation with in the last two months
530 Cochran, Wahleesee	NCher	45	F	Dead	No	
531 Chea	NCher	25	F	Dead	No	
532 Cramp, Brown	NCher	23	M	Dead	Yes	Farmer
533 Cramp, Sallie	NCher	20	F	Dead	Yes	
534 Cramp, Alsie	NCher	30	F	Dead	No	

Cooweescoowee District

Name	Race	Age	Sex	Census	Md	Remarks
535 Cramp, Ahlee	NCher	19	F	Dead	No	
536 Colston, Ike	NCher	1	M	D1481	No	
537 Cloud, Sam	NCher	48	M	Dead	Yes	Ferryman
538 Cloud, Lucy	NCher	30	F	Dead	Yes	
539 Cloud, Anna	NCher	13	F	2404	No	
540 Cloud, Wutty	NCher	11	F	Dead	No	
541 Cloud, Henry	NCher	7	M	5668	No	
542 Cloud, Joshua	NCher	3	M	9538	No	
543 Cloud, Lily	NCher	3m	F	2412	No	
544 Coats, Sam	NCher	26	M	5572	No	Farmer
545 Coats, Wm	NCher	21	M	4173	No	
546 Campbell, Alfred	AWhite	39	M	Dead	Yes	Farmer
547 Campbell, Sarah	NCher	28	F	Dead	Yes	
548 Campbell, John	NCher	10m	M	5550	No	
549 Chappy, Tom	AShaw	50	M	Dead	No	
550 Chappy, Tom, Jr	AShaw	18	M	Dead	No	
551 Crittenden, Tony	NCher	36	M	D1482	Yes	Farmer
552 Crittenden, Joanna	NCher	17	F	D1483	Yes	
553 Crittenden, Lewis	NCher	4m	M	D1484	No	
554 Cox, Claud	AShaw	27	M	5425	No	Marshall
555 Cox, Margaret	AShaw	53	F	3740	No	
556 Coker, Lewis	NCher	30	M	4493	Yes	Farmer
557 Coker, Charlotte	AWhite	23	F	4493	Yes	
558 Coker, Billy	NCher	6	M	4605	No	
559 Coker, Mattie T	NCher	2	F	4506	No	
560 Coney, George	AWhite	55	M	Dead	Yes	Butcher
561 Coney, Eliza J	NCher	25	F	3572	Yes	
562 Coney, Estella	NCher	10m	F	Dead	No	
563 Coon, James	A Del	40	M	Dead	Yes	Farmer
564 Coon, Rosa	A Del	20	F	Dead	Yes	
565 Coon, Whale	A Del	4	M	Dead	No	
566 Coon, Wane	A Del	2	M	Dead	No	
567 Caps, John	A Del	30	M	Dead	Yes	Farmer
568 Caps, Mrs John	A Del	33	F	Dead	Yes	
569 Chewlon,	A Del	26	F	Del225	No	
570 Chewlon, Mary	A Del	16	F	Del146	No	
571 Curleyhead, Albert	A Del	25	M	Del101	Yes	Dancer?
572 Curleyhead, Mrs	A Del	20	F	Del141	Yes	
573 Curleyhead, Lillie	A Del	22	F	Del101	No	
574 Curleyhead, Arter	A Del	5	M	Dead	No	
575 Cloud, Jane	NCher	35	F	D1485	No	Farmer
576 Cloud, Mary	NCher	9	F	D1486	No	

Name	Race	Age	Sex	Census	Md	Remarks
577 Candy, James	AWhite	30	M	Dead	No	Farmer
578 Cunningham, Alfred	NCher	19	M	5320	No	Smith
579 Cunningham, Ross	NCher	21	M	Dead	No	
580 Carr, N F	AWhite	35	M	4206	Yes	Farmer
581 Carr, S A	NCher	30	F	4206	Yes	
582 Carr, Jane A	NCher	10	F	4241	No	
583 Carr, J M	NCher	8	M	Dead	No	
584 Carr, Willie A	NCher	6	M	4355	No	
585 Carr, Marvin F	NCher	2	F	4246	No	
586 Charley, Delaware	A Del	76	M	Dead	No	Conjuror
587 Charley, Sarah	A Del	14	F	Dead	No	
588 Charley, Sam	A Del	17	M	Dead	Yes	
589 Charley, Mrs	A Del	19	F	Del118	Yes	
590 Choteau, Frank	AShaw	20	M	4628	No	Farmer
591 Choteau, Price	AShaw	17	M	Dead	No	
592 Choteau, Amanda	AShaw	16	F	4510	No	
593 Choteau, Minnie	AShaw	8	F	Dead	No	
594 Cary, Nannie	NCher	18	F	4951	Yes	
595 Cary, Gabriel	NCher	27	M	Dead	No	Blacksmith
596 Chambers, Charlie	A Col	45	M	F1017	Yes	Farmer
597 Chambers, Caroline	A Col	28	F	F938	Yes	
598 Chambers, John H	A Col	18	M	Dead	No	
599 Chambers, Eddie	A Col	2	M	F933	No	
600 Chambers, Mc	A Col	5	M	F934	No	
601 Choteau, Charlie	AShaw	30	M	4549	No	
602 Campbell, Charley	A Col	41	M	F846	No	Farmer
603 Campbell, Ed J	AWhite	32	M	5321	Yes	Merchant
604 Campbell, Emaline	A Del	26	F	Del329	Yes	
605 Campbell, Roby	A Del	19m	F	Del327	No	
606 Conner, Alex	A Del	37	M	Dead	Yes	Farmer
607 Conner, Lizzie	A Del	39	F	Dead	Yes	
608 Conner, Lucy	A Del	13	F	Dead	No	
609 Conner, Willie	A Del	7	M	Dead	No	
610 Conner, Nannie	A Del	5	F	Dead	No	
611 Conner, Minnie	A Del	5	F	Del214	No	
612 Conner, George	A Del	60	M	Dead	No	
613 Couch, N M	NCher	21	M	4539	Yes	Farmer
614 Couch, Rebecca J	AWhite	23	F	Dead	Yes	
615 Couch, Nancy J	NCher	3	F	4565	No	
616 Curry, Henry	AWhite	40	M	4399	Yes	Farmer
617 Curry, Margaret	NCher	22	F	4399	Yes	
618 Curry, Ida	NCher	9m	F	Dead	No	

Name	Race	Age	Sex	Census	Md	Remarks
619 Curl, James	AWhite	36	M	Dead	Yes	Stockman
620 Curl, Susan	AShaw	33	F	Dead	Yes	
621 Curl, Nellie	AShaw	6	F	3821	No	
622 Coodey, John H	NCher	24	M	4635	Yes	Farmer
623 Coodey, Mary	NCher	21	F	Dead	Yes	
624 Coodey, Henry	NCher	1	M	4631	No	
625 Coodey, Mrs B S	NCher	50	F	4531	No	
626 Carling, G	AWhite	34	M	D1487	Yes	
627 Carling, Emma J	NCher	46	F	D1487	Yes	
628 Carter, Riley	A Col	75	M	Dead	No	Jobber
629 Carter, John R	NCher	46	M	Dead	Yes	Farmer
630 Carter, Sarah	NCher	39	F	Dead	Yes	
631 Carpenter, Ben	AShaw	21	M	Dead	No	Gardener?
632 Carpenter, Mary	AShaw	50	F	3546	No	
633 Carpenter, Wm	AShaw	25	M	Dead	Yes	Pilfer
634 Carpenter, Fannie	AShaw	22	F	Dead	No	
635 Carpenter, Ben	AShaw	6	M	3526	No	
636 Carpenter, Lenia	AShaw	2	F	Dead	No	
637 Crutchfield, Thomas	NCher	25	M	2224	No	Convict at _____ for stealing horses
638 Coon, Sallie	A Del	59	F	Dead	No	
639 Camel, Rope, Hon	NCher	66	M	6292	Yes	The Is Rope Campbell Lowrey (BLB)
640 Camel, Betsy	NCher	65	F	Dead	No	
641 Camel, Alex	NCher	8	M	7743	No	On Dawes as Abraham Campbell (BLB)
642 Choteau, Nancy	NCher	14	F	R865	No	
643 Choteau, Vick	NCher	10	M	R866	No	
644 Cochran, Jesse	NCher	38	M	5684	Yes	Sheriff
645 Cochran, Susie	NCher	30	F	5684	Yes	
646 Cochran, Jesse Jr	NCher	6	M	5519	No	
647 Cochran, Henry	NCher	4	M	5678	No	
648 Cochran, Bill	NCher	40	M	Dead	No	
649 Chambers, John Jr	NCher	45	M	Dead	No	
650 Cochran, Chick	NCher	21	M	Dead	No	
651 Cochran, Thomas	NCher	20	M	Dead	No	Farmer
652 Choteau, Jip, Col	A Col	59	M	Dead	Yes	Farmer
653 Choteau, Martha	A Col	45	F	F597	No	
654 Choteau, Robert	A Col	26	M	Dead	No	
655 Cobb, J B	AWhite	50	M	Dead	Yes	Farmer
656 Cobb, Evaline	NCher	45	F	2283	Yes	
657 Cobb, Belle	NCher	21	F	2284	No	
658 Cobb, W C	NCher	20	M	Dead	No	

Name	Race	Age	Sex	Census	Md	Remarks
659 Cobb, Mattie	NCher	18	F	10235	No	
660 Cobb, J B, Jr	NCher	17	M	1852	No	
661 Cobb, E C	NCher	15	M	2286	No	
662 Cobb, Sam S	NCher	14	M	10277	No	
663 Cobb, Ada	NCher	10	F	7146	No	
664 Clinging, Bill	NCher	27	M	Dead	No	
665 Campton, Sarah	A Del	40	F	Del236	No	
666 Campton, Ella	A Del	11	F	Del236	No	
667 Campton, John	A Del	5	M	Del235	No	
668 Cunningham, Sarah	NCher	27	F	Dead	No	Farmer
669 Cunningham, Emma	NCher	3	F	2735	No	
670 Cunningham, Wm	NCher	1	M	6464	No	
671 Carter, George	AShaw	55	M	3122	No	Farmer
672 Christy, Nelly	NCher	25	F	D1490	No	Farmer
673 Chambers, Henry Sr	NCher	57	M	Dead	No	Farmer
674 Chambers, Parks	NCher	26	M	Dead	No	
675 Cambers, Maxfield W	NCher	21	M	5182	No	
676 Chambers, Nannie Jane	NCher	18	F	Dead	No	
677 Cat, Black	AShaw	45	M	Dead	No	
678 Crutchfield, James	NCher	33	M	Dead	Yes	Farmer
679 Crutchfield, Fannie	NCher	32	F	Dead	Yes	
680 Crutchfield, Kate	NCher	12	F	Dead	No	
681 Crutchfield, Emma	NCher	10	F	1440	No	
682 Crutchfield, Anna	NCher		F	Dead	No	
683 Clark, Sabra	NCher	42	F	3191	No	Is now Mrs Kelly, Osage
684 Chambers, Wm	NCher	43	M	4803	Yes	Smith ____
685 Chambers, P P	NCher	24	F	Dead	No	
686 Chambers, Ed	NCher	5	M	4798	No	Ezekiel Chambers (BLB)
687 Chambers, Dennie	NCher	2	M	4718	No	
688 Chambers, Henry	NCher	3m	M	Dead	No	
689 Chambers, John Sr	NCher	68	M	Dead	No	Politician
690 Chambers, Henry H	NCher	24	M	Dead	No	
691 Canon, Charley	NCher	10m	M	Dead	No	
692 Coker, D F	NCher	55	M	Dead	Yes	Minister
693 Coker, E E	AWhite	39	F	4764	Yes	
694 Coker, L R	NCher	20	F	4723	No	
695 Coker, M L A	NCher	17	F	Dead	No	
696 Coker, M E	NCher	15	F	4686	No	
697 Coker, D N	NCher	12	F	4785	No	
698 Coker, J R	NCher	10	M	4850	No	
699 Coker, S J	NCher	8	F	4852	No	
700 Coker, J A	NCher	4	F	4765	No	

Name	Race	Age	Sex	Census	Md	Remarks
701 Crump, Cynthie	NCher	72	F	Dead	No	
702 Cochran, Alex	NCher	35	M	Dead	Yes	Farmer
703 Cochran, Annie	NCher	30	F	7337	No	Dead
704 Cochran, Agness	NCher	12	F	Dead	No	
705 Cochran, Jesse	NCher	8	M	Dead	No	
706 Cochran, Martin	NCher	7	M	7337	No	Enrolled as Chickasaws census # 1397 (BLB)
707 Cochran, Jane	NCher	5	F	4995	No	
708 Cochran, Turner	NCher	4	M	7338	No	Enrolled as Chickasaws census # 1397 (BLB)
709 Crutchfield, J V	NCher	38	M	Dead	Yes	School Teacher
710 Crutchfield, Mary	NCher	25	F	Dead	Yes	
711 Choteau, John	A Col	19	M	F1135	Yes	Nothing
712 Choteau, Tobe	A Col	17	M	F1182	No	
713 Choteau, Will	A Col	13	M	F668	No	
714 Choteau, Eli	A Col	11	M	F1137	No	
715 Cowan, Andy	AWhite	50	M	9672	Yes	Farmer
716 Cowan, E J	NCher	50	F	Dead	Yes	
717 Cowan, C P	NCher	21	F	Dead	No	
718 Cowan, A C	NCher	18	M	2589	No	
719 Clingon, W D	NCher	46	M	2068	Yes	Farmer
720 Clingon, M J	NCher	33	F	2068	Yes	
721 Clingon, Maggie M	NCher	8	F	2073	No	
722 Clingon, Sherman	NCher	4	F	1935	No	
723 Clingon, Cora	NCher	2	F	2071	No	
724 Clingon, Mattie E	NCher	6m	F	2042	No	
725 Campton, Charles	AWhite	27	M	Dead	No	
726 Creason, John	NCher	34	M	Dead	Yes	None
727 Creason, Menerva	NCher	41	F	Dead	Yes	
728 Clark, Martha	NCher	5	F	3279	No	
729 Clark, Johnson	NCher	28	M	3457	No	
730 Cat, Polly	NCher	35	F	Dead	No	
731 Cat, Josie	NCher	12	F	Dead	No	
732 Chambers, Vann	NCher	30	M	4713	Yes	Farmer
733 Chambers, Jennie	NCher	23	F	4713	Yes	
734 Chambers, Juliet	NCher	6	F	4888	No	
735 Chambers, Lizzie	NCher	1	F	4977	No	
736 Chambers, Joseph	NCher	50	M	Dead	Yes	
737 Chambers, Nancy	NCher	49	F	5187	No	
738 Chambers, Pickins	NCher	8	M	5171	No	
739 Chambers, Nep	NCher	21	F	5366	No	
740 Chambers, Tuce	NCher	25	M	4886	No	
741 Chambers, Willie	NCher	21	M	4951	No	

Name	Race	Age	Sex	Census	Md	Remarks
742 Choteau, Martha	NCher	17	F	D1491	No	
743 Colins, Ann	AWhite	60	F	Dead	No	
744 Curlyhead, Old Man	A Del	46	M	Dead	Yes	Farmer
745 Curlyhead, Mrs	A Del	40	F	Dead	Yes	
746 Curlyhead, Lizzie	A Del	16	F	Del83	No	
747 Curlyhead, Lily	A Del	12	F	Del134	No	
748 Curlyhead, John	A Del	7	M	Dead	No	
749 Curlyhead, Dolly	A Del	6	F	Del143	No	
750 Curlyhead, Mary	A Del	3	F	Del206	No	
751 Conner, Susie	A Del	19	F	Dead	No	
752 Conner, Ben	A Del	16	M	Del243	No	
753 Conner, Ida	A Del	15	F	Dead	No	
754 Crutchfield, Rachel	NCher	19	F	Dead	No	
755 Crutchfield, Henry	NCher	21	M	Dead	No	
756 Cordry, Andy	A Col	19	M	F726	No	
757 Colier, Sam'l	AWhite	32	M		Yes	No census number given, not listed as dead (BLB)
758 Colier, Mary	NCher	30	F	Dead	Yes	
759 Colier, Charley	NCher	10	M	5157	No	
760 Colier, Mack	NCher	2	M	9918	No	
761 Colier, Carrie	NCher	3m	F	3769	No	
762 Cox, Bill	AWhite	22	M	D773	Yes	
763 Cox, J B	NCher	23	F	Dead	Yes	
764 Cox, R E	NCher	3	M	7059	No	
765 Cox, Vian	NCher	1	F	Dead	No	
766 Cump, Carter	NCher	26	M	Dead	No	Lawyer
767 Carter, Nancy Jane	NCher	5	F	Dead	No	
768 Carter, Oce	NCher	24	M	Dead	No	Mail Rider
769 Cochran, Nannie	NCher	10	F	Dead	No	Enrolled in N B Rowe's family
770 Canada, M F	NCher	25		4375		
771 Collins, Ida		25		5330		
772 Conner, Nancy		24		Dead		
773 Cole, Boon		25		2446		
774 Cole, Nancy		20		Dead		
775 Cole, Georgianna		3mo		2446		
776 Chamberlain, N B				3818		
777 Chamberlain, Emma				Dead		
778 Chamberlain, George				Dead		
779 Campbell, Ed	A Col			F837		
780 Campbell, Martha	A Col			F837		
781 Campbell, George				9633		George Tucker (BLB)
782 Campbell, Minnie				4387		

Cooweescoowee District

Name	Race	Age	Sex	Census	Md	Remarks
783 Campbell, Roseanna	A Col			Dead		
784 Campbell, Mary	A Col			F912		
785 Campbell, Keturah	A Col			Dead		
786 Campbell, Charlie	A Col					Duplicate 602
787 Campbell, Emma	A Col			F846		
788 Campbell, George	A Col			F1107		
789 Campbell, James	A Col			F827		
790 Campbell, Walter	A Col			F846		
791 Campbell, Charles Jr	A Col			F20		
792 Coker, Cynthia				4539		
793 Chambers, Robt	NCher	23	M	4717		
794 Cannon, L J				Dead		
795 Cannon, Josephine				5403		
796 Cannon, Mary P				5516		
797 Cannon, Wm C				Dead		
798 Cannon, Spencer W				5440		
799 Cannon, George L				5413		
800 Downing, Rachel	NCher	43	F	Dead	No	
801 Downing, Lizzie	NCher	12	F	2515	No	
802 Drew, W H	NCher	37	M	4198	Yes	
803 Drew, Ellen	NCher	35	F	4198	Yes	
804 Drew, Jesse B	NCher	9	M	3604	No	
805 Drew, Henrietta	NCher	6	F	Dead	No	
806 Drew, Sue	NCher	3	F	4766	No	
807 Drew, W P	NCher	13m	M	4768	No	
808 Duncan, J M	NCher	24	M	Dead	Yes	
809 Duncan, Nan	NCher	20	F	Dead	Yes	
810 Duncan, Rex	NCher	2	M	5921	No	
811 Duncan, Walter	NCher	3m	M	5917	No	
812 Dick, Jacob	NCher	28	M	4214	Yes	
813 Dick, Lucy	AWhite	28	F	4214	Yes	
814 Daugherty, Wm	AShaw	26	M	3039	Yes	Farmer
815 Daugherty, Hetty	A Del	23	F	Dead	Yes	
816 Dick, George	AShaw	27	M	3379	Yes	Farmer
817 Dick, Angeline	AShaw	36	F	Dead	Yes	
818 Dick, John	AShaw	4	M	Dead	No	
819 Dick, Willie	AShaw	9m	M	7522	No	
820 Dick, Sallie	AShaw	20	F	Dead	No	
821 Daugherty, Nancy	AShaw	22	F	3244	No	
822 Dick, James	AShaw	22	M	Dead	Yes	This mans wife Ruth we refused to enroll, she belongs to a band of Shawnee Spring River, Farmer

Name	Race	Age	Sex	Census	Md	Remarks
823 Drew, Sarah	NCher	18	F	Dead	Yes	
824 Drew, William	NCher	5m	M	2789	No	
825 Daniels, Henry	AWhite	42	M		Yes	Farmer
826 Daniels, Emma	NCher	31	F		Yes	Duplicates, 938, 939, 941, 943, 942, 940
827 Daniels, Mattie	NCher	6	F		No	
828 Daniels, Wm	NCher	4	M		No	
829 Daniels, Thomas	NCher	2	M		No	
830 Daniels, James	NCher	8	M		No	
831 Daniels, Henry A	AWhite	28	M	Dead	No	
832 Daniels, Becky	NCher	7	F	4453	No	
833 Daniels, Casinda	NCher	5	F	4502	No	
834 Daniels, Jo	NCher	10m	M	4455	No	
835 Dashade, David Jr	AShaw	57	M	Dead	Yes	Farmer (surname DuShane BLB)
836 Dushade, Martha	AShaw	32	F	Dead	Yes	
837 Dushade, Frank	AShaw	18	M	3683	No	
838 Dushade, Napoleon	AShaw	16	M	Dead	No	
839 Dushade, Lewis	AShaw	13	M	Dead	No	
840 Dushade, Dennis B	AShaw	6	M	Dead	No	
841 Dushade, Antonia	AShaw	2	M	Dead	No	
842 Denis, Mary	A Col	21	F	F956	No	
843 Denis, Isabel	A Col	3	F	Dead	No	
844 Denis, Bertha	A Col	1	F	Dead	No	
845 Denis, Laura	A Col	1m	F	Dead	No	
846 Daniels, L D	A Col	36	M	F875	Yes	Farmer
847 Daniels, Amanda	A Col	37	F	F1011	Yes	
848 Daniels, Bettie	A Col	14	F	F1012	No	
849 Daniels, Henry	A Col	13	M	Dead	No	
850 Daniels, Jessie	A Col	3	M	F1020	No	
851 Daniels, Ruth	A Col	18	F	F956	No	
852 Dawn, Malinda	A Col	45	F	Dead	Yes	
853 Daniels, Jo	NCher	25	M	Dead	Yes	
854 Daniels, Ida	AWhite	18	F	D1492	Yes	
855 Downing, Whale	NCher	27	M	Dead	Yes	Farmer
856 Downing, Sarah	NCher	30	F	Dead	Yes	
857 Downing, James	NCher	1	M	Dead	No	
858 Dirtpott, Robin	NCher	36		Dead	No	Farmer
859 Dirtpott, Susie	NCher	5		4216	No	
860 Drum, Alex	AShaw	35		3369	Yes	Farmer
861 Drum, Mrs A	A Del	35	F	Del21	Yes	see 134
862 Drum, George	A Del	7	M	Del137	No	
863 Drum, James	A Del	1	M	Del206	No	

Name	Race	Age	Sex	Census	Md	Remarks
864 Downing, Wm	NCher	30		4535	Yes	
865 Downing, Lou	A Col	25		Dead	Yes	
866 Downing, Mary J	A Col	4	F	F709	No	
867 Downing, Amanda	A Col	3	F	F839	No	
868 Downing, Thomas	A Col	1	M	F758	No	
869 Day, James	A Del	22	M	Del227	Yes	
870 Day, Lizzie	A Del	30	F	Dead	Yes	
871 Daniels, Wm	NCher	28	M	Dead	No	
872 Davis, R E	AWhite	43		Dead	Yes	Gardiner
873 Davis, Alice	NCher	6	F	Dead	No	
874 Davis, Dayon	NCher	4	F	4532	No	
875 Drake, John P	AWhite	35	M	5471	Yes	
876 Drake, Emma	NCher	35	F	5471	Yes	
877 Drake, Mary	NCher	2	F	5615	No	
878 Dower, W E	AWhite	20	M	5065	Yes	Worker (Surname Dowell BLB)
879 Dower, Mattie	NCher	20	F	Dead	Yes	
880 Drowningbear, Katie	NCher	45	F	Dead	No	
881 Drowningbear, Nancy	NCher	22	F	2584	No	
882 Davis, Jeff	NCher	19	M	4835	No	
883 Drawstring, Wakie	NCher	45	F	Dead	No	
884 Drawstring, John	NCher	18	M	Dead	No	
885 Drawstring, Young Jes	NCher	20	M	Dead	No	
886 Duck, Richard	NCher	42	M	8860	No	Politician
887 Duck, Sallie	NCher	15	F	Dead	No	
888 Duck, John	NCher	10	M	4926	No	
889 Delk, David	AWhite	37	M	Dead	No	Farmer
890 Davis, Monroe	NCher	28	M	Dead	Yes	
891 Davis, Eliza	NCher	23	F	Dead	Yes	This mans wife is disputed said to be half Negro and white
892 Davis, Lou A	NCher	6m	F	Dead	No	
893 Davis, Tom	NCher	35	M	5168	Yes	
894 Davis, Lizzie	NCher	26	F	Dead	Yes	
895 Davis, Martha	NCher	11	F	5130	No	
896 Davis, Lou V	NCher	8	F	Dead	No	
897 Davis, Wm	NCher	2	M	5141	No	
898 Davis, Bird	NCher	5m	M	5174	No	
899 Downing, Jack	NCher	35	M	7527	Yes	Farmer
900 Downing, Cahtayah	NCher	20	F	Dead	Yes	
901 Downing, George	NCher	6	M	3225	No	
902 Downing, Sophi	NCher	1	F	Dead	No	
903 Davis, Lizzie	NCher	45	F	Dead	No	
904 Davis, George	NCher	23	M	Dead	No	

Name	Race	Age	Sex	Census	Md	Remarks
905 Davis, Margaret	NCher	20	F	Dead	No	
906 Davis, John	NCher	18	M	Dead	No	
907 Davis, Wm	NCher	6	M	Dead	No	
908 Davis, Julia A	NCher	4	F	4874	No	
909 Duncan, John E	NCher	20	M	2536	No	Teacher
910 Drew, Mary	A Col	22	F	F1119	No	
911 Drew, Fannie	A Col	19	F	F476	No	
912 Downing, Wooster	NCher	22	M	Dead	Yes	
913 Downing, Eliza	NCher	34	F	Dead	Yes	
914 Downing, Wakie	NCher	1	F	Dead	No	
915 Davis, Wat	NCher	34	M	Dead	Yes	Farmer
916 Davis, Ida	AWhite	20	F	Dead	Yes	
917 Davis, Richard	NCher	6	M	Dead	No	
918 Davis, Jennie	NCher	4	F	Dead	No	
919 Daugherty, Jane	NCher	41	F	Dead	No	Farmer
920 Daugherty, Lizzie	NCher	17	F	2691	No	
921 Daugherty, Lydia	NCher	15	F	Dead	No	
922 Daugherty, Ellis	NCher	12	M	2687	No	
923 Daugherty, Charlie	NCher	5	M	2802	No	
924 Denton, Rufus	NCher	23	M	4724	Yes	Farmer
925 Denton, Hettie	NCher	20	F	Dead	Yes	
926 Denton, M E	NCher	4	F	4801	No	
927 Denton, Frank	NCher	1	M	4873	No	
928 Denton, Delila	NCher	13	F	5133	No	
929 Dunkard,	NCher	18	M	Dead	No	
930 Dick, Big	AShaw	28	M	Dead	Yes	Farmer
931 Dick, Polly	AShaw	45	F	Dead	Yes	
932 Denney, D L	AWhite	26	M	2426	Yes	Farmer
933 Denney, Lettee	NCher	20	F	Dead	Yes	
934 Denney, Coonskin	NCher	2w	M	Dead	No	
935 Duncan, Sallie	NCher	11	F	Dead	No	
936 Downing, Allie	NCher	8	F	7552	No	
937 Drew, Carry	A Col	18	F	F582	No	
938 Donley, Henry	AWhite	42	M	3782	Yes	Farmer
939 Donley, Emma	NCher	31	F	3782	Yes	
940 Donley, James	NCher	8	F	3470	No	
941 Donley, Mattie	NCher	6	F	3775	No	
942 Donley, Thomas	NCher	2	M	3787	No	
943 Donley, William	NCher	4	M	3846	No	
944 Day, Lilly	A Del	20	F	Dead	No	Racer
945 Day, Nanna	A Del	1	F	Del364	No	
946 Don Carloff, Fil	AWhite	40	M	Dead	Yes	Farmer

Cooweescoowee District

Name	Race	Age	Sex	Census	Md	Remarks
947 Don Carloff, Mary	NCher	20	F	6471	Yes	
948 Don Carloff, Louis	NCher	3	M	4313	No	
949 Don Carloff, Susie M	NCher	1	F	4332	No	
950 Dority, Nancy	AShaw	14	F	3244	No	Dup 821
951 Duncan, Rosy E	NCher	12	F	4990	No	
952 Downing, William	NCher	62	M	Dead	Yes	Farmer
953 Downing, Margaret	AWhite	47	F	Dead	No	
954 Downing, Richard	NCher	17	M	4615	No	
955 Downing, Watie	NCher	10	M	3738	No	
956 Duncan, Bill	A Del	18	M	Dead	No	
957 Duncan, Laura	A Del	12	F	4362	No	
958 Dick, Richard	A Del	12	M	Del139	No	Dup 3515 Coo Dist
959 Dick, Joseph	A Del	15	M	DLD28	No	
960 Dick, Emily	A Del	3	F	Dead	No	
961 Downing, Peggy	NCher	8	F	D193	No	Lives in Tah Dist
962 Davis, Willie	AShaw	16	M	D1494	No	
963 Duncan, Willie				2830		
964 Drum, Mary				Del21		
965 Deleware, Elisa				Del183		
966 Daniels, Ransom				Dead		
967 Everet, Caroline	A Del	29	F	Dead	No	
968 Everet, Mary	A Del	30	F	Dead	No	
969 Everet, Nancy	A Del		F	Dead	No	
970 Elliott, John W	AWhite	35	M	Dead	Yes	Farmer
971 Elliott, Lizzie	NCher	21	F	7260	No	
972 Elkhair, Charlie	A Del	28	M	Del169	Yes	Farmer
973 Elkhair, Mrs C	A Del	16	F	Del196	Yes	
974 Elridge, Jeff	NCher	60	M	Dead	Yes	Farmer
975 Elridge, L N	AWhite	31	F	Dead	Yes	
976 Elridge, Clin	NCher	6	M	4309	No	
977 Elridge, Wm J	NCher	3	M	5314	No	
978 Elridge, Martin E	NCher	5m	M	4819	No	
979 Easy, Jacob, Widow	A Del	40	F	Del133	No	Farmer
980 Easy, Wm	A Del	17	M	Del133	No	
981 Easy, Samuel	A Del	13	M	Dead	No	
982 Elliott, James	AShaw	37	M	4488	Yes	Farmer
983 Elliott, Emily	AShaw	28	F	4488	Yes	
984 Elliott, Emma	AShaw	13	F	Dead	No	
985 Elliott, Mary	AShaw	10	F	4489	No	
986 Elliott, Dora	AShaw	5	F	4490	No	
987 Elliott, Nancy	AShaw	2	F	Dead	No	
988 Elkhair, Mary	A Del	22	F	Dead	No	

Name	Race	Age	Sex	Census	Md	Remarks
989 Ecoowee, Arch	NCher	26	M	Dead	Yes	Farmer
990 Ecoowee, Sarah	NCher	19	F	Dead	Yes	
991 Ecoowee, Bunch	NCher	1	M	Dead	No	
992 Edwards, John W				2929		
993 Edwards, Easter				Dead		
994 Elridge, Turner	NCher	24	M	Dead	No	
995 Eaton, L F	AWhite	54	M	Dead	No	Black Smith
996 Eaton, W D	NCher	17	M	Dead	No	
997 Eaton, M E	NCher	14	F	3130	No	
998 Eaton, J B	NCher	9	M	Dead	No	
999 Eaton, Taylor	NCher	5	M	2889	No	
1000 Eaton, J A	NCher	4		Dead	No	
1001 Eaton, Jno A	NCher	2		2759	No	
1002 Eaton, G W	AWhite	34		4708	Yes	Farmer
1003 Eaton, N E	NCher	29		Dead	Yes	
1004 Eaton, R C	NCher	11		4743	No	
1005 Eaton, J C	NCher	9		4677	No	
1006 Eaton, M P	NCher	3		4744	No	
1007 Eaton, J M	NCher	6m		4682	No	
1008 Emerson, G W	NCher	30		D1495	Yes	Left County, Farmer
1009 Emerson, Mollie	AWhite	24	F	R690	Yes	
1010 Emerson, S E	NCher	2m		R690	No	
1011 Exondine, Fredrick	A Del	9m		DLD29	No	Caddo Allottee
1012 Elkhair, Charlie Jr	A Del	7		Dead	No	
1013 Elkhair, Lizzie	A Del	3		Del86	No	
1014 Elkhair, James	A Del	68		Del128	Yes	Hunter
1015 Elkhair, Telatoquah	A Del	48		Del128	Yes	
1016 Elkhair, Quartetee	A Del	16		Dead	No	
1017 Elkhair, Falling Leaf Mary	A Del	12		Dead	No	
1018 Eldridge, Armstrong	NCher	30		Dead	No	
1019 Francis, Richard	AShaw	32		Dead	Yes	
1020 Francis, Lizzie	AShaw	24	F	Dead	Yes	
1021 Francis, David	AShaw	3	M	Dead	No	
1022 Francis, Edmon	AShaw	5		Dead	No	
1023 Flint, A R	AWhite	39		4370	Yes	Farmer
1024 Flint, Vie	NCher	28		4370	Yes	
1025 Fields, James	NCher	47	M	Dead	Yes	Farmer
1026 Fields, Annie	NCher	26	F	4507	Yes	
1027 Fields, Charlie	NCher	4	M	4508	No	
1028 Fields, G W	AWhite	33	M	D1138	Yes	Farmer
1029 Fields, Eliza	NCher	32	F	Dead	Yes	
1030 Fields, Sarah	NCher	15	F	3953	No	

Name	Race	Age	Sex	Census	Md	Remarks
1031 Fields, L J	NCher	13	F	D1496	No	
1032 Fields, Pley	NCher	11	M	4138	No	
1033 Fields, Wm	NCher	9	M	4139	No	
1034 Fields, Margaret	NCher	6	F	3926	No	
1035 Fields, George	NCher	4	M	4027	No	
1036 Fox, Aaron	AShaw	40	M	Dead	Yes	Farmer
1037 Fox, Louisa	AShaw	35	F	3384	Yes	
1038 Fox, Thomas	AShaw	13	M	3468	No	
1039 Fox, Susie	AShaw	11	F	4981	No	
1040 Fox, Julia	AShaw	8	F	Dead	No	
1041 Fox, Nancy C	AShaw	5	F	Dead	No	
1042 Fish, Jake	A Del	50	M	Dead	Yes	Farmer
1043 Fish, Mary	A Del	30	F	Del92	Yes	
1044 Fish, Malinda	A Del	4	F	Dead	No	
1045 Fish, Minnie	A Del	5	F	Dead	No	
1046 Foster, Jerry	A Col	26	M	F997	Yes	
1047 Foster, Edney	A Col	25	F	F772	Yes	
1048 Falling, Henry	NCher	24	M	3233	No	Farmer
1049 Fields, H C	NCher	35	M	Dead	Yes	Farmer
1050 Fields, Amanda	AWhite	34	F	Dead	Yes	
1051 Fields, Henry	NCher	18	M	2629	No	
1052 Fields, Mary S	NCher	11	F	2472	No	
1053 Fields, Alice	NCher	12	F	2764	No	
1054 Fields, Josephine	NCher	7	F	2496	No	
1055 Fields, Willie	NCher	6	M	5695	No	
1056 Fields, Frances	NCher	3	F	2772	No	Henry Franklin Field (BLB)
1057 Fields, Elizabeth	NCher	5m	F	2574	No	
1058 Foreman, A W	NCher	24	M	3199	Yes	Physician
1059 Foreman, Emma	AWhite	23	F	Dead	Yes	
1060 Frazie, M	AWhite	42	M	3810	Yes	Physician
1061 Frazie, Susie	NCher	30	F	Dead	Yes	
1062 Fallingleaf, George	A Del	26	M	Del174	Yes	Farmer
1063 Fallingleaf, Lizzie	A Del	20	F	Del174	Yes	
1064 Fallingleaf, Cyrus	A Del	35	M	Dead	Yes	
1065 Fallingleaf, Mrs C	A Del	30	F	Del106	Yes	
1066 Fallingleaf, Auscusquee	A Del	16		Dead	No	
1067 Fallingleaf, Henry	A Del	13	M	Dead	No	
1068 Fallingleaf, Charles	A Del	5	M	DLD30	No	
1069 Fallingleaf, Wechelonkon	A Del	2	M	Del196	No	
1070 Flint, Wm	AShaw	25	M	Dead	No	
1071 Frenchman	A Del	50	M	Del85	Yes	
1072 Frenchman, Mrs	A Del	60	F	Dead	Yes	

Name	Race	Age	Sex	Census	Md	Remarks
1073 Frenchman, Ed	A Del	11	M	Del99	No	
1074 Foster, Malissie	A Col	30	F	F1006	No	Farmer
1075 Foster, Phil	A Col	29	M	F1008	No	
1076 Foster, Lou	A Col	27	F	F922	No	
1077 Foster, Percy	A Col	26	M	F1001	No	
1078 Foster, Lucinda	A Col	25	F	F1003	No	
1079 Foster, Clara	A Col	28	F	F1004	No	
1080 Foster, Ben	A Col	17	M	Dead	No	
1081 Foster, Fannie	A Col	16	F	F1013	No	
1082 Foster, Jeff	A Col	13	M	F1002	No	
1083 Foster, Dora	A Col	11	F	F1005	No	
1084 Foster, Frank	A Col	5	M	F1007	No	
1085 Frenchman, Frank	A Del	41	M	Del146	Yes	Farmer
1086 Frenchman, Lizzie	A Del	16	F	Dead	No	
1087 Fallingleaf, Widow	A Del	80	F	Dead	No	
1088 Fallingleaf, Lizzie	A Del	18	F	Del247	No	
1089 Fonts, Julius	A Del	14	M	Del208	No	
1090 Flanigan, Pat	AWhite	34	M	4517	Yes	Farmer
1091 Flanigan, Mary	NCher	20	F	4517	Yes	
1092 Flanigan, Jesse B	NCher	2	M	4558	No	
1093 Flanigan, Willie	NCher	5m	M	4517	No	
1094 Foreman, Link H	NCher	43	M	5289	Yes	Nothing
1095 Foreman, Mary	NCher	36	F	Dead	Yes	
1096 Foreman, Willie	NCher	5	M	Dead	No	
1097 Foreman, David	NCher	2	M	5289	No	
1098 Foster, Randal	A Col		M	Dead	Yes	
1099 Foster, Mary	A Col	34	F	FD895	No	
1100 Foster, Thomas	A Col	13	M	F1061	No	
1101 Foster, Susie	A Col	9	F	FD1136	No	
1102 Foster, Francis	A Col	7	F	Dead	No	
1103 Foster, Malinda	A Col	6	F	FD1137	No	
1104 Foster, Sarah	A Col	3	F	F1079	No	
1105 Foster, Lucinda	A Col	1	F	Dead	No	
1106 Foster, Philis	A Col	1m	F	F1078	No	
1107 Foreman, John W	NCher	21	M	Dead	No	
1108 Flint, James	AShaw	35	M	Dead	Yes	
1109 Flint, Alice	AShaw	26	F	3120	No	
1110 Flint, Susie	AShaw	9	F	5641	No	
1111 Flint, Kate	AShaw	6	F	4473	No	
1112 Flint, Jake	AShaw	38	M	Dead	Yes	Hunter
1113 Flint, Julia A	AShaw	37	F	4409	Yes	
1114 Fields, Moses	NCher	22	M	Dead	No	Runabout

Name	Race	Age	Sex	Census	Md	Remarks
1115 Fish, Anderson	NCher	21	M	Dead	Yes	
1116 Fish, Fannie	NCher	21	F	6958	Yes	On Dawes as Fannie Bigby (BLB)
1117 Falling, Jack	NCher	23	M	2530	No	
1118 Falling, Jess	NCher	25	M	4716	Yes	
1119 Falling, Betsey	NCher	20	F	dead	Yes	
1120 Falling, John	NCher	5	M	5309	No	
1121 Falling, Charlie	NCher	1	M	5006	No	
1122 Foster, Ed	A Col	20	M	F995	No	
1123 Foreman, John A	NCher	36	M	5244	No	Farmer
1124 Foreman, J E	NCher	8	F	5244	No	
1125 Foreman, J G	NCher	7	F	4828	No	
1126 Foreman, G A	NCher	4	M	Dead	No	
1127 Foreman, Taylor	NCher	30	M	Dead	Yes	Farmer
1128 Foreman, Ada C	AWhite	25	F	5256	Yes	
1129 Foreman, S L	NCher	5	F	4083	No	
1130 Foreman, J A	NCher	3	F	Dead	No	
1131 Foreman, J A	NCher	1	F	4825	No	
1132 Fields, R H	NCher	32	M	Dead	Yes	Merchant
1133 Fisher, Ben	NCher	36	M	2608	Yes	B Smith
1134 Fisher, Jennie	NCher	41	F	Dead	Yes	
1135 Fisher, Ro	NCher	10	M	2630	No	
1136 Fisher, Lucy	NCher	5	F	2479	No	
1137 Fisher, Jake	NCher	2	M	Dead	No	
1138 Fisher, Eliza	NCher	15	F	2608	No	
1139 Fields, James	NCher	36	M	Dead	Yes	Farmer
1140 Fields, Cynthia	AWhite	33	F	2738	Yes	
1141 Fields, Thomas D	NCher	6	M	7107	No	
1142 Falling, Bryant	AWhite	83	M	Dead	Yes	Farmer
1143 Falling, Kate	NCher	35	F	Dead	Yes	
1144 Frog, Bull	NCher	48	M	Dead	No	
1145 Fox, Chicken	NCher	28		Dead	Yes	Farmer
1146 Fox, Julia	NCher	22	F	Dead	Yes	
1147 Fair, Raper	AWhite	27	M	2480	Yes	Farmer
1148 Fair, Reener	NCher	24		2480	Yes	
1149 Foster, Sam	NCher	22	M	4686	No	
1150 Falkner, Lucy Jane	NCher	27	F	2878	Yes	Farmer (surname Fortner BLB)
1151 Falkner, Gracy	NCher	5	F	3805	No	
1152 Falkner, Lucile	NCher	1	F	3527	No	
1153 Forest, Man	A Del	45	M	Del353	Yes	Farmer
1154 Forest, Pachexquaie	A Del	34	F	Dead	Yes	
1155 Frye, Wm	AWhite	44	M	5023	Yes	Stone Mason
1156 Frye, Lettie	NCher	35	F	Dead	Yes	

Name	Race	Age	Sex	Census	Md	Remarks
1157 Frye, Wm	NCher	11	M	4831	No	
1158 Frye, Mc	NCher	9	M	5027	No	
1159 Frye, Kate	NCher	7	F	5326	No	
1160 Frye, Mary	NCher	3	F	5024	No	
1161 Frye, Alter	NCher	1	M	5225	No	
1162 Foster, James	NCher	37	M	Dead	Yes	Farmer
1163 Foster, Jane	NCher	35	F	4821	Yes	
1164 Foster, John	NCher	11	M	4710	No	
1165 Foster, Louisa	NCher	6	F	4890	No	
1166 Foster, Thomas	NCher	4	M	4818	No	
1167 Flint, D L	AWhite	25	M	3403	Yes	Farmer
1168 Flint, Delila	NCher	18	F	3403	Yes	
1169 Flint, Denny	NCher	2	F	3389	No	
1170 Flint, Willie	NCher	6m	M	3403	No	
1171 Foster, Wm	A Del	7	M	Dead	No	
1172 Foster, Lizzie	A Del	5	F	Dead	No	
1173 Fisher, Johnson	NCher	37	M	Dead	Yes	Farmer
1174 Fisher, Sarah	NCher	26	F	5125	Yes	
1175 Fisher, Walter	NCher	12	M	Dead	No	
1176 Fisher, Johnson Jr	NCher	8	M	5126	No	
1177 Fisher, Moses	NCher	6	M	5127	No	
1178 Fisher, Ella	NCher	4	F	2808	No	
1179 Fisher, Benj	NCher	2	M	Dead	No	
1180 Fisher, Isaac	NCher	2m	M	5123	No	
1181 Forbisch, W H	AWhite	36	M	Dead	Yes	Farmer (Surname Habbish BLB)
1182 Forbisch, M J	NCher	30	F	2948	Yes	
1183 Forbisch, Johney	NCher	10	F	3850	No	
1184 Forbisch, Mattie	NCher	9	F	3739	No	
1185 Forbisch, Elois	NCher	2	F	3746	No	
1186 Forbisch, S E	NCher	4m	F	Dead	No	
1187 Forbisch, G H	NCher	5	M	3898	No	
1188 Fourmile, Widow	A Del	70	F	Dead	No	
1189 Frazer, Robert	NCher	12	M	D1497	No	
1190 Fulsom, Jess	A Col	10	M	FD1138	No	
1191 French, David	A Col	45	M	F1000	Yes	Farmer
1192 French, Linda	A Col	40	F	Dead	Yes	
1193 French, Wash	A Col	20	M	F1124	No	
1194 French, Jennie	A Col	18	F	F995	No	
1195 French, Tom	A Col	13	M	F1074	No	
1196 French, Eli	A Col	10	M	F927	No	
1197 Flint, Mareen	AWhite	24	M	4869	Yes	Blacksmith
1198 Flint, Sabre	NCher	18	F	4869	Yes	

Name	Race	Age	Sex	Census	Md	Remarks
1199 Flint, Florence	NCher	2	F	5021	No	
1200 Fallingleaf, Fugerson	A Del	14	M	Dead	No	
1201 Fallingleaf, Mary	A Del	6	F	Del314	No	
1202 Fallingleaf, Nancy	A Del	4	F	Del123	No	
1203 Fallingleaf, Sulus Jr				Dead	No	
1204 Foster, Armstrong				FD907	No	
1205 Fish, Jane				Dead	No	
1206 Fountain, Isaac				D1498	No	1896 Del Dist
1207 Fountain, Aley	NCher	35	F	Dead	No	
1208 Greenway, A J	AWhite	44	M	Dead	No	Teacher
1209 Greenway, Alonzo	NCher	19	M	4624	No	
1210 Greenway, Minnie	NCher	13	F	Dead	No	
1211 Goodtraveler, J W	A Del	28	M	Dead	Yes	Farmer
1212 Goodtraveler, Susie	A Del	24	F	Del216	Yes	
1213 Goodtraveler, Martha	A Del	2	F	Del218	No	
1214 Grimmett, Ben	A Col	48	M	F923	Yes	Farmer
1215 Grimmett, Clarinda	A Col	39	F	Dead	Yes	
1216 Grimmett, George	A Col	18	M	F928	No	
1217 Grimmett, Henderson	A Col	17	M	F116	No	
1218 Grimmett, Edney	A Col	15	F	Dead	No	
1219 Grimmett, Elizabeth	A Col	9	F	Dead	No	
1220 Grimmett, Benj. Jr	A Col	8	M	Dead	No	
1221 Grimmett, Addie	A Col	7	F	Dead	No	
1222 Grimmett, Melgy	A Col	4	F	Dead	No	
1223 Grimmett, Samantha	A Col	8m	F	F1112	No	
1224 Goodykoontz, Arch	AWhite	35	M	Dead	Yes	Stockman
1225 Goodykoontz, Amanda	NCher	28	F	3432	Yes	
1226 Goodykoontz, George	NCher	6	M	Dead	No	
1227 Goodykoontz, Frank	NCher	2	M	3880	No	
1228 Griffith, Jno W	A Del	23	M	Dead	No	
1229 Graves, Charles	AWhite	35	M	Dead	Yes	Coal miner
1230 Graves, Abby	AShaw	34	F	Dead	Yes	
1231 Graves, Clarence	AShaw	8	F	4533	No	
1232 Goodman, Fred	AWhite	35	M	4297	Yes	Farmer
1233 Goodman, Catharine	NCher	20	F	4297	Yes	
1234 Goodman, E J	NCher	2	F	4298	No	
1235 Glass, Robert	A Col	30	M	F969	Yes	Farmer
1236 Glass, Lizzie	A Col	25	F	F969	Yes	
1237 Glass, Angeline	A Col	9	F	F964	No	
1238 Glass, Randal	A Col	5	M	F1071	No	
1239 Glass, John	A Col	2	M	F1072	No	
1240 Glass, Lewis	A Col	4m	M	F1110	No	

Name	Race	Age	Sex	Census	Md	Remarks
1241 Gunter, Keekee	NCher	34	M	Dead	Yes	Farmer
1242 Gunter, Sarah	NCher	28	F	4420	Yes	
1243 Gunter, G W	NCher	4	M	10262	No	
1244 Grass, Jennie	NCher	25	F	4221	No	Farmer
1245 Grass, Alice	NCher	5	F	10718	No	
1246 Grass, Delilah	NCher	6m	F	Dead	No	
1247 Goard, Loony R	NCher	35	M	4991	No	
1248 Goard, James R	NCher	7	M	5022	No	
1249 Goard, Henry R	NCher	3	M	5114	No	
1250 Grevey, Eliza	A Del	2	F	Dead	No	
1251 Grimmett, Melton	A Col	12	M	FD1139	No	
1252 Galketcher, Thomas	NCher	44	M	Dead	Yes	Sheriff Deputy
1253 Galketcher, Nancy	NCher	30	F	Dead	Yes	
1254 Galketcher, Lee	NCher	15	M	4678	No	
1255 Galketcher, Hetty	NCher	12	F	3729	No	
1256 Galketcher, Mary	NCher	9	F	Dead	No	
1257 Galketcher, Lou	NCher	7	F	4949	No	
1258 Glass, George	NCher	25	M	5553	Yes	Dead, Farmer
1259 Glass, Nellie	NCher	30	M	Dead	Yes	
1260 Glass, John	NCher	50	M	5524	No	Farmer
1261 Glass, Polly	NCher	30	F	8056	No	
1262 Glass, Sabra	NCher	2	F	Dead	No	
1263 Goard, Tim R	NCher	25	M	Dead	Yes	Farmer
1264 Goard, Julia R	AWhite	19	F	D1499	Yes	Left County, Married out
1265 Goard, Cora R	NCher	7m	F	Dead	No	
1266 Goodwin, Mary	NCher	45	F	Dead	No	Farmer
1267 Goodwin, Lucy	NCher	17	F	Dead	No	
1268 Goodwin, John	NCher	2	M	4237	No	
1269 Gray, Valentine	AWhite	47	M	2421	Yes	Stockman, half interest in steam mill and half in interest Dry goods store
1270 Gray, Mary A	NCher	54	F	2421	Yes	
1271 Gray, Fannie	NCher	19	F	2760	No	
1272 Gray, Anna	NCher	17	F	Dead	No	
1273 Gunter, Henry	NCher	17	M	5104	No	
1274 Glory, Mose	NCher	49	M	Dead	Yes	Farmer
1275 Glory, Mose Jr	NCher	16	M	Dead	Yes	
1276 Goback, Hettie	NCher	30	F	D1500	No	Right name Arsene
1277 Goback, Mary	NCher	1	F	D1501	No	Right name Arsene
1278 Goard, John R	NCher	29	M	Dead	Yes	Farmer
1279 Goard, Arteymesey r	NCher	23	F	4864	Yes	
1280 Goard, Eliza R	NCher	6	F	4867	No	

Name	Race	Age	Sex	Census	Md	Remarks
1281 Goard, Jesse R	NCher	2	M	Dead	No	
1282 Goard, William R	NCher	22	M	D1502	No	Left County years ago
1283 Gott, A M	AWhite	35	M	4515	Yes	Farmer
1284 Gott, Sue T	NCher	33	F	4515	Yes	
1285 Gage, John	NCher	32	M	Dead	Yes	Farmer
1286 Gage, Sarah F	AWhite	33	F	9629	Yes	
1287 Gibbs, James	A Del	18	M	Del143	No	
1288 Goard, Alex R	NCher	18	M	4895	No	
1289 Groundhog,	NCher	32	M	Dead	Yes	Farmer
1290 Groundhog, Sallie	NCher	25	F	2401	Yes	
1291 Goodtravler, H W	A Del	24	M	Dead	No	
1292 Gilstrap, Robert	NCher	20	M	Dead	No	
1293 Gunter, Russel	NCher	14	M	Dead	No	
1294 Gunter, Nanie	NCher	13	F	3537	No	
1295 Gunter, John	NCher	11	M	5267	No	
1296 Gunter, Blanch	NCher	8	F	Dead	No	
1297 Glory, Nancy				Dead		
1298 Gray, Laura A	NCher	34	F	4107	No	
1299 Gray, W A	NCher	10	M	4117	No	
1300 Gray, Mary B	NCher	8	F	Dead	No	
1301 Gray, L B	NCher	5	M	4108	No	
1302 Galliger, Malinda	NCher	18	F	Dead	No	
1303 Galliger, Andy				3313	No	
1304 Galliger, Nancy	NCher	inf't	F	D1503	No	lives in Oklahoma
1305 Goodtravler, Celia Ann				Dead		
1306 Grimmet, Ellis				F1125		
1307 Grimmet, Willie				F1126		
1308 Gourd, Thomas R	NCher	22	M	Dead		
1309 Gourd, Lou R	NCher	21	F	5350		
1310 Grimmit, Easter				F925		
1311 Grimmit, Nathan				Dead		
1312 Grimmit, Silvy				F925		
1313 Holderman, Mary	NCher	38	F	4076	Yes	Farmer
1314 Holderman, Bittie	NCher	9	F	Dead	No	
1315 Holderman, Curtus	NCher	7	M	7413	No	
1316 Holderman, Henry	NCher	5	M	7414	No	
1317 Holderman, Nellie	NCher	2	F	4159	No	
1318 Humphrey, John	AWhite	30	M	5207	Yes	Farmer
1319 Humphrey, Dora	NCher	20	F	Dead	Yes	
1320 Humphrey, Ellen	NCher	4	F	5240	No	
1321 Harrison, H M	AWhite	53	M	Dead	Yes	Carpenter
1322 Harrison, Susie	NCher	52	F	Dead	Yes	

Name	Race	Age	Sex	Census	Md	Remarks
1323 Helterbrand, John	NCher	35	M	5536	Yes	Farmer
1324 Helterbrand, Ellen	NCher	28	F	R858	Yes	
1325 Helterbrand, Jo	NCher	10	M	R859	No	Chelsea, IT Does not apply
1326 Helterbrand, James	NCher	11	M	R860	No	PO Bartlesville
1327 Helterbrand, David	NCher	8	M	R861	No	PO Bartlesville
1328 Helterbrand, Lizzie	NCher	5	F	R862	No	PO Bartlesville
1329 Helterbrand, Dick	NCher	2	M	R863	No	PO Bartlesville
1330 Hurst, John R	NCher	27	M	4773	Yes	
1331 Hurst, Sarah	NCher	25	F	4773	Yes	She should be listed as White (BLB)
1332 Hurst,				D3169	No	
1333 Hurst, S R	NCher	22	M	4184	No	
1334 Howey, Thomas	AWhite	52	M	3666	Yes	
1335 Howey, Mary	NCher	46	F	3666	Yes	
1336 Housebug, Blue	NCher	18	M	Dead	No	Rambler
1337 Hogan, Sarah A	NCher	10	F	D1510	No	
1338 Harvey, John	AShaw	32	M	3296	Yes	Fisherman
1339 Harvey, Louisa	AShaw	20	F	Dead	Yes	
1340 Harvey, Stealer	AShaw	2	M	9434	No	Is Stella Ann Grindstone lives at Quapaw Agency Siever, MO
1341 Harvey, Rachel	AShaw	1	F	Dead	No	
1342 Helterbrand, Malinda	NCher	46	F	Dead	No	Milkmaid
1343 Helterbrand, John O	NCher	18	M	D1511	No	
1344 Helterbrand, Nancy	NCher	13	F	D1512	No	
1345 Horsefly, James	NCher	40	M	3055	Yes	Farmer
1346 Horsefly, Aggie	NCher	30	F	3055	Yes	
1347 Henchoy, Jamie	NCher	19	F	5508	Yes	
1348 Henchoy, Ella	NCher	1	F	5508	No	
1349 Helterbrand, Wm	NCher	20	M	10257	No	
1350 Halfmoon, James	A Del	30	M	Dead	No	Farmer
1351 Halfmoon, Widow J	A Del	50	F	Dead	No	
1352 Halfmoon, Jo	A Del	50	M	Dead	Yes	Farmer
1353 Halfmoon, Mrs Jo	A Del	43	F	Del119	No	Died since enrolling
1354 Halfmoon, Rosy	A Del	15	F	Dead	No	
1355 Halfmoon, Stephen	A Del	18	M	Dead	No	
1356 Halfmoon, Tom	A Del	10	M	Dead	No	
1357 Hill, Mary	A Del	21	F	Dead	No	Seamstress
1358 Halfmoon, Eliza	A Del	20	F	Del211	No	
1359 Halfmoon, Edgar	A Del	28	M	Del202	Yes	Fiddler
1360 Halfmoon, Susan	A Del	30	F	Del169	Yes	
1361 Halfmoon, Willie	A Del	11	M	Del110	No	
1362 Halfmoon, Florence	A Del	5	F	Dead	No	
1363 Hill, John	A Del	21	M	Dead	No	Tramp

Name	Race	Age	Sex	Census	Md	Remarks
1364 Hallock, John	A Del	35	M	Del107	Yes	
1365 Hallock, Sallie	A Del	34	F	Dead	Yes	
1366 Hammer, George	A Col	40	M	6677	Yes	Farmer (He was 1/2 Cherokee and Half Black BLB)
1367 Hammer, Emma G	A Col	30	F	F1019	Yes	
1368 Hammer, Lizzie	A Col	19	F	F977	No	
1369 Hammer, Rachiel	A Col	15	F	F1034	No	
1370 Hammer, Mary	A Col	10	F	F1104	No	
1371 Hammer, Anna	A Col	8	F	F1029	No	
1372 Hammer, Isaac	A Col	21	M	Dead	No	
1373 Hammer, Silas	A Col	14	M	F1027	No	
1374 Hammer, Parley	A Col	2	F	F1028	No	
1375 Hammer, Arther	A Col	1	M	F1147	No	
1376 Halfmoon, Wm	A Del	41	M	Dead	Yes	Traveler
1377 Halfmoon, Matilda	A Del	30	F	Del127	Yes	
1378 Harrison, Lucy	A Del	42	F	Dead	No	
1379 Harrison, Henry	A Del	16	M	Dead	No	
1380 Harrison, John	A Del	10	M	Dead	No	
1381 Harlin, Josie	A Del	7	F	DLD31	No	Unknown to Delawares
1382 Harlin, Millie	A Del	5	F	DLD32	No	Unknown to Delawares
1383 House, D M	NCher	21	M	5092	No	Carpenter
1384 Hohensteen, John	AWhite	43	M	Dead	Yes	Farmer
1385 Hohensteen, Sallie	NCher	24	F	Dead	No	
1386 Hohensteen, Willie	NCher	1	M	Dead	No	
1387 Hohensteen, Samuel	NCher	1w	M	5478	No	
1388 Harrey, William	AShaw	25	M	3244	No	
1389 Herren, David	AShaw	21	M	Dead	No	
1390 Harnage, Ezekiel	NCher	38	M	5522	No	Farmer
1391 Heffington, S C	NCher	40	F	Dead	No	Teacher
1392 Heffington, I B	NCher	10	F	5647	No	
1393 Henry, Susie	NCher	20	F	4678	No	
1394 Henry, Lucy	NCher	2	F	Dead	No	
1395 Henry, Benj H	NCher	2m	M	Dead	No	
1396 Hayden, Clem	AWhite	34	M	2425	Yes	Mechanic
1397 Hayden, Carrie	NCher	30	F	2425	Yes	
1398 Hayden, Charles W	NCher	5	M	Dead	No	
1399 Hayden, Minnie	NCher	1	F	2419	No	
1400 Heary, Thomas	NCher	27	M	Dead	Yes	Farmer
1401 Heary, Charlotte	NCher	23	F	Dead	Yes	
1402 Hunt, Joe	AWhite	46	M	2982	Yes	Farmer
1403 Hunt, Ruth	NCher	33	F	2982	Yes	
1404 Hunt, Anna	NCher	6	F	4602	No	

Name	Race	Age	Sex	Census	Md	Remarks
1405 Hunt, Charles	NCher	4	M	3614	No	
1406 Hunt, Jane	NCher	2	F	3413	No	
1407 Hammer, Mose	NCher	37	M	Dead	Yes	Farmer
1408 Hammer, Betsy	NCher	30	F	Dead	Yes	
1409 Hammer, Lizzie	NCher	25	F	5239	No	
1410 Hanes, Charles	AWhite	32	M	4815	Yes	Farmer
1411 Hanes, D A	NCher	19	F	4815	Yes	
1412 Hanes, H C	NCher	1	M	4815	No	
1413 Hogan, John	AWhite	32	M	2744	Yes	Farmer
1414 Hogan, Margaret	NCher	30	F	2744	Yes	
1415 Hogan, Viella	NCher	8	F	2620	No	
1416 Hogan, Zallie	NCher	4	F	2535	No	
1417 Hogan, Ella	NCher	1	F	Dead	No	
1418 Haney, Robert	AShaw	26	M	3237	Yes	Farmer
1419 Haney, Anna	AShaw	36	F	9571	Yes	
1420 Haney, Runabout	AShaw	3	M	Dead	No	
1421 Haney, Saproney	AShaw	1m	F	3465	No	
1422 Haney, Malinda	AShaw	26	F	3243	No	
1423 Hubbard, Mose	NCher	24	M	6089	No	
1424 Hollars, Marlin	AWhite	40	M	D1513	Yes	Shoemanker, abandoned his wife
1425 Hollars, Sarah	NCher	23	F	2239	No	
1426 Hollars, John	NCher	4m	M	6084	No	On Dawes as John Haller (BLB)
1427 Hicks, John J	NCher	31	M	Dead	No	Clerk in Store
1428 Hawk, Adam	NCher	25	M	8890	Yes	Farmer
1429 Hawk, Susie	NCher	22	F	Dead	Yes	
1430 Hawk, John	NCher	5	M	9344	No	
1431 Hawk, Alsey	NCher	2	F	9341	No	
1432 Hawk, Katie	NCher	1m	F	Dead	No	
1433 Henson, John	NCher	23	M	Dead	No	Farmer
1434 Henson, Pigeon	NCher	3	M	3803	No	
1435 Henry, Eliza	NCher	24	F	Dead	No	
1436 Henry, Polly	NCher	40	F	4879	No	
1437 Henry, Levi	NCher	22	M	4879	No	
1438 Holt, John	NCher	20	M	Dead	No	
1439 Holt, W L	NCher	22	M	Dead	No	
1440 Hawk, Lacy	NCher	50	M	Dead	Yes	Farmer
1441 Hawk, Nancy	NCher	30	F	Dead	Yes	
1442 Hawk, Anna	NCher	60	F	Dead	No	Farmer
1443 Hammer, Ned	NCher	25	M	Dead	No	Hopper
1444 Hightman, Henry	AWhite	31	M	Dead	Yes	Farmer
1445 Hightman, Mary Jane	NCher	31	F	Dead	Yes	
1446 Hightman, F B	NCher	11	F	2972	No	

Name	Race	Age	Sex	Census	Md	Remarks
1447 Hightman, Mollie	NCher	6	F	4807	No	
1448 Hightman, Beatrice	NCher	3	F	4656	No	
1449 Hightman, Maud	NCher	1	F	4662	No	
1450 Harlin, Eli	NCher	18	M	Dead	No	Fisherman
1451 Harlon, E B	NCher	24	F	5305	Yes	Surname Harlow (BLB)
1452 Harlon, Laura	NCher	4	F	5308	No	Surname Harlow (BLB)
1453 Harlon, L M	NCher	2	F	Dead	No	Surname Harlow (BLB)
1454 Harlon, Bessie B	NCher	3w	F	5306	No	Surname Harlow (BLB)
1455 Harlon, Mary A	NCher	30	F	Dead	Yes	
1456 Hendricks, Charley	NCher	36	M	Dead	Yes	Farmer
1457 Hendricks, Aggy	NCher	30	F	Dead	Yes	
1458 Hendricks, Williams	NCher	7	M	Dead	No	
1459 Hendricks, Mary	NCher	2	F	4932	No	
1460 Hendricks, Marg	NCher	20	F	Dead	No	
1461 Hendricks, Juliet	NCher	4ds	F	D1514	No	
1462 Hefferfinger, Pace	AWhite	32	M	5154	No	Farmer
1463 Hefferfinger, Rosa	NCher	3	F	5153	No	
1464 Hefferfinger, Lizzie	NCher	20	F	5154	No	
1465 Hefferfinger, Bell	NCher	3	F	5303	No	
1466 Henderson, James	NCher	60	M	Dead	No	Seller?
1467 Halfbreed, Johnson	NCher	27	M	Dead	Yes	Farmer
1468 Halfbreed, Sallie	NCher	22	F	Dead	Yes	
1469 Halfbreed, Lucy	NCher	9	F	Dead	No	
1470 Halfbreed, Sallie Jr	NCher	5	F	Dead	No	
1471 Halfbreed, Jessie	NCher	3	M	Dead	No	
1472 Halfbreed, Malinda	NCher	1	F	Dead	No	
1473 Hatchet, Tom	NCher	48	M	Dead	Yes	Farmer
1474 Hatchet, Nancy	NCher	45	F	Dead	Yes	
1475 Hendrix, Robt	NCher	33	M	Dead	Yes	Farmer
1476 Hendrix, Ruth	NCher	31	F	Dead	Yes	
1477 Hendrix, Mack	NCher	5	M	Dead	No	
1478 Hendrix, S A	NCher	1	F	Dead	No	
1479 Hensley, Cherokee E	NCher	13	F	Dead	No	
1480 Hensley, Jennie J	NCher	8	F	1815	No	
1481 Henry, Josiah	NCher	30	M	2583	Yes	
1482 Henry, Alice	NCher	28	F	2583	Yes	
1483 Henry, Jesse	NCher	5	M	2592	No	
1484 Henry, Jo	NCher	3	M	Dead	No	
1485 Henry, William	NCher	3m	M	Dead	No	
1486 Henry, Peter	NCher	32	M	Dead	Yes	Clodhopper
1487 Henry, Kate	NCher	19	F	Dead	Yes	
1488 Henry, Ben	NCher	26	M	9402	No	

Name	Race	Age	Sex	Census	Md	Remarks
1489 Hicks, John R	NCher	46	M	Dead	Yes	Rootdigger
1490 Hicks, Mary E	AWhite	38	F	Dead	Yes	
1491 Hicks, Henry C	NCher	8	M	Dead	No	
1492 Hicks, Nancy	NCher	7	F	4724	No	
1493 Hicks, Cora	NCher	5	F	6766	No	
1494 Hilderbrand, Lucy	NCher	18	F	4498	No	
1495 Halfmoon, Phelin	A Del	20	M	Del100	No	
1496 Halfmoon, Silas	A Del	16	M	Dead	No	
1497 Harlan, Nannie	NCher	13	F	Dead	No	
1498 Harlin, Harriet,	NCher	11	F	Dead	No	
1499 Hill, Ben	A Del	5	M	Del170	No	
1500 Humphrey, Crissie	NCher	53	F	Dead		
1501 Humphrey, David		23		4188		
1502 Humphrey, Sarah				4188		
1503 Hodum, Rhoda				Dead		
1504 Hodum, Cora				Dead		
1505 Hendricks, Nellie				Dead		
1506 Henry, John	NCher	8	M	2420		
1507 Hogan, Georgiana	NCher	25	F	4496		
1508 Hughs, Andy				Dead		
1509 Hughs, Charlie				Dead		Lives in Tah Dist
1510 Henry, Tickeater	NCher	5	M	4833		On Dawes as George Coffee (BLB)
1511 Ironside, C C	AShaw	40	M	3927	Yes	Mechanic
1512 Ironside, Louisa	AWhite	35	F	3927	Yes	
1513 Ironside, Margaret	AShaw	65	F	Dead	No	
1514 Ivey, Guss	NCher	25	M	5958	Yes	Printer
1515 Ivey, Sarah	AWhite	22	F	Dead	Yes	
1516 Ivey, Lillian	NCher	4	F	Dead	No	
1517 Ivey, Birtha	NCher	2	F	5958	No	
1518 Jackson, Nancy	NCher	26	F	4650	No	Farmer
1519 Jackson, E B	NCher	6	M	7218	No	
1520 Jackson, J L	NCher	4	F	4964	No	
1521 Jackson, B B	NCher	2	M	4796	No	
1522 Journeycake, Jamima	A Del	46	F	Dead	No	
1523 Journeycake, Charles	A Del	62	M	Dead	Yes	Minister
1524 Journeycake, Jane	A Del	57	F	Dead	Yes	
1525 Journeycake, Anna	A Del	25	F	Del301	No	
1526 Journeycake, Cora	A Del	20	F	Dead	No	
1527 Journeycake, I N	A Del	21	M	Del252	No	Student
1528 Journeycake, Joseph	A Del	26	M	Dead	Yes	Farmer
1529 Journeycake, Mary	AWhite	20	F	4475	Yes	

Name	Race	Age	Sex	Census	Md	Remarks
1530 Jackson, Mack	NCher	31	M	Dead	No	
1531 John, James	A Del	35	M	Dead	Yes	
1532 John, Nulielononaquah	A Del	20	F	DLD33	Yes	
1533 Johnson, A F	AWhite	30	M	4616	Yes	Farmer
1534 Johnson, Louisa	NCher	20	F	Dead	Yes	
1535 John, Mrs.	AWhite	60	F	Dead	No	Farmer
1536 John, Emaline	NCher	20	F	D1515	No	Is a Delaware
1537 Journeycake, Alex	A Del	28	M	Dead	No	Farmer
1538 Jones, Lucy	NCher	16	F	4540	No	
1539 Jackson, Colonel	A Del	56	M	Del106	Yes	Farmer
1540 Jackson, Mrs. Col	A Del	45	F	Dead	Yes	
1541 Jackson, Lizzie	A Del	13	F	Dead	No	
1542 Jackson, John	A Del	10	M	Del177	No	
1543 Jack, Sampson	A Del	26	M	Dead	Yes	Farmer
1544 Jack, Anna L	A Del	26	F	Dead	Yes	
1545 Johnson, Sarah	NCher	25	F	Dead	Yes	
1546 Johnson, Moody	NCher	11	F	5231	No	
1547 Johnson, Doty	NCher	6	F	4919	No	
1548 Johnson, William	NCher	3	M	9654	No	
1549 Jackson, James	AWhite	37	M	2751	Yes	Farmer
1550 Jackson, Susie	NCher	30	F	Dead	Yes	
1551 Jackson, Betty	NCher	12	F	2752	No	
1552 Jackson, Lydia	NCher	11	F	2456	No	
1553 Jackson, John	NCher	7	M	2867	No	
1554 Jackson, Martha	NCher	5	F	2830	No	
1555 Jane	NCher	23	F	D1516	No	
1556 Jane, Walooky	NCher	2m	M	D1517	No	
1557 Jackson, Wm	AWhite	45	M	1848	Yes	Farmer
1558 Jackson, Martha	NCher	37	F	1848	Yes	
1559 Jackson, Mattie	NCher	16	M	1623	No	On census card as Walter H Jackson (BLB)
1560 Jackson, Anderson	NCher	14	M	6546	No	
1561 Jackson, Minnie	NCher	9	F	7296	No	
1562 Journeycake, Dolly	A Del	5	F	Del328	No	
1563 Jinkine, Henry	NCher	25	M	*474	No	
1564 Jinkine, J J	NCher	20	M	3283	No	
1565 Johnson, Mollie	NCher	9	F	Dead	No	
1566 Johnson, Robert	NCher	8	M	Dead	No	
1567 Journeycake, Malisse	A Del	12	F	Dead	No	
1568 Johnson, Oliver	A Col	6	M	Dead		
1569 Johnson, John	A Col	3	M	Dead		
1570 Journeycake, Benj S				Dead		

Name	Race	Age	Sex	Census	Md	Remarks
1571 Journeycake, Jinnie				Del98		
1572 Journeycake, Sarah				Dead		
1573 Jourdan, T J	NCher		M	2946		
1574 Jourdan, D P	NCher	23	F	2946		
1575 Jourdan, M Carrie	NCher	4	F	3826		
1576 Ketchum, Tom	A Del	20	M	Dead	Yes	Farmer
1577 Ketchum, Watson	A Del	18	M	Del193	Yes	
1578 Kinkade,	A Del	30	M	R261	No	Enrollment Refuse
1579 Kinkade, Ada	AWhite	18	F	Dead	Yes	
1580 Ketchum, W W	A Del	28	M	Del299	Yes	
1581 Ketchum, Sarah	A Del	30	F	Dead	Yes	
1582 Kiesheeakienow,	A Del	40	F	Del181	No	
1583 Kiesheeakienow, Nene	A Del	18	F	Dead	No	
1584 Kiesheeakienow, Wilson	A Del	2	M	Dead	No	
1585 Knaggs, A H	AWhite	41	M	4617	Yes	Farmer
1586 Knaggs, Sarah	NCher	44	F	Dead	Yes	
1587 Kinney, John	NCher	43	M	D579	Yes	Farmer
1588 Kinney, Eliza	NCher	40	F	Dead	Yes	
1589 Keys, John	A Col	19	M	F959	Yes	
1590 Kephart, J N	NCher	42	M	4794	Yes	___ Keeper
1591 Kephart, R E	NCher	49	M	4794	Yes	
1592 Ketcher,	NCher	26	M	Dead	No	
1593 Keekey,	NCher	25	M	Dead	No	Nothing
1594 Keekey, Sharptail	NCher	30	M	Dead	No	Nothing
1595 Keys, James	NCher	35	M	2692	Yes	Att at Law
1596 Keys, N J	NCher	29	M	2692	Yes	
1597 Keys, Dennis	NCher	2	M	7041	No	
1598 Keys, W E	NCher	3m	M	Dead	No	
1599 Keys, Osie	NCher	19	M	6172	No	
1600 Kilsey, Leaney	NCher	16	F	4439	No	On Dawes as Eleanor Hawkins (BLB)
1601 Keys, J W	NCher	44	M	Dead	Yes	Farmer
1602 Keys, J H	NCher	16	M	4255	No	
1603 Kirk, Silas	A Col	22	M	F756	No	
1604 Kiser, Henry	AShaw	30	M	Dead	Yes	Horse Racer
1605 Kiser, July	AShaw	20	F	3683	Yes	
1606 Kiser, Thomas	AShaw	16	M	Dead	No	
1607 Kiser, Nancy	AShaw	11	F	Dead	No	
1608 Keys, Monroe	NCher	54	M	Dead	Yes	Farmer
1609 Keys, Lucy	NCher	54	F	3096	Yes	
1610 Keys, Lydia	NCher	22	F	3938	No	
1611 Keys, Fannie	NCher	17	F	3993	No	

Cooweescoowee District

Name	Race	Age	Sex	Census	Md	Remarks
1612 Keys, Sallie	NCher	14	F	3744	No	
1613 Keys, Lizzie	NCher	12	F	3097	No	
1614 Keys, Munroe Jr.	NCher	10	M	6565	No	
1615 Keys, Lucy Jr.	NCher	8	F	3911	No	
1616 Keeler, G V	AWhite	30	M	4271	Yes	Farmer
1617 Keeler, Susie	NCher	24	F	Dead	Yes	
1618 Keeler, Charles	NCher	6	M	4354	No	
1619 Keeler, Willard	NCher	4	M	4315	No	
1620 Keeler, Frank	NCher	2	M	4245	No	
1621 Keeler, Albin	NCher	3m	M	4271	No	
1622 Ketcum, L P	A Del	42	M	Dead	No	Clerk of ___
1623 Keys, Charles	A Col	18	M	F960	No	
1624 Keener, John	A Del	27	M	Del84	Yes	
1625 Keener, Josa	A Del	22	F	Del79	Yes	
1626 Keys, T A	AWhite	22	M	D650	Yes	Farmer
1627 Keys, Mary	NCher	19	F	Del254	Yes	
1628 Keys, Cora	NCher	7m	F	Del297	No	
1629 King, William			M	Dead		
1630 Kelly, John			M	D1518		
1631 Long, Nancy	A Del	17	F	Del261	No	
1632 Long, Charley	A Del	10	M	Del293	No	Dup Coo 34
1633 Lawther, Leroy	NCher	25	M	4891	Yes	Farmer
1634 Lawther, Mahalie	AWhite	30	F	Dead	Yes	
1635 Lawther, Watson B	NCher	3	M	4894	No	
1636 Lawther, Jesse B	NCher	2	M	4953	No	
1637 Land, Joseph	NCher	22	M	3998	Yes	Nothing
1638 Land, Mary	AWhite	22	F	Dead	Yes	
1639 Land, Deloda	NCher	4	F	3964	No	
1640 Love, Andaline	A Del	27	F	Del338	No	Nothing
1641 Love, Charles H	A Del	7	M	Del352	No	
1642 Lowrey, Austin	NCher	30	M	Dead	No	Nothing
1643 Lowrey, Sallie	NCher	18	F	4481	No	
1644 Lowrey, Susie	NCher	1w	F	Dead	No	
1645 Longtail, Jacob	AShaw	22	M	308	Yes	
1646 Longtail, Sarah	AShaw	32	F	Dead	Yes	
1647 Longtail, Rosy	AShaw	7	F	3168	No	
1648 Longtail, Elizabeth	AShaw	60	F	Dead	No	
1649 Lenard, Hester	A Del	45	F	Dead	No	
1650 Lee, James	A Del	36	M	Dead	Yes	Farmer
1651 Lee, Mary	A Del	40	F	Del132	Yes	
1652 Longbone, Suse	A Del	24	F	Del310	No	
1653 Longbone, Johny	A Del	6	M	Del312	No	

Name	Race	Age	Sex	Census	Md	Remarks
1654 Levi, Charley	A Del	40	M	Del201	No	Farmer
1655 Landrum, Benj. Jr.	NCher	19	M	2662	No	
1656 Lee, Thomas	A Del	30	M	Dead	Yes	
1657 Lee, Lizzie	A Del	22	F	Dead	Yes	
1658 Lee, Daniel D	A Del	2	M	Dead	No	
1659 Lee, Susie L	A Del	4m	F	Dead	No	
1660 Longbone, Betsy	A Del	60	F	Dead	No	
1661 Lenonesho,	A Del	37	M	Dead	Yes	Farmer
1662 Lenonesho, Tahllanquahow	A Del	30	F	Dead	Yes	
1663 Lenonesho, Qualnaniscon	A Del	2	M	Dead	No	
1664 Lowrey, Harriet	A Col	24	F	Dead	No	
1665 Lowrey, Fannie	A Col	6	F	Dead	No	
1666 Lowrey, Austine	A Col	4	F	F1030	No	
1667 Lowrey, George	A Col	3	M	F1111	No	
1668 Love, Soloman	A Del	38	M	Dead	No	Root Digger
1669 Love, Benj. Jr.	A Del	9	M	Del350	No	
1670 Longbone, John	A Del	21	M	Dead	No	Farmer
1671 Leek, Albert	A Del	21	M	Dead	No	Tramp
1672 Longbone, Silas	A Del	8	M	Del134	No	Fiddler
1673 Landrum, Willie	NCher	3	M	3472	No	
1674 Lassley, George W	A Col	35	M	Dead	Yes	Farmer
1675 Lassley, Jane	A Col	28	F	F983	Yes	
1676 Lassley, M	A Col	9	F	F984	No	
1677 Lassley, Louis	A Col	6	M	F211	No	
1678 Lassley, Anna	A Col	1	F	Dead	No	
1679 Lassley, Osker	A Col	1w	M	Dead	No	
1680 Landrum, Susie	A Col	60	F	Dead	No	
1681 Landrum, John	A Col	38	M	F877	Yes	Farmer
1682 Landrum, Mary	A Col	31	F	F877	Yes	
1683 Landrum, Major	A Col		M	F838	No	
1684 Landrum, Martha	A Col	14	F	F962	No	
1685 Landrum, Polly	A Col	13	F	F878	No	
1686 Landrum, Andy	A Col	10	M	Dead	No	
1687 Landrum, Mariah	A Col	6	F	Dead	No	
1688 Landrum, Rhoda	A Col	3	F	Dead	No	
1689 Landrum, Harry	A Col	2	M	F971	No	
1690 Landrum, Nancy	A Col	2m	F	F792	No	
1691 Love, Margaret	A Del	33	F	Del320	No	
1692 Locust, Frank	A Del	19	M	Del274	No	Runabout
1693 Lindsey, Thomas	NCher	40	M	Dead	Yes	
1694 Lindsey, Susie	NCher	35	F	3570	Yes	
1695 Lindsey, William	NCher	8	M	3158	No	

Cooweescoowee District

Name	Race	Age	Sex	Census	Md	Remarks
1696 Lindsey, Ellie	NCher	2	F	Dead	No	
1697 Lacy, Wiles	NCher	19	M	Dead	No	
1698 Lizzie	NCher	100	F	Dead	No	
1699 Lizzie	NCher	40	F	Dead	No	
1700 Lizabeth,	NCher	30	F	Dead	No	
1701 Lizabeth, Wiley	NCher	2	M	Dead	No	
1702 Lipe, C C	NCher	33	M	4903	Yes	Dead
1703 Lipe, Maggie E	NCher	31	F	4903	Yes	
1704 Lipe, Herman V	NCher	4	M	5044	No	
1705 Lipe, John C	NCher	1	M	4574	No	Dead
1706 Love, Simon	A Del	25	M	Del321	No	
1707 Lane, A J	AWhite	30	M	Dead	Yes	Physician
1708 Lane, Lucinda	A Del	20	F	Del323	Yes	
1709 Lane, T L	A Del	1	M	Del322	No	
1710 Lane, Shoto	A Del	1m	F	Del350	Yes	
1711 Lindsey, Wallace	AWhite	29	M	2020	Yes	Wallace Lindsey (BLB)
1712 Lindsey, Leanie	NCher	23	F	2020	No	Lille Lindsey nee Starnes (BLB)
1713 Lindsey, Lillie	NCher	1	F	9515	Yes	On Dawes as Clara Cantrell (BLB)
1714 Lipe, D W	NCher	40	M	4699	No	
1715 Lipe, Mollie E	NCher	35	F	4699	No	
1716 Lipe, John G	NCher	15	M	5083	No	
1717 Lipe, Nannie	NCher	8	F	4813	No	
1718 Lipe, Vic T	NCher	6	F	4666	No	
1719 Lipe, Tola V	NCher	3	F	4810	No	
1720 Lowing, Nance	NCher	60	F	Dead	No	
1721 Lowing, Nellie	NCher	20	F	D1519	No	Dup 672 Coo
1722 Loing, Eli	NCher	9	M	Dead	No	
1723 Looking, Arch	NCher	34	M	5286	Yes	Coon Hunter
1724 Looking, Sophy	NCher	15	F	Dead	Yes	
1725 Lindsey, R W	AWhite	48	M	2590	Yes	Merchant
1726 Lindsey, Mariah	NCher	38	F	2590	Yes	
1727 Lindsey, Anna	NCher	18	F	2673	No	
1728 Lindsey, W D	NCher	13	M	Dead	No	
1729 Lindsey, J R	NCher	11	M	Dead	No	
1730 Lindsey, Hattie	NCher	9	F	2356	No	
1731 Lindsey, L C	NCher	7	F	2213	No	
1732 Lindsey, North	NCher	6	M	5038	No	
1733 Lindsey, Joel B	NCher	6	M	4991	No	
1734 Lindsey, F L V	NCher	2	F	2672	No	
1735 Login, Nancy	AShaw	40	F	Dead	No	
1736 Looney, John	NCher	20	M	3488	Yes	Farmer

Name	Race	Age	Sex	Census	Md	Remarks
1737 Looney, Sallie	NCher	26	F	Dead	Yes	
1738 Looney, Dianna	NCher	9	F		No	Is the wife of Wm Squirrell (no census card number BLB)
1739 Looney, Nellie	NCher	4	F	3213	No	On Dawes as Nellie Boot (BLB)
1740 Locus, James	A Del	15	M	Dead	No	
1741 Locus, John	A Del	26	M	Dead	Yes	Farmer
1742 Locus, Jacob	A Del	9	M	Del358	No	
1743 Locus, Rosie	A Del	11m	F	Del195	No	
1744 Lassley, Joe	NCher	45	M	Dead	Yes	Farmer
1745 Lassley, Nannie	NCher	33	F	4732	Yes	
1746 Lowther, Lune	AWhite	27	M	4731	Yes	
1747 Lowther, Josie	NCher	23	F	4731	Yes	
1748 Lowther, Jane	NCher	49	F	4892	No	
1749 Lovelady, Anna	NCher	51	F	D1520	No	
1750 Leffane, Elisa			F	Dead		
1751 Lassley, Jinnie			F	Dead		
1752 Lucas, Caroline			F	Dead		
1753 Lairy, John			M	Dead		
1754 Lairy, Elisa			F	2686		
1755 Lairy, James			M	2695		
1756 Lairy, Willis			M	2720		
1757 Lairy, Martha			F	2649		
1758 Miller, Jesse	A Del	41	M	Del291	Yes	
1759 Miller, Caroline	A Del	39	F	Dead	Yes	
1760 Miller, Ellis	A Del	14	M	Del231	No	
1761 Miller, Benj	A Del	13	M	Del342	No	
1762 Musgrove, Mary	A Col	50	F	F987	No	
1763 Musgrove, Rider	A Col	12	M	F990	No	
1764 Madden, Malinda	A Col	34	F	F732	Yes	Farmer
1765 Madden, Sarah	A Col	11	F	F843	No	
1766 Madden, John	A Col	9	M	F924	No	
1767 Madden, Willie	A Col	3	M	F926	No	
1768 Mane, Phrona	NCher	19	F	Dead	No	
1769 Mane, Ettney	NCher	1	F	Dead	No	
1770 Miller, Lucinda	NCher	24	F	4716	No	
1771 Moris, Albert	NCher	32	M	4552	Yes	Farmer (surname Morris BLB)
1772 Moris, Lucy	NCher	33	F	Dead	Yes	
1773 Moris, Johney	NCher	13	M	4417	No	
1774 Moris, Sarah	NCher	11	F	3935	No	
1775 Moris, Jorden	NCher	8	M	4402	No	
1776 Moris, Jermima	NCher	3	F	Dead	No	
1777 Martin, David	AWhite	40	M	Dead	Yes	Farmer

Name	Race	Age	Sex	Census	Md	Remarks
1778 Martin, Susan Q	NCher	23	F	Dead	Yes	
1779 Martin, Jennie	NCher	6	F	4552	No	
1780 Martin, Lizzie	NCher	3	F	4176	No	
1781 Martin, Jack	AWhite	28	M	Dead	Yes	Farmer
1782 Martin, Polly	NCher	17	F	4585	Yes	
1783 Martin, James	AWhite	47	M	4468	Yes	Farmer
1784 Martin, Amanda	NCher	35	F	4468	Yes	
1785 Martin, Barbra	A Del	15	F	Dead	No	
1786 Martin, Luella	A Del	10	F	3081	No	
1787 Martin, G W	NCher	7	M	4376	No	
1788 Martin, Susan	NCher	3	F	4485	No	
1789 Martin, Bill	AWhite	49	M	4391	Yes	Farmer
1790 Martin, Sarah	NCher	27	F	4391	Yes	
1791 Martin, George	NCher	5	M	4384	No	
1792 Martin, Joel	NCher	4	M	4391	No	
1793 Martin, James Jr.	NCher	18m	M	4395	No	
1794 Mule, Big	A Del	30	M	Dead	Yes	
1795 Mule, Mrs. Big	A Del	?	F	Dead	Yes	
1796 Mule, Big Jim	A Del	?	M	Del245	No	
1797 Meak, Abe	AWhite	28	M	D 456	Yes	No. should be 10985 (BLB)
1798 Meak, Barilla	NCher	25	F	Dead	Yes	
1799 Meak, James	NCher	5	M	Dead	No	
1800 Meak, Laura	NCher	2	F	4097	No	
1801 Meak, Anna D	NCher	1	F	3322	No	
1802 Mays, Jesse B	NCher	34	M	Dead	Yes	Farmer
1803 Mays, Cherokee	NCher	30	F	2755	Yes	
1804 Mays, Patsy	NCher	5	F	2755	No	
1805 Mays, Joel B	NCher	46	M	Dead	Yes	Farmer
1806 Mays, Mary	NCher	40	F	2703	Yes	
1807 Mays, Thompson	NCher	7	M	Dead	No	
1808 McNair, John	NCher	40	M	Dead	No	Carpenter
1809 McNair, Mary	NCher	8	F	Dead	No	
1810 McNair, Kinney	NCher	24	M	2659	Yes	Farmer
1811 McNair, Rachel	NCher	23	F	Dead	Yes	
1812 McNair, Oscer	NCher	2	M	2659	No	
1813 McNair, T B	NCher	24	M	Dead	Yes	Farmer
1814 McNair, Nellie	NCher	20	F	Dead	Yes	
1815 Mays, Sam	NCher	35	M	2704	Yes	
1816 Mays, Martha	NCher	23	F	2704	Yes	
1817 Mays, W M	NCher	6	M	2604	No	
1818 Mays, Jo F	NCher	3	M	2712	No	
1819 Mays, Carrie	NCher	1	F	2404	No	

Name	Race	Age	Sex	Census	Md	Remarks
1820 McLain, Jane	AShaw	37	F	Dead	No	
1821 McLain, L J	AShaw	7	F	Dead	No	
1822 Mays, W H	NCher	40	M	2624	Yes	
1823 Mays, Mat	NCher	32	F	Dead	Yes	
1824 Mays, George	NCher	15	M	Dead	No	
1825 Mays, Rachel	NCher	12	F	4931	No	
1826 Mays, Charlie	NCher	5	M	6276	No	
1827 Mays, Mary	NCher	2	F	2617	No	
1828 Mays, Wiley B	NCher	27	M	2734	Yes	Farmer
1829 Mays, Maggie	AWhite	21	F	Dead	Yes	
1830 Mays, Susie	NCher	5	F	2716	No	
1831 Mays, Lola	NCher	5m	F	6757	No	
1832 Melton, David	NCher	23	M	2740	Yes	Farmer
1833 Melton, Francis	AWhite	2	F	Dead	Yes	
1834 Muncell, Bell	NCher	8	F	D1521	No	Suppose to be Colored
1835 Mayes, George W Jr.	NCher	31	M	2611	Yes	Farmer
1836 Mayes, Susie	NCher	36	F	2611	Yes	
1837 Mayes, Teppy	NCher	7	M	5708	No	
1838 Mayes, Carrie	NCher	3	F	2621	No	
1839 Mayes, Pixie	NCher	3	M	2644	No	
1840 Mayes, Sisie Jr.	NCher	1w	F	Dead	No	
1841 McCrairy, N B	NCher	40	M	Dead	Yes	Farmer
1842 McCrairy, Joannah	AWhite	37	F	3165	Yes	
1843 McCrairy, Frank	NCher	9	M	Dead	No	
1844 McCrairy, James	NCher	8	M	3082	No	
1845 McCrairy, William	NCher	5	M	3621	No	
1846 McCrairy, Amanda	NCher	3	F	Dead	No	
1847 McCrairy, Alizra	NCher	7m	F	3165	No	
1848 Martin, John R	NCher	24	M	Dead	No	Farmer
1849 Martin, Hernando A	NCher	18	M	Dead	No	
1850 Martin, Victoria R	NCher	15	F	4367	No	
1851 Mills, Lloyd	AWhite	50	M	Dead	No	Farmer
1852 Mills, William	NCher	23	M	5395	No	
1853 Mills, Marion	NCher	21	M	Dead	No	
1854 Mills, Lee	NCher	16	M	7108	No	
1855 Martin, Jos L	NCher	60	M	Dead	Yes	
1856 Martin, Jennie	NCher	31	F	4372	Yes	
1857 Martin, Jesse B	NCher	6	M	4346	No	
1858 Martin, Granvil A	NCher	4	M	2612	No	
1859 Martin, Willie A	NCher	1	M	4373	No	
1860 Mghealen, James	AWhite	38	M	4503	Yes	Farmer (Surname Mehlin BLB)
1861 Mghealen, Elizabeth	NCher	26	F	4503	Yes	

Name	Race	Age	Sex	Census	Md	Remarks
1862 Mghealen, Charlie	NCher	5	M	5521	No	
1863 Machine, Charlie	A Del	43	M	Dead	Yes	Farmer
1864 Machine, Mrs C	A Del	42	F	Dead	Yes	
1865 Miller, Nancy	A Del	40	F	Dead	No	Farmer
1866 Miller, Silas	A Del	22	M	Del164	No	
1867 Miller, John	A Del	17	M	Dead	No	
1868 Miller, Andrew	A Del	39	M	Dead	Yes	
1869 Miller, Mary	A Del	35	F	Del135	Yes	
1870 Miller, Stephen	A Del	10	M	Del272	No	
1871 Miller, Lucinda	A Del	14	F	Del29	No	
1872 Miller, Caroline	A Del	4	F	Dead	No	
1873 Miller, Jacob	A Del	19	M	Dead	No	
1874 Miller, Jacob	A Del	2	M	Del135	No	
1875 Moonshine,	A Del	90	F	Dead	No	
1876 Maun, Frank	A Del	15	M	Dead	No	Farmer
1877 Maun, John	A Del	10	M	Dead	No	
1878 Maun, Patatquenow	A Del	4	M	Dead	No	
1879 Mack, Ellis	A Col	28	M	F252	Yes	Farmer
1880 Mack, Pigg	A Col	23	F	FD26	Yes	
1881 Mack, Kate	A Col	1	F	Dead	No	
1882 Musgrove, George W Jr.	A Col	45	M	F1024	Yes	Farmer
1883 Musgrove, Becky	A Col	40	F	F1024	Yes	
1884 Musgrove, William	A Col	20	M	F1064	No	
1885 Musgrove, Becky Ann	A Col	6	F	F1077	No	
1886 McPherson, Elmira	A Del	50	F	Dead	No	
1887 Melton, Billy	A Col	65	M	Dead	Yes	Farmer
1888 Melton, Sallie	A Col	65	F	Dead	Yes	
1889 Melton, Sam	A Col	6	M	Dead	No	
1890 Marshall, W H	A Del	24	M	Dead	Yes	Farmer
1891 Marshall, Susan	A Del	24	F	Dead	Yes	
1892 Marshall, Ida M	A Del	1	F	Del303	No	
1893 Marshall, Rosie	A Del	28	F	Dead	No	Cook
1894 McCoy, Jack	A Col	51	M	FD1141	No	
1895 McCartle, John	A Del	23	M	Dead	Yes	Shoemaker
1896 McCartle, Lizzie	A Del	20	F	DLD34	Yes	
1897 McCartle, Anna	A Del	2	F	Dead	No	
1898 McQugan, Willie	A Del	30	M	Del96	Yes	Farmer
1899 McQugan, Susie	A Del	24	F	Del96	Yes	
1900 McQugan, Lily	A Del	4	F	Dead	No	
1901 McQugan, Sra A	A Del	2	F	Del166	No	
1902 McQugan, Susie Jr.	A Del	1w	F	Dead	No	
1903 McCoy, Cloa	A Col	100	F	Dead	No	___ at Mission

Name	Race	Age	Sex	Census	Md	Remarks
1904 Morgin, Tom	A Col	86	F	Dead	No	Old Tom Morgan is an intruder his mother a White woman and father Col.
1905 Melton, Henry	A Col	45	M	F904	Yes	Farmer
1906 Melton, Araminta	A Col	44	F	F904	Yes	
1907 Melton, Nancy	A Col	13	F	F908	No	
1908 Melton, Sallie	A Col	25	F	F904	No	
1909 Melton, Stephen	A Col	7	M	F904	No	
1910 Melton, Lizzie	A Col	11m	F	Dead	No	
1911 McCracken, Wm	NCher	41	M	Dead	Yes	Horse Racer
1912 McCracken, Dora	NCher	38	F	2486	Yes	
1913 McCracken, J L	NCher	19	M	Dead	No	
1914 McCracken, R O	NCher	16	M	2190	No	
1915 McCracken, Nannie	NCher	13	F	Dead	No	
1916 Miller, Joe	NCher	52	M	Dead	Yes	Farmer
1917 Miller, Jane	NCher	47	F	Dead	Yes	
1918 Miller, Susie	NCher	8	F	4710	No	
1919 Miller, Willie	NCher	26	M	4700	No	
1920 Mice, Joe	NCher	27	M	Dead	No	
1921 Mills, George	NCher	36	M	5148	Yes	
1922 Mills, Wakie	NCher	30	F	Dead	Yes	
1923 Mills, Rachel	NCher	12	F	Dead	No	
1924 McClellan, Wm	AWhite	24	M	4740	Yes	Stone mason
1925 McClellan, Rachel	NCher	21	F	4740	Yes	
1926 McClellan, Mary	NCher	1	F	4770	No	
1927 McClellan, C M	AWhite	33	M	10152	Yes	Farmer
1928 McClellan, J L	NCher	29	F	5193	Yes	
1929 McClellan, J F	NCher	7	M	5189	No	
1930 McClellan, M E	NCher	5	F	4922	No	
1931 McClellan, S W	NCher	4	M	5190	No	
1932 Morris, Ollivia	NCher	23	F	3507	Yes	Surname Marrs (BLB)
1933 Morris, Ollivia	NCher	6m	F	3505	No	Surname Marrs (BLB)
1934 Munroe, George	NCher	36	M	Dead	No	
1935 Moneyminder,	NCher	40	M	Dead	No	
1936 Moneyminder, Mrs.	NCher	35	F	Dead	No	
1937 Moneyminder, Yawkinney	NCher	10	F	Dead	No	
1938 Moneyminder, Alex	NCher	1	M	7881	No	
1939 Markham, Willis	A Col	65	M	Dead	No	Farmer
1940 Markham, Mariah	A Col	50	F	Dead	No	
1941 Markham, Johnson	A Col	19	M	FD1142	No	
1942 Markham, Jacob	A Col	14	M	Dead	No	
1943 Markham, Osewego	A Col	11	M	F534	No	

Name	Race	Age	Sex	Census	Md	Remarks
1944 Markham, Fred	A Col	44	M	Dead	Yes	Farmer
1945 Markham, July	A Col	50	F	Dead	Yes	
1946 Markham, Wm	A Col	15	M	F623	No	
1947 Markham, Sarah	A Col	10	F	F794	No	
1948 Martin, Wm	NCher	32	M	Dead	Yes	Farmer
1949 Martin, Maragaret	NCher	30	F	Dead	Yes	
1950 Martin, Westley	NCher	9	M	Dead	No	
1951 Martin, Hettie	NCher	4	F	7129	No	
1952 Martin, Tom Wright	NCher	1	M	5128	No	
1953 McLain, J B	AWhite	38	M	4792	Yes	___Maker
1954 McLain, Martha	NCher	23	F	4792	Yes	
1955 McLain, W H	NCher	10	M	5341	No	
1956 McLain, Minnie	NCher	3	F	4809	No	
1957 McLain, Mary	NCher	8	F	4793	No	
1958 McLain, Anna	NCher	5	F	5009	No	
1959 Melton, Latita	NCher	62	F	Dead	No	
1960 McPherson, Ulec	NCher	19	M	6935	No	
1961 Miller, G W	NCher	37	M	Dead	Yes	
1962 Miller, Louisa	AWhite	36	F	3515	Yes	
1963 Miller, J L	NCher	12	F	3514	No	
1964 Miller, Warren	NCher	9	F	3947	No	
1965 Miller, A E	NCher	2	F	Dead	No	
1966 Marmittuse, Widow	A Del	90	F	Del120	No	
1967 Melton, George	A Col	34	M	F1011	No	Farmer
1968 McIntosh, John	NCher	44	M	7824	Yes	
1969 McIntosh, Jane	NCher	34	F	Dead	Yes	
1970 McIntosh, J R	NCher	14	M	5430	No	
1971 McIntosh, Ellen	NCher	11	F	Dead	No	
1972 McIntosh, Susie	NCher	9	F	Dead	No	
1973 McIntosh, Cherokee	NCher	7	F	4288	No	
1974 McIntosh, Nicholas	NCher	3	M	Dead	No	
1975 McIntosh, Ocra	NCher	1	F	Dead	No	
1976 Morris, Gid	NCher	21	M	Dead	No	Farmer
1977 McLeod, M	AWhite	44	M	4906	Yes	Carpenter
1978 McCoy, J L	NCher	67	M	Dead	Yes	Begger
1979 McCoy, Lucy	NCher	42	F	Dead	Yes	
1980 McCoy, Ida	NCher	15	F	27	No	
1981 McCoy, Anna	NCher	13	F	6376	No	
1982 McCoy, Chester	NCher	21	M	3960	No	Log_____
1983 McCoy, W T	NCher	23	M	6417	Yes	
1984 McCoy, Lou	NCher	21	F	6417	Yes	
1985 Murry, Alex	NCher	45	M	4933	Yes	Runabout

Name	Race	Age	Sex	Census	Md	Remarks
1986 Murry, Susie	NCher	30	F	Dead	Yes	
1987 Murry, Jack	NCher	5	M	Dead	No	
1988 Murry, Frank	NCher	3	M	Dead	No	
1989 Murry, Harry	NCher	1w	M	4933	No	
1990 McDaniel, Martin	NCher	22	M	4956	No	
1991 McCoy, Stealer	NCher	25	M	Dead	Yes	__ Man
1992 McCoy, Anna	NCher	27	F	Dead	Yes	
1993 McCoy, Jefferson	NCher	1	M	Dead	No	
1994 Monroe, Adolphus	NCher	30	M	Dead	Yes	Farmer
1995 Monroe, Nancy	NCher	36	F	Dead	Yes	
1996 Musgrove, Wm S	NCher	30	M	Dead	Yes	Stockman
1997 Musgrove, Cynthia	NCher	22	F	R871	No	Bartlesville
1998 Musgrove, L E	NCher	3	F	R872	No	Bartlesville, Now Mrs Fred McDaniel
1999 Musgrove, W N	NCher	2	M	R873	No	Bartlesville
2000 Musgrove, Frank	NCher	33	M	Dead	Yes	Stockman
2001 Musgrove, Clara E	NCher	34	F	5179	Yes	
2002 Musgrove, Lizzie	NCher	12	F	5754	No	
2003 Musgrove, James T	NCher	11	M	Dead	No	
2004 Musgrove, Sallie	NCher	8	F	4912	No	
2005 Musgrove, W A	NCher	6	M	4978	No	
2006 Musgrove, M A	NCher	4	F	4928	No	
2007 Musgrove, Cora	NCher	1	F	4846	No	
2008 McPherson, Jack	NCher	45	M	Dead	Yes	Farmer
2009 McPherson, Sarah	NCher	30	F	5144	Yes	
2010 McCoy, Lettie	NCher	57	F	Dead	No	Farmer
2011 McCoy, James T	NCher	57	M	Dead	Yes	Farmer
2012 McCoy, Malinda	NCher	47	F	Dead	Yes	
2013 McCoy, J S	NCher	13	M	Dead	No	
2014 McCoy, John	NCher	35	M	Dead	Yes	Coon Hunter
2015 McCoy, Jane	NCher	43	F	Dead	Yes	
2016 Markham, Nancy	NCher	67	F	Dead	No	Farmer
2017 Miller, Anna	NCher	65	F	Dead	No	
2018 Mathis, Sallie	A Col	40	F	Dead	No	
2019 Mathis, Angeline	A Col	9	F	F1139	No	
2020 McKinsey, Simon	NCher	35	M	7578	Yes	Farmer
2021 McKinsey, Morning	AWhite	47	F	Dead	Yes	
2022 McKinsey, Jeff	NCher	10	M	Dead	No	
2023 McKinsey, Nancy	NCher	6	F	10377	No	
2024 Marsh, W A	NCher	36	M	Dead	No	Mechanic
2025 Marsh, L C	NCher	7	F	3361	No	
2026 Marsh, Ella P	NCher	5	F	6581	No	

Name	Race	Age	Sex	Census	Md	Remarks
2027 Marsh, F W	NCher	3	M	6584	No	
2028 Millner, James	AWhite	32	M	Dead	Yes	Farmer
2029 Millner, Mary	NCher	24	F	5026	No	
2030 Millner, Wm	NCher	4	M	Dead	No	
2031 Millner, Florence	NCher	3	F	4948	No	
2032 Millner, John	NCher	3m	M	5026	No	
2033 Moonshine, Louisa	AShaw	9	F	Dead	No	
2034 Markham, John	NCher	29	M	Dead	Yes	Runabout
2035 Markham, Martha	NCher	25	F	Dead	Yes	
2036 Markham, John Jr.	NCher	3	M	7086	No	
2037 Markham, D Walker	NCher	6m	M	Dead	No	
2038 Mize, Jose	NCher	3	F	6520	No	
2039 Moore, Susan	NCher	15	F	Dead	No	
2040 McDaniel, Winona	NCher	8	F	4371	No	
2041 McNair, Susie	NCher	14	F	Dead	No	
2042 McNair, Lee	NCher	8	M	Dead	No	
2043 Miller, Tobe	A Col	12	M	F671	No	
2044 Mosier, Hattie	A Col	9	F	F665	No	
2045 Meadows, Leonard	NCher	3	M	2539	No	
2046 McSpaden, Jo C	AWhite	30	M	Dead	Yes	Mechanic
2047 McSpaden, Florence	NCher	21	F	5405	Yes	
2048 McSpaden, Tom E	NCher	6m	M	5405	No	
2049 McDaniel, George	NCher	28	M	4218	Yes	
2050 McDaniel, Sarah	NCher	25	F	Dead	Yes	
2051 McDaniel, Phillipps	NCher	7	M	Dead	No	
2052 McDaniel, Alie	NCher	1	F	Dead	No	
2053 McDaniel, Lizzie	NCher	6	F	Dead	No	
2054 Marshall, Ella P	A Col	8m	F	F1026	No	
2055 Madden, Ira	NCher	7	F	4556	No	
2056 McCay, Mary	NCher	48	F	2681	No	
2057 McCay, Haley	NCher	19	M	4711	No	
2058 McCay, Daniel	NCher	17	M	Dead	No	
2059 McCay, Nannie	NCher	15	F	2682	No	
2060 McGhee, F H		24	M	3992	Yes	Nothing
2061 McGhee, Elizabeth		25	F	Dead	Yes	
2062 McClellan, Ella P			F	2182		On Dawes as Jessie L Wilson (BLB)
2063 McCoy, Arch	NCher	27	M	4855		
2064 Musgrove, Tuck				Dead		
2065 McPherson, B F				Dead		
2066 Morton, Jim				4468		
2067 Mills, James	NCher	8	M	4923		

Name	Race	Age	Sex	Census	Md	Remarks
2068 McLaughlin, Joshua				3086		
2069 McLaughlin, Cela				Dead		
2070 McLaughlin, Babe				3086		
2071 McNair, Columbus	A Col			F698	No	
2072 Nobles, Wm	AWhite	38	M	4100	Yes	Farmer
2073 Nobles, Ellen	NCher	21	F	4090	Yes	
2074 Nobles, Walssee	NCher	6	M	3241	No	
2075 Nave, Moses	A Col	69	M	Dead	Yes	Farmer
2076 Nave, Darkist	A Col	50	F	Dead	Yes	
2077 Nave, Westley	A Col	15	M	Dead	No	
2078 Nave, Louis	A Col	27	M	FD1143	Yes	Dead
2079 Nave, Flora	A Col	20	F	Dead	Yes	
2080 Nichols, Big	A Del	57	M	Dead	Yes	Farmer
2081 Nichols, Nancy	A Del	55	F	Dead	Yes	
2082 Nichols, Sarah	A Del	18	F	Del326	No	
2083 Nichols, Willie	A Del	13	M	Del295	No	
2084 Nelaleetoepakenow,	A Del	50	F	Dead	No	
2085 Nelaleechepahkinow,	A Del	85	F	Dead	No	
2086 Noise, Nancy	A Del	49	F	Dead	No	
2087 Noise, John	A Del	13	M	Dead	No	
2088 Nave, John	A Col	19	M	F1059	Yes	
2089 Nave, Lucinda	A Col	21	F	Dead	Yes	
2090 Nave, Arta	A Col	6	F	F1025	No	
2091 Nave, Ellen	A Col	22	F	F1075	No	
2092 Nave, Cora	A Col	4	F	F998	No	
2093 Nave, Charlotte	A Col	3	F	Dead	No	
2094 Nave, Esaw	A Col	1	M	F1053	No	
2095 Necom, Widow	A Del	70	F	Dead	No	
2096 Nicholson, Sallahlah	NCher	31	M	Dead	Yes	Farmer
2097 Nicholson, Lizzie	NCher	23	F	Dead	Yes	
2098 Nicholson, Richard	NCher	2	M	4843	No	
2099 Newcomb, Syrus	A Del	26	M	Dead	Yes	Farmer
2100 Newcomb, Mary	A Del	26	F	Dead	Yes	
2101 Newcomb, James	A Del	4	M	Dead	No	
2102 Newcomb, Famrose	A Del	1	M	Del305	No	
2103 Newcomb, Jack	A Del	33	M	Dead	Yes	Preacher
2104 Newcomb, Amanda	A Del	30	F	Del268	Yes	
2105 Newcomb, Edward	A Del	7	M	Del354	No	
2106 Newcomb, Aford	A Del	6	M	Del285	No	
2107 Newcomb, Lizzie J	A Del	4	F	Del295	No	
2108 Newcomb, Benj J	A Del	2	M	Dead	No	
2109 Newcomb, Tom	A Del	23	M	Del344	Yes	

Name	Race	Age	Sex	Census	Md	Remarks
2110 Newcomb, Julia	A Del	20	F	Dead	Yes	
2111 Newcomb, Mary R	A Del	26	F	Del220	No	
2112 Nelums, Arch	NCher	38	M	Dead	Yes	
2113 Nelums, Nancy	NCher	28	F	Dead	Yes	
2114 Nelums, Arch Jr.	NCher	5	M	5194	No	
2115 Nelums, Adam	NCher	11m	M	7571	No	
2116 Nelums, John	NCher	26	M	Dead	Yes	Farmer
2117 Nelums, Ibby	NCher	22	F	5195	Yes	
2118 Nelums, John	NCher	2	M	7583	No	
2119 Nelums, Nancy	NCher	30	F	Dead	No	
2120 Nelums, Levi	NCher	5	M	7584	No	
2121 Nakey, Tee	NCher	25	M	Dead	Yes	
2122 Nakey, Eny	NCher	20	F	5196	Yes	
2123 Norwood, A H	AWhite	29	M	4321	Yes	
2124 Norwood, Susie	A Del	22	F	Dead	Yes	
2125 Norwood, William	A Del	2m	M	Dead	No	
2126 Nelums, Felix	NCher	28	M	5554	Yes	Farmer
2127 Nelums, Ida	NCher	30	F	Dead	Yes	
2128 Nelums, Mary J	NCher	5	F	5634	No	
2129 Nelums, Louis	NCher	2	M	Dead	No	
2130 Norman, C A	NCher	51	M	Dead	Yes	Farmer
2131 Norman, M J	NCher	44	F	2214	Yes	
2132 Norman, Jay	NCher	19	M	2009	No	
2133 Norman, M J Jr.	NCher	15	F	6385	No	
2134 Norman, A C	NCher	13	M	2305	No	
2135 Norman, C W	NCher	12	M	2240	No	
2136 Norman, W B	NCher	11	M	Dead	No	
2137 Nellums, Minnie				5418		
2138 Nave, Eli				F1092		
2139 Nave, Jane				F1092		
2140 Nave, Mary				F1102		
2141 Nave, Ellis				F1101		
2142 Nave, Elisa				F1113		
2143 Nave, Anna				F1103		
2144 Nave, George				Dead		
2145 Nave, Aggy				F1062		
2146 Nave, Chilc				F1063		
2147 Oskerson, Sarah	NCher	12	F	4003	No	Sarah Ann Calvert nee Crittenden (BLB)
2148 Oskerson, John	NCher	5	M	10306	No	
2149 Oskerson, Richard	NCher	2	M	3832	No	
2150 Oskerson, Willie	NCher	8	M	3430	No	

Name	Race	Age	Sex	Census	Md	Remarks
2151 Oer, Tom	A Col	30	M	FD1144	No	
2152 Oer, Margaret	A Col	30	F	FD1144	No	
2153 Opossom, John	AShaw	35	M	Dead	No	Hunter
2154 Ootahyahtah,				Dead		
2155 Pedige, Mary	AShaw	30	F	Dead	No	
2156 Patton, W C	AWhite	50	M	5644	Yes	Merchant
2157 Patton, Jane	NCher	39	F	5644	Yes	
2158 Patton, Pauline	NCher	16	F	4709	No	
2159 Patton, Julia T	NCher	12	F	13	No	
2160 Patton, Eva E	NCher	3	F	144	No	
2161 Perry, James	AShaw	38	M	Dead	Yes	Farmer
2162 Perry, Mariah	AShaw	36	F	3986	Yes	
2163 Perry, Emma	AShaw	15	F	Dead	No	
2164 Perry, Frank	AShaw	19	M	3104	No	
2165 Parish, Hallen	AWhite	32	M	4427	Yes	Farmer
2166 Parish, T J	NCher	31	F	Dead	Yes	
2167 Parish, Alvin	NCher	9	F	4456	No	
2168 Parish, Rebecca	NCher	8	F	Dead	No	
2169 Parish, Walter	NCher	6	M	4461	No	
2170 Parish, N J	NCher	4	F	4466	No	
2171 Parish, Betsy	NCher	16m	F	Dead	No	
2172 Paskell, John	A Del	38	M	Del23	Yes	Farmer
2173 Paskell, Lizzie	A Del	30	F	Dead	Yes	
2174 Parks, J B	A Del	34	M	Del204	Yes	Farmer
2175 Parks, Caroline	A Del	33	F	Dead	Yes	
2176 Parks, J F	A Del	7	M	Del205	No	
2177 Parks, James	A Del	4	M	Dead	No	
2178 Parks, D W B	A Del	10m	M	Del208	No	
2179 Purcell, Josh B	AWhite	50	M	Dead	Yes	
2180 Peter, John	A Del	41	M	Dead	Yes	Farmer
2181 Peter, Mary	A Del	30	F	Del81	Yes	
2182 Peter, Henry	A Del	2	M	Del83	No	
2183 Perry, William	A Del	23	M	Dead	No	Farmer
2184 Parson, Eneas	AWhite	34	M	R254	Yes	Enrollment Refused
2185 Parson, Mary	NCher	30	F	Dead	Yes	
2186 Parson, Henry F	NCher	3	M	4338	No	
2187 Parson, Wm E	NCher	1	M	4339	No	
2188 Paolenow,	A Del	25	M	Del86	No	
2189 Pumpkin, Jane James	A Del	36	F	Dead	No	
2190 Pumpkin, Mary James	A Del	5	F	4544	No	
2191 Pumpkinpile, George	NCher	42	M	2713	Yes	Farmer
2192 Pumpkinpile, Peggy	NCher	46	F	2713	Yes	

	Name	Race	Age	Sex	Census	Md	Remarks
2193	Pack, Joe	A Col	25	M	F1148	No	
2194	Prophet, James	AShaw	45	M	Dead	Yes	Farmer
2195	Prophet, Mary	AShaw	25	F	Del198	Yes	
2196	Prophet, Jacob	AShaw	8	M	Dead	No	
2197	Prophet, Sam	AShaw	6	M	Dead	No	
2198	Prophet, Minnie	AShaw	3	F	Del199	No	
2199	Prophet, Peggy	AShaw	1	F	Del197	No	
2200	Prophet, Susan	AShaw	18	F	7524	Yes	Dead
2201	Prophet, Margaret	AShaw	2	F	Dead	No	
2202	Panther, George	A Del	16	M	DLD35	No	Root Digger, Absentee Shawnee Allottee
2203	Phillipps, S	AWhite	34	M	Dead	Yes	
2204	Phillipps, Susie	NCher	18	F	4296	Yes	
2205	Phillipps, Ida J	NCher	5	F	4360	No	
2206	Phillipps, Percy	NCher	8m	M	Dead	No	
2207	Phillipps, Myrtle	NCher	8	F	4310	No	
2208	Patton, A F	NCher	17	F	4512	Yes	Farmer
2209	Patton, Charlie L	NCher	2	M	4505	No	
2210	Patton, W W	NCher	1	M	4541	No	
2211	Payne, Thomas	NCher	32	M	Dead	Yes	Farmer
2212	Payne, C L	NCher	23	F	Dead	Yes	
2213	Payne, Charles H	NCher	5	M		No	No census card number given, nor is he listed as dead (BLB)
2214	Payne, A J Lane	NCher	3m	M	9373	No	
2215	Partsel, Wm E	AWhite	29	M	D951	Yes	
2216	Partsel, Eugeaney	NCher	19	F	4013	Yes	
2217	Partsel, Roly	NCher	3m	M	4013	No	
2218	Potatoe, Charlie	NCher	23	M	Dead	No	Marble Player
2219	Prewett, James	AWhite	34	M	Dead	Yes	Farmer
2220	Prewett, Mary Jane	NCher	24	F	Dead	Yes	
2221	Prewett, George	NCher	2	M	5376	No	
2222	Prewett, Dolly	NCher	1	M	2142	No	
2223	Peter, Nellie	NCher	30	F	D1526	No	
2224	Peter, Sallie	NCher	4	F	D1527	No	
2225	Parris, Susie	NCher	24	F	6702	No	See 5116 (census card BLB)
2226	Parris, Rosa	NCher	1	F	D1528	No	
2227	Parks, S P	NCher	19	M	5666	No	
2228	Parks, Samuel	NCher	30	M	Dead	Yes	Farmer
2229	Parks, Clara	NCher	22	F	Dead	Yes	
2230	Polone, Jane	NCher	23	F	Dead	No	
2231	Pecan, John	AShaw	30	M	5082	No	P"ecan"___ Hunter
2232	Pecan, Nancy	AShaw	25	F	Dead	No	
2233	Pecan, Lizzie	AShaw	10	F	Dead	No	

Name	Race	Age	Sex	Census	Md	Remarks
2234 Pigeon, Wm	NCher	35	M	9018	Yes	
2235 Pigeon, Mary	NCher	44	F	Dead	Yes	
2236 Pigeon, Loney	NCher	16	M	5676	No	
2237 Pumpkin, Jim	NCher	37	M	Dead	Yes	Carpenter
2238 Pumpkin, Sallie	NCher	20	F	Dead	Yes	
2239 Potts, Lewis	NCher	7	M	Dead	No	
2240 Parks, John	A Del	18	M	Del195	No	
2241 Parks, Mary	A Del	16	F	Dead	No	
2242 Parks, George	A Del	6	M	Del197	No	
2243 Pratt, Nannie	A Del	19	F	DLD17	No	
2244 Pratt, Ella	A Del	17	F	Del318	No	
2245 Pratt, Ida	A Del	13	F	Del163	No	
2246 Purcell, Charles	AShaw	19	M	3091	No	
2247 Purcell, Alice	AShaw	16	F	3138	No	
2248 Purcell, Westley	AShaw	14	M	3145	No	
2249 Purcell, Lincoln	AShaw	12	M	4448	No	
2250 Peak, Nannie	A Del	14	F	Dead	Yes	
2251 Partridge, Widow	NCher	40	F	Dead	No	
2252 Partridge, Wm	NCher	50	M	Dead	No	
2253 Parris, Malissa	NCher	13	F	Dead	No	
2254 Price, James	NCher	13	M	5214	No	
2255 Price, Charlie	NCher	10	M	5200	No	
2256 Payne, Lula	NCher	5	F	D1529	No	
2257 Potatoe, Ned	NCher	12	M	8861		
2258 Parris, Billie	NCher	11	M	5116		
2259 Perry, Samuel			M	4429		
2260 Perry, John			M	Dead		
2261 Qualespenow	A Del	18	F	Dead	No	
2262 Quatuckache,				Del269		
2263 Robins, Nancy	NCher	23	F	5538	No	
2264 Robins, Frank	NCher	3	M	5540	No	On Dawes as Ben F Bice (BLB)
2265 Rice, James A	NCher	23	M	Dead	No	Clerk
2266 Rogers, Mary G	A Del	60	F	Dead	No	Farmer
2267 Rogers, Sam	AShaw	60	M	Dead	Yes	Farmer
2268 Rogers, Lizzie	AShaw	40	F	Dead	Yes	
2269 Rogers, Frank	AShaw	18	M	3229	No	
2270 Rogers, Charles	AShaw	11	M	Dead	No	
2271 Rogers, Lewis	NCher	42	M	Dead	Yes	Farmer
2272 Rogers, Jane	AWhite	40	F	Dead	Yes	
2273 Rogers, Mary	NCher	19	F	3549	No	
2274 Rogers, Thomas	NCher	17	M	3940	No	
2275 Rogers, Robert	NCher	13	M	Dead	No	

Cooweescoowee District

Name	Race	Age	Sex	Census	Md	Remarks
2276 Rogers, James	NCher	11	M	3341	No	
2277 Rogers, Henry	NCher	9	M	4866	No	
2278 Rogers, Charles	NCher	2	M	2709	No	
2279 Read, Luman	AWhite	38	M	Dead	Yes	Farmer
2280 Read, M J	NCher	19	F	Dead	Yes	
2281 Read, Eddie	NCher	1	M	Dead	No	
2282 Rogers, Eli	AShaw	38	M	Dead	Yes	Farmer
2283 Rogers, Sarah	AShaw	40	F	Dead	Yes	
2284 Ratlinggourd, D	NCher	30	M	Dead	Yes	Farmer
2285 Ratlinggourd, Mintie	NCher	22	F	Dead	No	
2286 Ratlinggourd, Sarah	NCher	3	F	Dead	No	
2287 Rogers, Wellington	NCher	24	M	D708	Yes	Farmer
2288 Rogers, Mary	NCher	21	F	Dead	Yes	
2289 Rogers, Ida May	NCher	2	F	4935	No	
2290 Rogers, M E	NCher	2m	F	3915	No	
2291 Rogers, Charlotte	NCher	22	F	3827	No	
2292 Rogers, Maggie	NCher	5	F	3929	No	
2293 Rogers, William	NCher	3	M	Dead	No	
2294 Rogers, Willis	A Col	30	M	F1044	Yes	Farmer
2295 Rogers, Sarah	A Col	20	F	F1044	Yes	
2296 Rogers, M J	A Col	7	M	Dead	No	
2297 Rosey, Nig	A Col	25	F	FD1145	No	
2298 Rosey, Alberty	A Col	8m	F	FD1146	No	
2299 Raymond, A C	AWhite	52	M	3009	Yes	Mechanic
2300 Raymond, Amanda J	NCher	42	F	3009	Yes	
2301 Raymond, Mary	NCher	10	F	5416	No	
2302 Roach, A A	AWhite	32	M	3305	Yes	
2303 Roach, Mattie	NCher	21	F	3305	Yes	
2304 Roach, W A	NCher	4m	M	Dead	No	
2305 Rogers, N B	NCher	36	M	Dead	Yes	Farmer
2306 Rogers, Annie C	NCher	30	F	Dead	Yes	
2307 Rogers, Mary E	NCher	9	F	Dead	No	
2308 Rogers, John Jr.	NCher	6	M	Dead	No	
2309 Rogers, John	AShaw	25	M	Dead	No	
2310 Rogers, Wm L	NCher	15	M	Dead	No	
2311 Ross, Lizzie	A Col	30	F	Dead	No	
2312 Ross, Tom	A Col	7	M	Dead	No	
2313 Ross, Rachiel	A Col	10	F	F1046	No	
2314 Ross, Sam	A Col	5	M	Dead	No	
2315 Rider, Henry	A Col	44	M	Dead	Yes	Farmer
2316 Rider, Mariah	A Col	42	F	F1031	Yes	
2317 Rider, Polly	A Col	27	F	Dead	No	

Name	Race	Age	Sex	Census	Md	Remarks
2318 Rider, Tony	A Col	19	M	Dead	No	
2319 Rider, Hannah	A Col	13	F	F960	No	
2320 Rider, Jennie	A Col	9	F	F949	No	
2321 Rider, Sallie	A Col	4	F	FD1147	No	
2322 Rider, Maglin	A Col	2	F	F1050	No	
2323 Rider, Charlie	A Col	3m	M	F1032	No	
2324 Rogers, Sallie Vann	A Col	20	F	Dead	No	
2325 Rogers, Nelson Vann	A Col	2	M	F853	No	
2326 Runnells, E F	AWhite	28	M	D1530	Yes	Married out, Farmer
2327 Runnells, Mary E	NCher	23	F	Dead	Yes	
2328 Runnells, Williams	NCher	5	M	Dead	No	
2329 Runnells, C N D	NCher	4m	M	Dead	No	
2330 Runnells, B P	NCher	3	F	Dead	No	
2331 Rogers, Clem V	NCher	41	M	4747	Yes	Policeman
2332 Rogers, Mary	NCher	41	F	Dead	Yes	
2333 Rogers, Sallie	NCher	17	F	5461	No	
2334 Rogers, Robert	NCher	13	M	Dead	No	
2335 Rogers, Maud	NCher	10	F	5630	No	
2336 Rogers, May	NCher	7	F	4899	No	
2337 Rogers, Col W P	NCher	7m	M	4747	No	
2338 Ross, Charlie	A Col	65	M	Dead	Yes	Farmer
2339 Ross, Sarah	A Col	60	F	Dead	Yes	
2340 Randle, F H	A Del	25	M	Del230	No	
2341 Rider, Wm L	A Col	32	M	F670	Yes	
2342 Rider, Eadie	A Col	20	F	F670	Yes	
2343 Rider, Bob	A Col	7	M	F793	No	
2344 Rider, Lizzie	A Col	5	F	Dead	No	
2345 Rider, Mary	A Col	2	F	F809	No	
2346 Riley, John	NCher	53	M	Dead	Yes	Farmer
2347 Riley, Mrs. John	AWhite	43	F	Dead	Yes	
2348 Riley, Louis	NCher	16	M	4428	No	
2349 Riley, Ellen	NCher	12	F	Dead	No	
2350 Riley, James	NCher	10	M	4525	No	
2351 Riley, Sallie	NCher	4	F	4583	No	Sallie McMains (BLB)
2352 Riley, Rufus	NCher	49	M	Dead	Yes	Farmer
2353 Riley, Betty	AWhite	34	F	4521	Yes	
2354 Riley, George	NCher	13	M	Dead	No	
2355 Riley, Samuel	NCher	10	M	4543	No	
2356 Riley, Hotwood	NCher	3	F	4432	No	
2357 Riley, Looney	NCher	79	M	Dead	Yes	Farmer
2358 Riley, Mrs. L	AWhite	79	F	Dead	Yes	
2359 Riley, Ida	NCher	3	F	4603	No	

Name	Race	Age	Sex	Census	Md	Remarks
2360 Riley, R R	NCher	2	M	4526	No	
2361 Rogers, Henry	AShaw	45	M	3384	Yes	
2362 Rogers, Mary	AShaw	42	F	Dead	Yes	
2363 Rogers, Dora	AShaw	2	F	Dead	No	
2364 Rowe, N B	NCher	31	M	2390	Yes	Farmer
2365 Rowe, Letha	NCher	29	F	2390	Yes	
2366 Rowe, Lattie	NCher	5	F	6404	No	
2367 Rowe, Lizzie	NCher	3	F	2391	No	
2368 Rowe, David Jr.	NCher	7d	M	Dead	No	
2369 Ross, Kate	NCher	24	F	3956	No	
2370 Rogers, Nig	A Col	28	M	Dead	Yes	Farmer
2371 Rogers, Ester	A Col	24	F	F615	Yes	
2372 Rogers, Tom	A Col	3w	M	FD143	No	
2373 Rogers, Wm	A Col	3	M	F584	No	
2374 Ruddles, Joe	AWhite	55	F	Dead	Yes	Farmer (He should be listed as male and Cherokee, it is his wife Cynthia was white, JF is his daughter BLB)
2375 Ruddles, J F	NCher	24	F	5161	Yes	
2376 Ruddles, J L	NCher	23	M	9624	No	
2377 Ruddles, C B	NCher	20	M	Dead	No	
2378 Ruddles, Mary E	NCher	16	F	Dead	No	
2379 Ruddles, Emma	NCher	13	F	5230	No	
2380 Ruddles, Augustus	NCher	11	M	Dead	No	
2381 Ruddles, Oliver	NCher	9	M	Dead	No	
2382 Ruddles, Nora	NCher	3	M	5142	No	On Dawes as Norris Ruddles (BLB)
2383 Ruddles, Cynthia	NCher	46	F	Dead	No	
2384 Rider, Charles R	NCher	22	M	2726	Yes	Farmer
2385 Rider, Jane	AWhite	15	F	Dead	Yes	
2386 Riley, Major O P	NCher	25	M	Dead	No	
2387 Rider, Blue W	NCher	33	M	5472	Yes	Farmer
2388 Rider, Lydia	NCher	31	F	5472	Yes	
2389 Rider, Maude	NCher	3	F	5474	No	
2390 Risemon, Fred	AWhite	35	M	Dead	Yes	Farmer
2391 Risemon, Polly	NCher	30	F	3242	Yes	Should be Martha (BLB)
2392 Risemon, Joe	NCher	10	M	Dead	No	
2393 Risemon, L E	NCher	8	F	3245	No	
2394 Risemon, John	NCher	5m	M	3242	No	
2395 Ralph, Joe	AWhite	25	M	Dead	No	A Widower
2396 Ross, Bark	NCher	22	M	Dead	No	
2397 Riders, Hon A M	NCher	40	M	Dead	Yes	Officer of ____
2398 Riders, Minnie	AWhite	19	F	4390	Yes	

Name	Race	Age	Sex	Census	Md	Remarks
2399 Riders, Kate	NCher	15	F	5417	No	
2400 Riders, Austin	NCher	12	M	4618	No	
2401 Riders, John	NCher	6	M	5618	No	
2402 Riders, James O Hall	NCher	3	M	4683	No	
2403 Richards, Hannah	NCher	50	F	Dead	No	
2404 Rogers, Rabb	A Col	45	M	F1021	Yes	
2405 Rogers, Rhoda	A Chic	35	F	F1021	Yes	
2406 Rogers, Nic	A Col	12	M	Dead	No	
2407 Rogers, Jack	A Col	10	M	F1179	No	
2408 Rogers, Huston Jr,	A Col	9	M	F1032	No	
2409 Rogers, Clem Vicious	A Col	7	M	F1106	No	
2410 Rogers, Jasper	A Col	4	M	F1108	No	
2411 Rogers, Andy	A Col	3	M	F1129	No	
2412 Rogers, Rose	A Col	11m	F	F1105	No	
2413 Rogers, Lucy	A Col	100	F	Dead	No	Granny
2414 Rogers, Lucinda	A Col	15	F	F1018	No	
2415 Rogers, Betsy	A Col	12	F	F469	No	
2416 Rogers, Houston Sr.	A Col	39	M	F955	Yes	
2417 Rogers, Sidney	A Col	36	F	Dead	Yes	
2418 Rogers, R O	A Col	11	M	F1073	No	
2419 Rogers, Mollie	A Col	10	F	Dead	No	
2420 Rogers, Susy	A Col	7	F	F1150	No	
2421 Rogers, Charles R	A Col	5	M	F1149	No	
2422 Rogers, Eli	A Col	3	F	F1115	No	
2423 Rogers, Jack	A Col	3m	M	F955	No	
2424 Rogers, Lizzie	A Col	22	F	Dead	No	
2425 Ross, Perry	A Col	36	M	F1088	Yes	Fiddler
2426 Ross, Mariah	A Col	29	F	f1080	Yes	
2427 Ross, Rutha	A Col	9	F	Dead	No	
2428 Ross, Jesse	A Col	3	M	f1083	No	
2429 Reed, Andy	NCher	27	M	4349	Yes	
2430 Reed, Emeline	NCher	45	F	5310	Yes	
2431 Reed, David	NCher	24	M	Dead	No	
2432 Rowe, Haywood	A Col	22	M	F1018	No	
2433 Ragsdale, Jonah	A Col	40	M	F779	Yes	
2434 Ragsdale, Annaca	A Col	26	F	F779	Yes	
2435 Ragsdale, I J	A Col	9	M	Dead	No	
2436 Rogers, Nancy	AShaw	60	F	Dead	No	
2437 Reese, Jesse	NCher	40	M	F705	Yes	Farmer
2438 Reese, Betsy	NCher	40	F	F705	Yes	
2439 Reese, Benny	NCher	6	M	F708	No	
2440 Reese, Jennie	NCher	3	F	F707	No	

Name	Race	Age	Sex	Census	Md	Remarks
2441 Rogers, Ellis	NCher	20	M	Dead	No	
2442 Richards, John A	AWhite	53	M	Dead	No	Mormon Preacher
2443 Rider,	NCher	30	M	Dead	No	
2444 Ratliff, Sam	NCher	28	M	Dead	Yes	Senator?
2445 Ratliff, July	NCher	27	F	6834	Yes	
2446 Ratliff, John Beck	NCher	10	M	6829	No	
2447 Rider, Lige	A Col	45	M	F718	Yes	Preacher
2448 Rider, Lucy	A Col	50	F	Dead	Yes	
2449 Rider, Jerry	A Col	22	M	F585	Yes	Farmer
2450 Rider, Anna	A Col	19	F	F585	Yes	
2451 Rider, Frank	A Col	2	M	F620	No	
2452 Rider, Lucy	A Col	2m	F	FD1148	No	
2453 Rider, James	A Col	35	M	F624	Yes	Farmer
2454 Rider, Tildy	A Col	25	F	Dead	Yes	
2455 Rider, Alsie	A Col	11	F	Dead	No	
2456 Rider, Sam	A Col	9	M	F588	No	
2457 Rider, John	A Col	8	M	F614	No	
2458 Rider, Tom	A Col	5	M	F619	No	
2459 Raper, John A	NCher	44	M	2529	Yes	Teaser
2460 Raper, M A	AWhite	25	F	2529	Yes	
2461 Raper, W P	NCher	30	M	5237	No	
2462 Raper, H M	NCher	10	M	Dead	No	
2463 Raper, Callie	NCher	8	F	2499	No	
2464 Rogers, Thomas	NCher	12	M	5675	No	
2465 Ross, George	A Col	28	M	F1095	Yes	Farmer
2466 Ross, Malissa	A Col	25	F	9620	No	
2467 Ragsdale, Riley	NCher	24	M	504	No	
2468 Rosenthall, L A	A Jew	35	M	Dead	Yes	Farmer
2469 Rosenthall, Lizzie	NCher	28	F	4955	Yes	
2470 Richards, Joe A	NCher	21	M	Dead	No	
2471 Roland, Joe	AWhite	29	M	4992	Yes	
2472 Roland, Elmina	NCher	26	M	4992	Yes	
2473 Rogers, Hon Charles	NCher	62	M	Dead	Yes	Fiddler
2474 Rogers, Joanna A	NCher	19	F	2596	No	
2475 Rogers, Chicken	NCher	16	M	Dead	No	
2476 Rogers, Bink	NCher	13	M	Dead	No	
2477 Rogers, Jane	NCher	31	F	Dead	Yes	
2478 Rogers, D B	NCher	2	M	5341	No	
2479 Rowe, D C	NCher	26	M	2449	Yes	Farmer
2480 Rowe, Eliza	NCher	22	F	2449	Yes	
2481 Rowe, Martin	NCher	4	M	2489	No	
2482 Rowe, Richard	NCher	1	M	Dead	No	

Name	Race	Age	Sex	Census	Md	Remarks
2483 Rogers, William C	NCher	31	M	6199	No	Merchant
2484 Ragsdale, Francis	A Col	20	F	Dead	No	Shagger
2485 Rogers, Emma	NCher	13	F	4218	No	
2486 Rogers, Hanna	NCher	7	F	D543	No	
2487 Robins, Thomas	NCher	14	M	D1531	No	
2488 Robins, Betsey	NCher	16	F	Dead	No	
2489 Ross, Frank	A Col	36	M	F882	Yes	Farmer
2490 Ross, Susie	A Col	33	F	Dead	Yes	
2491 Ross, Nathan	A Col	15	M	F887	No	
2492 Ross, Lizzie	A Col	13	F	F1121	No	
2493 Ross, Matilda	A Col	10	F	F982	No	
2494 Ross, Aggy	A Col	7	F	F888	No	
2495 Ross, Anna	A Col	3	F	F935	No	
2496 Ross, George	NCher	15	M	Dead	No	
2497 Ross, Frank	A Col					Crossed out Duplicate of above
2498 Ross, Susan	A Col					"
2499 Ross, Nathan	A Col					"
2500 Ross, Lizzie	A Col					"
2501 Ross, Matilda	A Col					"
2502 Ross, Aggy	A Col					"
2503 Ross, Anna	A Col					"
2504 Rogers, Reuben	A Col	5	M	F795		
2505 Rogers, Anna	NCher	16	F	4513	No	
2506 Rogers, John	NCher	18	M	2029	No	
2507 Riley, Bell	NCher	5	F	2609	No	
2508 Rogers, Gabe	A Col	30	M	9767	No	
2509 Rogers, Betsy	NCher	27	F	1638	No	
2510 Rogers, Susan	NCher	1	F	1648	No	
2511 Rowe, Perry	NCher	6	M	F828	No	Duplicate
2512 Rowe, Seely	NCher	4	F	F706	No	Duplicate
2513 Ridge, A E				Dead		
2514 Ross, Jack	NCher	24	M	Dead		
2515 Right, Nancy			F	Del222		
2516 Rowe, Davis Jr.			M	Dead		
2517 Spencer, J W T	NCher	40	M	Dead	Yes	Street___er
2518 Spencer, Bettie	NCher	40	F	Dead	Yes	
2519 Spencer, Nannie	NCher	12	F	4235	No	Adopted child of J M T Spencer
2520 Sarah, Boot	NCher	30	F	9402	No	
2521 Skinner, J W	AWhite	32	M	R150	Yes	Enrollment Refused, Miller
2522 Skinner, Lucy	NCher	28	F	Dead	Yes	
2523 Skinner, Louisa	NCher	1	F	3051	No	
2524 Shotpouch, Bill	NCher	22	M	2358	No	

Cooweescoowee District

Name	Race	Age	Sex	Census	Md	Remarks
2525 Skinner, Frank	AWhite	37	M	3288	Yes	Engineer
2526 Skinner, Mattie	NCher	27	F	Dead	Yes	
2527 Skinner, Dora	NCher	1	F	3644	No	
2528 Swain, John	AWhite	51	M	3577	Yes	Shoemaker, to the best of my knowledge this man has never been divorced from his first wife who is in California _____ he is an intruder
2529 Swain, R M	NCher	16	F	3577	Yes	
2530 Sam, Old Man	NCher	29	M	Dead	Yes	Farmer
2531 Sam, Peggy	NCher	28	F	Dead	Yes	
2532 Sam, Ezekiel	NCher	1	M	7580	No	On Dawes as Zeke Knightkiller (BLB)
2533 Still, Coon	A Col	30	F	Dead	No	
2534 Schrimpsher, Jume	NCher	50	F	Dead	Yes	Farmer
2535 Schrimpsher, Laura L	NCher	12	F	3634	Yes	
2536 Schrimpsher, Maggie	NCher	10	F	3871	No	
2537 Stewart, W W	AWhite	28	M	Dead	Yes	Farmer
2538 Stewart, Marianne	AShaw	23	F	Dead	Yes	
2539 Stewart, Edward	AShaw	5	M	5694	No	
2540 Stewart, James	AShaw	5	M	3057	No	
2541 Sanders, Daniels	A Col	36	M	F1122	Yes	Farmer
2542 Sanders, Malinda	A Col	33	F	F1122	Yes	
2543 Sanders, Benj	A Col	11	M	F1120	No	
2544 Sanders, Mary	A Col	9	F	Dead	No	
2545 Sanders, Anna	A Col	6	F	F1058	No	
2546 Sanders, Josie	A Col	4	F		No	No census number given, or listed as dead (BLB)
2547 Sanders, Daniel Jr.	A Col	4m	M	F1048	No	
2548 Sanders, Daniel	A Col	98	M	Dead	Yes	Farmer
2549 Sanders, Polly	A Col	55	F	Dead	Yes	
2550 Sanders, Ella	A Col	6	F	Dead	No	
2551 Smith, Houston	AWhite	46	M	78	Yes	Coal miner
2552 Smith, Elizabeth	NCher	38	F	78	Yes	
2553 Smith, S F	NCher	20	F	2445	No	
2554 Smith, Anna A	NCher	8	F	Dead	No	
2555 Stout, Wesley	A Del	34	M	Del263	Yes	Nothing
2556 Stout, Elizabeth	A Del	33	F	Del263	Yes	
2557 Squirrel, Daniel	AShaw	30	M	Dead	Yes	Farmer
2558 Squirrel, Anna	AShaw	20	F	3203	Yes	
2559 Squirrel, Lizzie	AShaw		F	4436	No	
2560 Squirrel, Amanda	AShaw	3	F	4429	No	
2561 Secondine, Filmore	A Del	40	M	Del307	Yes	Farmer
2562 Secondine, Jane	A Del	24	F	Dead	Yes	

Name	Race	Age	Sex	Census	Md	Remarks
2563 Secondine, Rosie Sr.	A Del	11	F	Del288	No	
2564 Secondine, Isaac	A Del	6	M	Del348	No	
2565 Secondine, Anna	A Del	3	F	Del289	No	
2566 Secondine, Rosie Jr.	A Del	3	F	Del231	No	
2567 Secondine, Charlie	A Del	7m	M	Del307	No	
2568 Smith, Alvin	AWhite	38	M	Dead	Yes	Farmer
2569 Smith, Sallie	NCher	44	F	Dead	Yes	
2570 Southerland, Enoch	AWhite	40	M	3901	Yes	Farmer
2571 Southerland, Abigail	NCher	23	F	3901	Yes	
2572 Schrimpsher, Ruth	NCher	18	F	3575	No	
2573 Scraper, Noisy	NCher	37	M	Dead	Yes	
2574 Scraper, Tooniah	NCher	35	F	Dead	Yes	
2575 Sanders, Wm	NCher	45	M	Dead	Yes	Possum Hunter
2576 Sanders, Jinnie	NCher	25	F	6123	Yes	
2577 Sanders, Loura	NCher	12	F	Dead	No	
2578 Sanders, Polly	NCher	5	F	6149	No	
2579 Sanders, Johnson	NCher	2	M	D1532	No	Dead, In Tahl Dist if alive
2580 Skillman, John	AWhite	36	M	D481	Yes	Farmer
2581 Skillman, Jane	AShaw	40	F	Dead	Yes	
2582 Smith, John T	AWhite	46	M	Dead	Yes	Farmer
2583 Smith, S O	A Del	40	F	Del260	Yes	
2584 Smith, W C	A Del	17	M	Del261	No	
2585 Smith, Nannie M	A Del	14	F	Del259	No	
2586 Smith, L E	A Del	3	M	Del348	No	
2587 Skinner, Nat	AWhite	30	M	R381	Yes	Rejected, Married out, Stockman
2588 Skinner, Nan	NCher	22	F	Dead	Yes	
2589 Skinner, Mollie	NCher	5m	F	3724	No	On Dawes as Louie J Green (BLB)
2590 Sitzler, Henry	AWhite	25	M	2801	Yes	
2591 Sitzler, Jane	NCher	20	F	Dead	Yes	
2592 Shawnee, John	AShaw	33	M	Dead	Yes	Squirrell Hunter
2593 Shawnee, Julia	AShaw	26	F	Del114	Yes	
2594 Shawnee, Charley	AShaw		M	Del94	No	
2595 Shawnee, Ada	AShaw	1m	F	Del280	No	
2596 Shawnee, Lizzie	A Del	17	F	Dead	No	
2597 Swannock, J M	A Del	27	M	Dead	Yes	Farmer
2598 Swannock, Martha	A Del	30	F	Del131	Yes	
2599 Soldier,	A Del	50	M	Del81	Yes	Farmer
2600 Soldier, Wahlalunah,	A Del	30	F	Dead	Yes	
2601 Soldier, Wilson Sallie	A Del	6	F	Del142	No	
2602 Sarcoxey, John	A Del	34	M	Del207	Yes	Farmer
2603 Sarcoxey, Elizabeth	A Del	27	F	Dead	Yes	

Name	Race	Age	Sex	Census	Md	Remarks
2604 Sarcoxey, Henry	A Del	15	M	Dead	No	
2605 Sarcoxey, Reuben	A Del	5	M	Del95	No	
2606 Spybuck, Jack	AShaw	25	M	Dead	Yes	Farmer
2607 Shelar, Jack	A Del	25	M	Del173	Yes	Farmer
2608 Shelar, Mrs. Jack	A Del	30	F	Dead	Yes	
2609 Shelar, Anna	A Del	7	F	Dead	No	
2610 Shelar, Emma	A Del	3	F	Dead	No	
2611 Shelar, Sallatee	A Del	5	F	Dead	No	
2612 Shelar, Bock	A Del	1	M	D Del10	No	
2613 Swannock, George	A Del	43	M	Dead	No	
2614 Swannock, Qaaschispit	A Del	36	F	Dead	No	
2615 Swannock, Sallie	A Del	18	F	Dead	No	
2616 Swannock, Mary	A Del	15	F	Del274	No	
2617 Swannock, Henry	A Del	13	M	Dead	No	
2618 Scullawl, Aggy	NCher	40	F	4220	No	
2619 Scullawl, Blunt	NCher	18	M	4221	No	
2620 Scullawl, Peggy	NCher	13	F	Dead	No	
2621 Scullawl, Bear	NCher	8	M	4226	No	
2622 Secondine, Tom	NCher	40	M	Del15	Yes	
2623 Secondine, Jane	A Del	36	F	Dead	Yes	
2624 Secondine, Lizzie	A Del	15	F	Del303	No	
2625 Secondine, Joseph	A Del	12	M	Del355	No	
2626 Secondine, Anderson	A Del	10	M	Del61	No	
2627 Secondine, Silas	A Del	3	M	Dead	No	
2628 Secondine, Jacob	A Del	4	M	Del28	No	
2629 Secondine, Lucinda	A Del	2	F	Dead	No	
2630 Sarcoxey, John	A Del	59	M	Dead	Yes	Minister
2631 Sarcoxey, Lizzie	A Del	44	M	Dead	Yes	
2632 Sarcoxey, Henry	A Del	9	M	Dead	No	
2633 Simmons, Alice	A Del	19	F	Dead	No	
2634 Secondine, Simon	A Del	25	M	Del310	No	
2635 Swannock, John	A Del	40	M	Dead	Yes	
2636 Swannock, Jane	A Del	21	F	Del121	Yes	
2637 Swannock, Josie	A Del	13	F	Del137	No	
2638 Swannock, Willie	A Del	6m	M	Dead	No	
2639 Swannock, Widow	A Del	80	F	Dead	No	
2640 Swannock, Lilie	A Del	15	F	Dead	No	
2641 Swannock, Lucy	A Del	9	F	Dead	No	
2642 Swannock, Emma	A Del	7	F	Dead	No	
2643 Sequoyah, Aggy	NCher	8	F	Dead	No	
2644 Swannock, Bill	A Del	47	M	Dead	Yes	Farmer
2645 Swannock, Mrs. Bill	A Del	47	F	Del180	Yes	

Name	Race	Age	Sex	Census	Md	Remarks
2646 Simon, Jackson	A Del	36	M	Dead	Yes	Farmer
2647 Simon, Mrs. Jackson	A Del	27	F	Dead	Yes	
2648 Simon, Alice	A Del	3	F	Dead	No	
2649 Simon, Neguatshe	A Del	115	F	Dead	No	
2650 Silas, John	A Del	28	M	Dead	Yes	Farmer
2651 Silas, Mary	A Del	22	M	Dead	Yes	
2652 Sarcoxey, Wm	A Del	38	M	Dead	Yes	Farmer
2653 Sarcoxey, Lizzie	A Del	16	F	Del144	Yes	
2654 Sarcoxey, Nancy	A Del	16	F	Dead	No	
2655 Sarcoxey, Jeff	A Del	14	M	Del351	No	
2656 Sarcoxey, Anderson	A Del	9	M	Dead	No	
2657 Sanders, Reuben	A Col	27	M	F892	Yes	Farmer
2658 Sanders, Alice	A Col	24	F	F892	Yes	
2659 Sanders, Lillie	A Col	11	F	F895	No	
2660 Sanders, Rosie	A Col	12	F	F1146	No	
2661 Sanders, Mike	A Col	5	M	F1045	No	
2662 Sanders, George	A Col	3	M	Dead	No	
2663 Sanders, Dennis B	A Col	3m	M	Dead	No	
2664 Smith, Thompson	A Del	37	M	Dead	Yes	Farmer
2665 Smith, Mary	A Del	33	F	Del308	Yes	
2666 Smith, Solomon	A Del	14	M	Del270	No	
2667 Smith, Thomas	A Del	4m	M	Dead	No	
2668 Secondine, John	A Del	31	M	Del62	No	Farmer
2669 Sanders, Harry	AWhite	45	M	Dead	Yes	Farmer
2670 Sanders, Susan	NCher	45	F	Dead	Yes	
2671 Stout, John	A Del	30	M	Del271	Yes	Farmer
2672 Stout, Susie	A Del	17	F	Del271	Yes	
2673 Stout, Wm	A Del	10	M	Dead	No	
2674 Smith, Samuel	A Del	49	M	Dead	No	Farmer
2675 Smith, George	A Del	15	M	Del29*	No	
2676 Smith, Willie	A Del	12	M	Dead	No	
2677 Sanders, Louis	A Col	19	M	F655	No	Farmer
2678 Sullivan, James	NCher	30	M	2584	Yes	Farmer
2679 Sullivan, M A	NCher	28	F	Dead	Yes	
2680 Sullivan, Wm	NCher	12	M	7428	No	
2681 Sullivan, Frank	NCher	2	M	2587	No	
2682 Smokes, Charles	NCher	26	M	Dead	No	Roustabout
2683 Snow, W H	AWhite	30	M	Dead	No	
2684 Schrimpsher, John G	NCher	44	M	5165	Yes	Policeman
2685 Schrimpsher, Juliet	NCher	38	F	5165	Yes	
2686 Schrimpsher, Kittie	NCher	13	F	Dead	No	
2687 Schrimpsher, Betsy Bell	NCher	7	F	5183	No	

Name	Race	Age	Sex	Census	Md	Remarks
2688 Schrimpsher, Earnest	NCher	4	M	4979	No	
2689 Schrimpsher, Juliet Jr.	NCher	2	F	4918	No	
2690 Sunday, Ed	NCher	28	M	4840	Yes	Farmer
2691 Sunday, Nancy	NCher	27	F	Dead	Yes	
2692 Sunday, Jane	NCher	4	F	5317	No	
2693 Sunday, Wm Jr.	NCher	2	M	4840	No	
2694 Sunday, Sunday	NCher	5m	F	4944	No	Lucy Sunday (BLB)
2695 Sunday, Mary Ellen	NCher	22	F	5319	No	
2696 Silk, Mose	NCher	35	M	Dead	Yes	Farmer
2697 Silk, Peggy	NCher	24	F	Dead	Yes	
2698 Silk, James	NCher	12	M	Dead	No	
2699 Silk, Alice	NCher	4	F	Dead	No	
2700 Silk, John	NCher	2	M	Dead	No	
2701 Silk, Charles	NCher	6m	M	Dead	No	
2702 Shybuck, George	AShaw	26	M	D1534	Yes	Farmer
2703 Shybuck, Nancy	AShaw	40	F	Dead	No	
2704 Shybuck, Jane	AShaw	10	F	D529	No	
2705 Stopp, Clem	NCher	26	M	Dead	Yes	Farmer
2706 Stopp, Sarah	NCher	30	F	Dead	Yes	
2707 Sequoyah, Dick	NCher	20	M	D1533	Yes	Roustabout
2708 Sequoyah, Charlotte	NCher	18	F	Dead	Yes	
2709 Sequoyah,	NCher	2	M	Dead	No	
2710 Sardine,	NCher	30	M	Dead	Yes	Farmer
2711 Sardine, Dumpy	NCher	25	F	Dead	Yes	
2712 Sanders, Ed	NCher	23	M	5014	Yes	Farmer
2713 Starr, Caleb W	NCher	22	M	6789	No	Policeman
2714 Sanders, Frank	NCher	25	M	Dead	No	
2715 Starr, Watt S	NCher	35	M	4889	Yes	Farmer
2716 Starr, Ruth	NCher	34	F	Dead	Yes	
2717 Starr, Emmerett	NCher	9	M	890	No	
2718 Starr, Coll	NCher	3	M	4889	No	
2719 Starr, Mary	NCher	6m	F	4889	No	
2720 Swim, Wm	AWhite	47	M	Dead	Yes	Blacksmith
2721 Swim, M E	NCher	29	F	4848	Yes	
2722 Swim, M J	NCher	7	F	4861	No	
2723 Swim, J L	NCher	2	M	4863	No	
2724 Stinger, David	AWhite	38	M	4059	Yes	Farmer
2725 Stinger, Mrs. David	NCher	34	F	4059	Yes	
2726 Stinger, Mattie	NCher	12	F	3947	No	
2727 Stinger, John	NCher	8	M	4180	No	
2728 Silk, Polly	AWhite	80	F	Dead	No	
2729 Silk, Levi	NCher	32	M	4703	Yes	Fisherman

Cooweescoowee District

Name	Race	Age	Sex	Census	Md	Remarks
2730 Silk, Melvina	NCher	26	F	4703	Yes	
2731 Silk, Nannie	NCher	6	F	4970	No	
2732 Silk, W M	NCher	1	M	4720	No	
2733 Sullahteeskee,	NCher	49	M	5222	Yes	On Dawes on John Ridge (BLB)
2734 Sullahteeskee, Rachel	NCher	30	F	Dead	Yes	
2735 Sullahteeskee, David	NCher	10	M	7374	No	
2736 Sullahteeskee, Polly	NCher	7	F	Dead	No	
2737 Shawnee,	NCher	25	M	Dead	Yes	
2738 Shawnee, Lydia	NCher	19	F	Dead	Yes	
2739 Sanders, Bird	NCher	45	M	Dead	No	Farmer
2740 Sanders, Joe	NCher	23	M	5069	No	
2741 Sanders, Jesse	NCher	3	M	6661	No	
2742 Soney, Goosy	NCher	40	M	2456	No	
2743 Saesar, James	AShaw	45	M	4254	Yes	Farmer
2744 Saesar, Nancy	AShaw	33	F	Del94	Yes	
2745 Saesar, Lucy	AShaw	6	F	Dead	No	
2746 Saesar, Mary	AShaw	2	F	Del94	No	
2747 Saesar, Dick	AShaw	7m	M	Dead	No	
2748 Sarah, Widow	AShaw	60	F	Dead	No	
2749 Sanders, John	NCher	30	M	5163	No	Farmer
2750 Shone, Sallie	A Del	18	F	Dead	No	
2751 Sanders, George	NCher	26	M	Dead	Yes	
2752 Sanders, Margaret	AWhite	20	F	4840	Yes	On Dawes as Maggie Sunday (BLB)
2753 Sanders, T J	NCher	9	M	Dead	No	
2754 Sanders, Charles	NCher	7	M	5011	No	
2755 Sanders, Clem	NCher	4m	M	4842	No	
2756 Saesar, George	AShaw	22	M	D1535	No	Not known to Shawnee's
2757 Squirrel, Rosie	NCher	30	F	D1537	No	
2758 Squirrel, Mary	NCher	14	F	D1538	No	
2759 Smith, Sophy	NCher	40	F	Dead	No	Farmer
2760 Starr, Edward	NCher	30	M	Dead	Yes	Farmer
2761 Starr, Rachel	NCher	25	F	5375	Yes	
2762 Starr, Ida	NCher	6	F	5373	No	
2763 Starr, Mose	NCher	2	M	5197	No	On Dawes as Arch Starr (BLB)
2764 Starr, Delila	NCher	2w	F	6221	No	
2765 Sequitchie, Martha	NCher	55	F	Dead	No	Farmer
2766 Sequitchie, Mary	NCher	25	F	Dead	No	
2767 Sequitchie, Sallie	NCher	18	F	Dead	No	
2768 Sequitchie, Joe	NCher	11	M	5486	No	
2769 Sequitchie, Martha J	NCher	14	F	5430	No	
2770 Sequitchie, Arch	NCher	5	M	5653	No	

Name	Race	Age	Sex	Census	Md	Remarks
2771 Still, Thomas	NCher	21	M	Dead	No	Farmer
2772 Still, George	NCher	19	M	Dead	No	
2773 Sanders, Rat	NCher	27	M	5087	Yes	Farmer
2774 Sanders, Anna	NCher	30	F	5087	Yes	
2775 Sanders, Polly	NCher	2	F	5084	No	
2776 Still, Aggy	NCher	25	F	2393	No	Skiver, (on Dawes as Aggie Keener BLB)
2777 Still, Sam	NCher	9	M	Dead	No	
2778 Stealer, Lydia	NCher	65	F	Dead	No	Dancer
2779 Sullivan, William	NCher	21	M	2531	No	Farmer
2780 Sullivan, Jeff Davis	NCher	18	M	2581	No	
2781 Sullivan, George Lee	NCher	13	M	5140	No	
2782 Starr, Thomas	NCher	24	M	Dead	No	Skunk Catcher
2783 Shanahan, Mary	NCher	1	F	3822	No	
2784 Sullivan, Robert	NCher	23	M	Dead	Yes	
2785 Sullivan, Sarah	AWhite	21	F	Dead	Yes	
2786 Sullivan, Jim W	NCher	5m	M	Dead	No	
2787 Sullivan, Willis	NCher	20	M	2534	No	
2788 Six, Old Man	NCher	35	M	Dead	Yes	Carpenter
2789 Six, Jennie	NCher	35	F	Dead	Yes	
2790 Smith, J L A	NCher	47	M	Dead	Yes	Racer
2791 Smith, E B	NCher	39	F	Dead	Yes	
2792 Smith, Martha	NCher	15	F	Dead	No	
2793 Smith, May	NCher	10	F	5371	No	
2794 Smith, Florence	NCher	7	F	Dead	No	
2795 Smith, H E	NCher	4	F	1937	No	
2796 Smith, Joe	NCher	5	M	9371	No	
2797 Smith, J B	NCher	4m	M	5176	No	
2798 Sixkiller, Martin	NCher	22	M	Dead	Yes	
2799 Sixkiller, Charlotte	NCher	18	F	5146	No	
2800 Scott, George	NCher	55	M	D1539	Yes	Farmer
2801 Scott, Alcy	NCher	21	F	D1540	Yes	
2802 Scott, Big Road	NCher	11	M	D1541	No	
2803 Scott, Osago	NCher	8	M	D1542	No	
2804 Scott, Mary	NCher	5	F	D1543	No	
2805 Southerland, George	AWhite	35	M	5216	Yes	
2806 Southerland, Tempy	NCher	30	F	Dead	Yes	
2807 Southerland, Anna	NCher	4	F	2944	No	
2808 Southerland, George	NCher	2	M	6539	No	
2809 Stop,	NCher	26	M	Dead	Yes	
2810 Stop, Nancy	NCher	21	F	Dead	Yes	
2811 Stop, Alcy	NCher	1	F	9893	No	

	Name	Race	Age	Sex	Census	Md	Remarks
2812	Spoon, Sarah	AShaw	39	F	5086	No	
2813	Spoon, Wm	AShaw	4	M	5085	No	
2814	Spoon, John	AShaw	33	M	Dead	No	
2815	Sanders, John	NCher	30	M	4806	No	Farmer
2816	Squirrel, Wm	NCher	30	M	Dead	No	
2817	Squirrel, Lizzie	NCher	1	F	D1544	No	In Tah if alive
2818	Smith, Nancy	NCher	37	F	5255	No	
2819	Smith,					No	
2820	Smith, Nelly	NCher	8	F	4692	No	
2821	Squirrel, Mary	NCher	14	F	D1537	No	Duplicate #2751
2822	Squirrel, Rosa	NCher	30	F	D1538	No	Duplicate #2753
2823	Sunday, Wm	NCher	48	M	Dead	Yes	Farmer
2824	Sunday, Eliza	NCher	37	F	2663	Yes	
2825	Sunday, Ezekiel	NCher	5	M	Dead	No	
2826	Sunday, Cuntakea	NCher	8	F	Dead	No	
2827	Sunday, James	NCher	27	M	Dead	Yes	Farmer
2828	Sunday, Elvina	NCher	27	F	Dead	Yes	
2829	Sunday, Susie	NCher	3	F	2719	No	
2830	Sunday, Betsy	NCher	3m	F	Dead	No	
2831	Sanders, Lewis	NCher	36	M	D1545	Yes	
2832	Sanders, Lizzie	NCher	26	F	D1545	Yes	
2833	Starr, Blue	NCher	21	F	5105	No	Farmer
2834	Stones, Susie	NCher	25	F	7374	No	On Dawes as Susan Tucker (BLB)
2835	Stones, Lydia	NCher	1	F	D1546	No	Dead
2836	Stealer, James	NCher	23	M	2520	No	
2837	Sanders, Ann	A Col	25	F	F871	No	Washerwoman
2838	Sanders, Minnie	A Col	9	F	F929	No	
2839	Spybuck, Henry	AShaw	28	M	4346	Yes	Dancer
2840	Spybuck, Mary	AShaw	20	F	Del182	No	
2841	Spybuck, Becky	AShaw	4	F	Del182	No	
2842	Spybuck, Frank	AShaw	2	M	Del182	No	
2843	Spybuck, Wm	AShaw	2m	M	Dead	No	
2844	Spybuck,	AShaw	16	M	3487	No	
2845	Scott, Daniel	NCher	18	M	624	No	Creek Card roll 2043
2846	Sanders, G M	A Col	11m	M	FD1149	No	
2847	Swimmer, Alex	NCher	7	M	D1548	No	
2848	Sequoyah, John	NCher	1	M	Dead	No	Dup 48 Coo
2849	Sidney, John	NCher	66	M	Dead	No	
2850	Shaw, James	A Del	28	M	Del345	No	
2851	Secondine, Polly	A Del	16	F	Dead	No	
2852	Smith, Malinda	A Col	17	F	FD1150	No	
2853	Spybuck, Peter	AShaw	17	M	4091	No	

Cooweescoowee District

Name	Race	Age	Sex	Census	Md	Remarks
2854 Street, Jake	AShaw	7	M	4320	No	
2855 Smith, James	NCher	10	M	4595		
2856 Stealer, Nancy			F	Dead		
2857 Smith, John			M	5515		
2858 Smith, Susan	NCher	39	M	5515		
2859 Smith, Ada	NCher	5	M	5489		
2860 Stand, Charlie			M	Dead		
2861 Stand, Josephine			F	Del118		
2862 Snow, Rachel	NCher	8	F	1441		
2863 Taylor, C C	NCher	38	M	Dead	No	Farmer
2864 Taylor, Davie Jr.	NCher	7	M	5339	No	
2865 Taylor, David Sr.	NCher	56	M	Dead	Yes	Farmer
2866 Taylor, Fannie	AWhite	50	F	Dead	Yes	
2867 Tittle, J M	NCher	33	M	3276	Yes	Hotel Keeper
2868 Tittle, Henryetta	NCher	32	F	Dead	Yes	
2869 Tittle, Anna E	NCher	9	F	3260	No	
2870 Tittle, Manora	NCher	7	F	3282	No	
2871 Tittle, Lula J	NCher	6	F	3272	No	
2872 Tittle, Orena	NCher	4	F	3280	No	
2873 Tittle, Lila Ada	NCher	1	F	3284	No	
2874 Tickeater,	NCher	40	M	Dead	Yes	Farmer
2875 Tickeater, Nancy	NCher	42	F	Dead	Yes	
2876 Tielee, Wm	AWhite	40	M	Dead	Yes	Farmer
2877 Tielee, Pauline	NCher	32	F	Dead	Yes	
2878 Tielee, Abe	NCher	8	M	4905	No	
2879 Tielee, Ida	NCher	6	F	3584	No	
2880 Tielee, Joe	NCher	3	M	Dead	No	
2881 Tanner, Nelson	AWhite	46	M	Dead	Yes	Farmer
2882 Tanner, Rachel	A Del	40	F	Dead	Yes	
2883 Tanner, Charles	NCher	19	M	Del90	No	
2884 Tanner, Louisa	NCher	14	F	Del227	No	
2885 Tanner, Linly	NCher	11	F	Del298	No	
2886 Tanner, Jas	NCher	5	M	Del223	No	
2887 Thornburgh, James	NCher	37	M	4412	Yes	Farmer
2888 Thornburgh, Hortenuse	NCher	24	F	4412	Yes	
2889 Thomas, Jess	AWhite	27	M	2978	Yes	Farmer
2890 Thomas, Joanna	NCher	25	F	2978	Yes	
2891 Thomas, E J	NCher	5	F	3753	No	
2892 Thomas, Levisa	NCher	3	F	3036	No	
2893 Thomas, T C	NCher	10m	F	3540	No	
2894 Thomas, F J	NCher	10	M	3253	No	
2895 Thomas, J L	NCher	12	M	3152	No	On Dawes roll as Joseph Williams

Cooweescoowee District

Name	Race	Age	Sex	Census Md	Remarks
					(BLB)
2896 Tartle, Campbell	A Mex	45	M	D1549	No Gone to Mexico
2897 Tartle, Martin	NCher	2	M	D1550	No Gone to Mexico
2898 Tartle, Emma	NCher	4	F	D1551	No Gone to Mexico
2899 Timpson, Bear	NCher	45	M	Dead	Yes Farmer
2900 Timpson, Lizzie	NCher	38	F	Dead	Yes
2901 Tucker, Charles	AShaw	65	M	Dead	Yes Preacher
2902 Tucker, Harriet	AWhite	45	F	10241	Yes
2903 Thompson, Nick	NCher	20	M	D1552	No Ex Treasurer of Osage Nation
2904 Timberlake, A W	NCher	45	M	Dead	Yes Teacher
2905 Timberlake, M L	NCher	45	F	3769	Yes
2906 Timberlake, Jennie W	NCher	21	F	3967	No
2907 Timberlake, Kate	NCher	19	F	3767	No
2908 Timberlake, Bob	NCher	17	M	Dead	No
2909 Thompson, Jesse	NCher	50	M	Dead	Yes Farmer
2910 Thompson, Lizzie	NCher	33	F	Dead	Yes
2911 Tigers, Ellen	NCher	14	F	3453	No
2912 Tigers, Sallie	NCher	14	F	3439	No
2913 Tongienoxie, Charles	A Del	28	M	Dead	Yes Farmer
2914 Tongienoxie, Mrs.	A Del	20	F	Dead	Yes
2915 Tongienoxie, Ellalnoquah	A Del	6	F	Dead	No
2916 Tongienoxie, Paoteaquah	A Del	3	F	Del313	No
2917 Tyner, Prince	A Col	19	M	F124	No
2918 Tiblow, Henry (widow)	A Del	95	F	Dead	No
2919 Tyner, Nancy	A Col	21	F	Dead	No
2920 Taylor, Nancy	A Col	45	F	F978	No Farmer
2921 Taylor, Patsy	A Col	16	F	F776	No
2922 Taylor, Henry	A Col	10	M	FD1151	No
2923 Taylor, Mary	A Col	9	F	Dead	No
2924 Taylor, Joannah	A Col	4	F	Dead	No
2925 Taylor, Sissie	A Col	2m	F	F1053	No
2926 Thompson, Martin	NCher	56	M	Dead	Yes Farmer
2927 Thompson, Jane M	AWhite	39	F	5492	Yes
2928 Thompson, Johnson	NCher	15	M	Dead	No
2929 Thompson, H D	NCher	13	M	5556	No
2930 Tiger, Susie	NCher	21	F	4845	No Washerwoman
2931 Trimble, Mary A	NCher	40	F	Dead	No
2932 Trimble, Mary L	NCher	10	F	4518	No
2933 Tyner, Reuben	NCher	30	M	4406	Yes Farmer
2934 Tyner, Mary A	NCher	27	F	Dead	Yes
2935 Tyner, John H	NCher	8	M	Dead	No
2936 Tiblow, Overleer	AShaw	36	M	4222	No On Dawes roll as Obediah (BLB)

Cooweescoowee District

Name	Race	Age	Sex	Census	Md	Remarks
2937 Tiblow, Bean	AShaw	5	M	4318	No	
2938 Tiger, Charlie	NCher	26	M	Dead	Yes	Farmer
2939 Tiger, Lizzie	NCher	27	F	4844	Yes	
2940 Tiger, Louis	NCher	7m	M	Dead	No	
2941 Timpson, John	NCher	50	M	Dead	No	Farmer
2942 Timpson, Charlie	NCher	20	M	Dead	No	
2943 Thomas, Wm	AShaw	25	M	Del137	Yes	
2944 Thomas, Nancy	AShaw	23	F	4302	Yes	
2945 Thomas, Betsy	AShaw	1	F	4270	No	
2946 Tramper,	NCher	30	M	Dead	Yes	
2947 Tramper, Beck	NCher	20	F	Dead	Yes	
2948 Tramper, Jesse	NCher	1	M	Dead	No	
2949 Tyner, Wm	AWhite	60	M	Dead	No	Nurse?
2950 Tallow, James	NCher	48	M	Dead	Yes	Farmer
2951 Tallow, Kate	NCher	30	F	Dead	Yes	
2952 Tallow, Whitegal	NCher	14	F	Dead	No	
2953 Tallow, Nancy	NCher	6	F	Dead	No	
2954 Tallow, Mary	NCher	4	F	Dead	No	
2955 Tallow, A B	NCher	6m	M	Dead	No	
2956 Trapp, Joe	NCher	22	M	5166	No	
2957 Tyner, James F	NCher		M	4329		
2958 Tyner, S C	NCher	42		Dead		
2959 Tyner, Sarah	NCher	12	F	4322		
2960 Thompson, D G	AWhite	39	M	2564	Yes	Farmer
2961 Thompson, C C	NCher	36	F	2564	Yes	
2962 Thompson, M C	NCher	12	M	2586	No	
2963 Thompson, D S	NCher	9	F	5672	No	
2964 Thompson, Thos L	NCher	7	M	2504	No	
2965 Thompson, A L	NCher	5	F	3676	No	
2966 Thomas, John	AWhite	37	M	Dead	Yes	Farmer
2967 Thomas, Jane	NCher	38	F	Dead	Yes	
2968 Thomas, Oscar	NCher	3	M	4474	No	
2969 Thomas, Ada	NCher	1	F	5620	No	
2970 Towers, Wm	AWhite	31	M	Dead	Yes	
2971 Towers, Theodonsia	NCher	17	F	Dead	Yes	
2972 Towers, T B	NCher	7w	M	Dead	No	
2973 Tadpole, David	NCher	41	M	Dead	Yes	Farmer
2974 Tadpole, Mollie	NCher	42	F	2461	Yes	
2975 Tadpole, Tiger	NCher	14	M	2447	No	
2976 Tadpole, Darkie	NCher	10	F	5126	No	
2977 Tadpole, Rosie	NCher	8	F	Dead	No	
2978 Tyner, George	NCher	30	M	4284	Yes	Farmer

Name	Race	Age	Sex	Census	Md	Remarks
2979 Tyner, Mary	NCher	21	F	Dead	Yes	
2980 Tyner, Edward	NCher	4m	M	Dead	No	
2981 Tyner, Reuben (Big)	NCher	39	M	4261	Yes	Farmer
2982 Tyner, A V	AWhite	29	F	4261	Yes	
2983 Tyner, Fannie	NCher	11	F	Dead	No	
2984 Tyner, Emma	NCher	9	F	4280	No	
2985 Tyner, F M	NCher	3	M	4240	No	
2986 Tyner, Lenard	NCher	10m	M	4306	No	
2987 Tiblow, Simon	AShaw	50	M	Dead	Yes	Farmer
2988 Tiblow, Mary	AShaw	40	F	Dead	Yes	
2989 Tickeater, Swan	NCher	36	M	Dead	Yes	Farmer
2990 Tickeater, Susie	NCher	35	F	5595	Yes	
2991 Tickeater, B N	NCher	15	M	7552	No	
2992 Tickeater, Chaselouee	NCher	11	F	5665	No	
2993 Tickeater, Susie jr.	NCher	7	F	Dead	No	
2994 Thornton, Polly	NCher	5m	F	Dead	No	
2995 Taylor, Marion	NCher	21	M	Dead	No	
2996 Taylor, Joe	NCher	26	M	Dead	Yes	Trapper
2997 Taylor, Kate	NCher	31	F	Dead	Yes	
2998 Taylor, Esaw	NCher	6m	M	Dead	No	
2999 Tassel, Wm	NCher	26	M	D1553	Yes	Farmer
3000 Tassel, Lucy	NCher	22	F	D1554	Yes	
3001 Tassel, Ida	NCher	5m	F	D1357	No	
3002 Tyner, Carter	NCher	24	M	4228	Yes	Peddler
3003 Tyner, Jane	AShaw	22	F	Dead	Yes	
3004 Tyner, T J	NCher	2	M	4345	No	
3005 Tyner, S T	NCher	35	M	Dead	No	Peddler
3006 Tyner, Kate	AShaw	22	F	4242	Yes	
3007 Terrill, T J	NCher	26	M	Dead	Yes	Farmer
3008 Terrill, Betsy	NCher	25	F	5527	Yes	
3009 Terrill, Mary Carr	NCher	13	F	2742	No	
3010 Thompson, Ezekiel	NCher	31	M	Dead	No	Farmer
3011 Trent, Nancy	NCher	23	F	Dead	No	
3012 Trent, Jeter	NCher	1	M	Dead	No	
3013 Trent, R O	AWhite	26	M	Dead	Yes	M D
3014 Trent, Mollie	NCher	20	F	1846	Yes	
3015 Trent, Georgie	NCher	2	F	1845	No	
3016 Tatserqusee,	NCher	45	M	Dead	Yes	Hunter
3017 Tatserqusee, Betsy	NCher	30	F	Dead	Yes	
3018 Thomas, David	A Del	28	M	Dead	Yes	Farmer
3019 Thomas, Mrs. David	A Del	29	F	Del340	Yes	
3020 Thermon, Joe	A Del	6	M		No	Not know to Delawares DelD36

Name	Race	Age	Sex	Census	Md	Remarks
3021 Thompson, Ida	A Del	14	F	Dead	No	
3022 Timberlake, Ruth	NCher	18	F	Dead	No	
3023 Timberlake, Willie	NCher	11	M	4930	No	
3024 Tyner, Clinton			M	6638		
3025 Tyner, May	NCher	17	F	D1556		
3026 Teeapaky,				Dead		
3027 Tyner, Fraiser	NCher	2	M	4307		
3028 Tarpin, Jimmie				Dead		
3029 Tyner, Mollie	NCher	17	F	4229		
3030 Vann, Stephen	A Col	20	M	F847	No	Roustabout
3031 Vann, Sophrona	A Col	20	M	R1	No	
3032 Vann, James	A Col	5	F	Dead	No	
3033 Vann, Dank	A Col	28	M	F850	Yes	
3034 Vann, Chick	A Col	28	F	F850	Yes	
3035 Vann, Caroline	A Col	14	F	Dead	No	
3036 Vann, Lizzie	A Col	12	F	Dead	No	
3037 Vann, Ellen	A Col	7	F	F856	No	
3038 Vann, Ben	A Col	6	M	F851	No	
3039 Vann, Andy	A Col	1	M	Dead	No	
3040 Vann, George	A Col	30	M	F699	Yes	Farmer
3041 Vann, Susan	A Col	23	F	Dead	Yes	
3042 Vann, John	A Col	36	M	Dead	Yes	Farmer
3043 Vann, Sarah	A Col	25	F	F1047	Yes	Enrollment Refused R263
3044 Vann, George	A Col	5	M	F1050	No	
3045 Vann, Reed	A Col	1	M	F1047	No	Enrollment Refused R263
3046 Vann, Joe	A Col	3m	M	F1047	No	Enrollment Refused R263
3047 Vann, Gilbert	A Col	25	M	F991	Yes	Nothing
3048 Vann, Sophia	A Col	22	F	F764	Yes	
3049 Vann, Katie	A Col	45	F	Dead	Yes	Nothing
3050 Vann, Willie	A Col	16	M	Dead	Yes	
3051 Vann, Rachel	A Col	18	F	Dead	No	
3052 Vann, Jane	A Col	13	F	Dead	No	
3053 Vann, Mary	A Col	40	F	Dead	No	
3054 Vann, Susie	A Col	12	F	Dead	No	
3055 Vann, Eli	A Col	25	M	Dead	Yes	Nothing
3056 Vann, Pursonnet	A Col	23	F	Dead	Yes	
3057 Vann, Vie	A Col	10	F	F985	No	
3058 Vann, Lizzie	A Col	5	F	F986	No	
3059 Vann, Dave	A Col	7	M	F1009	No	
3060 Vann, Laura	A Col	2	F	F6594	No	
3061 Vann, Jesse	A Col	39	M	Dead	Yes	Farmer
3062 Vann, Cynthia	A Col	39	F	Dead	Yes	

Name	Race	Age	Sex	Census	Md	Remarks
3063 Vann, Susan	A Col	12	F	Dead	No	
3064 Vann, George	A Col	5	M	F998	No	
3065 Vann, Cora	A Col	2	F	Dead	No	
3066 Vann, Jennie	A Col	35	F	F664	No	
3067 Vann, Sam	A Col	49	M	Dead	Yes	Farmer
3068 Vann, Katie	A Col	39	F	F872	Yes	
3069 Vann, Joe	A Col	21	M	Dead	No	
3070 Vann, Amanda	A Col	9	F	F945	No	
3071 Vann, Willie	A Col	7	M	F944	No	
3072 Vann, Rosie	A Col	3	F	F1099	No	
3073 Vinitia, John	A Mex	40	M	Dead	Yes	Farmer
3074 Vinitia, Sallie	NCher	21	F	4437	Yes	
3075 Vinitia, Johney	NCher	2	M	5670	No	
3076 Vinitia, Albert	NCher	1	M	4437	No	
3077 Vinitia, Mariah	NCher	2w	F	Dead	No	
3078 Vann, David	A Col	30	M	Dead	Yes	Farmer
3079 Vann, Polly	A Col	36	F	F875	Yes	
3080 Vann, Eli	A Col	4	M	T941	No	
3081 Vann, Josh	A Col	2	M	F953	No	
3082 Vann, Louis	A Col	3m	M	F945	No	
3083 Vann, Edmond	A Col	36	M	F906	Yes	Farmer
3084 Vann, Dinah	A Col	40	F	F906	Yes	
3085 Vann, Sarah	A Col	13	F	F1049	No	
3086 Vann, James	A Col	10	M	Dead	No	
3087 Vann, Willie	A Col	11	M	Dead	No	
3088 Vann, Eddy	A Col	8	M	F172	No	
3089 Vann, Malinda	A Col	14	F	Dead	No	
3090 Vann, D W	NCher	35	M	2566	Yes	Farmer
3091 Vann, Clarinda	NCher	29	F	2566	Yes	
3092 Vann, Jennie	NCher	9	F	Dead	No	
3093 Vann, Joe	NCher	6	M	Dead	No	
3094 Vann, S M	NCher	7m	F	Dead	No	
3095 Vann, Alice	NCher	23	M	2723	Yes	Farmer
3096 Vann, Susan	NCher	5	F	2675	No	
3097 Vann, Reldy	A Col	30	F	Dead	No	
3098 Vann, Henry	A Col	10	M	F818	No	
3099 Vann, Stephen	NCher	19	M	6797	No	
3100 Vann, Joe	NCher	48	M	Dead	Yes	Farmer
3101 Vann, Martha	NCher	29	F	2770	Yes	
3102 Vann, James	NCher	19	M	2701	Yes	
3103 Vann, Joe Jr.	NCher	15	M	Dead	No	
3104 Vann, Ella	NCher	12	F	2433	No	

Name	Race	Age	Sex	Census	Md	Remarks
3105 Vann, Jesse	NCher	9	M	5071	No	
3106 Vann, Emma	NCher	7	F	2707	No	
3107 Vann, Sallie	NCher	85	F	Dead	No	Farmer
3108 Vann, Lucy	NCher	24	F	Dead	No	
3109 Vann, Jennie	A Col	25	F	FD794	No	Farmer
3110 Vann, Sarah E	A Col	5	F	FD1152	No	
3111 Vann, Arch Jr.	NCher	24	M	7665	No	
3112 Vann, Rutha	NCher	19	F	3877	No	
3113 Vann, Sarah	NCher	2m	F	3877	No	
3114 Vann, Dave	A Col	25	M	Dead	Yes	Farmer
3115 Vann, Mary	A Col	22	F	F649	Yes	
3116 Vann, Tildy	A Col	7	F	F901	No	
3117 Vann, Sam	A Col	5	M	FD1153	No	
3118 Vann, Lindsay	A Col	3	M	FD1154	No	
3119 Vann, July	A Col	1	M	F966	No	
3120 Vann, Johnson	A Col	40	M	F745	Yes	Johnson Vann was sold out of the Nation during the war, after the war he returned like a white man and obtained license and married his wife as required by law for a white man, Farmer
3121 Vann, Delilah	A Col	36	F	Dead	Yes	
3122 Vann, Lena	A Col	18	F	F248	No	
3123 Vann, Johnson Jr.	A Col	16	M	F844	No	
3124 Vann, Cora	A Col	11	F	F623	No	
3125 Vann, Upton	A Col	9	M	Dead	No	
3126 Vann, Henry	A Col	7	M	F970	No	
3127 Vann, Wed Hampton	A Col	3	M	Dead	No	
3128 Vann, Cunigam	A Col	1	M	F822	No	
3129 Vann, James	A Col	25	M	F865	No	
3130 Vann, Rosie	A Col	22	F	F668	No	
3131 Vann, Ben	A Col	23	M	F794	No	
3132 Vann, Wm Jr.	A Col	27	M	F657	Yes	
3133 Vann, Sarah	A Col	22	F	F657	Yes	
3134 Vann, Tildy	A Col	1	F	F778	No	
3135 Vann, Arch	NCher	69	M	Dead	No	Mechanic
3136 Vann, George	NCher	25	M	6925	No	
3137 Vann, Lem	NCher	12	M	Dead	No	
3138 Vann, Rhoda	NCher	9	F	5415	No	
3139 Vann, Henry	NCher	12	M	FD1155	No	
3140 Vann, J D	NCher	21	M	4915	No	
3141 Vann, Sissie	A Col	13	F	FD1156	No	
3142 Vann, Wm Jr.	A Col	8	M	FD1157	No	Dead

Name	Race	Age	Sex	Census	Md	Remarks
3143 Vann, Ed	A Col	6	M	FD1158	No	
3144 Vann, C E	NCher	13	M	Dead	No	
3145 Vann, Ben	A Col	23	M	F737	No	Farmer
3146 Ward, Bryant	NCher	62	M	Dead	No	Farmer
3147 Ward, Ester	NCher	21	F	5439	No	
3148 Ward, Neal	NCher	20	M	4921	No	
3149 Wilson, Albers	NCher	23	M	D766	Yes	Nothing
3150 Wilson, Mary	NCher	18	F	D491	Yes	
3151 Whitmire, Lewis	A Col	38	M	F879	Yes	Farmer
3152 Whitmire, Betsy	A Col	35	F	F879	Yes	
3153 Whitmire, Nathan	A Col	18	M	F1117	No	
3154 Whitmire, Peggy	A Col	11	F	F880	No	
3155 Whitmire, Jesse W	A Col	9	M	F905	No	
3156 Whitmire, Jenny	A Col	8	F	F884	No	
3157 Whitmire, Josie	A Col	5	F	F883	No	
3158 Whitmire, Willie	A Col	3	M	F967	No	
3159 Whitmire, Aaron Jr.	A Col	17m	M	F903	No	
3160 White, David	AShaw	40	M	Dead	Yes	Nothing
3161 White, Peggy	AShaw	30	F	Dead	Yes	
3162 Winpedler, George	AWhite	30	M	Dead	Yes	Nothing
3163 Winpedler, Ellen	NCher	22	F	1100	Yes	
3164 Winpedler, Hattie	NCher	4	F	1101	No	
3165 Winpedler, Lydia M	NCher	19m	F	Dead	No	
3166 Williamson, G W	AWhite	46	M	D1555	Yes	Married out, Nothing
3167 Williamson, Lizzie	NCher	19	F	Dead	Yes	
3168 Williamson, Mackalone	NCher	2m	F	3802	No	
3169 White, Minnie	AShaw	12	F	D1557	No	
3170 Wolfe, Lizzie	NCher	22	F	Dead	No	
3171 Walker, George W	NCher	30	M	3933	Yes	Farmer
3172 Walker, Mary J	AWhite	29	F	3933	Yes	
3173 Walker, Dan'l H	NCher	11	M	3637	No	
3174 Walker, James	NCher	3	M	4557	No	
3175 Walker, Rosy	NCher	1	F	3991	No	
3176 Walker, Mary	NCher	6	F	3934	No	
3177 Whitmire, Moses	NCher	30	M	Dead	Yes	Farmer
3178 Whitmire, Mariah	A Col	26	F	F857	Yes	
3179 Whitmire, Johnson	A Col	15	M	Dead	No	
3180 Whitmire, Segal	A Col	14	M	F863	No	
3181 Whitmire, Susan	A Col	9	F	F858	No	
3182 Whitmire, Birthie	A Col	7	F	F1081	No	
3183 Whitmire, Eliza	A Col	5	F	F859	No	
3184 Whitmire, Gettie	A Col	3	M	F1082	No	

Name	Race	Age	Sex	Census	Md	Remarks
3185 Whitmire, Minnie	A Col	2	F	Dead	No	
3186 Whitmire, Willie	A Col	4m	M	F861	No	
3187 Whitmire, Dick	A Col	56	M	Dead	Yes	Farmer
3188 Whitmire, Hannah	A Col	20	F	Dead	Yes	
3189 Whitmire, Becky	A Col	7	F	Dead	No	
3190 Whitmire, Mattie	A Col	3	F	Dead	No	
3191 Whitmire, Margaret	A Col	2	F	FD1159	No	
3192 Wren, Widow	A Del	80	F	Dead	No	Nothing
3193 Whitmire, Dennis	A Col	30	M	F975	Yes	Farmer
3194 Whitmire, Lucy	A Col	25	F	Dead	Yes	
3195 Whitmire, Joe	A Col	6	M	F852	No	
3196 Whitmire, L J	A Col	5	F	F976	No	
3197 Whitmire, Nelson	A Col	46	M	Dead	Yes	Farmer
3198 Whitmire, Lizzie	A Col	45	F	F902	Yes	
3199 Whitmire, Tom	A Col	2	M	F974	No	
3200 Whitmire, Dick Jr.	A Col	29	M	F1060	No	
3201 Whitmire, Betsy	A Col	59	F	Dead	No	Nothing
3202 Whitmire, Looney	A Col	22	M	F937	No	
3203 Whitmire, Mary	A Col	33	F	F937	No	
3204 Whitmire, Maggie	A Col	2	F	F973	No	
3205 Whitmire, Josie	A Col	5	F	F968	No	
3206 Whitmire, Mose Sr.	A Col	50	M	F972	Yes	Farmer
3207 Whitmire, Kate	A Col	40	F	Dead	Yes	
3208 Whitmire, Dave	A Col	2	M	F1085	No	
3209 Whitmire, Aaron	A Col	45	M	F718	Yes	Farmer
3210 Whitmire, Ann	A Col	40	F	FD432	Yes	
3211 Whitmire, Mose	A Col	33	M	Dead	No	
3212 Whitmire, Nelson	A Col	16	M	Dead	No	Nelson Grimmet instead of Whitmire
3213 Whitmire, Ellen	A Col	14	F	Dead	No	
3214 Whitmire, Mattie	A Col	12	F	F920	No	
3215 Whitmire, Charles	A Col	10	M	Dead	No	
3216 Whitmire, Sarah	A Col	8	F	F921	No	
3217 Whitmire, Rachel	A Col	25	F	Dead	Yes	Farmer
3218 Whitmire, Georgia	A Col	3	M	9783	No	
3219 Whitmire, Jack	A Col	1	M	FD1160	No	
3220 White, Jack	AShaw	37	M	Dead	Yes	Nothing
3221 White, Nancy	AShaw	38	F	3178	No	daughter of widow White
3222 White, Beckey	AShaw	2	F	Dead	No	
3223 White, Rosie	AShaw	1	F	3982	No	
3224 Wilson, Willie	A Del	30	M	Dead	No	Farmer
3225 Webber, Hannah	A Del	37	F	Del292	No	

Name	Race	Age	Sex	Census	Md	Remarks
3226 Williams, Francis	A Col	40	F	F836	No	
3227 Williams, Nancy	A Col	20	F	F840	No	
3228 Williams, Julia	A Col	8	F	F1036	No	
3229 Williams, Alice	A Col	6	F	F1037	No	
3230 Williams, George	A Col	4	M	F909	No	
3231 Williams, Amanda	A Col	1	F	F038	No	
3232 Wilson, Joshua	A Del	40	M	Del340	Yes	Nothing
3233 Wilson, Mary	A Del	30	F	Dead	Yes	
3234 Wilson, Lizzie	A Del	10	F	Dead	No	
3235 Winblow, John	A Del	32	M	Dead	Yes	Farmer
3236 Winblow, Susan	A Del	26	F	Dead	Yes	
3237 Winblow, James	A Del	6	M	Del191	No	
3238 White, Mary	A Del	30	F	Del93	No	
3239 White, Eugene	A Del	30	M	Del175	Yes	Nothing
3240 White, Mary Jane	A Del	25	F	Dead	Yes	
3241 Washington, Charles	A Del	29	M	Dead	Yes	Farmer
3242 Washington, Noah Bettie	A Del	26	M	Del262	Yes	
3243 Washington, George	NCher	26	M	Del198	No	
3244 Wahlookie, Lizzie	NCher	20	F	Dead	No	
3245 Wahlookie, Ukie	NCher	6	F	Dead	No	
3246 Wahlookie, Daniel	NCher	6m	M	Dead	No	
3247 Wilson, Mary	A Del	23	F	Dead	No	
3248 WhiteTurkey, Mrs. Widow	A Del	46	F	Del185	No	
3249 White Turkey, Dutch	A Del	22	M	Del168	No	
3250 White Turkey, Sam	A Del	20	M	Del192	No	
3251 White Turkey, Liender	A Del	21	F	Dead	No	
3252 White Turkey, Robt	A Del	19	M	Del118	No	
3253 White Turkey, Katie	A Del	18	F	Del209	No	
3254 White Turkey, Albert	A Del	12	M	Del89	No	
3255 White Turkey, Willis	A Del	10	M	Del186	No	
3256 White Turkey, Lelie	A Del	8	F	Del103	No	
3257 Wilson, George	A Del	80	M	Dead	Yes	
3258 Wilson, Nancy	A Del	39	F	Del2	Yes	
3259 Wilson, Mary	A Del	19	F	Dead	No	
3260 Wilson, Lucy	A Del	2	F	Del200	No	
3261 Wilson, Lizzie	A Del	25	F	DLD37	No	
3262 Wilson, Young John	A Del	6	M	DLD38	No	
3263 Walker, Thomas	A Del	30	M	Dead	Yes	Farmer
3264 Walker, Jennie	A Del	20	F	Dead	Yes	
3265 Walker, Mary	A Del	3	F	Del210	No	
3266 Walker, Wm	A Del	2m	M	Del332	No	
3267 White, Widow	A Del	45	F	Dead	No	

Name	Race	Age	Sex	Census	Md	Remarks
3268 Wilson, Joe	A Del	18	M	Dead	No	
3269 Wilson, Wm	A Del	13	M	Del184	No	
3270 White, Wm	A Del	13	M	Del160	No	
3271 Wilson, George	A Del	23	M	Dead	Yes	Fiddler
3272 Wilson, Mrs. George	A Del	20	F	Dead	Yes	
3273 Wilson, John H	A Del	6m	M	DLD39	No	
3274 Woodie, Jennie	A Del	30	F	4199	No	
3275 Wilson, Sam'l	A Del	30	M	Del77	Yes	Farmer
3276 Wilson, Mrs. Sam	A Del	33	F	Del77	Yes	
3277 Wilson, Wetahloquah	A Del	7	F	Del178	No	
3278 Wilson, Lilley	A Del	6	F	Del82	No	
3279 Wilson, George	A Del	3	M	Del147	No	
3280 Wilson, Mack	A Del	1	M	Del72	No	
3281 White Feather, Frank	A Del	25	M	Dead	No	Farmer
3282 White Feather, Old Widow	A Del	50	F	Dead	No	
3283 White Feather, Charlie	A Del	15	M	4639	No	
3284 White Feather, Nancy	A Del	7	F	Dead	No	
3285 White Feather, Almenow	A Del	5	F	Dead	No	
3286 Wells, Randolph	AShaw	35	M	4397	Yes	Stockman
3287 Wells, July	AShaw	27	M	4397	Yes	
3288 Wells, Jonah	AShaw	7	M	43696	No	
3289 Wells, Wah	AShaw	19	M	2836	No	
3290 Wells, Fred	AShaw	2	M	4551	No	
3291 Willie, John	AShaw	30	M	Del302	No	Farmer
3292 Wilson, Haven	A Del	28	M	Dead	No	Roustabout
3293 Wilson, Lucinda	A Col	70	F	Dead	No	
3294 Wilson, James	A Del	54	M	Del144	No	Preacher
3295 Wilson, Lizzie	A Del	16	F	Dead	No	
3296 Wilson, Rosie	A Del	10	F	5158	No	
3297 Wilson, Cun	A Del	5	M	Del176	No	
3298 Wilson, Horace	A Del	2	M	Dead	No	
3299 Wheeler, Jack	A Del	49	M	Dead	Yes	Hunter
3300 Wheeler, Mary	A Del	30	F	Dead	Yes	
3301 Wheeler, Robert	A Del	14	M	Del156	No	
3302 Wheeler, Anna	A Del	13	F	Del188	No	
3303 Wheeler, John	A Del	6	M	Del359	No	
3304 Wheeler, Cataline	A Del	3	M	Del186	No	
3305 Wheeler, Jacob	A Del	19	M	Dead	Yes	Skiver
3306 Wheeler, Amanda	NCher	16	F	DLD40	Yes	
3307 Wilson, Ice	A Del	30	M	Dead	Yes	Farmer
3308 Wilson, Lattie	A Del	33	F	Dead	Yes	
3309 Wilson, Reed	A Del	4	M	Del398	No	

	Name	Race	Age	Sex	Census	Md	Remarks
3310	Wilson, Anna	A Del	2	F	Del110	No	
3311	Williams, Peter	A Col	70	M	F703	Yes	Farmer
3312	Williams, Judy	A Col	65	F	Dead	Yes	
3313	Williams, Rosie	A Col	26	F	F704	No	
3313a	Williams, Perry	A Col	6	M			Dup of 2511 Coo Dist
3313b	Williams, Seely	A Col	4	F			Dup of 2512 Coo Dist
3314	Williams, Amanda	A Col	39	F	FD98	No	
3315	Williams, Joanna	A Col	14	F	F841	No	
3316	Wagon, Mrs.	A Del	50	F	Del80	No	
3317	Wagon, Joe	A Del	23	M	Dead	No	
3318	Wagon, Lelie	A Del	19	F	Dead	No	
3319	Wilson, George	A Del	18	M	Dead	No	
3320	Wilson, Joseph	A Del	17	M	Dead	No	
3321	Wing, J	AWhite	60	M	Dead	Yes	Farmer
3322	Wing, Margaret	NCher	28	F	4352	Yes	
3323	Wing, Minnie	NCher	3	F	4504	No	
3324	Wing, Vic	NCher	1	M	4404	No	
3325	Wing, Victor	NCher	1	M	Dead	No	
3326	Wilson, Tom	A Del	38	M	Del343	No	
3327	Wilson, Mrs. Tom	A Del	30	F	Del343	No	
3328	Wilson, (infant)	A Del	3ds	M	Del343	No	
3329	Wilson, Mary	A Del	40	F	Dead	Yes	
3330	Wilson, Adam	A Murs	36	M	Del368	Yes	Preacher
3331	Wilson, Mary Jr.	A Del	16	F	Dead	No	
3332	Walker, Wm	NCher	29	M	4392	Yes	Farmer
3333	Walker, Georgia A	AWhite	17	F	4392	Yes	
3334	Walker, C F	AWhite	35	M	D1556	No	Married out, Doctor
3335	Walker, Joe E	NCher	28	F	Dead	Yes	
3336	Walker, Carrie	NCher	4	F	2423	No	
3337	Walker, William	NCher	3	M	4940	No	
3338	Wright, Isaac	A Col	18	M	Dead	No	None
3339	Wilson, James	NCher	24	M	1151	Yes	
3340	Wilson, Minty	AWhite	21	F	1151	Yes	
3341	Wilson, Frank	NCher	3	M	Dead	No	
3342	Wilson, Jesse	NCher	3m	M	1144	No	
3343	Wright, Wm W	NCher	22	M	4702	No	
3344	Wright, Elis B	NCher	25	M	2691	No	
3345	Whirlwind, Sam	NCher	29	M	Dead	Yes	Farmer
3346	Whirlwind, Kate	NCher	24	F	Dead	Yes	
3347	Whirlwind, Arch	NCher	4	M	Dead	No	
3348	Whirlwind, George	NCher	2	M	Dead	No	
3349	Whirlwind, Lydia	NCher	2m	F	5491	No	

Name	Race	Age	Sex	Census	Md	Remarks
3350 Wolfe, Foster	NCher	10	M	3889	No	Stepson name Wolf
3351 Ward, T F	NCher	30	M	4832	Yes	
3352 Ward, Lizzie	NCher	21	F	4832	Yes	Adopted White (BLB)
3353 Ward, Wm	NCher	6	M	4963	No	
3354 Ward, Moses	NCher	4	M	5117	No	
3355 Ward, Cora	NCher	1	F	Dead	No	
3356 Ward, C D	NCher	26	M	4929	No	
3357 Williams, Harrison	NCher	36	M	5475	Yes	Farmer
3358 Williams, Kate	NCher	36	F	Dead	Yes	
3359 Williams, Jack	NCher	18	M	5638	No	
3360 Williams, George	NCher	14	M	5433	No	
3361 Williams, Lucy	NCher	12	F	Dead	No	
3362 Williams, T	NCher	10	M	Dead	No	
3363 Williams, Josie	NCher	8	F	Dead	No	
3364 Worford, John	NCher	42	M	Dead	Yes	Farmer
3365 Worford, Jennie	AWhite	38	F	Dead	Yes	
3366 Worford, James M	NCher	12	M	4722	No	
3367 Worford, Joe V	NCher	10	M	5101	No	
3368 Worford, Wm McCracken	NCher	5	M	4812	No	
3369 Worford, Belford W	NCher	3	M	4742	No	
3370 Worford, Dora McCracken	NCher	1m	F	4733	No	
3371 Whitewater,	NCher	19	M	5232	No	Tramp (On Dawes as Whitewater Tassel BLB)
3372 Wilson, Wm	NCher	18	M	Dead	No	
3373 White, Washington	AShaw	23	M	Dead	No	
3374 White, Lucinda	AShaw	4	F	Dead	No	
3375 Walker, Cora	AShaw	3m	F	Dead	No	
3376 Walker, James	AShaw	40	M	4353	Yes	Farmer
3377 Walker, Susan	AShaw	40	F	Dead	Yes	
3378 Walker, Nannie	AShaw	11	F	Dead	No	
3379 Washington, James	AShaw	50	M	Dead	No	
3380 Ward, Jasper	NCher	31	M	4657	No	
3381 Wilkerson, John	NCher	32	M	4675	No	
3382 Wilkerson, Sis	NCher	22	F	Dead	No	
3383 Wilkerson, Jack	NCher	6	M	Dead	No	
3384 Wilkerson, Tom	NCher	3	M	Dead	No	
3385 Wilkerson, Lewis	NCher	8m	M	4737	No	
3386 White, Tom	AShaw	35	M	Dead	Yes	Farmer
3387 White, Nancy	AShaw	39	F	3988	Yes	
3388 White, Reuben	AShaw	13	M	4292	No	
3389 White, Peter	AShaw	2	M	4068	No	
3390 White, Joe V	AShaw	21	M	5648	No	

Name	Race	Age	Sex	Census	Md	Remarks
3391 Walker, Daniel	A Col	30	M	F1091	Yes	Cow Driver
3392 Walker, Aggy	A Col	18	F	F1091	Yes	
3393 Walker, Charlotte	A Col	1d	F	F1095	No	
3394 Woodruff, J M	AWhite	59	M	Dead	Yes	Blacksmith
3395 Woodruff, Malinda	NCher	49	F	Dead	Yes	
3396 Williams, George	AShaw	40	M	Dead	Yes	Digger
3397 Williams, Martha	AShaw	40	F	Dead	Yes	
3398 Williams, George Jr.	AShaw	17	M	3182	No	Dup 2822 Del Dist
3399 Williams, Thos W	AShaw	9	M	5569	No	
3400 Whitmire, Martha	NCher	23	F	2974	No	
3401 Walkingstick, Peggy	NCher	30	F	2427	No	
3402 Walkingstick, Nannie	NCher	13	F	5185	No	
3403 Walkingstick, Charlie	NCher	13	M	Dead	No	
3404 Writer, Mrs. (widow)	NCher	43	F	8860	No	Wife of Dick Duck
3405 Writer, Jesse	NCher	14	M	Dead	No	
3406 Writer, Jennie	NCher	11	F	7241	No	
3407 Writer, Thomas	NCher	8	M	Dead	No	
3408 Writer, Joe V	NCher	6	M	Dead	No	
3409 Writer, Nancy	NCher	6	F	Dead	No	
3410 Writer, James	NCher	4	M	Dead	No	
3411 Wich, William	NCher	45	M	Dead		
3412 Webber, Rosie	A Col	45	F	Dead	Yes	Farmer
3413 Webber, Johnie	A Col	10	M	Dead	No	
3414 Webber, Ellen	A Col	5	F	F477	No	
3415 Wyska,	NCher	20	M	Dead	Yes	
3416 Wyska, Kate	NCher	19	F	5671	Yes	
3417 Watt, Sallie	NCher	27	F	Dead	No	
3418 Watt, Charlie	NCher	3	M	4685	No	
3419 Ward, James	NCher	19	M	6466	No	
3420 Washington, Thomas Sr	AShaw	42	M	Dead	Yes	Farmer
3421 Washington, Mrs. Thomas	AShaw	30	F	4278	Yes	
3422 Washington, Sallie	AShaw	22	F	Dead	No	
3423 Washington, Lizzie	AShaw	16	F	Dead	No	
3424 Washington, Lydia	AShaw	13	F	Dead	No	
3425 Walker, Sam Sr.	AShaw	35	M	Dead	Yes	Farmer
3426 Walker, Nancy	AShaw	16	F	Dead	Yes	
3427 Walker, John	AShaw	28	M	Del185	Yes	
3428 Walker, Mary	AShaw	17	F	4086	Yes	
3429 Walker, Mrs. Nancy	AShaw	16	F	D1559	No	
3430 Walker, Sam Jr.	AShaw	7m	M	Dead	No	
3431 White Feather, Sallie A	AShaw	26	F	Dead	No	
3432 White Feather, Jane	AShaw	3	F	3482	No	

Cooweescoowee District

Name	Race	Age	Sex	Census	Md	Remarks
3433 Wright, Nancy	AShaw	35	F	3234	Yes	
3434 Wright, Sarah M	AShaw	3w	F	3181	No	
3435 Wright, G W	AShaw	3w	M	Dead	No	
3436 Wiley,	NCher	25	M	Dead	Yes	
3437 Wiley, Martha	NCher	20	F	Dead	Yes	
3438 Wolf, Dennis	NCher	24	M	Dead	Yes	Carpenter
3439 Wolf, Deaka	NCher	20	F	Dead	Yes	
3440 Wolf, Susie	NCher	1	F	Dead	No	
3441 Writer, John	NCher	32	M	Dead	Yes	Farmer
3442 Writer, Sallie	NCher	30	F	Dead	Yes	
3443 Writer, Squash	NCher	7	M	Dead	No	
3444 Writer, Becky	NCher	1	F	Dead	No	
3445 Walkley, Wm	AWhite	43	M	Dead	Yes	Mason
3446 Walkley, Alcy J	NCher	27	F	4714	Yes	
3447 Walkley, George	NCher	12	M	4695	No	
3448 Walkley, Henry	NCher	5	M	4741	No	
3449 Walkley, S C	NCher	3	F	4719	No	
3450 Wayburn, W L	NCher	23	M	10242	Yes	
3451 Wayburn, C P	NCher	33	F	2510	Yes	
3452 Wayburn, R W	NCher	2	M	9541	No	
3453 Wayburn, Ada	NCher	1	F	2521	No	
3454 Whirlwind, Ticumseh	NCher	26	M	Dead	No	Farmer
3455 Wind, Anna W	NCher	50	F	Dead	No	
3456 Wind, Lewis W	NCher	14	M	5149	No	
3457 Wolf, Lewis	NCher	32	M	2434	Yes	Farmer
3458 Wolf, Ellen	NCher	25	F	Dead	Yes	
3459 Wright, T B	NCher	29	M	Dead	No	Lawyer
3460 Wood, A J	NCher	30	F	Dead	Yes	
3461 Woods, Geo	NCher	6	M	D524	No	Transferred to census card 10059 (BLB)
3462 Woods, W E	NCher	9	M	2550	No	
3463 Ward, John	NCher	59	M	Dead	Yes	Farmer
3464 Ward, Jane	NCher	35	F	Dead	Yes	
3465 Ward, Susie	NCher	14	F	Dead	No	
3466 Ward, Maggie	NCher	12	F	2631	No	
3467 Ward, Delvia	NCher	11	F	5304	No	
3468 Ward, Joel	NCher	7	M	6484	No	
3469 Ward, Vie	NCher	5	M	2811	No	
3470 Ward, J T N	NCher	3	M	Dead	No	
3471 Wolfe,	A Mex	36	M	Dead	Yes	Hog man
3472 Wolfe, Susie	NCher	36	F	Dead	Yes	
3473 Wolfe, French	NCher	18	M	Dead	No	

Name	Race	Age	Sex	Census	Md	Remarks
3474 Wolfe, Sophy	NCher	15	F	Dead	No	
3475 Wilson, French	A Del	34	M	Dead	Yes	Tramp
3476 Wilson, Mary	A Del	33	F	Del126	Yes	
3477 Walker, Marriah	A Del	25	F	Dead	No	
3478 Walker, Mary	NCher	5	F	Dead	No	
3479 Ward, Will	NCher	18	M	3516	No	
3480 Wilson, Ellen	NCher	7	F	D1560	No	
3481 West, Hessie	NCher	32	F	3578	No	
3482 West, Anna W	NCher	8	F	3834	No	
3483 West, Jesse	NCher	11	M	3732	No	
3484 Williams.Lucy	NCher	30	F	Dead	No	
3485 Winddaalaquah,	NCher	30	M	Del11	No	Farmer
3486 Wechelaquah,	A Del	26	F	Dead	No	
3487 Warlookee,	A Del	2m	M	Dead	No	
3488 Wiskepake,	A Del	19	F	Del78	No	
3489 Wright, Widow'd	A Del	30	M	Del253	No	
3490 Wilson, L W	NCher	12	M	D1561	No	
3491 Webber, Samuel	A Col	34	M	F1132	Yes	Farmer
3492 Webber, Sarah	A Col	24	F	F1132	Yes	
3493 Webber, Nancy	A Col	11	F	Dead	No	
3494 Webber, Lewis	A Col	9	M	Dead	No	
3495 Webber, Aaron	A Col	6	M	F1058	No	
3496 Webber, Manerva	A Col	4	F	F1066	No	
3497 Webber, Davis	A Col	18m	F	Dead	No	
3498 Webber, David	A Col	18m	M	F1127	No	
3499 Wolf, Abby	A Col	15	F	Dead	No	
3500 Wolf, Nancy	A Col	11	F	Dead	No	
3501 Wilson, Annice T	NCher	19	M	Dead	No	
3502 Williams.Bettie	A Col	18	F	Dead	No	
3503 Warford, Charlie	NCher	5	F	6834	No	
3504 Wolf, Henry	A Del	20	M	Del72	No	Hunter
3505 Williams.Thomas	NCher	3	M	6148	No	
3506 Washington, George	AShaw	35	M	3465	No	
3507 Williams.John	A Del	20	M	Dead	No	
3508 Washington, Anna	AShaw	25	F	Dead	No	
3509 Williams.Jane	NCher	66	F	Dead	No	
3510 Williams.Lucy	NCher	24	F	Dead	No	
3511 Williams.Alf	NCher	11	M	F1181	No	
3512 Wilson, Mary	NCher	23	F	Dead	No	
3513 Wind, Big	NCher	30	M	Dead	No	
3514 Wilson, Ephamanoquah	NCher	40	F	Del130	No	
3515 Wilson, James	NCher	8	M	Del139		Dup 958 Coo Dist

Cooweescoowee District

Name	Race	Age	Sex	Census	Md	Remarks
3516 Wilson, Deck	NCher	6	M	Del113		
3517 Wilson, Martin	NCher		M	Dead		
3518 Wilson, Lucinda	NCher		M	Dead		
3519 Wilson, Susan	NCher		M	F961		
3520 Whitmire, Mike			M	Dead		
3521 Whitmire, Harriet			F	FD1162		
3522 Whitmire, Levi			M	FD1163		
3523 Whitmire, Marshall			M	FD1164		
3524 Wear, Sue	NCher	32	F	2624		
3525 Williams.Leonard			M	2742		
3526 Williams.Sarah			F	Dead		
3527 Williams.L B				Dead		
3528 Yellowjacket, John	NCher	21	M	Del149	No	
3529 Young, John Sr	A Del	36	M	Del74	Yes	Farmer
3530 Young, Eley T	A Del	19	F	Del74	Yes	
3531 Young, Edmund	A Del	1	M	Del122	No	
3532 Young, Old Mrs.	A Del	71	F	Dead	No	
3533 Yearbob, Alex	NCher	25	M	2450	Yes	Farmer
3534 Yearbob, Jane	NCher	25	F	Dead	Yes	
3535 Yearbob, George	NCher	1	M	7375	No	
3536 Yellowleaf, Sarah	A Del	29	F	Del224	No	
3537 Zanes, Jeff	A Del	41	M	4462	Yes	
3538 Zanes, Matilda	A Del	26	F	Del232	Yes	
3539 Zanes, Mary	A Del	6	F	Del264	No	
3540 Zanes, Lillie	A Del	9	F	Del42	No	
3541 Ziegler, Henry	A Del	36	M	Del279	Yes	Farmer
3542 Ziegler, Mrs.	A Creek	22	F	Dead	Yes	

	Name	Race	Age	Sex	Census	Md	Remarks
1	Angel, Thomas	A White	27	M	Dead	Yes	This man claims citizenship says he is from Sequoyah Dist his wife name Sharp, Farmer
2	Angel, Rebecca	N cher	23	F	178	Yes	
3	Angel, Ida	N cher	3m	F	178	No	
4	Allen, John Thos	A White	30	M	Dead	Yes	
5	Allen, Sarah	N cher	27	F	1456	Yes	
6	Allen, George W	N cher	4	M	1572	No	
7	Allen, Layfayette M	N cher	2	M	1454	No	
8	Allen, Emily B	N cher	6m	F	1528	No	
9	Allen, F G	A White	37	M	Dead	Yes	
10	Allen, Sarah E	A shaw	30	F	3563	No	
11	Aleck, Caroline	A shaw	7	F	Dead	No	
12	Aleck, Henry	A shaw	43	M	5649	Yes	
13	Aleck, Phebe	A shaw	28	F	Dead	Yes	
14	Aleck, Benjamin	N cher	2	M	5649	No	
15	Akin, James H	A White	29	M	D520	Yes	
16	Akin, Fannie C	N cher	23	F	3596	Yes	
17	Akin, Reubin L	N cher	4	M	3685	No	
18	Adin, Willie	N cher	2	M	3765	No	
19	Annie	N cher	60	F	Dead	No	
20	Aleck, James	N cher	27	M	8388	Yes	
21	Aleck, Nelly	N cher	23	F	8388	Yes	
22	Aleck, Nannie	N cher	4m	F	8388	No	
23	Ainsey,	N cher	55	F	Dead	No	
24	Aleck, Thomas	N cher	25	M	3653	Yes	
25	Aleck, Ailsey	N cher	30	F	3653	Yes	
26	Aleck, Chuco-na	N cher	1	F	Dead	No	
27	Ailsey	N cher	80	F	Dead	No	
28	Adair, Squire	A col	60	M	Dead	Yes	Farmer
29	Adair, Eliza	A col	29	F	Dead	Yes	
30	Ainsey,	N cher	18	F	Dead	No	
31	Ailsey,	N cher	2m	F	Dead	No	
32	Armstrong, P F	A White	28	M	D1582	No	Left Country 16 years ago
33	Armstrong, Darcus	N cher	27	F	Dead	Yes	
34	Armstrong, Thos F	N cher	4	M	7025	No	
35	Armstrong, Albert	N cher	2	M	Dead	No	
36	Ah-mer-su-yah,	N cher	24	M	Dead	Yes	
37	Ah-mer-su-yah, Kulst-iah	N cher	20	F	8965	No	
38	Adair, Mattie	N cher	14	F	3454	No	Correct census number 3464 (BLB)
38	Armstrong, Geo A	A White	33	M	4022	Yes	
39	Armstrong, Panola	A shaw	22	F	Dead	Yes	

Name	Race	Age	Sex	Census	Md	Remarks
40 Armstrong, Richard	A shaw	5	M	3037	No	
41 Armstrong, Jennie	A shaw	2	F	3973	No	
42 Armstrong, Sophia	A del	16	F	Del 116	No	
43 Adam, Cora	N col	20	F	Dead	No	A daughter of Ruben Downing citizen under the Treaty of 1866
44 Adam, Frank	N col	9	M	Dead	No	
45 Adam, Grace	N col	5	F	F919	No	
46 Adam, Ida	N col	3	F	F786	No	
47 Adam, Squire	N col	15m	M	F979	No	
48 Adam, Grant	N col	1m	M	Dead	No	
49 Armstrong, Ferndades	A del	21	M	Dead	No	Farmer
50 Angel, Wm	AWhite	29	M	178	No	
51 Awy	N cher	18	F	Dead	No	
52 Awa	N cher	31	F	Dead	No	
53 Alexander, Elmer,	N cher	10	M	2970	No	
54 Agent,	N cher	26	M	D1563	No	
55 Arthur, Surbina	N cher	13	F	D1564	No	Not found on Original Census rolls
56 Adam,	N cher	9	M	Dead	No	
57 Allen, C H	AWhite	46	M	6343	Yes	
58 Allen, Nancy A	N cher	40	F	6343	Yes	
59 Allen, Henry F	N cher	18	M	5081	No	
60 Allen, Charley W	N cher	16	M	7425	No	
61 Allen, John D	N cher	14	M	Dead	No	
62 Allen, Lewis B	N cher	12	M	6371	No	
63 Allen, Alferetta	N cher	10	F	4694	No	
64 Allen, Mikeral	N cher	8	M	8807	No	
65 Allen, Cora A	N cher	4	F	5700	No	
66 Allen, Oscar	N cher	2	M	6372	No	
67 Agin,	N cher	3	F	D1565	No	
68 Authar, Sabina	N cher	73	F	Dead	Yes	
69 Alex, Jones	N cher	9	M	D3173	No	
70 Anderson, Wm	N cher	10	M	6950	No	
71 Anderson, Cleopatra	N cher	9	F	339	No	
72 Ah-me-ta,				2465	No	
73 Beamer, Lucy	N cher	30	F	Dead	No	
74 Beamer, Aisey	N cher	13	F	Dead	No	
75 Beamer, Oo-yos-tah	N cher	8	F	7501	No	
76 Blevins, Jackson	AWhite	47	M	Dead	Yes	Farmer
77 Blevins, Nancy	N cher	23	F	3022	Yes	
78 Blevins, Jeff	N cher	7	M	3859	No	
79 Blevins, Ross	N cher	5	M	3754	No	
80 Blevins, Augusta	N cher	1	F	3645	No	

Name	Race	Age	Sex	Census	Md	Remarks
81 Blevins, Birl	AWhite	40	M	Dead	Yes	
82 Blevins, Sarah	N cher	23	F	6842	Yes	
83 Blevins, Joseph	N cher	11	M	6541	No	
84 Blevins, Pleasant	N cher	7	M	7479	No	
85 Blevins, Calvin T	N cher	3	M	Dead	No	
86 Blevins, Geo W	N cher	1	M	6543	No	
87 Byers, John Evart	N cher	6	M	D1566	No	Dead
88 Bates, John L	AWhite	20	M	_55	Yes	Farmer (first number on census card, unreadable (BLB)
89 Bates, Pauline	N cher	22	F	197	Yes	
90 Bates, Charles	N cher	4m	M	197	No	
91 Browning, Roberts	AWhite	33	M	Dead	Yes	
92 Browning, Mary	N cher	24	F	3628	No	
93 Blevins, Leroy	N cher	19	M	2987	Yes	
94 Blevins, Louisa	AWhite	19	F	D1567	Yes	Married out
95 Ballard, Randolph	N cher	26	M	3523	Yes	
96 Ballard, Minnie	N cher	26	F	3523	Yes	
97 Ballard, Fannie	N cher	6	F	3005	No	
98 Ballard, Archibald	N cher	2	M	3699	No	
99 Ballard, Roberts	N cher	1m	M	3523	No	
100 Ballard, Anna	N cher	48	F	Dead	No	
101 Ballard, Martha	N cher	22	F	4079	No	Martha Grazier on 83 census roll
102 Ballard, Thos	N cher	20	M	3617	No	
103 Ballard, Susan	N cher	10	F	2821	No	
104 Ballard, Wm	N cher	27	M	139	Yes	
105 Ballard, Charlotte	N cher	28	F	139	Yes	
106 Ballard, Jane Anna	N cher	5	F	139	No	
107 Ballard, Anna	N cher	2	F	139	No	
108 Ballard, Lucinda	N cher	10m	F	139	No	
109 Blalock, Henry	N cher	37	M	Dead	Yes	
110 Blalock, Nancy	AWhite	19	F	D1568	No	
111 Blalock, Gano	N cher	11	M	Dead	No	
112 Blalock, Charley	N cher	9	M	D394	No	
113 Beck, Sut	N cher	33	M	Dead	Yes	Farmer
114 Beck, Susan E	N cher	24	F	4160	Yes	
115 Beck, Wm A	N cher	4	M	3006	No	
116 Beck, Beula	N cher	6m	F	Dead	No	
117 Burns, Joseph M	AWhite	32	M	Dead	Yes	This family located in Coo Dist
118 Burns, Victoria	N cher	31	F	Dead	Yes	
119 Burns, Bernard D	N cher	9m	M	3035	No	
120 Bluejacket, Emma	A shaw	24	F	3383	No	
121 BerryMartin	AWhite	50	M	45	No	

Name	Race	Age	Sex	Census	Md	Remarks
122 BerryEliha C	N cher	20	F	57	No	
123 BerryAmos Ehie	N cher	16	M	56	No	
124 Breedlove, Napoleon B	AWhite	54	M	158	Yes	There are 55 acres of cotton given in that is in Sequoyah Dist
125 Breedlove, Emily W	N cher	43	F	158	Yes	
126 Breedlove, Lelia	N cher	20	F	Dead	No	
127 Breedlove, Walter	N cher	19	M	1911	No	
128 Breedlove, Emily M	N cher	16	F	Dead	No	
129 Breedlove, Florence	N cher	10	F	1061	No	
130 Breedlove, Jennie	N cher	7	F	Dead	No	
131 Barnet, Elsora	N cher	14	F	3909	No	
132 Barnet, Frank	N cher	11	M	135	No	
133 Barnet, Edward	N cher	8	M	196	No	
134 Bird, Osborn	AWhite	33	M	3866	Yes	
135 Bird, Julia	N cher	32	F	Dead	Yes	
136 Bird, Bettie	N cher	5	F	3878	No	
137 Bird, Dimaria	N cher	3	M	4154	No	
138 Bird, Decater F	N cher	1	F	4089	No	
139 Boyle, F W	AWhite	39	M	Dead	Yes	This man's name was spelled Bowles, he is AWhite man of the Shawnee tribe his first wife died he afterwards married AWhite woman, Farmer
140 Boyle, Amanda	AWhite	34	F	727	Yes	
141 Boyle, Willie	A shaw	21	M	Dead	No	
142 Boyle, Ambrose	A shaw	6	M	172	No	
143 Boyle, Charley	A shaw	5	M	D1569	No	1896 Del Dist #75 Shawnee
144 Boyle, Mary	A shaw	2	F	Dead	No	
145 Bluejacket, Dave	A shaw	33	M	3914	Yes	
146 Bluejacket, Eliza	A shaw	33	F	3914	No	
147 Bluejacket, Rosanna	A shaw	14	F	Dead	No	
148 Bluejacket, Catherine	A shaw	12	F	Dead	No	
149 Bluejacket, Cinderella	N cher	6	F	4028	No	
150 Bluejacket, Mollie	N cher	3	F	5603	No	
151 Brown, Theresa	A shaw	75	F	Dead	No	
152 Brown, Thompson	A shaw	40	M	3347	No	
153 Blythe, Elijah	N cher	29	M	4282	No	
154 Blythe, Mary F	N cher	5	F	Dead	No	
155 Blythe, Melvin	N cher	3	F	4300	No	
156 Bluejacket, Charles	A shaw	63	M	Dead	Yes	
157 Bluejacket, Louisa	A shaw	30	F	3876	Yes	
158 Bluejacket, Silas	A shaw	22	M	9751	No	
159 Bluejacket, Henry	A shaw	20	M	3722	No	

Name	Race	Age	Sex	Census	Md	Remarks
160 Bluejacket, Richard	A shaw	14	M	Dead	No	
161 Bluejacket, Cora	N cher	21	F	3948	No	
162 Bluejacket, Simon	N cher	8m	M	7431	No	
163 Bluejacket, Willis	A shaw	24	M	Dead	Yes	Farmer
164 Bluejacket, Eliza	A shaw	19	F	3958	Yes	
165 Bluejacket, Minnie	N cher	1	F	4062	No	
166 Brown, Ella	N cher	20	F	Dead	No	
167 Brown, James Henry	N cher	3m	M	3736	No	
168 Brock, Maud	N cher	7	F	827	No	
169 Brock, Charley	N cher	6	M	4106	No	
170 Brock, Walter	N cher	4	M	7092	No	
171 Brock, George	N cher	3	M	Dead	No	
172 Butler, Darcus	N cher	45	F	Dead	No	
173 Butler, James	N cher	20	M	151	No	
174 Butler, John	N cher	18	M	5687	No	
175 Butler, Elizabeth	N cher	9	F	Dead	No	
176 Blackfox, Cheater	N cher	35	M	7485	Yes	
177 Blackfox, Ka-haw-kee	N cher	30	F	7485	Yes	
178 Budder, James	N cher	21	M	Dead	No	
179 Buzzard, Walker	N cher	60	M	Dead	Yes	
180 Buzzard, Mary	N cher	30	F	Dead	Yes	
181 Buzzard, Ned	N cher	17	M	Dead	No	
182 Barbee, John	A shaw	14	M	3756	No	
183 Barnett, Ella	A shaw	23	F	3574	Yes	
184 Barnett, Edmon	A shaw	10m	M	3574	No	
185 Blythe, James	N cher	52	M	4204	Yes	
186 Blythe, Sallie	N cher	40	F	3585	Yes	
187 Bowling, Gilbert	A White	52	M	Dead	Yes	Ferryman, keeps a farm Grand River
188 Bowling, Eliza	N cher	48	F	Dead	Yes	
189 Barlow, John	A mex	50	M	9886	No	Was adopted with Shawnees, Farmer
190 Barlow, Phebe	A shaw	30	F	Dead	No	Enrollment refused
191 Barlow, Julia	A shaw	13	F	Dead	No	
192 Barlow, Julias	A shaw	10	M	5090	No	
193 Boney, Steve	N cher	28	M	Dead	Yes	
194 Boney, Betsy	N cher	25	F	8541	Yes	
195 Boney, Sam	N cher	6	M	8349	No	
196 Budder,	N cher	47	M	Dead	Yes	
197 Budder, Rachel	N cher	30	F	Dead	Yes	
198 Budder, Jesse	N cher	20	M	3481	No	
199 Budder, Lewis	N cher	15	M	3408	No	
200 Budder, David	N cher	12	M	7741	No	

Name	Race	Age	Sex	Census	Md	Remarks
201 Budder, Bettie	N cher	9	F	7326	No	
202 Budder, Annie	N cher	7	F	Dead	No	
203 Budder, Ollie	N cher	2	F	2467	No	
204 Buzzard, Falling	N cher	28	M	Dead	Yes	
205 Buzzard, Jennie	N cher	41	F	Dead	Yes	
206 Buzzard, Chick	N cher	20	F	8327	No	
207 Buzzard, Sam	N cher	18	M	8326	No	
208 Buzzard, Oo-nun-gawn	N cher	14	M	Dead	No	
209 Buzzard, Boudinott	N cher	10	M	8331	No	
210 Buzzard, Will Ross	N cher	8	M	7959	No	
211 Buzzard, Jackson	N cher	5	M	8529	No	
212 Buzzard, Sallie	N cher	2	F	8329	No	
213 Buzzard, Cho-we-ake	N cher	1m	F	4078	No	
214 Buzzard, Sarah	N cher	2	F	D1570	No	
215 Buzzard, Aleck	N cher	2m	M	Dead	No	
216 Blackbird,	N cher	50	M	Dead	Yes	Farmer
217 Blackbird, Rasey	N cher	50	F	Dead	Yes	
218 Blackbird, Joseph	N cher	9	M	8769	No	
219 Blackbird, James	N cher	6	M	8372	No	
220 Buckskin, Joseph	N cher	49	M	8342	Yes	
221 Buckskin, Wahley	N cher	40	F	5369	Yes	
222 Buckskin, Sic-a-towie	N cher	12	M	8363	No	
223 Birchfield, W F	A White	55	M	Dead	Yes	Mill Man
224 Birchfield, Mary F	N cher	29	F	477	Yes	
225 Birchfield, Thos Jefferson	N cher	14	M	Dead	No	
226 Bannon, John W	A White	56	M	7082	Yes	Farmer
227 Bannon, Delilah	N cher	44	F	7082	Yes	
228 Bannon, Angeline	N cher	7	F	6031	No	
229 Blackfox,	N cher	45	M	Dead	Yes	
230 Blackfox, Nancy	N cher	45	F	8542	Yes	
231 Blackfox, Tar-go-na-sene	N cher	15	M	8912	No	
232 Blackfox, Sallie	N cher	11	F	6281	No	
233 Blackfox, Jennie	N cher	9	F	Dead	No	
234 Batt, Lizzie	N cher	30	F	8376	No	On Dawes as Lizzie Cobb (BLB)
235 Batt, Joshua	N cher	9	M	8506	No	
236 Batt, Cora	N cher	6	F	8512	No	
237 Batt, Aggy	N cher	4	F	8509	No	
238 Bony, Peggy	N cher	40	F	8333	No	
239 Bony, Jinsey	N cher	25	F	Dead	No	
240 Bony, Jinnie	N cher	11	F	8332	No	
241 Bony, Lydia	N cher	9	F	Dead	No	
242 Bony, Nakey	N cher	14	F	Dead	No	

Name	Race	Age	Sex	Census	Md	Remarks
243 Blue, Sam	N cher	28	M	Dead	Yes	Farmer
244 Blue, Anny	N cher	22	F	Dead	Yes	
245 Blue, Isaac	N cher	2	M	Dead	No	
246 Blue, Susan	N cher	3	F	Dead	No	
247 Bullfrog, Dave	N cher	40	M	Dead	No	
248 Bullfrog, Wah-le-ah	N cher	18	F	8346	No	
249 Bullfrog, Kal-taw-klun-ah	N cher	4	F	8533	No	
250 Buzzard, Yellowbird	N cher	27	M	Dead	Yes	
251 Buzzard, Tu-ni-ka	N cher	24	F	Dead	Yes	
252 Buzzard, Akiny	N cher	1	F	Dead	No	
253 Bucket, David	N cher	20	M	7473	Yes	
254 Bucket, Aggy	N cher	26	F	7473	No	
255 Brown, Steven A	AWhite	39	M	5593	Yes	
256 Brown, Lucy A	N cher	35	F	Dead	No	
257 Ballard, Wm	N cher	27	M	5998	Yes	
258 Ballard, Fannie	N cher	26	F	5998	Yes	
259 Ballard, Finnie L	N cher	8	F	5993	No	
260 Ballard, Will Henry	N cher	4	M	5905	No	
261 Ballard, Martha A	N cher	2	F	Dead	No	
262 Beck, Henry	N cher	23	M	3131	Yes	Farmer
263 Beck, Martha	N cher	19	F	Dead	Yes	
264 Beck, Ezekiel	N cher	45	M	2522	Yes	
265 Beck, Mary F	N cher	25	F	Dead	Yes	
266 Beck, Donpedro	N cher	1	M	Dead	Yes	
267 Beck, Dave	N cher	14	M	2523	No	
268 Beck, John W	N cher	8	M	6003	No	
269 Beck, Willie	N cher	7	M	5887	No	
270 Beck, Jefry	N cher	66	M	Dead	Yes	Farmer
271 Beck, Sallie	N cher	68	F	Dead	Yes	
272 Beck, Robert	N cher	26	M	3119	No	Robert Beck is a cripple and unable to take care of himself
273 Beck, George	N cher	19	M	Dead	No	
274 Beck, Wm	N cher	32	M	Dead	Yes	
275 Beck, Hannah	N cher	23	F	Dead	Yes	
276 Bird, Lucy A	N cher	26	F	Dead	No	
277 Bird, Cho-wah-chuck	N cher	7	M	Dead	No	
278 Birch, Thos	AWhite	35	M	3028	Yes	
279 Birch, Martha	N cher	22	F	3028	Yes	
280 Beck, Weatherford	N cher	41	M	Dead	Yes	
281 Beck, Sabra	N cher	35	F	412	Yes	
282 Beck, Joseph	N cher	12	M	412	No	
283 Beck, Jeffrey	N cher	10	M	412	No	

Name	Race	Age	Sex	Census	Md	Remarks
284 Beck, Harling	N cher	9	M	412	No	
285 Beck, Samuel	N cher	8	M	412	No	
286 Beck, Rutherford	N cher	5	M	6029	No	
287 Beck, John	N cher	2	M	412	No	
288 Beck, Weatherford	N cher	2m	M	412	No	
289 Barnett, Jim	N cher	27	M	R714	Yes	
290 Barnett, Eliza	N cher	25	F	Dead	Yes	
291 Barnett, Margaret	N cher	3	F	5999	No	
292 Barnett, Jesse	N cher	2	M	7089	No	
293 Buffington, W W	N cher	48	M	3278	Yes	
294 Buffington, Callie E	AWhite	40	F	Dead	Yes	
295 Ballard, Sallie	N cher	50	F	2913	Yes	Farmer
296 Ballard, Sam	N cher	21	M	R901	No	
297 Ballard, Lucy	N cher	19	F	3444	No	
298 Ballard, Henry	N cher	18	M	3068	No	
299 Ballard, Freeman	N cher	17	M	2928	No	
300 Ballard, Sabina	N cher	16	F	2954	No	
301 Beck, D M	N cher	44	M	5462	Yes	
302 Beck, Manda	AWhite	24	F	5462	Yes	
303 Beck, Belle D	N cher	14	F	5539	No	
304 Beck, Charles M	N cher	7	M	5534	No	
305 Beck, Emma	N cher	6	F	4048	No	
306 Beck, Willa	N cher	5	M	4151	No	Stepson of Dave Beck proper name Wm New and is white
307 Beck, Ellis	N cher	5m	M	5463	No	
308 Blackfox, Budder	N cher	50	M	Dead	Yes	Farmer
309 Blackfox, Martha	N cher	50	F	D1571	Yes	
310 Beamer, John W	N cher	25	M	7681	No	Farmer
311 Blythe, Napoleon	N cher	22	M	Dead	No	
312 Blythe, Monroe	A col	22	M	F730	No	Citizen under Treaty 1866
313 Burl, Franklin	N Col	20	M	F829	No	Duplicate of 2165, This boy better known as Frank Ratliff is citizen under Treaty 1866, raised by Winnie Ratliff
314 Buzzard, Thos	N cher	29	M	Dead	No	
315 Burris, John	AWhite	65	M	Dead	No	
316 Barbee, Billy	A shaw	18	M	Dead	No	Carpenter
317 Batt, Ned	N cher	23	M	7489	No	
318 Bryant, John	N cher	18	M	3519	No	Farmer
319 Buffington, L W	N cher	21	M	3537	No	
320 Ballard, James	N cher	22	M	2697	No	
321 Ballard, George	N cher	23	M	2967	No	Farmer
322 Beck, John	N cher	22	M	Dead	No	School Teacher

Name	Race	Age	Sex	Census	Md	Remarks
323 Beckie	N cher	50	F	Dead	No	
324 Beck, Orin	N cher	53	M	2542	No	This man is blind
325 Bean, Lucinda	A col	25	F	F747	Yes	
326 Bean, Alice	A col	8	F	F714	No	
327 Bean, Patsy	A col	2	F	Dead	No	
328 Bean, Philis	A col	25	F	F755	Yes	Wife of Lander Bean She is a citizen, daughter of Lucy Vann
329 Bean, Hattie	A col	9	F	F734	No	
330 Bean, Eliza	A col	2	F	F774	No	
331 Bean, Walker	A col	4m	M	Dead	No	
332 Blackfeather, David	A shaw	42	M	Dead	Yes	Farmer
333 Blackfeather, Martha	A shaw	40	F	Dead	Yes	
334 Blackfeather, John	A shaw	26	M	Dead	No	
335 Blackfeather, Mary	A shaw	9	F	Dead	No	
336 Blackfeather, Nancy	A shaw	6	F	Dead	No	
337 Blackfeather, Robt	A shaw	11	M	Dead	No	
338 Brown, John A	AWhite	35	M	3881	Yes	
339 Brown, Francis O	A del	26	F	Del 50	Yes	
340 Brown, Henry	A del	6	M	Dead	No	
341 Brown, Daniel	N cher	4	M	Del 50	No	
342 Brown, George	N cher	2	M	Del 44	No	
343 Bell, L B	N cher	47	M	3560	Yes	
344 Bell, Mary F	N cher	37	F	3560	Yes	
345 Bell, Hoolie	N cher	17	F	Dead	No	
346 Berry, Charley	N cher	12	M	3050	No	
347 Berry, Wm	N cher	10	M	3623	No	
348 Barber, Lizzie	N cher	33	F	Dead	No	
349 Buffington, Josaphine	N cher	2	F	3471	No	
350 Buffington, G F	A shaw	19	M	D1572	No	Not known to Shawnees
351 Buffington, Samuel	A shaw	14	M	D1573	No	Not known to Shawnees
352 Buffington, Thomas M	N cher	25	M	4073	Yes	
353 Buffington, Susan H	N cher	22	F	Dead	Yes	
354 Blackstone, Henry	N cher	7	M	Dead	No	
355 Benton, V L	AWhite	53	M	Dead	Yes	Farmer
356 Benton, Mary Jane	N cher	47	F	Dead	Yes	
357 Buffington, Rachel	N cher	45	F	Dead	No	
358 Buffington, Charles	N cher	18	M	3452	No	
359 Buffington, John	N cher	17	M	Dead	No	
360 Buffington, James	N cher	13	M	3443	No	
361 Boudinot,	N cher	6	M	D1574	No	
362 Buffington, Mary	A col	20	F	Dead	No	
363 Buffington, Florence	A col	2m	F	F739	No	

Name	Race	Age	Sex	Census	Md	Remarks
364 Brown, Charles	N cher	7	M	6735	No	
365 Barbee, Anna	A shaw	18	F	3646	No	
366 Bigknife, Emma	N shaw	8	F	Dead	No	
367 Bigknife, Sam	N shaw	6	M	3423	No	
368 Blackfeather, Johnathan	A shaw	36	M	3238	Yes	Farmer
369 Blackfeather, Nancy	A shaw	40	F	3238	Yes	
370 Bailey, Samuel	A shaw	19	M	5769	No	
371 Bailey, G F	A shaw	14	M	7392	No	
372 Bowen, M W				R216	No	Enrollment Refused
373 Co-nel-sah,	N cher	25	M	6105	No	On Dawes as Cornelius Mouse (BLB)
374 Chopper, Bettie	N cher	78	F	Dead	No	
375 Colston, James	N cher	20	M	Dead	No	
376 Chism, Rose	A col	80	F	F784	No	
377 Che-kah-che-lah-lah,	N cher	10	M	8354	No	
378 Che-ah-nuh-nah,	N cher	8	F	Dead	No	
379 Buffington, Alex	A col	25	M	Dead	Yes	Farmer
380 Buffington, Ruth	A col	24	F	10341	No	
381 Buffington, James	A col	3	M	FD1165	No	
382 Buffington, Willie	A col	10m	M	FD1166	No	
383 Britton, Mary	Supplement rolls (Adopted Shawnee BLB)					Nee Wheeler (BLB)
384 Britton, WM	" "					
385 Britton, Caroline	" "					
386 Britton, Lotta	" "					Left the country years ago
387 Britton, John	" "					Left the country years ago
388 Baldridge, Jack	Supplement rolls					
389 Baldridge, Nancy	Supplement rolls					
390 Baldridge, Luveinia	Supplement rolls					
391 Baldridge, Lucy	Supplement rolls					
392 Bean, Lee	Supplement rolls					Duplicate of Lucinda Bean #326 Del Dist
393 Bean, Alice	Supplement rolls					Duplicate of Alice Bean #327 Del Dist
394 Bean, Patsy	Supplement rolls					
395 Bean, Ellen	Supplement rolls					
396 Bean, Pola	Supplement rolls					
397 Bean, Margaret	Supplement rolls					
398 Buffington, Gus	Supplement rolls					
399 Buffington, Mary	Supplement rolls					
400 Buffington, Ellis	Supplement rolls					
401 Buffington, Eliza	Supplement rolls					
402 Buffington, Lucy	Supplement rolls					
403 Buffington, John	Supplement rolls					

Name	Race	Age	Sex	Census	Md	Remarks
404 Buffington, Emet	Supplement rolls					
405 Brown, Margaret	Supplement rolls					
406 Chu-wa-looky, Dave	N cher	39	M	3204	Yes	Farmer, also known as Dave Vann (BLB)
407 Chu-wa-looky, Dick	N cher	20	M	3607	Yes	
408 Chu-wa-looky, Leann	N cher	8	F	3204	No	
409 Chu-wa-looky, Celia	N cher	5	F	3202	No	On Dawes as Celia On-the hill (BLB)
410 Chu-wa-looky, Nannie	N cher	13	F	3201	No	On Dawes as Nannie White (BLB)
411 Chu-wa-looky, Teek-ah-nah-chut	N cher	10	M	Dead	No	
412 Chick-a-lee-lee,	N cher	38	M	3680	No	
413 Chick-a-lee-lee, Nakey	N cher	50	F	Dead	No	
414 Chick-a-lee-lee, Darkey	N cher	15	F	6105	No	
415 Chick-a-lee-lee, Runaway	N cher	2	M	3657	No	
416 Chu-wa-looky, Davis	N cher	37	M	Dead	Yes	
417 Chu-wa-looky, Uqua	N cher	40	F	4192	No	
418 Chu-wa-looky, Becky	N cher	1	F	4192	No	
419 Constitution, Dave	N cher	35	M	8375	Yes	
420 Constitution, Betsy	N cher	25	F	Dead	Yes	
421 Constitution, Peter	N cher	9	M	8520	No	On Dawes as Peter James (BLB)
422 Constitution, Nelly	N cher	6	F	D1577	No	Dead
423 Constitution, Teacher	N cher	2	M	8500	No	
424 Constitution, Betty	N cher	2m	F	7948	No	
425 Colarche, Will	N cher	27	M	Dead	No	
426 Cheater, Lucy	N cher	30	F	8364	Yes	Should be Lacey Cheater male (BLB)
427 Cheater, Katy	N cher	27	F	8364	Yes	
428 Cheater, John	N cher	13	M	8370	No	
429 Cheater, Hicks	N cher	9	M	8335	No	
430 Cheater, Ool-stah-stay	N cher	7	F	Dead	No	
431 Cheater, Benjamin	N cher	3	M	8534	No	
432 Cheater, Che-aw-sa	N cher	1	F	Dead	No	
434 Cheater, Nelly	N cher	25	F	D1578	Yes	
435 Cheater, Lydia	N cher	18	F	Dead	No	
436 Cheater, George	N cher	15	M	8373	No	
437 Cheater, Locust	N cher	8	M	Dead	No	
438 Cheater, Che-lo-nah-cha	N cher	5	F	Dead	No	
439 Chopper, Daniel	N cher	31	M	Dead	Yes	Farmer
440 Chopper, Elia	N cher	30	F	3218	No	
441 Chopper, Sewa	N cher	10	F	3227	No	
442 Chopper, Waser	N cher	3	M	Dead	No	
443 Chopper, Tookah	N cher	2m	F	3218	No	

Name	Race	Age	Sex	Census	Md	Remarks
444 Chanler, B G	AWhite	39	M	3337	Yes	Readmitted by Citizenship court
445 Chanler, Anna E	N cher	31	F	3337	Yes	
446 Chanler, Alberta	N cher	11	M	3156	No	
447 Chanler, Kitty	N cher	8	F	3123	No	
448 Chanler, Milton	N cher	7	M	Dead	No	
449 Chanler, Claude	N cher	3	M	3579	No	
450 Chanler, Calvin	N cher	1	M	Dead	No	
451 Chuck, Ben	N cher	50	M	Dead	Yes	
452 Chuck, Jennie	N cher	50	F	D1579	Yes	Dead
453 Chuck, Olley	N cher	10	F	Dead	No	
454 Chuck, Sallie	N cher	7	F	Dead	No	
455 Chuck, John	N cher	1	M	D1580	No	
456 Cornshucker, John	N cher	27	M	9044	Yes	
457 Cornshucker, Tehking	N cher	24	F	8334	Yes	
458 Chopper, Daylight	N cher	26	M	3649	Yes	
459 Chopper, Jennie	N cher	28	F	3649	Yes	
460 Chopper, Ester	N cher	4m	F	Dead	No	
461 Chelawtetakee,	N cher	70	M	Dead	Yes	
462 Chelawtetakee, Lizzie	N cher	70	F	8497	Yes	
463 Chelawtetakee, George	N cher	16	M	8498	No	
464 Chelawtetakee, Lailie	N cher	8	F	8503	No	
465 Chelawtetakee, Abraham	N cher	6	M	8522	No	
466 Colarche, Nick	N cher	70	M	Dead	No	
467 Colarche, Ailsey	N cher	60	F	8353	Yes	
468 Colarche, Peter	N cher	22	M	8908	No	
469 Colarche, Chinconah	N cher	15	F	8672	No	Dead
470 Colarche, Nancy	N cher	9	F	8353	No	
471 Colarche, Adam	N cher	40	M	Dead	Yes	
472 Colarche, Sofkin	N cher	25	F		Yes	No census card number given, nor is she listed as dead (BLB)
473 Colarche, Younbird	N cher	6m	M	Dead	No	
474 Chunkerhunsk,	N cher	29	M	3636	Yes	
475 Chunkerhunsk, Bettie	N cher	30	F	3636	Yes	
476 Chunkerhunsk, Kahtate	N cher	1	F	4175	No	
477 Chunkerhunsk, Wahlease	N cher	50	F	Dead	No	
478 Chunkerhunsk, Sakie	N cher	20	F	Dead	No	
479 Chunkerhunsk, Joe	N cher	2	M	Dead	No	
480 Chunkerhunsk, Lydia	N cher	1	F	6656	No	
481 Chunkerhunsk, Ann	N cher	16	F	4163	No	
482 Colins, John	N cher	25	M	Dead	Yes	
483 Colins, Sabra	N cher	35	F	Dead	Yes	
484 Colins, Henry	N cher	5	M	3586	No	

Name	Race	Age	Sex	Census	Md	Remarks
485 Colins, Joseph	N cher	3	M	Dead	No	
486 Colins, Sallie	N cher	1	F	3920	No	
487 Chandler, Pink	AWhite	40	M	6444	Yes	
488 Chandler, Susie	N cher	26	F	6444	Yes	
490 Chandler, Mattie	N cher	12	F	370	No	
491 Chandler, Wm	N cher	10	M	6806	No	
492 Chandler, Adam	N cher	7	M	7395	No	
493 Chandler, John	N cher	5	M	6807	No	
494 Chandler, Sam	N cher	3	M	6505	No	
495 Chandler, Eliza	N cher	6m	F	6919	No	
496 Chennestudy, Wm	N cher	36	M	8339	No	Farmer
497 Chennestudy, Josiah	N cher	10	M	7910	No	
498 Chennestudy, Rachel	N cher	7	F	8340	No	
499 Chennestudy, Sohking	N cher	2	F	8539	No	
500 Chennestudy,	N cher	70	M	Dead	Yes	
501 Chennestudy, Canhene	N cher	20	F	7499	Yes	
502 Chennestudy, Thirsty	N cher	11	M	7477	No	On Dawes as Houston Downing (BLB)
503 Chennestudy, Lydia	N cher	19	M	8339	No	
504 Chennestudy, Susie	N cher	2	F	Dead	No	
505 Chennestudy, Joe	N cher	5m	M	8540	No	
506 Clay, Nicholas	AWhite	57	M	Dead	Yes	
507 Clay, Nancy Ann	N cher	42	F	100	No	
508 Cary, Edmon	N cher	48	M	65	Yes	
509 Cary, Lydia Ann	N cher	29	F	65	Yes	
510 Cary, Joseph Shelby	N cher	15	M	Dead	No	
511 Cary, Robert EL	N cher	11	M	64	No	
512 Cary, Stonewall Jackson	N cher	8	M	66	No	
513 Cary, David L	N cher	6	M	4131	No	
514 Cary, Darkes	N cher	5m	F	Dead	No	
515 Cary, Nancy	N cher	21	F	2943	No	
516 Cary, Susan	N cher	17	F	167	No	Susan Kelly on census of 83
517 Cary, Lucy	N cher	1	F	133	No	
518 Cowles, James	AWhite	21	M	3726	Yes	Farmer
519 Cowles, Martha	N cher	17	F	3726	Yes	
520 Cowles, Charles	N cher	8m	M	5582	No	
521 Carr, E E	A choc	31	M	3691	Yes	
522 Carr, Susan M	N cher	30	F	3691	Yes	
523 Carr, Hattie A	N cher	12	F	6109	No	
524 Carr, Mary A	N cher	8	F	3776	No	
525 Carr, Wm	N cher	6	M	Dead	No	
526 Carr, Addie	N cher	3	F	3777	No	

The Delaware District

Name	Race	Age	Sex	Census	Md	Remarks
527 Carr, Frank Jr.	N cher	1	M	Dead	No	
529 Cohee, James	AWhite	48	M	110	Yes	
530 Cohee, Martha	N cher	44	F	110	Yes	
531 Currie, G W	AWhite	57	M	8358	Yes	Age should be 37 (BLB)
532 Currie, F S	N cher	25	F	8358	No	
533 Currie, Emma E	N cher	8	F	3957	No	
534 Currie, F B	N cher	3	F	41	No	
535 Currie, Cora M	N cher	2	F	4040	No	
536 Currie, C E	N cher	1m	M	8358	No	
537 Cox, Stephen C	AWhite	30	M	Dead	Yes	
538 Cox, Rebecca L	N cher	30	F	449	Yes	
539 Cox, Elizabeth L	N cher	16	F	4123	No	
540 Cox, John S	N cher	10	M	4124	No	
541 Cox, Celia J	N cher	6	F	6375	No	
542 Cox, Geo E	N cher	3	M	6303	No	
543 Cowles, Frank	N cher	26	M	D1581	Yes	Left the country years ago
544 Cowles, Jane	N cher	20	F	Dead	Yes	
545 Cheek, Pleasant	N cher	36	M	Dead	Yes	Farmer
546 Cheek, Sarah N	AWhite	37	F	2855	Yes	
547 Cheek, Mary Ann	N cher	13	F	2818	No	
548 Cheek, Augusta F	N cher	7	F	Dead	No	
549 Cheek, Corbin R	N cher	5	F	3870	No	
550 Cheek, Della G	N cher	13m	F	3512	No	
551 Cunigin, Lizzie	N cher	27	F	Dead	No	
552 Cunigin, Johnson	N cher	19	M	Dead	No	
553 Cunigin, Ester	N cher	14	F	Dead	No	
554 Cunigin, Mary	N cher	19	F	8499	No	
555 Cunigin, Lucy	N cher	13	F	7959	No	
556 Cunningham, Geo	N cher	21	M	7490	No	
557 Countryman, Geo	N cher	39	M	3365	Yes	
558 Countryman, Minerva	N cher	38	F	3365	Yes	
559 Countryman, Hollie	N cher	15	M	3796	Yes	
560 Countryman, John	N cher	8	M	4070	No	
561 Countryman, James	N cher	6	M	4099	No	
562 Courteney, J L	AWhite	29	M	3374	Yes	
563 Courteney, Eliza A	N cher	17	F	3374	Yes	
564 Countryman, John	N cher	41	M	3372	Yes	
565 Countryman, Ester	N cher	43	F	Dead	Yes	
566 Countryman, Martha	N cher	13	F	3841	No	Martha E Wall on census of 83
567 Countryman, Andrew	N cher	31	M	2874	Yes	
568 Countryman, Ezmere	N cher	26	F	2874	Yes	
569 Countryman, Geo	N cher	6	M	2960	No	

Name	Race	Age	Sex	Census	Md	Remarks
570 Countryman, Rosama	N cher	3	F	2926	No	
571 Countryman, Rebecca	N cher	8m	F	3126	No	
572 Charlie, John	A Peoria	62	M	Dead	Yes	Farmer
573 Charlie, Louisa	N cher	31	F	40	Yes	
574 Charlie, Eliza	N cher	14	F	Dead	No	
575 Clark, Jordan	AWhite	41	M	Dead	Yes	
576 Clark, Endosia F	N cher	33	F	Dead	Yes	
577 Clark, Annsey M	N cher	7	F	3252	No	
578 Clark, Ann Eliza	N cher	6	F	3011	No	
579 Clark, Alice	N cher	2	F	Dead	No	
580 Clark, Joel B	N cher	2m	M	3011	No	
581 Courtney, Mande	N cher	5m	F	3984	No	
582 Cricket, Mary	A col	55	F	Dead	No	
583 Cricket, Alice	N cher	24	F	Dead	No	
584 Cooley, John	A shaw	38	M	D1582	Yes	Dead
585 Cooley, Mary	A shaw	26	F	113	Yes	
586 Cooley, Robt	N cher	2	M	113	No	
587 Connor, Francis M	AWhite	28	M	192	Yes	
588 Connor, Rebecca J	N cher	21	F	192	Yes	
589 Connor, Alonzo	N cher	3	M	198	No	
590 Connor, Lee	N cher	2m	M	Dead	No	
591 Campbell, Hugh	AWhite	36	M	10144	Yes	
592 Campbell, Alice	A shaw	36	F	Dead	Yes	
593 Craig, Granville	AWhite	31	M	3844	Yes	
594 Craig, Jane	N cher	30	F	3844	Yes	
595 Craig, Lee	N cher	11	M	4071	No	
596 Craig, Laura	N cher	8	F	3595	No	
597 Craig, Carl	N cher	6	M	3839	No	
598 Craig, Geo	N cher	4	M	3852	No	
599 Coats, H D	AWhite	32	M	3955	Yes	Farmer
600 Coats, Louisa J	N cher	27	F	3955	Yes	
601 Coats, James E	N cher	10	M	3941	No	
602 Coats, Charles F	N cher	6	M	3945	No	
603 Coats, John Wm	N cher	2	M	4036	No	
604 Colston, Wilson	N cher	25	M	Dead	No	
605 Colston, Ceilia	N cher	42	F	Dead	No	
606 Colston, Charley	N cher	20	M	Dead	No	
607 Cockran, Geo W	N cher	7	M	4874	No	Age should probably be 17 (BLB)
608 Caldwell, John J	AWhite	30	M	4101	Yes	
609 Caldwell, Callie M	N cher	18	F	Dead	Yes	
610 Cramp, Little	N cher	30	M	Dead	Yes	
611 Cramp, Willie	N cher	40	F	Dead	Yes	

Name	Race	Age	Sex	Census	Md	Remarks
612 Cornsilk, Flora	N cher	18	F	7489	No	
613 Cornatzer, Cyrus C	A shaw	24	M	3919	Yes	
614 Cornatzer, Lydia O	A White	29	F	Dead	Yes	
615 Cornatzer, Caroline B	A shaw	8	F	3414	No	
616 Cornatzer, W Jane	A shaw	6	F	3761	No	
617 Cornatzer, Cornelia A	A shaw	5	F	3394	No	
618 Cornatzer, Walter C	A shaw	2	M	3541	No	
619 Choteau, Benj	A shaw	42	M	3556	Yes	
620 Choteau, Mariah H	A shaw	19	F	3556	Yes	
621 Carlton, Elizabeth	A del	13	F	Del 365	No	
622 Cheater, Betsy	N cher	11	F	7498	No	
623 Cheater, Ailsy	N cher	10	F	Dead	No	
624 Cheater, Charlie	N cher	7	M	3618	No	
625 Cheater, Swimmer	N cher	4	M	Dead	No	
626 Carter, Willie	N cher	9	M	Dead	No	
627 Colston, Richard	N cher	25	M	Dead	Yes	Farmer
628 Colston, Millie Jane	N cher	25	F	4249	Yes	
629 Chinarche, John	N cher	9	M	3779	No	
630 Cooheest,	N cher	12	F	Dead	No	
631 Cornatzer, Samuel M	A White	55	M	Dead	Yes	
632 Cornatzer, Caroline	A shaw	45	F	Dead	Yes	
633 Cornatzer, Lieurgus	A shaw	23	M	3460	No	
634 Cornatzer, Minna E	A shaw	21	F	Dead	No	
635 Cornatzer, Adelia A	A shaw	18	F	5635	No	
636 Cornatzer, Samuel L	A shaw	12	M	D1583	No	Dead, left the country 10 years ago, Gone to Colorado
637 Cunningham, J T	N cher	35	M	5758	Yes	
638 Cunningham, K C	N cher	28	F	5758	Yes	
639 Cunningham, Andrew	N cher	12	M	5858	No	
640 Cunningham, Kate A	N cher	10	F	1693	No	
641 Cunningham, Jeter T	N cher	8	M	5724	No	
642 Cunningham, Betsy	N cher	6	F	5790	No	
643 Cunningham, James F	N cher	3	M	Dead	No	
644 Cunningham, May	N cher	1	F	6474	No	
645 Cunningham, Mariah	N cher	65	F	Dead	No	
646 Colston, Susanna	N cher	30	F	2992	No	
647 Chouteau, Alexander	A shaw	24	M	Dead	No	Farmer
648 Coody, Daniel	N cher	21	M	2245	No	
649 Che-kah-na-gai-hees,	N cher	20	M	D1584	No	
650 Chick-coo-ie	N cher	27	F	D1585	No	Widow of George Raper
651 Coming,	N cher	20	M	8347	No	
652 Chopper, Bird	N cher	20	M	8494	No	

	Name	Race	Age	Sex	Census	Md	Remarks
653	Chee-naw Anna	N cher	7	F	Dead	No	This little farm belongs to these two children whose mother is died, but they have a living father
654	Chee-naw, Wilson	N cher	2	M	Dead	No	
655	Chee-wah-see	N cher	5m	F	D1586	No	Enrolled on original roll with Frank Howard as family pg 99
656	Cowan, Richard	N cher	42	M	Dead	Yes	
657	Cowan, Elsade	A White	37	F	3310	Yes	
658	Cowan, Felix	N cher	13	M	3513	No	
659	Cowan, Sarah	N cher	10	F	3309	No	
660	Cornwall, Mary	N cher	48	F	4358	No	
661	Cornwall, James	N cher	13	M	4357	No	
662	Conner, Silas	A del	20	M	Dead	No	
663	Connell, James	A White	25	M	Dead	Yes	
664	Connell, Acenith	A shaw	24	F	Dead	Yes	
665	Curtis, W H	N cher	35	M	2957	Yes	Mechanic
666	Curtis, Loulie H	N cher	18	F	2957	Yes	
667	Coslowie, James	N cher	30	M	3939	Yes	Farmer
668	Coslowie, Kate	N cher	26	F	3937	Yes	
669	Coslowie, Susan E	N cher	6	F	2536	No	
670	Coslowie, James R	N cher	5	M	5651	No	
671	Coslowie, Annie E	N cher	3	F	3879	No	
672	Cephas, Sallie	N cher	20	F	5697	No	
673	Charlesworth, J F	A White	24	M	3535	Yes	Dup of 689
674	Charlesworth, Mary Jane	N cher	17	F	3535	Yes	Dup of 690
675	Charlotte,	N cher	30	F	Dead	No	
676	Collins, Geo W	A White	30	M	D1587	Yes	Dead, married out
677	Collins, Martha E	N cher	29	F	Dead	Yes	
678	Copeland, Alexander	N cher	40	M	74	Yes	
679	Copeland, Sarah	N cher	39	F	2871	Yes	
680	Copeland, J R	N cher	18	M	4156	No	
681	Chunaw,	N cher	22	M	7973	No	
682	Colier, Jane	N cher	62	F	Dead	No	
683	Cox, Lydia Ann	N cher	9	F	D1588	No	Citizen under the Treaty of 1866 raised by Winnie Ratliff
684	Choctaw Aslsey	N cher	45	F	Dead	No	
685	Corne,	N cher	9	F	Dead	No	
686	Crain, Hattie			F	3961	No	
687	Crain, Israel			M	D1589	No	
688	Charlesworth, J F			M	3535		
689	Charlesworth, Mary Jane			F	3535		
690	Collier, Jane			F	Dead		
691	Cely In-cha-was-kah				Dead		

Name	Race	Age	Sex	Census	Md	Remarks
692 Chou-u-ka,				Dead		
693 Coleman, Samuel			M	6998		
694 Dick, Lydia Ann	N cher	14	F	Dead	No	
695 Downing, Reuben	A col	65	M	Dead	No	Farmer
696 Downing, Zebedee	A col	25	M	F780	Yes	
697 Downing, Jennie	A col	22	F	F781	Yes	
698 Downing, Luvena	A col	7	F	F781	No	
699 Downing, Henry	A col	4	M	F783	No	
700 Downing, Walter	A col	6m	M	F782?	No	
701 Davesy,	N cher	49	M	Dead	No	
701 Daniel,	N cher	25	M	3258	Yes	
702 Dolly, Arch	N cher	50	M	Dead	No	
703 Dick, Charley	N cher	21	M	Dead	Yes	
704 Dick, Niesee	N cher	22	F	Dead	Yes	
705 Denton, John	AWhite	40	M	3417	Yes	
706 Denton, Dora	N cher	18	F	D1591	Yes	Left the County ___ from husband
707 Davis, David	N cher	30	M	Dead	Yes	Farmer
708 Davis, Kate	N cher	26	F	Dead	Yes	
709 Davis, Geo	N cher	9	M	8379	No	
710 Davis, Jack	N cher	2	M	8380	No	
711 Davis, Jennie	N cher	5	F	8494	No	
712 Davis, Tookah	N cher	1	F	8389	No	
713 Deamer, Nannie	N cher	60	F	Dead	No	
714 Dial, Abram	AWhite	62	M	Dead	No	
715 Dial, Martha	N cher	23	F	4920	No	
716 Dial, Rebecca	N cher	21	F	3416	No	
717 Dial, Nancy	N cher	16	F	Dead	No	
718 Dial, Isaac	N cher	26	M	Dead	Yes	
719 Dial, Martha	AWhite	22	F	Dead	Yes	
720 Dial, Mary	N cher	6	F	Dead	No	
721 Dial, Vida May	N cher	1	F	2507	No	
722 Dobkins, Melvina	N cher	8	F	3491	No	
723 Dobkins, Mary M	N cher	6	F	Dead	No	
724 Dobkins, Hannah C	N cher	4	F	Dead	No	
725 Dick, Charley	N cher	45	M	Dead	Yes	
726 Dick, Peggy	N cher	40	F	Dead	Yes	
727 Dick, Robert	N cher	18	M	569	No	On Dawes as Robert B Stand (BLB)
728 Dick, Andy	N cher	15	M	6873	No	
729 Dick, John	N cher	12	M	7423	No	
730 Dick, Sarah	N cher	9	F	Dead	No	
731 Dick, Taylor	N cher	7	M	Dead	No	

Name	Race	Age	Sex	Census	Md	Remarks
732 Dick, George	N cher	5	M	6874	No	
733 Dick, Charley	N cher	9m	M	9859	No	
734 Downing, Mose	N cher	30	M	Dead	Yes	Farmer
735 Downing, Anna	N cher	27	F	6873	Yes	
736 Downing, Colsicuntny	N cher	2	M	Dead	No	
737 Dobkins, John Robert	AWhite	32	M	D1592	No	In Texas, married out
738 Dobkins, Emma S	N cher	25	F	Dead	Yes	
739 Dobkins, Benjamin	N cher	8	M	4061	No	
740 Dobkins, Ada	N cher	8	F	3837	No	
741 Dean, James H	AWhite	34	M	Dead	Yes	Correct surname is Deems (BLB)
742 Dean, Eliza	N cher	24	F	Dead	Yes	""
743 Dean, Martha	N cher	6	F	2936	No	""
744 Dean, Abigal	N cher	3	F	4181	No	""
745 Dean, John	N cher	10m	M	5138	No	""
746 Dick, Ellis	N cher	40	M	Dead	Yes	
747 Dick, Mary	N cher		F	3175	Yes	
748 Dick, Washington	N cher		M	3551	No	
749 Dick, Lorenzo	N cher		M	Dead	No	
750 Dick, Ruth Jane	N cher		F	5452	No	
751 Dick, Geo	N cher		M	3469	No	
752 Dick, Thomas	N cher		M	Dead	No	
753 Dick, Rosetta	N cher		F	5454	No	
754 Denbo, Joseph	AWhite	36	M	4897	Yes	
755 Denbo, Lettia	N cher	35	F	4897	Yes	
756 Denbo, Eli H	N cher	15	M	Dead	No	
757 Denbo, Martha J	N cher	11	F	Dead	No	
758 Denbo, Mary E	N cher	8	F	4984	No	
759 Denbo, John L	N cher	6	M	4983	No	
760 Denbo, Minnie M	N cher	4	F	4993	No	
761 Denbo, Ida May	N cher	2	F	Dead	No	
762 Daniels, Marma D	N cher	33	M	3083	Yes	Farmer
763 Daniels, Orra	AWhite	23?	F	3083	Yes	
764 Daniels, Jackie	N cher	18m	F	3115	No	
765 Duncan, James H	N cher	78	M	3044	Yes	
766 Duncan, Susie	AWhite	40	F	3044	Yes	
767 Duncan, Darcas	N cher	18	F	Dead	No	Darcas Kelly on Census of 83
768 Duncan, Rebecca J	N cher	15	F	2959	No	
769 Duncan, James A	N cher	53	M	Dead	Yes	
770 Duncan, Lucy Ann	N cher	32	F	2849	Yes	
771 Duncan, Delen R	N cher	6	F	2953	No	
772 Duncan, Annie Ellen	N cher	4	F	4250	No	
773 Duncan, Jinnie	N cher	5m	F	2951	No	

Name	Race	Age	Sex	Census	Md	Remarks
774 Duncan, Blueford	N cher	30	M	Dead	Yes	
775 Duncan, Samantha	N cher	32	F	96	No	
776 Duncan, Ellen Frances	N cher	2	F	88	No	
777 Duncan, James	N cher	5m	M	96	No	
778 Donalson, Edward	A Shaw	17	M	Dead	No	
779 Daugharty, Narcisa	A Col	31	F	Dead	No	
780 Duncan, Logan H	A White	47	M	Dead	Yes	
781 Duncan, Narcisa	N cher	39	F	3695	Yes	
782 Duncan, James	N cher	18	M	8047	No	
783 Duncan, Walter	N cher	14	M	5372	No	
784 Duncan, Lena	N cher	10	F	3946	No	
785 Duncan, Nattie	N cher	7	F	4083	No	
786 Duncan, Fredrick	N cher	6	M	4083	No	
787 Duncan, Nellie	N cher	4m	F	5695	No	
788 Daugharty, David	A Shaw	41	M	3103	No	
789 Daugharty, Eliza	A Shaw	9	F	4143	No	
790 Daugharty, Mary	A Shaw	30	F	Dead	No	
791 Daugharty, Martin	A Shaw	4	M	D1593	No	In Oklahoma 12 years his wife drew land with Absentee Shawnee
792 Daugharty, Rosa	A Shaw	8	F	3382	No	
793 Daugharty, Ridley	A Shaw	25	M	5682	No	
794 Daugharty, Albert	N Shaw	6	M	Dead	No	
795 Daugharty, Thos	A Shaw	35	M	3496	Yes	
796 Daugharty, Mollie	A Shaw	25	F	5648	Yes	
797 Donalson, Wm H	A White	46	M	3171	Yes	
798 Donalson, Rachel S	N cher	25	F	3171	Yes	
799 Donalson, Franklin	N cher	16m	M	2947	No	
800 Donalson, Walter	N cher	2m	M	3171	No	On Dawes as William C Donaldson (BLB)
801 Daugharty, Joshua	A Shaw	27	M	Dead	Yes	
802 Daugharty, Mary	A Shaw	33	F	Dead	Yes	
803 Daugharty, James	N cher	7	M	9108	No	
804 Daugharty, Edward	N cher	5	M	3693	No	
805 Daugharty, Geo	N cher	1	M	Dead	No	
806 Daniel, John M	N cher	35	M	2914	Yes	
807 Daniel, Alice R	N cher	28	F	2914	Yes	
808 Daniel, Marina D	N cher	2	M	2898	No	
809 Daniel, James H	N cher	1	M	3786	No	
810 Dick, Mary	A Shaw	40	F	3176	No	
811 Dick, Amos	A Shaw	17	M	3564	No	
812 Daniel, Lucy Ann	N cher	22	F	4150	No	
813 Daniel, Johny	N cher	2	M	5659	No	
814 Dick, Oclola	N cher	22	M	7521	No	Farmer

Name	Race	Age	Sex	Census	Md	Remarks
815 Dick, Josie	N cher	24	F	3127	No	
816 Dick, Jeffrey	N cher	19	M	Dead	No	
817 Daugharty, Wm H	A Shaw	16	M	D1595	No	
818 Daugharty, Robert	A Shaw	25	M	5682	No	Enrolled as Ridley Daugherty
819 Duncan, John H	N cher	21	M	D1596	No	
820 Donalson, Wm M	A Shaw	30	M	7204	No	Merchant
821 Denis, Peter	N cher	22	M	8499	No	Farmer
822 Day, Cumming M	A Shaw	24	M	Dead	No	
823 Duncan, Charlotte C	N cher	18	F	D333	No	
824 Duncan, Joshua L	N cher	16	M	3373	No	
825 Davis, Jonah	N cher	28	M	Dead	No	Nothing, this man is a cripple
826 Davis, Sarah	N cher	19	F	6740	No	
827 Dianne,	N cher	18	F	Dead	No	
828 Dave, Mary	A Shaw	17	F	Dead	No	
829 Dirteater, Joseph	N cher	37	M	Dead	Yes	Farmer
830 Dirteater, Nancy	N cher	40	F	7962	Yes	
831 Daugherty, Isaac	A Shaw	29	M	Dead	Yes	Farmer
832 Daugherty, Frances	N cher	28	F	5069	Yes	Is the wife of Joe Sanders
833 Daugherty, Albert	N cher	6	M	Dead	No	
834 Daugherty, Dora	N cher	2	F	3701	No	
835 Davidson, Dan'l W	N cher	30	M	Dead	Yes	
836 Davidson, Mary E	N cher	31	F	Dead	Yes	
837 Daugherty, Lizzie	A Shaw	25	FF	3179	Yes	
838 Damerrson, Nancy	N cher	52	F	Dead	No	
839 Damerrson, John	N cher	23	M	3474	No	
840 Daugharty, Joseph	A Shaw	36	M	3800	Yes	Farmer
841 Daugharty, Matilda A	A White	33	F	Dead	Yes	
842 Daugharty, Josephine	A Shaw	13	F	Dead	No	
843 Daugharty, Lanexa F	A Shaw	10	F	3904	No	
844 Daugharty, Loula A	A Shaw	5	F	3640	No	On Dawes as Lula A Bailey (BLB)
845 Daugharty, Louella	A Shaw	5	F	3385	No	
846 Davison, Wm	N cher	8	M	D1597	No	
847 Davis, Wm F	A White	30	M	D1598	No	Ketchum, It
848 Davis, Frances C	N cher	25	F	Dead	Yes	
849 Davis, John W	N cher	6	M	4179	No	
850 Davis, Geo W	N cher	4	M	7520	No	
851 Davis, Minesota	N cher	2	F	Dead	No	
852 Davis, Thos H	N cher	2m	M	Dead	No	
853 Davis, Emily	A col	20	F	F936	Yes	Wife of Wm Davis rejected daughter of Betsy Glass, formerly Betsy Whitmire (Col) of Coo and Claims citizenship under treaty of

Name	Race	Age	Sex	Census	Md	Remarks
				1866		
854 Davis, Jackie	N col	3m	M	Dead	No	
855 Daniel, Hester	A del	20	F	Del 41	No	
856 Downing, James H	N cher	40	M	Dead	Yes	Farmer
857 Downing, Annewake	N cher	20	F	Dead	Yes	
858 Downing, Aleck	N cher	1	M	Dead	No	
859 Downing, John	N cher	30	M	Dead	Yes	
860 Downing, Nicoti	N cher	28	F	7574	Yes	
861 Downing, Emma	N cher	3	F	D1599	No	Is the wife of 1896 Saline mother 1896 Sal 1747
862 Downing, Smith	N cher	3	M	Dead	No	
863 Downing, Thompson	N cher	3m	M	Dead	No	
864 Daniel, Ana	N cher	38	F	Dead	No	
865 Davis, Jim	N cher	21	M	Dead	Yes	
866 Davis, Olsey	N cher	20	F	8523	Yes	
867 Davis, Ahquisah	N cher	6	F	8495	No	On Dawes as Susan Owens (BLB)
868 Davis, Sallie	N cher	3	F	2839	No	
869 Davis, Phillip	N cher	1	M	6658	No	
870 Dolly, Arch	N cher	50	M	Dead	No	
871 Dolly, Ahtanah	N cher	30	F	8833	Yes	
872 Dolly, Lydia	N cher	5	F	8514	No	On Dawes as Lydia Snell nee Backwater (BLB)
873 Dolly, Ada	N cher	4	F	Dead	No	
874 Daniel, Robert	N cher	25	M	3258	No	
875 Daniel, Martha	N cher	63	F	Dead	No	
876 Daugharty, Jane	A Shaw	19	F	4085	No	
877 Dean, Nancy	N cher		F	Dead		
878 Dean, Frank	N cher		M	Dead		
879 Deganoogoweeski, Solole	N cher			8377		Known as Charley Squirrell
880 Driver,	N cher			Dead		
881 Daris, Sarah	N cher		F	2839	No	
882 Emmons, Dallas	A White	36	M	R733	No	Carpenter
883 Emmons, Theodore P	A Shaw	10	M	D1344		Lives in MO, lived there may years
884 Emmons, Bettie J	A Shaw	8	F	Dead	No	
885 Emmons, Adelia	A Shaw	6	F	Dead	No	
886 Evert, Betsy	A del	35	F	Dead	No	
887 Elliotte, Geo W	N cher	30	M	Dead	Yes	Farmer
888 Elliotte, Rachel	N cher	20	F	Dead	Yes	
889 Elliotte, John W	N cher	7	M	D1600	No	1896 Coo 1589, he is scouting (running from the law BLB) brother of James Elliott, Pensacola, IT
890 Elliotte, James H	N cher	5	M	3247	No	
891 Elliotte, Elizabeth	N cher	2	F	Dead	No	

Name	Race	Age	Sex	Census	Md	Remarks
892 Elliotte, Arch	N cher	35	M	Dead	Yes	
893 Elliotte, Jess W	N cher	18	M	Dead	Yes	
894 Elliotte, Abigal	N cher	30	F	Dead	No	
895 Elliotte, Annie	N cher	35	F	5238	No	
896 Elliotte, Hiram	N cher	22	M	3449	No	
897 England, Joseph	N cher	55	M	Dead	No	Miller
898 England, Joseph	N cher	10	M	4033	No	
899 England, Lucy	N cher	6	F	4047	No	
900 England, Joseph	N cher	56	M	Dead	Yes	Farmer
901 England, Mary	AWhite	35	F	R672	Yes	
902 England, Mary T	N cher	13	F	2888	No	On Dawes as Josephine Buchanan (BLB)
903 England, Viola J	N cher	5	F	3714	No	
904 Evans, Minnie	N cher	16	F	4886	No	
905 Emery, Sarah Jane Blanc	N cher	5	F	3371	No	
906 England, Geo W	N cher	4	M	5219	No	
907 England, L W	N cher	40	M	Dead	Yes	
908 England, Sarah R	AWhite	29	F	3784	Yes	
909 England, Mary L	N cher	1w	F	4185	No	
910 Ellen, Manda	A Shaw	3	F	D1601	No	Not known to the Shawnees
911 Eiffert, Henry	N cher	32	M	2307	Yes	
912 Eiffert, Susan	N cher	28	F	2307	No	
913 Eiffert, Maude	N cher	7	F	2194	No	
914 Eiffert, Cecil E	N cher	5	M	2045	No	
915 Eiffert, Caria Etta	N cher	3	F	6011	No	
916 Eiffert, Margaret E	N cher	5m	F	2307	No	
917 Evans, W N	AWhite	20	M	Dead	Yes	School Teacher
918 Evans, Fannie J	N cher	20	F	Dead	Yes	
919 Evans, James P	N cher	10m	M	5102	No	
920 England, Charles	N cher	4	M	D1602	Yes	
921 Emily,	N cher	60	F	8923	No	
922 England, Jackson	N cher	49	M	Dead	Yes	Farmer
923 England, Salina	N cher	40	F	7500	Yes	
924 England, Washington	N cher	23	M	7499	No	
925 England, John W	N cher	20	M	5539	No	
926 England, Kate	N cher	14	F	2856	No	
927 England, Maude	N cher	13	F	3212	No	
928 England, Fannie J	N cher	6	F	3209	No	
929 England, Martin	N cher	4	M	8383	No	
930 Edmonson, M S	AWhite	26	M	6564	Yes	
931 Edmonson, Florence	N cher	19	F	6564	Yes	
932 Edmonson, Cherokee B	N cher	5m	F	2758	No	

The Delaware District

	Name	Race	Age	Sex	Census	Md	Remarks
933	England, Mary	N cher	48	F	Dead	No	
934	Elijah,	N cher	14	M	Dead	No	
935	England, Benj	N cher	31	M	3094	Yes	Originally in census under the name of Cornelius
936	England, Jensey C	AWhite	30	F	3094	No	
937	England, Susan C	N cher	10	F	3751	No	
938	England, James C	N cher	8	M	Dead	No	
939	England, Mary C	N cher	6	F	3163	No	
940	England, Pet C	N cher	4	M	4094	No	
941	Emery, Willie	AWhite	30	M	Dead	No	Stone Mason, Citizen by marriage but lost his wife
942	Edmonson, A V	AWhite	51	M	Dead	Yes	Farmer
943	Edmonson, Nancy M	N cher	41	F	214	Yes	
944	Edmonson, James T	N cher	3	M	213	No	
945	Edmonson, Chas D	N cher	1m	M	Dead	No	
946	Edmons, Mary	A Shaw	14	F	2883		These are children of Henry W Edmonds by a Shawnee------------ who has since died He has since married Susan Harris (nee England BLB) who live on Neutral Lands
947	Edmons, Sam'l	A Shaw	12	M	7213		
948	Edmons, David	N Shaw	19	M	Dead		
949	Edmons, Frank	N Shaw	8	M	5597		
950	Edmons, Anna	N Shaw	4	F	5479		
951	Flyer, Dirteater	N cher	25	M	Dead	Yes	Farmer
952	Flyer, Becky	N cher	25	F	9428	Yes	
953	Flyer, Jim	N cher	2	M	Dead	No	
954	Flyer, Peter	N cher	3m	M	Dead	No	
955	Flute,	N cher	67	M	Dead	Yes	
956	Flute, Nelly	N cher	60	F	Dead	Yes	
957	Flute, Annie	N cher	18	F	Dead	No	
958	Flute, Ahne	N cher	2	F	8534	No	
959	Fields, Samuel J	N cher	41	M	3715	Yes	
960	Fields, Caroline D	AWhite	31	F	3715	Yes	
961	Fields, Susie	N cher	4	F	Dead	No	
962	Fields, Maggie	N cher	3	F	Dead	No	
963	Fields, Mirtie B	N cher	10m	F	4166	No	
964	Foreman, Yerkinney	N cher	50	F	8344	No	
965	Foreman, Johaky	N cher	35	M	Dead	No	
966	Foreman, Bettie	N cher	25	F	Dead	No	
967	Foreman, Elam	N cher	22	M	8903	No	
968	Foreman, Sallie	N cher	18	F	Dead	No	
969	Foreman, Watt	N cher	49	M	8342	Yes	Farmer

Name	Race	Age	Sex	Census	Md	Remarks
970 Foreman, Setahnie	N cher	30	F	8342	Yes	
971 Foreman, Dick	N cher	3	M	Dead	No	
972 Foreman, Hugh	N cher	7m	M	8521	No	
973 Foreman, Jim	N cher	25	M	4516	Yes	
974 Foreman, Eliza	N cher	30	F	Dead	No	
975 Foreman, Andy	N cher	4	M	Dead	No	
976 Foreman, Bettie	N cher	4	F	5962	No	
977 Fields, James S	N cher	45	M	Dead	Yes	
978 Fields, Charlotte E	N cher	28	F	3069	Yes	
979 Fields, Mattie	N cher	16	F	Dead	No	
980 Fields, O M	N cher	12	M	3070	No	
981 Fields, Carrie	N cher	10	F	5803	No	
982 Fields, Nannie	N cher	10	F	271	No	
983 Fields, Alice L	N cher	6	F	4983	No	
984 Fields, Robertt W	N cher	4	M	6485	No	
985 Fields, Maud E	N cher	2m	F	5039	No	
986 Freeman, Mattie	N cher	18	F	61	No	
987 Freeman, Minnie J	N cher	16	F	2965	No	
988 Freeman, G J	N cher	25	M	60	Yes	
989 Freeman, Luella	N cher	18	F	60	Yes	
990 Freeman, Vina Maud	N cher	1m	F	Dead	No	
991 Freeman, D W	N cher	28	M	91	Yes	
992 Freeman, R S	AWhite	24	F	91	Yes	
993 Freeman, L P	N cher	3	F	Dead	No	
994 Fields, Timothy	N cher	20	M	4133	Yes	
995 Fields, Laura	AWhite	20	F	4133	Yes	
996 Fields, Mahala	AWhite	68	F	Dead	No	
997 Fields, Saffrona	N cher	32	F	169	No	
998 Fields, Susan	N cher	30	F	Dead	No	
999 Fields, Geo	N cher	42	M	4095	Yes	Farmer
1000 Fields, Sarah	N cher	25	F	4095	Yes	
1001 Fields, Jane	N cher	12	F	3917	No	
1002 Fields, Albert	N cher	10	M	4096	No	
1003 Fields, Susanna	N cher	8	F	3868	No	
1004 Fields, Redmond	N cher	5	M	7270	No	
1005 Fields, Walker	N cher	5	M	7471	No	
1006 Fields, Thomas	N cher	2	M	5652	No	
1007 Fields, Charlotte	N cher	5m	F	3026	No	
1008 Fields, Mack	N cher	1m	M	4130	No	
1009 Fields, Elizabeth	N cher	18	F	D1603	No	
1010 Fox, Joseph	N cher	33	M	7502	Yes	
1011 Fox, Anna	N cher	21	F	7502	Yes	

Name	Race	Age	Sex	Census	Md	Remarks
1012 Fox, Walter	N cher	2	M	5915	No	
1013 Fox, Lucy	N cher	11m	F	7470	No	
1014 Fields, Jefferson	N cher	28	M	5345	Yes	
1015 Fields, Linia	N cher	26	F	4463	Yes	
1016 Fields, Lizzie	N cher	7	F	3667	No	
1017 Fields, Layfaette	N cher	7	M	Dead	No	
1018 Fields, Charley	N cher	3	M	5343	No	
1019 Fields, Jeff	N cher	2m	M	5344	No	
1020 Fields, Thompson	N cher	36	M	Dead	Yes	
1021 Fields, Caroline	N cher	33	F	3188	Yes	
1022 Fields, Johnson	N cher	9	M	3965	No	
1023 Fields, Victoria	N cher	6	F	3189	No	
1024 Fields, Mathew	N cher	4	M	3615	No	
1025 Fluke, Frederick	AWhite	36	M	3858	Yes	Farmer
1026 Fluke, Susanna	N cher	39	F	Dead	Yes	
1027 Fluke, Geo	N cher	2m	M	3849	No	
1028 Foreman, Gertrude	N cher	2m	F	Dead	No	
1029 Fields, Thomas M	N cher	50	M	3908	Yes	
1030 Fields, Martha J	AWhite	52	F	3908	Yes	
1031 Fields, Wm	N cher	19	M	3942	No	
1032 Fields, Thos	N cher	14	M	3907	No	
1033 Fields, Alice J	N cher	9	F	Dead	No	
1034 Foreman, Worcestor	N cher	35	M	Dead	Yes	
1035 Foreman, Elizabeth	N cher	25	F	Dead	Yes	
1036 Foreman, Minerva	N cher	2	F	Dead	No	
1037 Frazer, E B	AWhite	31	M	3320	Yes	Farmer
1038 Fields, Ezekiel	N cher	30	M	3620	Yes	
1039 Frazer, Mary E	N cher	29	F	3620	Yes	Farmer
1040 Fields, Sabra	N cher	25	F	4035	No	
1041 Fields, Elizabeth	N cher	9	F	3393	No	
1042 Fields, Richard	N cher	7	M	4055	No	
1043 Fields, Isabell	N cher	5	M	3959	No	
1044 Fields, Emily	N cher	3	F	4053	No	
1045 Fox, Joseph Jr.	N cher	2	M	D1604	No	
1046 Fox, Joseph Sr.(Jr.?)	N cher	3m	M	6399	No	
1047 Fox, Rachel	N cher	6	F	152	No	
1048 Fields, Lewis	N cher	22	M	Dead	No	
1049 Fields, Ezekiel	N cher	38	M	4052	Yes	Farmer
1050 Fields, Margaret	N cher	35	F	4052	Yes	
1051 Fields, Westley	N cher	12	M	4054	No	
1052 Fields, Richard	N cher	10	M	2919	No	
1053 Fields, Mary Ann	N cher	7	F	128	No	

Name	Race	Age	Sex	Census	Md	Remarks
1054 Fields, Martha J	N cher	5	F	4052	No	
1055 Fields, Cynthia	N cher	1	F	Dead	No	
1056 Falling, Johnson	N cher	24	M	3263	No	
1057 Flyer, Lucy	N cher		F		No	No census card number given, nor is she listed as dead (BLB)
1058 Freeman, Wm S	N cher	23	M	Dead	No	School Teacher
1059 Foster, Eva	N cher	21	F	4029	No	These young folks own a farm near the Kansas lines but are themselves in Texas
1060 Foster, Robert	N cher	14	M	Dead	No	
1061 Franklin, Frances	A Shaw	20	F	3330	No	
1062 Franklin, John	A Shaw	18	M	7127	No	
1063 Franklin, Alex B	A Shaw	12	M	7126	No	
1064 Foster, Anika	A Col	31	M	Dead	No	Anika is a daughter of Reubin Downing who is a citizen under the treaty of 1866
1065 Fritz, Meldo	N Col	2m	F	Dead	No	
1066 Fritz, Francis	A White	44	M	3426	Yes	Well Digger
1067 Fritz, Agnes	N cher	22	F	Dead	Yes	
1068 Fritz, Joseph	A Shaw	3	M	2482	No	
1069 Fritz, Fannie	N cher	6m	F	3174	No	
1070 Flint, Jane	A Shaw	60	F	Dead	No	
1071 Flint, Joseph	A Shaw	46	M	3236	Yes	
1072 Flint, Subatab	A Shaw	26	F	D1605	No	Not known to Shawnee
1073 Frye, Andrew	A Col	46	M	F802	Yes	Farmer
1074 Frye, Milly	A Col	41	M	F802	Yes	
1075 Frye, Joseph	A Col	19	M	Dead	No	
1076 Frye, Mary Jane	A Col	17	F	F833	No	
1077 Frye, Sarah	N col	12	F	F852	No	
1078 Frye, Susan	N col	10	F	F834	No	
1079 Frye, Manda	N col	8	F	F817	No	
1080 Frye, Viola	N col	6	F	Dead	No	
1081 Frye, Ruth	N col	4	F	F1057	No	
1082 Frye, Carry	N col	2	F	F474	No	
1083 Frye, Safronia	N col	4m	F	F823	No	
1084 Ferrill, Mary	N cher	45	F	2875	No	
1085 Ferrill, Lizzie	N cher	5	F	3906	No	
1086 Ferrill, Girtie	N cher	4	F	3327	No	
1087 Forkedtail, Lewis	N cher	38	M	Dead	Yes	
1088 Forkedtail, Jinnie	N cher	26	F	8368	No	
1089 Foreman, Rachel A	N cher	18	F	4092	No	
1090 Fishtrap, Jim	N cher	21	M	2975	No	Know as James Musk on this roll, as Jim McLaughlin also
1091 Groves, Lydia	N cher	26	F	4957	No	

Name	Race	Age	Sex	Census	Md	Remarks
1092 Groves, Johnie	N cher	7	M	Dead	No	
1093 Groves, Joseph	N cher	2	M	Dead	No	
1094 Gobiner, Stephen	A White	53	M	Dead	Yes	
1095 Gobiner, Sarah	N cher	42	F	3772	Yes	
1096 Gobiner, Mary	N cher	17	F	3793	No	
1097 Gobiner, Martha	N cher	15	F	3797	No	
1098 Gobiner, Kate	N cher	11	F	3785	No	
1099 Gobiner, Dan'l	N cher	9	M	Dead	No	
1100 Gobiner, Sarah Jr.	N cher	6	F	3773	No	
1101 Green, W L Jr.	A Shaw	8	M	3783	No	
1102 Green, Bennette	N Shaw	4	M	10311	No	
1103 Goddard, Henry	N cher	22	M	3997	No	Farmer
1104 Greenfeather, John	A Shaw	25	M	3400	No	
1105 Grasshopper, Jack	N cher	39	M	8058	No	
1106 Going-to-count,	N cher	2m	M	Dead	No	
1107 Glass, Joe	N cher	23	M	D1606	Yes	
1108 Glass, Louisa	N cher	24	F	D1606	Yes	
1110 Gossett, James	A White	29	M	3045	Yes	
1111 Gossett, Demaris	N cher	20	F	Dead	Yes	
1112 Gossett, Geo	N cher	2m	M	3045	No	
1113 Glenn, Sam'l	A White	32	M	2846	Yes	
1114 Glenn, Ann	N cher	23	F	2846	Yes	
1115 Glenn, Wm	N cher	3m	M	Dead	No	
1116 Guess, Mose	N cher	40	M	Dead	No	Farmer
1117 Guess, Sakie	N cher	7	F	8349	No	
1118 Guess, Geo	N cher	5	M	8492	No	
1119 Goddard, James	N cher	45	M	5579	Yes	Farmer
1120 Goddard, Phebe	A White	33	F	5579	Yes	
1121 Goddard, Nerva	N cher	6	F	5436	No	
1122 Goddard, Henry M	N cher	5	M	5435	No	
1123 Grant, Edward	A White	30	M	Dead	Yes	School Teacher
1124 Grant, Susan	N cher	35	F	Dead	Yes	
1125 Gibney, Geo	A White	27	M	R176	Yes	Enrollment Refused, Farmer
1126 Gibney, Josephine	N cher	27	F	Dead	Yes	
1127 Gibney, Nettie	N cher	3	F	3134	No	On Dawes as Mittie A Bazzell (BLB)
1128 Gibney, Ida	N cher	2	F	3102	No	
1129 Gore, Johnathan	A White	46	M	107	Yes	Trader
1130 Gore, Sarah	A Shaw	35	F	107	Yes	
1131 Gore, Hattie	A Shaw	13	F	107	No	
1132 Gore, Blake	A Shaw	10	M	3885	No	
1133 Gore, Mary	N cher	6	F	3884	No	

Name	Race	Age	Sex	Census	Md	Remarks
1134 Gore, Johnathan	N cher	4	M	107	No	
1135 Gore, Sallie	N cher	7m	F	107	No	
1136 Guess, Jesse	N cher	35	M	Dead	No	Farmer
1137 Guess, Kate	N cher	12	F	7681	No	Wife of John Beamer in Saline
1138 Guess, Jesse Jr.	N cher	3	M	3246	No	Jessie Corntassle (BLB)
1139 Gilispie, John	A White	26	M	R686	Yes	
1140 Gilispie, Susan	N cher	19	F	Dead	Yes	
1141 Green, W L	A White	43	M	3494	Yes	Painter?
1142 Green, Sarah	A Shaw	40	F	Dead	Yes	
1143 Greenfeather, Wm	A Shaw	55	M	3235	Yes	Farmer
1144 Greenfeather, Eliza	A Shaw	50	F	3235	Yes	
1145 Greenfeather, Alice	A Shaw	19	F	3281	No	
1146 Greenfeather, Isaac	A Shaw	17	M	3504	No	
1147 Greenfeather, Alec	A Shaw	2	M	Dead	No	
1148 Gibson, John	A Shaw	6	M	4368	No	
1149 Gibson, John	N cher	18	M	2852	No	At the Male Seminary going to school
1150 Goodwin, Wm	N cher	30	M	Dead	Yes	
1151 Goodwin, Rosa	A White	20	F	Dead	Yes	
1152 Gunter, Sam Ella	N cher	6	F	5858	No	
1153 Graham, Wm	N cher	9	M	47	No	
1154 Guess, Nelson	N cher	26	M	Dead	No	
1155 George,	N cher	66	M	Dead	Yes	
1156 George, Kate	N cher	66	F	Dead	Yes	
1157 Graham, John	A Shaw	15	M	D1607	No	
1158 Gray, Isaac	N cher	21	M	Dead	No	
1159 Goingwater,	N cher	30	M	Dead	No	
1160 Goingwater, Rachel	N cher	6	F	Dead	No	
1161 Goingwater, Susanna	N cher	60	F	Dead	No	
1162 Grass, Benj	N cher	20	M	4826	No	
1163 Guess, David			M	Dead		
1164 Guthry, Nancy			F	Dead		
1165 Guthry, Jas			M	3534		
1166 Guthry, Jacob			M	10328		
1167 Hawkins, Charley	A Shaw	10	M	3349	No	
1168 Hawkins, Lucy	N cher	7	F	5396	No	
1169 Hawkins, Eva	N cher	5	F	D1608	No	Daughter of Jno Hawkins
1170 Hardiman, Wm	A Col	31	M	Dead	No	
1171 Hardiman, Jinnie	A Col	14	F	F722	No	
1172 Hardiman, Joseph	A Col	10	F?	F1068	No	
1173 Howard, Frank	A White	40	M	281	Yes	___ Lawyer
1174 Howard, Josaphine	N cher	27	F	Dead	Yes	

The Delaware District

Name	Race	Age	Sex	Census	Md	Remarks
1175 Howard, Ollie	N cher	9	F	5254	No	
1176 Howard, Frank	N cher	7	M	498	No	
1177 Howard, Percy P	N cher	5	M	7366	No	
1178 Hilburn, J W	A White	44	M	Dead	Yes	Farmer
1179 Hilburn, Amanda	N cher	27	F	Dead	Yes	
1180 Hilburn, Harvey	N cher	3	M	Dead	No	
1181 Hilburn, William H	N cher	2	M	Dead	No	
1182 Horn, William	N cher	25	M	Dead	Yes	
1183 Horn, Eliza	N cher	24	F	3446	Yes	
1184 Hall, James O	A White	34	M	3321	Yes	
1185 Hall, Mary	N cher	34	F	3321	Yes	
1186 Hall, Clinton D	N cher	5	M	Dead	No	
1187 Hall, Luda C	N cher	3	F	3336	No	
1188 Hampton, Alfred Corn	A White	24	M	Dead	No	
1189 Hampton, Mary Ellen	N cher	21	F	D1609	No	Wyandot Indians lived in Cherokee Nation
1190 Hampton, Florence C	N cher	2m	F	D1610	No	
1191 Harlin, Jas E	N cher	49	M	199	Yes	Farmer
1192 Harlin, Nancy A	N cher	36	F	199	Yes	
1193 Harlin, Rosa Lee	N cher	12	F	4632	No	
1194 Harlin, Geo Ellis	N cher	6	M	7421	No	
1195 Harlin, Lotta Bell	N cher	4	F	Dead	No	
1196 Harlin, Aloeso V	N cher	1	M	199	No	
1197 Harlin, J B	N cher	41	M	2998	Yes	Farmer
1198 Harlin, Mary	N cher	35	F	Dead	Yes	
1199 Harlin, Jane	N cher	11	F	4111	No	
1200 Harlin, Ruth	N cher	9	F	2998	No	
1201 Harlin, Fannie	N cher	7	F	2859	No	
1202 Harlin, John	N cher	5	M	4136	No	
1203 Harlin, Ada	N cher	3	F	6616	No	
1204 Hanna, Jerry	A White	38	M	Dead	Yes	Farmer
1205 Hanna, Joanna	N cher	25	F	4024	Yes	
1206 Hanna, Anna	N cher	2	F	3943	No	
1207 Hanna, Leola	N cher	7m	F	3948	No	
1208 Hitchens, Dick	A White	35	M	Dead	Yes	Farmer
1209 Hitchens, Sweetie	A Shaw	10	F	4446	Yes	
1210 Hitchens, Cricket	N cher	7m	F	4447	No	
1211 Hawkins, Susan	N cher	44	F	Dead	No	
1212 Henderson, Jas	N cher	12	M	Dead	No	
1213 Hensley, John Anna	N cher	19	F	6058	No	
1214 Hilderbrand, Benj	N cher	30	M	3216	Yes	Farmer
1215 Hilderbrand, Delilah	N cher	25	F	Dead	Yes	

Name	Race	Age	Sex	Census	Md	Remarks
1216 Hilderbrand, Sarah	N cher	8	F	Dead	No	
1217 Helderbrand, Eliza	N cher	13	F	D1612	No	
1218 Helderbrand, Joseph	N cher	6m	M	4249	No	
1219 Helderbrand, Sam'l	N cher	2m	M	3174	No	
1220 Hilderbrand, Dennis	N cher	27	M	Dead	Yes	Farmer
1221 Hilderbrand, Lucy	AWhite	28	F	5867	Yes	
1222 Hilderbrand, Wm	N cher	4	M	4069	No	
1223 Hilderbrand, Joseph	N cher	1m	M	2306	No	
1224 Hilderbrand, Thos	N cher	2	M	3287	No	On Dawes as Wallace Hilderbrand (BLB)
1225 Hitchcock, J B	AWhite	55	M	R720	Yes	Enrollment Refused
1226 Hitchcock, E A D	N cher	47	F	Dead	Yes	
1227 Hitchcock, Etta	N cher	19	F	3500	No	Etta Burns enrolled Census of 83
1228 Hitchcock, J D	N cher	15	M	2961	No	
1229 Hawk, Alexander	N cher	44	M	Dead	Yes	
1230 Hawk, Sarah	A Shaw	35	F	2857	Yes	
1231 Hawk, Lydia	N cher	14	F	3063	No	
1232 Hawk, Benj	N cher	7	M	2857	No	
1233 Hawk, Lahowie	N cher	4	M	Dead	No	
1234 Hawk, Noah	N cher	1	M	3672	No	
1235 Haycock, Mary	N cher	48	F	3013	No	This name should have been Hickox
1236 Haycock, Wm	N cher	19	M	Dead	No	
1237 Haycock, Henry	N cher	10	M	53	No	
1238 Haycock, Anna	N cher	6	F	5241	No	
1239 Hereford, Elkanna	AWhite	65	M	Dead	No	Merchant
1240 Hereford, Wm B	AWhite	28	M	R202?	No	Enrollment Refused, by mistake these men are on the wrong list, they are citizens living together, father and son
1241 Hudson, Thos	N cher	50	M	Dead	Yes	
1242 Hudson, Sallie	N cher	48	F	3806	Yes	
1243 Hudson, James	N cher	18	M	4150	No	
1244 Hudson, Sylvannus	N cher	12	M	4019	No	
1245 Hudson, Alfred	N cher	8	M	Dead	No	
1246 Howell, Wm	AWhite	30	M	3397	Yes	Farmer
1247 Howell, Eliza	N cher	30	F	3397	Yes	
1248 Howell, Mary	N cher	7	F	163	No	
1249 Howell, Martha	N cher	4	F	3401	No	
1250 Howell, Minnie	N cher	2	F	2958	No	
1251 Hawkins, Thos	AWhite	40	M	Dead	Yes	
1252 Hawkins, Sarah C	N cher	25	F	39	Yes	
1253 Hawkins, Martha Ellen	N cher	1m	F	2822	No	
1254 Hall, Suel	N cher	12	M	4037	No	These boys are sons of D D Hall

Name	Race	Age	Sex	Census	Md	Remarks
						by his first wife who was Cherokee (Mary Elizabeth Scrimsher census 4147 BLB)
1255 Hall, Edward	N cher	10	M	4074	No	
1256 Hall, Jesse	N cher	7	M	Dead	No	
1257 Haff, Israel	A Del	66	M	Dead	Yes	Farmer
1258 Haff, Mary	A Del	55	F	Del 30	Yes	
1259 Haff, Cyrus	A Del	26	M	Del 60	No	
1260 Haff, Joseph	A Del	24	M	Dead	No	
1261 Haff, Sarah	A Del	20	M	Del 48	No	
1262 Haff, Hiram	A Del	18	M	Del 32	No	
1263 Haff, Wm	A Del	18	M	Del 31	No	
1264 Haff, Carrie	A Del	14	M	Del 49	No	
1265 Haff, Benj	A Del	12	M	Del 65	No	
1266 Haff, Dood	N Del	8	M		No	No census card number given, nor is he listed as dead (BLB)
1267 Hider, Andrew	N cher	24	M	7516	Yes	
1268 Hider, Anna	N cher	24	F	Dead	Yes	
1269 Hider, Joel	N cher	7	M	8913	No	
1270 Hider, Susan	N cher	7	F	3224	No	
1271 Hider, Joel	N cher	4	M	7592	No	
1272 Hilderbrand, Elijah	N cher	24	M	7529	Yes	
1273 Hilderbrand, Dianna	N cher	40	F	Dead	Yes	
1274 Hogshooter, Ned	N cher	33	M	8752	Yes	
1275 Hogshooter, Nundy	N cher	25	F	8752	Yes	
1276 Hogshooter, Oce	N cher	12	M	9048	No	
1277 Hogshooter, Jim	N cher	6	M	8830	No	
1278 Hogshooter, Betsy	N cher	3	F	Dead	No	
1279 Hogshooter,	N cher	40	M	Dead	No	
1280 Hogshooter, Jessie	N cher	25	F	6676	Yes	
1281 Hogshooter, Peggy	N cher	19	F	6676	No	
1282 Hogshooter, Teequeske	N cher	1	M	6675	No	
1283 Hogshooter, Anna	N cher	1m	F	6658	No	
1284 Harrison, D W	AWhite	34	M	3274	Yes	
1285 Harrison, Mary F	N cher	40	F	3274	Yes	
1286 Harrison, Julia	N cher	11	F	3547	No	
1287 Harrison, Andrew P	N cher	9	M	3680	No	
1288 Harrison, Zada	N cher	5	F	3674	No	
1289 Harrison, Nathan C	N cher	1	M	3661	No	
1290 Horsefly, Watt	N cher	37	M	Dead	Yes	
1291 Horsefly, John	N cher	8	M	8366	No	
1292 Horsefly, Rachel	N cher	4	F	4348	No	
1293 Harrison, Jack	AWhite	60	M	Dead	Yes	

Name	Race	Age	Sex	Census	Md	Remarks
1294 Harrison, Letha	N cher	40	F	3019	Yes	
1295 Harrison, W T	A White	38	M	5823	Yes	
1296 Hasting, Louisa J	N cher	40	F	5823	Yes	
1297 Hasting, John R	N cher	15	M	5830	No	
1298 Hasting, W W	N cher	13	M	617	No	
1299 Hasting, C D	N cher	10	F	73	No	On Dawes as Delilah Victor (BLB)
1300 Hawkins, Jasper	A White	28	M	R522	Yes	Enrollment Refuse, Farmer
1301 Hawkins, Catherine	N cher	26	F	Dead	Yes	
1302 Hawkins, Emma	N cher	6	F	3721	No	
1303 Hawkins, Geo	N cher	4	M	3971	No	
1304 Hawkins, Robert	N cher	1	M	3592	No	
1305 Hill, H L	A White	44	M	Dead	Yes	
1306 Hill, E A	N cher	45	F	2850	Yes	
1307 Hill, John	N cher	14	M	2915	No	
1308 Hill, Minnta	N cher	11	F	9550	No	
1309 Hill, James F	N cher	9	M	Dead	No	
1310 Hill, Oliver M	N cher	7	M	2933	No	
1311 Hill, Rollin R	N cher	5	M	2882	No	
1312 Hizer, F M	A White	31	M	6492		
1313 Hizer, Martha E	N cher	36	F	6492		
1314 Hizer, Lilian E	N cher	6	F	6633		
1315 Hizer, Marah F	N cher	4	F	6492		
1316 Hizer, Lucy F	N cher	2	F	6493		
1317 Hilderbrand, Wm	N cher	19	M	D969	No	
1318 Hawkins, John	A White	30	M	3679	No	
1319 Haw, Black	N cher	18	M	Dead	No	Mill hand
1320 Handle, Wm	N cher	24	M	8325	No	Farmer
1321 Hummingbird, Flint	N cher	26	M	2992	No	
1322 Hummingbird, Randolp	N cher	20	M	7420	No	
1323 Hummingbird, Jim	N cher	28	M	2989		Mill hand
1324 Hilderbrand, Watt	N cher	25	M	Dead	Yes	Farmer
1325 Hilderbrand, Caroline	N cher	21	F	8537	Yes	
1326 Hilderbrand, John	N cher	3	M	8508	No	
1327 Hilderbrand, Chas	N cher	3m	M	Dead	No	
1328 Hendrick, Ella	A del	13	F	Dead	No	
1329 Hendrick, Susie	A del	11	F		No	Dup 39 of Sal Dist
1330 Hendrick, Louisa J	A del	8	F	Dead	No	
1331 Harlin, Nancy	N cher	70	F	Dead	No	
1332 Hogshooter, Tyanee	N cher	11	F	Dead		
1333 Hall, Newton			M	4120		
1334 Harlin, Matilda			F	184		

Name	Race	Age	Sex	Census	Md	Remarks
1335 Harlin, Albert			M	184		
1336 Inlow, Thomas	N cher	17	M	5587	No	
1337 Inlow, Laura	N cher	14	F	649	No	
1338 Inlow, Henry	N cher	11	M	5586	No	
1339 Inlow, Caroline	N cher	8	F	3086	No	
1340 Ironsides, Susan	A Shaw	35	F	3335	No	
1341 Ironsides, Charley	A Shaw	19	M	10269	No	
1342 Jones, Newton	N cher	19	M	Dead	No	
1343 Steve or John on the Hill	N cher	22	M	3202	Yes	
1344 Steve, Josty,	N cher	30	M	Dead	Yes	
1345 Steve, Allick	N cher	1	M	Dead	No	
1346 Jackson, Jackson	N cher	7	M	D1611	No	
1347 Johnson, Andrew	N cher	37	M	Dead	No	Sheriff
1348 Jones, Jackson	N cher	30	M	Dead	Yes	Farmer
1349 Jones, Lucy	N cher	40	F	Dead	Yes	
1350 Jones, Lizzie	N cher	20	F	Dead	No	
1351 Jones, James	N cher	5	M	D1217	No	
1352 Jones, Peter	N cher	3	M	Dead	No	
1353 Jones, Isaac	AWhite	40	M	Dead	Yes	
1354 Johnson, Martha E	N cher	34	F	3611	Yes	
1355 Johnson, Mart	N cher	18	M	Dead	No	
1356 Johnson, Berry	N cher	45	M	Dead	Yes	White, adopted by Shawnees (BLB)
1357 Johnson, Charlotte	N cher	30	F	2879	Yes	
1358 Johnson, Wm R	A Shaw	15	M	Dead	No	
1359 Johnson, Lewis	N cher	8	M	2881	No	Should be a female and on the Dawes as Louisa F Cunningham (BLB)
1360 Johnson, John L	N cher	4m	M	2879	No	
1361 Johnson, Geo W	AWhite	28	M	10280	Yes	
1362 Johnson, Eliza	N cher	28	F	Dead	Yes	
1363 Johnson, Matilda	N Shaw	8	F	D1613	No	
1364 Johnson, Rebecca	N Shaw	6	F	D1614	No	
1365 Johnson, Berry Jr.	N cher	15m	M	D1615	No	Transferred to census card 2879 (BLB)
1366 James, Solon	AWhite	37	M	82	Yes	
1367 James, P J	N cher	31	F	82	Yes	
1368 James, Calvin	N cher	12	M	46	No	
1369 Johnos, Anna	N Shaw	12	F	3824	No	
1370 James, Alonzo	N cher	9	M	84	No	
1371 James, Clara D	N cher	6	F	82	No	
1372 James, Albert	N cher	2	M	85	No	
1373 Johnson, Chas	AWhite	35	M	Dead	Yes	Carpenter

Name	Race	Age	Sex	Census	Md	Remarks
1374 Johnson, Josephine	N cher	24	F	4601	Yes	
1375 Johnson, Fred G	N cher	17m	M	4440	No	
1376 Jones, Nellie	N cher	27	F	3479	No	
1377 Jones, Levi	N cher	7	M	3480	No	
1378 John,	N cher	22	M	9431	Yes	On Dawes as Jack Redbird (BLB)
1379 John,	N cher	20	M	D1617	No	
1380 Jackaliar,	N cher	3	M	3608	No	On Dawes as Jack Summerfield (BLB)
1381 Joab,	N cher	25	M	D1618	Yes	
1382 Jennie,	N cher	18	F	Dead	Yes	
1383 Jennie	N cher	21	F	Dead	No	
1384 Josiah, Teekamasky	N cher	12	M	Dead	No	
1385 Josinna, Ahleecher	N cher	1m	M	Dead	No	
1386 Josinna,	N cher	29	M	Dead	Yes	Farmer
1387 Josinna, Anna	N cher	16	F	Dead	Yes	
1388 Johnson,	N cher	8	M	9134	No	Dead
1389 Jase, E	N cher	1	M	Dead	No	
1390 Josiah,	N cher	22	M	8324	Yes	Farmer
1391 Josiah, Oolooche	N cher	20	F	8324	Yes	
1392 Josiah, Ailsey	N cher	2	F	Dead	No	
1393 Jones, Jesse	N cher	26	M	Dead	Yes	Farmer
1394 Jones, Anna	N cher	29	F	Dead	Yes	
1395 Jones, Phillip	N cher	9	M	Dead	No	
1395 Jacksin,	N cher	16	M		No	
1396 Jumper, Chelawnata	N cher	19	F	8535	Yes	
1397 Jumper, Pheasant	N cher	10m	M	8517	No	
1398 Jumper,	N cher	18	M	8535	Yes	
1399 Jefferson,	N cher	20	M	9430	Yes	Farmer
1400 Jefferson, Ahsunyah	N cher	20	F	Dead	Yes	
1401 James, Preston S	AWhite	25	M	155	Yes	
1402 James, Mattie E	N cher	21	F	155	Yes	
1403 James, Mirtle B	N cher	2	F	156	No	
1404 James, Zula G	N cher	2m	F	155	No	
1405 Juahlate,	N cher	39	M	Dead	Yes	
1406 Juahlate, Polly	N cher	33	F	Dead	Yes	
1407 Juahlate, Celia	N cher	3	F	Dead	No	
1408 Juahlate, Lizzie	N cher	16	F		No	Dup of 2096
1409 James, Garret	AWhite	28	M	4102	Yes	
1410 James, Mary E A	N cher	28	F	4102	Yes	
1411 James, Evin M	N cher	1	M	7054	No	
1412 Journeycake, Eliza	N Del	9	F	Del 7	No	
1413 Johnson, Thos	Supplemental roll		M	6262		

The Delaware District

Name	Race	Age	Sex	Census	Md	Remarks
1414 Johnson, Rebecca	""		F	6262		
1415 Johnson, Jas	""		M	6488		
1416 Johnson, Eddie	""		M	Dead		
1417 Johnson, Sherman	""		M	6498		
1418 Johnson, Mary	""		F	6474		
1419 Johnson, Martha	""		F	6467		
1420 Jimmie,	""		F	Dead		
1421 Johnson, Hiram	A Shaw	23	M	Dead	No	Farmer
1422 Johnson, Altabena	N cher	19	F	D1620	No	Lives in Arkansas
1423 Kahtayah,	N cher	25	F	9430	Yes	
1424 Klaus, Robert	A White	39	M	R140	Yes	Enrollment Refused
1425 Klaus, Mary Ann	N cher	32	F	Dead	Yes	
1426 Klaus, Wm	N cher	6	M	3696	No	
1427 Klaus, Mary A	N cher	2	F	2864	No	On Dawes as Alice Klaus (BLB)
1428 Kahtayah,	N cher	2	F	Dead	No	
1429 Kahtayah, Lewis	N cher	5m	M	Dead	No	
1430 Kahyawah,	N cher	30	M	Dead	Yes	Farmer
1431 Kahyawah, Taky	N cher	20	F	3605	Yes	
1432 Kuhucha,	N cher	2	F	Dead	No	
1433 Kerucha,	N cher	18	F		No	Dup of 2005
1434 Kahtahyah,	N cher	5	F	8356	No	On Dawes as Nancy Sharp nee Buck (BLB)
1435 Kahnoogeesky,	N cher	21	M	8371	Yes	On Dawes as Ike Cheater his parents on census 8367 (BLB)
1436 Kahnoogeesky, Ahtekla	N cher	24	F	8371	No	
1437 Ketcher,	N cher	30?	M	Dead	No	
1438 Kannoskees,	N cher	25	M	8516	Yes	
1439 Kahnoskees, Nelsin	N cher	30	F	8516	Yes	
1440 Kahnoskees, Tuneree	N cher	3	F	8515	No	
1441 Kaywood, John T	A White	29	M	Dead	Yes	Farmer
1442 Kaywood, Nancy M	N cher	20	F	Dead	Yes	
1443 Kaywood, Moses S	N cher	3	M	6029	No	
1444 Kaywood, Herbert T	N cher	1	M	6027	No	
1445 Kahawka,	N cher	20	F	Dead	No	
1446 Ketcher, Johnson	N cher	12	M	7488	No	
1447 Ketcher, Ross	N cher	10	M	Dead	No	
1448 Ketcher, Levi	N cher	6	M	3609	No	
1449 Ketcher, Mary	N cher	3	F	4016	No	
1450 Knight, Robert D	N cher	34	M	3502	Yes	Saddle & Harness Maker
1451 Knight, Martha L	A White	24	F	3502	Yes	
1452 Knight, Herman	N cher	2	M	7017	No	
1453 Knight, Robert F	N cher	2m	M	3502	No	
1454 Kelly, Willie	N cher	14	M	3854	No	

Name	Race	Age	Sex	Census	Md	Remarks
1455 Kelly, Lula	N cher	12	F	3706	No	
1456 Ketcher, Charley	N cher	21	M	Dead	No	
1457 Ketcher, Thos E	A Del	23	M	Del 26	No	
1458 Katahyah,	N cher	20	F	6665	No	
1459 Kahnell,	N cher	23	M	D1651	No	
1460 Kinney, Charles D	N cher	23	M	4165	No	
1461 Kayyan,	N cher	50	F	Dead	No	
1462 Ketcher, John	N cher	41	M	Dead	No	
1463 Ketcher, Malinda	N cher	12	F	Dead	No	
1464 Ketcher, Rhoda	N cher	9	F	Dead	No	
1465 Knight, Thomas	N cher	35	M	Dead	Yes	Farmer
1466 Knight, Rachel	N cher	30	F	3576	Yes	
1467 Knight, Victora	N cher	10	F	Dead	No	
1468 Knight, Joseph	N cher	8	M	3792	No	
1469 Knight, Morris	N cher	6	M	3308	No	
1470 Knight, Thos	N cher	4	M	3405	No	
1471 Knight, Henry	N cher	2	M	4121	No	
1472 Keener, Ned	N cher	67	M	Dead	Yes	
1473 Keener, Nannie	N cher	60	F	Dead	Yes	
1474 King, Catherine	A Shaw	50	F	3823	No	
1475 King, James	A Shaw	30	M	3824	No	
1476 King, Geo	A Shaw	25	M	Dead	No	
1477 King, Elizabeth	A Shaw	15	F	Dead	No	
1478 King, Patrick Henry	N cher	7	M	3833	No	
1479 Ketchum, Wm R	A Del	50	M	Dead	Yes	
1480 Ketchum, Lucy	A Del	50	F	Dead	Yes	
1481 Ketchum, Caroline	A Del	21	F	Dead	No	
1482 Ketchum, Jas Sr.	A Del	62	M	Dead	Yes	
1483 Ketchum, Elizabeth	A Del	45	F	Del 70	Yes	
1484 Ketchum, Jas Jr.	A Del	13	M	Dead	No	
1485 Ketchum, Jane Anna	N Del	9	F	Del 59	No	
1486 Ketchum, Lucinda	N Del	7	F	Del 71	No	
1487 King, Kate	A Shaw	19	F	3552	No	
1488 Kell, James	N cher	4	M	5577	No	
1489 Kootiee	N cher	70	F	Dead	No	
1490 Kahletawchee,	from sup. Rolls		M	Dead	No	
1491 Landrum, Winnie	A Col	45	F	F702	No	Admitted under the Treaty of 1866
1492 Landrum, Spencer	A Col	25	M	F743	Yes	
1493 Landrum, Sam'l	A Col	10	M	Dead	No	
1494 Lewis,	N cher	3	M	D1620	No	
1495 Lydia	N cher	100	F	Dead	No	

The Delaware District

Name	Race	Age	Sex	Census	Md	Remarks
1496 Lucky, N B	A White	53	M	2796	Yes	Mill man, owns a stream and mill
1497 Lucky, Lucy	N cher	50	F	Dead	Yes	
1498 Lindsey, Malinda	N cher	18	F	D1622	No	
1499 Lamar, F B F	N cher	29	M	Dead	Yes	Farmer
1500 Lamar, Mary	N cher	25	F	44	Yes	
1501 Lamar, Mariah	N cher	2	F	129	No	
1502 Lucas, Jennie	N cher	40	F	Dead	No	
1503 Lucas, Julia	N cher	14	F	Dead	No	
1504 Lucas, Betsy	N cher	12	F	6042	No	
1505 Lucas, Johney	N cher	9	M	6081	No	
1506 Lucas, Mary	N cher	7	F	D1624	No	
1507 Lucas, Nannie	N cher	3	F	497	No	
1508 Landrum, H T	N cher	40	M	Dead	Yes	Farmer
1509 Landrum, A C	N cher	36	F	Dead	Yes	
1510 Landrum, Joseph V	N cher	18	M	Dead	No	
1511 Landrum, Johnathan W	N cher	11	M	Dead	No	
1512 Landrum, James Kell	N cher	3	M	2837	No	
1513 Lundy, Robert J	A White	44	M	Del 24	Yes	
1514 Lundy, Louisa	A Del	40	F	Dead	Yes	
1515 Lundy, Edward E	A Del	18	M	Del 4	No	
1516 Lundy, Rosa E	A Del	16	F	Del 17	No	
1517 Lundy, Elulah G	A Del	14	F	Del 46	No	
1518 Lundy, Robert L	A Del	9	M	Del 54	No	
1519 Lundy, Leander	A Del	7	M	Del 43	No	
1520 Lundy, Flora D	A Del	4	F	Del 3	No	
1521 Lundy, Cleora A	A Del	2	F	Del 45	No	
1522 Landrum, Charlotte	N cher	20	F	7417	Yes	
1523 Landrum, James P	N cher	2	M	7418	No	
1524 Landrum, Alonza	N cher	2m	M	7419	No	
1525 Landrum, Elizabeth	N cher	47	F	3836	No	
1526 Landrum, Benj	N cher	25	M	3311	No	
1527 Landrum, Cicero	N cher	21	M	3789	No	
1528 Landrum, Louisa	N cher	13	F	Dead	No	
1529 Landrum, Charles F	N cher	10	M	3612	No	
1530 Landrum, Wm A	N cher	7	M	Dead	No	
1531 Landrum, Ada	N cher	5	F	3835	No	
1532 Lasater, Wm L	A White	23	M	Dead	Yes	
1533 Lasater, Betsy	A Del	43	F	Dead	Yes	
1534 Longtail, Samuel	A Shaw	20	M	Dead	No	
1535 Longtail, Amanda	A Shaw	18	F	Dead	No	
1536 Longtail, Barney	A Shaw	10	M	3173	No	
1537 Lamar, J R	A White	31	M	Dead	Yes	Farmer

Name	Race	Age	Sex	Census	Md	Remarks
1538 Lamar, Lydia	N cher	46	F	Dead	Yes	
1539 Lamar, Jesse	N cher	14	M	2955	No	
1540 Lamar, Jas	N cher	10	M	3438	No	
1541 Lamar, Charley	N cher	7	M	4146	No	
1542 Lamar, Alex	N cher	16m	M	Dead	No	
1543 Lamar, Pollie	N cher	23	F	3770	No	
1544 Lamar, Jas	N cher	4	M	4125	No	
1545 Lamar, Eddie	N cher	2	M	7503	No	
1546 Lamar, Ewing	N cher	20	M	Dead	Yes	
1547 Lamar, Jennie	N cher	28	F	4183	Yes	
1548 Lamar, Sallie	N cher	8	F	4139	No	
1549 Lynch, Allen	A Col	40	M	F700	Yes	
1550 Lynch, Cynthia	N cher	30	F	3364	No	
1551 Lynch, Florence	N Col	11	M	3893	No	Children are listed as Colored because their father was Colored (BLB)
1552 Lynch, Eddie	N Col	9	M	3781	No	Census card cancelled transferred to 10084 (BLB)
1553 Lynch, Birtie	N Col	7	M	3364	No	
1554 Lynch, Andrew	N Col	3	M	4536	No	
1555 Lynch, Mary	N Col	6m	F	3631	No	Card was cancelled and transferred to Freedman's card 1257 (BLB)
1556 Landrum, David D	N cher	21	M	Dead	No	Citizen by marriage but having lost his wife
1557 Log, Big	N cher	33	M	D1625	No	Pos Error or Cornstalk and wife at Vinita
1558 Lynch, Anderson	A Col	40	M	F791	Yes	Crape Lynch better know by that name is a citizen under the Treat of 1866, (married to Ruth E Downing 1/2 Cherokee, 1/2 Colored on census 10341 BLB)
1559 Lynch, Rhoda	N cher	15	F	D1626	No	Colored
1560 Lynch, Dinah	N cher	12	F	FD825	No	
1561 Lynch, Wm	N cher	9	M	D1627	No	
1562 Lynch, Tobias	A Col	25	M	F763	Yes	Farmer
1563 Lynch, Martha	A Shaw	18	F	Dead	Yes	
1564 Lynch, Susie	A Shaw	17m	F	3239	No	
1565 Lucky, Geo	AWhite	38	M	Dead	Yes	Wagon maker
1566 Luckey, Martha	N cher	39	F	Dead	Yes	
1567 Luckey, Sarah F	N cher	10	F	3117	No	
1568 Luckey, Sabina	N cher	5	F	3132	No	
1569 Luckey, Jackie	N cher	10m	M	3133	No	
1570 Lynch, Johney	A Col	18	M	F326	No	
1571 Large, Benj	AWhite	64	M	Dead	Yes	Blacksmith
1572 Large, Sabina	N cher	55	F	Dead	Yes	

Name	Race	Age	Sex	Census	Md	Remarks
1573 Large, Benj F	N cher	20	M	3264	No	Farmer
1574 Large, Oceola Q	N cher	16	M	Dead	No	
1575 Large, Wm C	N cher	13	M	3164	No	
1576 Lindsley, L E	N cher	20	F	5544	No	
1577 Leach, John W	N cher	22	M	4839	Yes	
1578 Leach, Lizzie Merrita	N cher	23	F	4839	Yes	
1579 Langley, Rachel E	A White		F	Dead	No	
1580 Langley, Cynthia C	N cher		F	6085	No	
1581 Langley, Wm J	N cher		M	6967	No	
1582 Langley, Noah	N cher		M	6038	No	
1583 Landrum, Nellie	N cher	43	F	3742	No	
1584 Landrum, Francis D	N cher	22	M	Dead	No	
1585 Landrum, Johnson	N cher	20	M	3785	No	Farmer
1586 Landrum, Samuel	N cher	13	M	3742	No	
1587 Landrum, Edward	N cher	9	M	3755	No	
1588 Landrum, David D	N cher	55	M	Dead	Yes	___ Smith
1589 Landrum, Susan	N cher	50	F	5201	Yes	
1590 Landrum, Nancy	N cher	23	F	6945	No	
1591 Landrum, Rachel	N cher	20	F	5262	No	
1592 Landrum, Chas L	N cher	18	M	Dead	No	
1593 Landrum, Elias Mc	N cher	14	M	5771	No	
1594 Lane, Mabel	N cher	6	F	Dead	No	
1595 Lawrence, J W	A White	45	M	D1628	No	1896 Del Dist 234 (734?BLB) been in California for 15 years, Citizen by marriage but lost his wife
1596 Lynch, Charley	A White	30	M	Dead	Yes	Stone mason
1597 Lynch, Alice J	A Del	22	M	Del 57	Yes	
1598 Lynch, Luther L	A Del	3	M	Dead	No	
1599 Landrum, Jo				Dead		
1600 Landrum, John			M	Dead		
1601 Leek, Edward			M	Dead		
1602 Leek, Elizabeth			F	F1043		
1603 Leek, Ed Jr.			M	F114		
1604 Leek, Henry			M	F951		
1605 Lafalier, Louis			M	4115		
1606 Lafalier, Sarah F			F	Dead		
1607 Lafalier, Franklin			M	4116		
1608 Lafalier, Ama E			F	4075		
1609 Martin, Wilson	A Col	40	M	Dead	Yes	Farmer
1610 Martin, Martha	A Col	35	F	Dead	Yes	
1611 Martin, Ida	N Col	11	F	F790	No	
1612 Martin, Frank	N Col	10	M	F695	No	

Name	Race	Age	Sex	Census	Md	Remarks
1613 Martin, Jinnie	N Col	7	F	F697	No	
1614 Martin, Mary	N Col	5	F	F866	No	
1615 Martin, Gen Blunt	N Col	4	M	F873	No	
1616 Martin, Frederick	A Col	50	M	Dead	Yes	Citizen under Treaty of 1866, Never left the county
1617 Martin, Juno	A Col	60	F	F805	Yes	
1618 Martin, Amy	N Col	25	F	F725	No	
1619 Martin, Isaac	N Col	19	M	F712	No	
1620 Martin, Hattie	N Col	7	F	F719	No	
1621 Martin, Sallie	N Col	4	F	F733	No	
1622 Martin, Love	N Col	2	F	F947	No	
1623 Mitchell, Mary	N cher	37	F	Dead	No	__ Store, This woman came from Gilmore with her husband was ___ man says she is Cherokee looks like one, Mitchell has since died (Mary Dawson Old Settler BLB)
1624 Mitchell, Franklin	N cher	10	M	10302	No	
1625 Mitchell, Mary	N cher	6	F	399	No	
1626 Mitchell, Margaret	N cher	3	F	D1629	No	
1627 Mitchell, Joseph	N cher	1	M	441	No	
1628 Martin, Richard L	N cher	31	M	3114	Yes	Farmer
1629 Martin, Nancy E	N cher	25	F	Dead	Yes	
1630 Martin, John	N cher	6	M	D1630	No	
1631 Martin, Robert Lee	N cher	3	M	D1631	No	
1632 Martin, Joseph E	N cher	15m	M	D1632	No	
1633 Morris, Wm L	A White	51	M	D1633	No	
1634 Miller, Martin	N cher	30	M	2816	No	Trader
1635 Miller, Nancy M	N cher	19	F	3735	No	
1636 Miller, Daniel D	N cher	1	M	2817	No	
1637 Mayfield, Elijah	A White	50	M	4648	Yes	Farmer
1638 Mayfield, Sarah	N cher	42	F	4648	Yes	
1639 Martin, Susin	A Col	19	F	F742	No	
1640 Martin, Nathaniel	N Col	5	M	F788	No	
1641 Martin, Sallie	A Col	28	F	Dead	Yes	
1642 Martin, Arthur	N Col	10	M	F738	No	
1643 Martin, Joseph	N Col	8	M	Dead	No	
1644 Martin, Wm	N Col	6	M	Dead	No	
1645 Martin, John	N Col	3	M	Dead	No	
1646 Martin, Worcester	N Col	8	M	Dead	No	
1647 Miller, Ezekiel	N cher	53	M	Dead	Yes	Carpenter
1648 Miller, Minerva	N cher	39	F	Dead	Yes	
1649 Miller, Stand	N cher	14	M	3890	No	
1650 Miller, Henry	N cher	12	M	Dead	No	

Name	Race	Age	Sex	Census	Md	Remarks
1651 Miller, Elmira	N cher	9	F	Dead	No	
1652 Miller, William	N cher	19	M	7212	No	Farmer, Nancy Miller his mother lives in Tahlequah
1653 McDaniel, Mollie	N cher	20	F	D1634	No	Wife of Bill Woodard
1654 Melton, Chas F	N cher	23	M	2866	No	Farmer
1655 Melton, Bettie	N cher	22	F	2826	No	
1656 Melton, Willey J	N cher	21	M	108	No	
1657 Mills, John Andrew	A Shaw	19	M	5674	No	Trader, doing business with his father, son of Abram Mills (census card 3919 BLB)
1658 Monroe, Thos J	N cher	26	M	136	No	Trader
1659 Muskrat, David	N cher	21	M	Dead	No	
1660 Miller, Jas	A White	25	M	Dead	No	His wife abandon him
1661 Moore, Nelson	A Col	27	M	F810	Yes	
1662 Moore, Rose	A Col	27	F	F810	Yes	
1663 Moore, Rhedas	N Col	7	F	F862	No	
1664 Moore, Emily F	N Col	5	F	F811	No	
1665 Moore, Chany	N Col	3	F	Dead	No	
1666 Moore, Mary	N Col	9m	F	F715	No	
1667 Mann, Marshall	A White	30	M	4735	No	
1668 Mann, Pauline	N cher	26	F	4735	Yes	
1669 Mann, Fannie	N cher	2m	F	Dead	No	
1670 Mike, Will	N cher	30	M	Dead	Yes	
1671 Mike, Lucy	N cher	18	F	Dead	Yes	
1672 Mike, Robin	N cher	6	M	8533	No	
1673 Mike, Becke	N cher	1	M	8373	No	On Dawes as Becky Cheater (BLB)
1674 Mike, Ainsey	N cher	16	M	Dead	No	
1675 Minnie,	N cher	3	F	D1635	No	
1676 Mouse, Jim	N cher	30	M	Dead	Yes	
1677 Mouse, Awa	N cher	25	F	6093	No	
1678 Mouse, Wahcooly	N cher	3	M	3652	No	
1679 Mouse, Lewis	N cher	1	M	4186	No	
1680 Martha	N cher	1	F	D1636	No	
1681 Mouse, Degine	N cher	50?	M	8381	Yes	
1682 Mose, Oosquina	N cher	38	F	Dead	Yes	
1683 Mouse, Blossom	N cher	15	M	3924	No	
1684 Mouse, Sahnahna	N cher	12	M	8919	No	
1685 Mouse, Cheawsoly	N cher	6	F	8528	No	
1686 Mouse, Jinnie	N cher	2	F	Dead	No	
1687 McLaughlin, Geo	N cher	43	M	Dead	Yes	Farmer
1688 McLaughlin, Susie E	N cher	10	F	Dead	Yes	
1689 McLaughlin, Sabra Ann	N cher	6	F	3124	No	

Name	Race	Age	Sex	Census	Md	Remarks
1690 Mouse, Tiah	N cher	45	M	Dead	Yes	
1691 Mouse, Susanna	N cher	35	F	Dead	Yes	
1692 Mouse, Hummingbird	N cher	12	M	Dead	No	
1693 Mouse, Chowweuke	N cher	6	F	Dead	No	
1694 Mouse, Chewanes	N cher	7	F	3680	No	
1695 Mouse, Nahner	N cher	1	F	8379	No	
1696 Melton, S W	N cher	58	M	Dead	Yes	
1697 Melton, Mary Ann	N cher	40	F	124	Yes	
1698 Melton, Willie T	N cher	17	M	2831	No	
1699 McLaughlin, Wm	N cher	42	M	3998	Yes	
1700 McLaughlin, Anna	N cher	46	F	Dead	Yes	
1701 McLaughlin, Jim	N cher	21	M	2975	No	Same as Jim Fishtrap
1702 McLaughlin, Sallie	N cher	19	F	7585	No	
1703 McLaughlin, Geo	N cher	16	M	3209	No	
1704 McLaughlin, Frank	N cher	12	M	Dead	No	
1705 McCamish, Jas	AWhite	34	M	3848	Yes	
1706 McCamish, Sarah A	A Del	38	F	Del 47	Yes	
1707 McCamish, R W C	N cher	2	M	Del 52	No	
1708 McCamish, Betsy	A Del	17	F	Del 51	No	
1709 McCamish, Florence	N Del	7m	F	Del 5	No	
1710 Mitchell, Geo	AWhite	25	M	4041	Yes	Farmer
1711 Mitchell, Susan	N cher	20	F	Dead	Yes	
1712 Mitchell, Robert Lee	N cher	4	M	4147	No	
1713 Mitchell, Levia	N cher	3	F	6336	No	
1714 Martin, John	N cher	44	M	Dead	Yes	
1715 Martin, Lucinda	N cher	44	F	413	Yes	
1716 Martin, Wm	N cher	9	M	7090	No	
1717 Martin, Susie E	N cher	7	F	2485	No	
1718 Martin, Mary	N cher	5	F	3794	No	
1719 Martin, Abraham	N cher	2	M	413	No	
1720 McAffrey, Hugh	AWhite	42	M	3542	Yes	
1721 McAffrey, Fannie	N cher	27	F	3542	Yes	
1722 McAffrey, Andrew	N cher	6	M	3524	No	
1723 McAffrey, John	N cher	4	M	3543	No	
1724 McAffrey, Mary	N cher	2	F	4010	No	
1725 McAffrey, Albert	N cher	2m	M	3542	No	
1726 Matoy, Wm	N cher	60	M	Dead	No	
1727 Matoy, Sonora	N cher	6	F	194	No	
1728 Murphy, Isabel	N cher	34	F	51	No	
1729 Murphy, Susie E	N cher	7	F	4433	No	
1730 Murphy, Mand E	N cher	6	F	101	No	
1731 Muskrat, McNair	N cher	25	M	8340	Yes	

Name	Race	Age	Sex	Census	Md	Remarks
1732 Muskrat, Ov MC	N cher	27	M	Dead	Yes	
1733 Mode, Isaac	A White	43	M	3072	Yes	School Teacher
1734 Mode, Sarah A	N cher	34	F	3072	Yes	
1735 Mode, Henrietta	N cher	5	F	3921	No	
1736 Mode, Charlotte	N cher	3	F	3696	No	
1737 Mode, John Ross	N cher	1	M	3694	No	
1738 Mellir, Robert	A White	50	M	3008	Yes	Farmer
1739 Mellir, Mary	N cher	30	F	3008	Yes	
1740 Mellir, Margrete	N cher	10	F	3010	No	
1741 Mellir, Sarah Anne	N cher	8	F	64	No	
1742 Mellir, Louella	N cher	7	F	2823	No	
1743 Mellir, Susan Jane	N cher	3	F	Dead	No	
1744 Mellir, Robert P	N cher	1	M	4114	No	
1745 Mellir, Jesse	N cher	1	M	4105	No	
1746 McGee, T J	N cher	36	M	179	Yes	
1747 McGee, M J	A White	32	F	Dead	Yes	
1748 McGee, F E	N cher	11	M	4032	No	
1749 McGee, R E	N cher	9	M	3442	No	
1750 McGee, S B	N cher	8	M	3959	No	
1751 McGee, J M	N cher	7	M	4043	No	
1752 McGee, T J	N cher	4	M	4174	No	
1753 McGee, M V	N cher	2	M	3112	No	
1754 Mayes, Wm P	N cher	24	M	3828	Yes	
1755 Mayes, Annie H	N cher	25	F	3828	Yes	
1756 Mayes, Maggie M	N cher	20m	F	5812	No	
1757 McGee, Susan	N cher	47	F	3484	No	
1758 McGee, Cynthia Ann	N cher	19	F	118	No	
1759 McGee, David	N cher	28	M	3985	Yes	
1760 McGee, Mary C	A White	24	F	3985	Yes	
1761 McGee, Francis C	N cher	6	M	4009	No	
1762 McGee, Rose Anna	N cher	4	F	5598	No	
1763 McGee, David A	N cher	2	M	4008	No	
1764 McGee, Dennis Bushyhead	N cher	5m	M	3985	No	
1765 Mitchell, Sallie Ann	N cher	45	F	4056	No	
1766 Mitchell, Don Juan	N cher	20	M	4057	No	
1767 Mitchell, Walker	N cher	19	M	7037	No	
1768 McCollough, M H	A White	39	M	4007	Yes	Farmer
1769 McCollough, Rachel J	N cher	33	F	4007	Yes	
1770 McCollough, John W	N cher	10	M	93	No	
1771 McCollough, William P	N cher	8	M	4000	No	
1772 McCollough, Peter	N cher	7	M	5357	No	
1773 McCollough, James F	N cher	6	M	59	No	

Name	Race	Age	Sex	Census	Md	Remarks
1774 McCollough, George E	N cher	2	M	3111	No	
1775 McCollough, Joseph H	N cher	8m	M	4001	No	
1776 Moore, Ellis	N cher	28	M	3678	Yes	Carpenter
1777 Moore, Mary E	A White	18	F	3678	Yes	Mary E Moore is in Idaho has been there since last Spring expects to come home soon
1778 Monroe, J M	N cher	28	M	Dead	Yes	Farmer
1779 Monroe, Mary Frances	A White	19	F	D1637	Yes	Married out, does not apply
1780 Moore, Allcut	N cher	37	M	Dead	Yes	
1781 Moore, Elizabeth	N cher	30	F	Dead	Yes	
1782 Moore, Richard	N cher	13	M	Dead	No	
1783 Moore, Lewis	N cher	8	M	Dead	No	
1784 Moore, Lee	N cher	4	M	4161	No	
1785 Moore, John	N cher	18m	M	2621	No	
1786 Miller, John	N cher	36	M	2950	Yes	
1787 Miller, Lucinda	N cher	30	F	2950	Yes	
1788 Miller, Avry	N cher	8	M	5570	No	
1789 Miller, Wm P	N cher	2	M	3071	No	
1790 Miller, Sarah J	N cher	2m	F	3595	No	
1791 Miller, Edward	N cher	6	M	3962	No	
1792 Miller, Andrew	N cher	33	M	2981	Yes	Farmer
1793 Miller, Martha Ann	A White	22	F	2981	Yes	
1794 Miller, Flora	N cher	2	F	154	No	
1795 Miller, Ida	N cher	1	F	3521	No	
1796 McGinnis, Charley	A White	40	M	10121	Yes	
1797 McGinnis, Sarah R	N cher	30	F	Dead	Yes	
1798 McGinnis, Wm F	N cher	2m	M	5155	No	
1799 McBain, Ida J	N cher	13	F	2820	No	
1800 McBain, Thos	N cher	8	M	Dead	No	
1801 McGannon, Jas T	A White	24	M	Dead	Yes	
1802 McGannon, Lucy Ann	N cher	24	F	Dead	Yes	
1803 McGannon, Anna F	N cher	19	F	Dead	No	
1804 Mills, Abraham	A White	54	M	3913	Yes	Trader, this man and his wife live in Senaca but own some property in the Nation. The woman is a daughter of James Ordrain, They expect to return soon (this note looks incorrect but it is off the original census records of 1880, on her Dawes card she is listed as the daughter of George and Polly Dodge George is listed as a Shawnee and Polly as an AS Delaware BLB)
1805 Mills, Eliza	A Shaw	41	F	3913	Yes	

Name	Race	Age	Sex	Census	Md	Remarks
1806 Mills, Francis	A Shaw	17	M	4026	No	
1807 Mills, Cyrus	A Shaw	11	M	4028	No	
1808 Mills, Benjamin	N cher	6	M	5662	No	
1809 Mills, Mary Jane	N cher	3	F	4058	No	
1810 Mills, William	N cher	18m	M	4149	No	
1811 McLaughlin, Betsy	N cher	63	F	Dead	Yes	
1812 McLaughlin, Franklin	N cher	24	M	3950	No	Farmer
1813 McLaughlin, Chas	N cher	22	M	Dead	No	
1814 McLaughlin, Benj	N cher	26	M	Dead	No	
1815 McLain, Franklin P	AWhite	23	M	Dead	Yes	
1816 McLain, Senora	N cher	22	F	Dead	Yes	
1817 Muskrat, Betsy	N cher	25	F	6934		
1818 McGannon, Lucy Ann			F	Dead		
1819 McGannon, Jas F			M	Dead		
1820 Marker, John D	AWhite	54	M	Del 5	Yes	Farmer
1821 Marker, Jane	N cher	35	F	Del 5	Yes	
1822 Marker, Eliza Ann	N cher	10	F	Del 35	No	
1823 Marker, John B Jr	N cher	8	M	Del 16	No	
1824 Marker, Cyrus	N cher	6	M	Dead	No	Enrolled as Delaware
1825 Marker, Robert J	N cher	4	M	3266	No	
1826 Marker, Sarah E	N cher	3	F	Del 25	No	
1827 Marker, Josephine	N cher	1	F	Del 18	No	
1828 Muskrat, Johnson	N cher	20	M	Dead	Yes	
1829 Muskrat, Mary	N cher	25	F	120	Yes	
1830 Muskrat, Jacob	N cher	44	M	Dead	Yes	
1831 Muskrat, Martha	N cher	47	F	Dead	Yes	
1832 Muskrat, Jas	N cher	21	M	4137	No	
1833 Muskrat, Nancy	N cher	24	F	151	No	Dup 1847 Del
1834 Muskrat, Cynthia	N cher	14	F	6355	No	
1835 Muskrat, Nannie	N cher	9	F	4144	No	
1836 Muskrat, William	N cher	5	M	Dead	No	
1837 Moore, Lewis	AWhite	25	M	3297	Yes	
1838 Moore, Bettie	N cher	25	F	3297	Yes	
1839 Moore, Wm	N cher	3	M	3325	No	
1840 McSpadden, Thos	AWhite	28	M	5461	Yes	McSpadden farm and stock are in Cooweescoowee District
1841 McSpadden, Eliza	N cher	25	F	3692	Yes	
1842 Muskrat, Daniel	N cher	60	M	Dead	Yes	
1843 Muskrat, Polly	N cher	70	F	Dead	Yes	
1844 Muskrat, J D	N cher	28	M	116	No	
1845 Muskrat, T J	N cher	22	M	7494	No	
1846 Muskrat, Nancy	N cher	25	F	151	No	

Name	Race	Age	Sex	Census	Md	Remarks
1847 Muskrat, Nancy	N cher	23	F	5325	No	
1848 Moon or Moore, Thos			M	D1640		
1849 Miers, Geo W	N cher	22	M	89	No	This young man is blind
1850 Miers, Maud			F	D1641		
1851 Merrill, Oscar	N cher	9	M	Dead	No	
1852 McDaniel, Alice	N cher	18	F	Dead	No	
1853 McNair, Lizzie	N cher	17	F	Dead	No	
1854 Melton, Sampson			M	51		
1855 McLaughlin, Jas	N cher	34	M	Dead	Yes	Farmer
1856 McLaughlin, Sarah	N cher	26	F	Dead	Yes	
1857 McLaughlin, Rachel	N cher	6	F	Dead	No	
1858 McLaughlin, Ida May	N cher	4	F	6660	No	
1859 Muskrat, Thalax	N cher	9	M	2870	No	On Dawes as Daniel Muskrat (BLB)
1860 Martin, Noolie E	N cher	16	F	5547	No	
1861 Martin, Mary Ann	A Del		F	Dead		
1862 McAlister, J H			M	Dead		
1863 McAlister, Louisa			F	D1642		
1864 McAlister, Ellen			F	5080		
1865 McAlister, Chas Edward			M	Dead		
1866 Neighbors, L S	AWhite	65	M	Dead	Yes	Farmer
1867 Neighbors, Cynthia	N cher	26	F	Dead	Yes	
1868 Neighbors, Isaac	N cher	9m	M	1308	No	
1869 Nix, Robert K	AWhite	35	M	3780	Yes	
1870 Nix, Sabina	N cher	29	F	3780	Yes	
1871 Nix, Ada	N cher	7	F	4043	No	
1872 Nix, Robert	N cher	6	M	6271	No	
1873 Nix, Sarah	N cher	1	F	3899	No	
1874 Nix, John	N cher	4	M	2525	No	
1875 Neidiffer, Isaac	AWhite	61	M	Dead	Yes	Farmer
1876 Neidiffer, Lucy	N cher	51	F	Dead	Yes	
1877 Neidiffer, Geo W	N cher	19	M	3343	No	
1878 Neidiffer, Rachel	N cher	10	F	3647	No	
1879 Neidiffer, Lucy	N cher	7	F	3038	No	
1880 Neidiffer, Foreman	N cher	31	M	3351	Yes	
1881 Neidiffer, Mary R	A Del	30	F	Del 20	Yes	
1882 Neidiffer, Edward O	N cher	3	M	Del 347	No	Census card 10676 (BLB)
1883 Neidiffer, Louisa Sabina	N cher	1	F	Del 39	No	
1884 Neighbors, Robert B	AWhite	29	M	3002	Yes	
1885 Neighbors, Nancy C	N cher	23	F	Dead	Yes	
1886 Neighbors, Lucy F	N cher	20m	F	4045	No	
1887 Neighbors, Luvenia L	N cher	20m	F	4038	No	

Name	Race	Age	Sex	Census	Md	Remarks
1888 Neidiffer, Samuel	N cher	31	M	50	Yes	
1889 Neidiffer, Emma	N cher	21	F	50	Yes	
1890 Neidiffer, Mary	N cher	11	F	3882	No	
1891 Neidiffer, Charley	N cher	9	M	3910	No	
1892 Neidiffer, Isaac Jr.	N cher	2	M	111	No	
1893 Neidiffer, Samuel J	N cher	6m	M	50	No	
1894 Nancy,	N cher	45	F	Dead	No	
1895 Neidiffer, Felix	N cher	20	M	Dead	Yes	
1896 Neidiffer, Joanna	N cher	19	F	3261	Yes	
1897 Neidiffer, Erminia F	N cher	2	F	3262	No	
1898 Noster, Taylor	N cher	20	M	Dead	Yes	
1899 Noster, Kahawker	N cher	26	F	Dead	Yes	
1900 Noster, Taylor	N cher	3	M	8323	No	Rider Goodmoney (BLB)
1901 Necotia,	N cher	50	M	Dead	No	
1902 Nipp, Joseph	N cher	13	M	3912	No	Citizen under the treaty with the Shawnee two Nipps
1903 Nipp, Frank	N cher	9	M	Dead	No	
1904 Nakee	N cher	18	F	Dead	No	
1905 Nepoleon, Edward O	N cher	18	M	D1639	No	
1906 Ootahlun,	N cher	20	M		No	Farmer, (no census card number given nor is he listed as dead (BLB)
1907 Oobskasety,	N cher	20	F	8066	No	
1908 Oolawnahstesky,	N cher	70	M	Dead	Yes	
1909 Oosowee,	N cher	33	M	Dead	Yes	
1910 Oosowee, Sarah	N cher	29	F	3668	Yes	
1911 Oosowee, Harry	N cher	11	M	3665	No	
1912 Oosowee, Anna	N cher	9	F	3671	No	
1913 Oosowee, Ailsy	N cher	5	F	Dead	No	
1914 Oosowee, Sarah	N cher	9	F	Dead	No	
1915 Oosowee, Ailsy	N cher	3	F	7496	No	
1916 Oosquina	N cher	60	F	Dead	No	
1917 Oaksy,	N cher	25	M	D1643	Yes	Dead, Farmer
1918 Olty, Lucy	N cher	40	F	D1644	No	
1919 Olty, Annie	N cher	10	F	D1645	No	
1920 Olty, Lewis	N cher	8	M	D1646	No	
1921 Ootaneter,	N cher	28	M	D1647	Yes	Farmer
1922 Ootaneter, Ahtoouke	N cher	18	F	D1647	Yes	
1923 Ootaneter, Charity	N cher	1m	M	D1648	No	
1924 Ootie	N cher	80	F	Dead	No	
1925 Ordrain, Jas P	AWhite	55	M	Dead	Yes	Surname should be Audrain (BLB)
1926 Ordrain, Mary J	N cher	57	F	Dead	Yes	

Name	Race	Age	Sex	Census	Md	Remarks
1927 Ordrain, Wingfield	N cher	24	M	174	No	
1928 Ordrain, F G	N cher	20	M	4135	No	
1929 Ookillah,	N cher	27	F	5069	No	
1930 Olking,	N cher	3	F	8522	No	
1931 Ooscuntny,	N cher	2	M	D1649	No	
1932 Okeryanty,	N cher	52	M	Dead	No	
1933 O'Fields, Dick	N cher	50	M	8345	Yes	
1934 O'Fields, Lizzie	N cher	45	F	8345	Yes	
1935 O'Fields, Aggy	N cher	21	F	8363	No	
1936 O'Fields, Martha	N cher	19	F	7958	No	
1937 O'Fields, Lizzie	N cher	17	F	3219	No	
1938 O'Fields, Robert	N cher	12	M	7513	No	
1939 O'Fields, Henry	N cher	8	M	6006	No	
1940 O'Fields, Anna	N cher	7	F	3656	No	On Dawes as Annie Tanner(BLB)
1941 O'Fields, Charley	N cher	28	M	8502	Yes	Mill hand
1942 O'Fields, Nancy	N cher	19	F	Dead	Yes	
1943 O'Fields, Ben	N cher	22	M	7953	Yes	
1944 O'Fields, Sam	N cher	2	M	7954	No	
1945 O'Fields, Anna	N cher	22	F	7953	Yes	
1946 O'Fields, Chickalelee	N cher	6m	M	7953	No	
1947 Old Fields, Willie	N cher	20	M	Dead	No	
1948 O'Fields, Mose	N cher	18	M	3650	No	
1949 O'Fields, Johnson	N cher	46	M	Dead	Yes	
1950 O'Fields, Sarah	AWhite	37	F	9468	Yes	
1951 O'Fields, Samuel	N cher	13	M	3031	No	
1952 O'Fields, Peter	N cher	7	M	Dead	No	
1953 O'Fields, Lizzie	N cher	7	F	3109	No	
1954 O'Fields, Louella	N cher	3	F	3043	No	
1955 O'Fields, Sarah Ellen	N cher	1	F	Dead	No	
1956 Ooyouseetter,	N cher	3	M	7893	No	
1957 Pyeatt, Morgan	AWhite	29	M	Dead	Yes	Farmer
1958 Pyeatt, Senora	N cher	21	F	4808	Yes	
1959 Pyeatt, Caledonia	N cher	6m	F	Dead	No	
1960 Pigeon, Webster	N cher	12	M	7424	No	On Dawes as Webster Halfbreed (BLB)
1961 Perry, O V	N cher	38	M	Dead	Yes	
1962 Perry, Eliza	AWhite	34	F	2861	Yes	
1963 Perry, Columbus	N cher	7	M	3095	No	
1964 Perry, Artemus	N cher	1	M	3012	No	
1965 Parks, Johnson C	N cher	28	M	3346	Yes	
1966 Parks, Minerva	AWhite	25	F	3346	Yes	
1967 Parks, Melvin	N cher	9m	M	3750	No	

Name	Race	Age	Sex	Census	Md	Remarks
1968 Parks, T J	N cher	59	M	Dead	Yes	
1969 Parks, Mevia Ann	N cher	49	F	Dead	Yes	
1970 Parks, Annie	N cher	20	F	3136	No	
1971 Parks, Jeffrey	N cher	18	M	6805	No	
1972 Parks, Elmira	N cher	15	F	3038	No	
1973 Parks, James A T	N cher	13	M	10213	No	
1974 Parks, Fannie E	N cher	9	F	3466	No	
1975 Polson, Dr. W D	A White	49	M	Dead	No	
1976 Polson, Mary E	N cher	16	F	2985	No	
1977 Polson, F A	N cher	13	F	Dead	No	
1978 Polson, John Henry	N cher	6	M	2938	No	
1979 Polson, Wm Dudley	N cher	4	M	2925	No	
1980 Pigeon, Lyda	N cher	13	F	Dead	No	
1981 Pitcher, Horrace	A Shaw	18	M	Dead	No	
1982 Padon, Ben J	N cher	20	M	Dead	Yes	Farmer
1983 Padon, Johnnie	A White	10	F	Dead	Yes	
1984 Padon, Thos	N cher	18m	M	6669	No	
1985 Poorbear, Laura	N cher	10	F	3318	No	
1986 Pate, Louis	A White	50	M	Dead	Yes	
1987 Pate, Letha	N cher	43	F	141	Yes	
1988 Pate, Albert Newton	N cher	18	M	140	No	
1989 Pate, Joesph Baxter	N cher	13	M	142	No	
1990 Payne, Henry	A White	33	M	Dead	Yes	
1991 Payne, Susan	A Shaw	22	F	3029	Yes	
1992 Payne, Lillian	A Shaw	4	F	5067	No	Daughter of Henry Hardin Trott, Cherokee (BLB)
1993 Payne, Fleet	A Shaw	18m	M	2947	No	Should be a female, on Dawes as Fleety Donaldson (BLB)
1994 Pott, Falling	N cher	25	M	6123	Yes	Dead
1995 Pott, Aiking	N cher	30	F	Dead	Yes	
1996 Pott, Grant	N cher	11	M	6435	No	
1997 Pott, Eve	N cher	7	F	8391	No	
1998 Pott, Lucy	N cher	3	F	8518	No	
1999 Pott, Betty	N cher	5	F	7943	No	
2000 Pott, Dobkins	N cher	1	M	6782	No	
2001 Priceo, (Pricer)	N cher	30	M	8977	Yes	On Dawes as Price Parchcorn (BLB)
2002 Priceo, Nellie	N cher	25	F	Dead	Yes	
2003 Priceo, Zebedee	N cher	3	M	Dead	No	
2004 Priceo, Josiah	N cher	20	M	8973	No	
2005 Pricer, Kereecha	N cher	18	F	Dead	No	
2006 Pig, Runabout	N cher	30	M	Dead	Yes	
2007 Pig, Aggy	N cher	16	F	Dead	Yes	

Name	Race	Age	Sex	Census	Md	Remarks
2008 Pig, Nancy	N cher	12	F	Dead	No	
2009 Perch, Sun	N cher	22	M	Dead	Yes	Sun Perch and his wife Wakee having separated, the property given to him to said woman and his children, Farmer
2010 Perch, Weekee	N cher	40	F	Dead	Yes	
2011 Perch, Rider	N cher	9	M	8384	No	
2012 Perch, Jessee	N cher	5	M	8385	No	
2013 Parchmeal,	N cher	18	M	Dead	No	Farmer
2014 Parchmeal, Betty	N cher	15	F	8507	No	
2015 Parchcorn, Will	N cher	25	M	Dead	Yes	
2016 Parchcorn, Solkin	N cher	25	F	Dead	Yes	
2017 Parchcorn, Sutoowah	N cher	8	M	Dead	No	
2018 Parchcorn, Ooghwe	N cher	1	M	Dead	No	
2019 Peter,	N cher	20	M	8491	Yes	Peter is almost blind
2020 Peter, Bettie	N cher	15	F	8491	Yes	
2021 Parris, Geo	N cher	53	M	Dead	No	
2022 Parris, Letha	N cher	38	F	2542	No	
2023 Parris, Nellie	N cher	26	F	6425	No	
2024 Parris, John	N cher	19	M	D1652	No	
2025 Parris, Rachel	N cher	17	F	5983	No	
2026 Parris, Jane	N cher	17	F	5978	No	
2027 Parris, Jim	N cher	28	M	2546	Yes	
2028 Parris, Nancy	N cher	32	F	2546	Yes	
2029 Parris, Rachel	N cher	8	F	Dead	No	
2030 Parris, Annie	N cher	6	F	2753	No	
2031 Parris, Cherokee	N cher	4	F	2746	No	
2032 Parris, Willis	N cher	3	M	5977	No	
2033 Parris, Nellie	N cher	1	F	2739	No	
2034 Parris, Pollie	AWhite	60	F	Dead	No	
2034 Panther, Rachel	N cher	40	F	6653	No	
2035 Pigeon, Young	N cher	24	M	6996	Yes	Farmer
2036 Pigeon, Kate	N cher	25	F	Dead	Yes	
2037 Pigeon, Rigoo	N cher	2	M	6996	No	
2038 Pigeon, Ookillah	N cher	1m	M	6996	No	
2039 Pott, Kehuhnecker	N cher	32	M	Dead	Yes	
2040 Pott, Awa	N cher	25	M	Dead	Yes	
2041 Phillips, Jinnie	N cher	30	F	Dead	No	
2042 Phillips, M H	AWhite	37	M	4570	Yes	
2043 Phillips, Joseph B	N cher	23	M	4570	Yes	
2044 Phillips, Frank	N cher	11	M	4640	No	
2045 Phillips, Penn	N cher	9	M	4081	No	
2046 Phillips, Augusta C	N cher	8	F	4568	No	

The Delaware District

Name	Race	Age	Sex	Census	Md	Remarks
2047 Phillips, Vienna	N cher	6	F	Dead	No	
2048 Phillips, Julia Ann	N cher	2	F	213	No	
2049 Phillips, John B	N cher	3	M	Dead	No	
2050 Phillips, Susan P	N cher	1	F	4546	No	
2051 Parrish, Virginia	A Shaw	44	F	Dead	No	Mrs Parrish lives in Del. but her farm is in Saline
2052 Parrish, Orin	A Shaw	18	M	3281	No	
2053 Parrish, Nancy Jane	A Shaw	16	F	4668	No	
2054 Parrish, Cadison	A Shaw	13	M	3270	No	
2055 Parrish, Anna	A Shaw	8	F	94	No	
2056 Parrish, Geo	A Shaw	8	M	3240	No	
2057 Payne, Cicero	N cher	42	M	Dead	Yes	Shoemaker
2058 Payne, Caroline	N cher	39	F	Dead	Yes	
2059 Payne, Johnathan	N cher	20	M	2805	No	
2060 Payne, Susanna	N cher	16	F	4728	No	On Dawes as Susanna Picaman (BLB)
2061 Payne, Julins	N cher	10	M	2557	No	
2062 Parks, G W	N cher	60	M	Dead	Yes	Farmer
2063 Parks, Louisa	AWhite	54	F	Dead	Yes	
2064 Parks, Cherokee	N cher	30	F	Dead	No	
2065 Parks, Dondeneah	N cher	20	F	3151	No	Dondemat Couch on census roll of 1883
2066 Parks, Geo W	N cher	18	M	Dead	No	
2067 Parks, Ruth	N cher	12	F	3467	No	
2068 Perry, E H	N cher	26	M	208	No	
2069 Perry, N M	N cher	24	M	7191	No	N M Perry is a brother of S M and E H Perry who were admitted by the citizenship courts
2070 Perry, S M	N cher	23	M	112	No	
2071 Pursel, Sallie	N cher	67	F	Dead	No	
2072 Paden, Jas	N cher	23	M	49	No	
2073 PitcherGeo	A Shaw	21	M	5612	No	
2074 Powell, Wash	N cher	27	M	166	No	
2075 Powder, Falling Jim	N cher	23	M	D1653	No	
2076 Payne, Herman	AWhite	30	M	D1654	Yes	This man married a Cherokee but is now at his father's in Illinois but ___ property here
2077 Payne, Delora E	N cher	16	F	Dead	Yes	
2078 Preston, Chas H	N cher	42	M	186	Yes	Physician
2079 Preston, Martha E	N cher	18	F	67	Yes	
2080 Preston, Clara	N cher	7m	F	3462	No	
2081 Pool, Lulu N	N cher	19	F	3593	No	
2082 Powell, Alex	N cher	14	M	F785	No	
2083 Polly	N cher	13	F	D1655	No	
2084 Powell, Johnnie	N cher	11	F	2940	No	

Name	Race	Age	Sex	Census	Md	Remarks
2085 Panther, John	N cher	25	M	Dead	No	Farmer
2086 Proctor, Ruthy	N cher	35	F	D1656	No	
2087 Perdee, Dorothy			F	3205	No	
2088 Parchmeal, Water			M	8971	No	On Dawes as John Parchmeal (BLB)
2089 Queen, Geo	N cher	7	F	5169	No	
2090 Queen, Josphine	N cher	3	F	3490	No	
2091 Quahlecha,	N cher	1	F	Dead	No	
2092 Qualate,	N cher	39	M	Dead	Yes	Farmer
2093 Qualate, Pollie	N cher	33	F	Dead	Yes	
2094 Qualate, Celia	N cher	3	F	Dead	No	
2095 Qualate, Lissie	N cher	16	F	8326	No	
2096 Raper, Sarah Jane	AWhite	30	F	Dead	No	
2097 Raper, John H	N cher	11	M	3906	No	
2098 Raper, Frank	N cher	9	M	D1657	No	
2099 Raper, E J	N cher	2	F	Dead	No	
2100 Ridge, Moses	N cher	38	M	6093	Yes	Farmer
2101 Ridge, Jinnie	N cher	35	F	Dead	Yes	
2102 Ridge, John	N cher	15	M	7376	No	
2103 Ridge, Jeremiah	N cher	7	M	7377	No	
2104 Ridge, Elijah	N cher	2	M	6102	No	
2105 Ridge,	N cher	25	M	Dead	Yes	
2106 Ridge, Annie	N cher	20	F	D1658	Yes	
2107 Ridge, Oosquina	N cher	2	F	D1659	No	
2108 Ridge, Susanna	N col	3m	F	D1660	No	
2109 Rowe, Louis	N col	48	M	Dead	Yes	Farmer
2110 Rowe, Chana	N col	45	F	Dead	Yes	
2111 Rowe, Jessee	N col	18	M	F830	No	
2112 Rowe, Eliza	N col	17	F	F800	No	
2113 Rowe, Sophia	N col	14	F	F807	No	
2114 Rowe, Laura	N col	12	F	F813	No	
2115 Rowe, Martha Ann	N col	9	F	F824	No	
2116 Rowe, Jim	N cher	7	M	Dead	No	
2117 Roach, John	N cher	30	M	6823	Yes	
2118 Roach, Nellie	N cher	20	F	6823	Yes	
2119 Roach, Annie	N cher	6m	F	6823	No	
2120 Raven, Osin	N cher	28	F	8336	Yes	
2121 Raven, Jinnie	N cher	10	F	Dead	No	
2122 Raven, Betsy	N cher	8	F	8337	No	
2123 Raven,	N cher	25	M	8336	No	
2124 Russel, Sam	N cher	30	M	8490	Yes	
2125 Russel, Susan	N cher	24	F	Dead	Yes	

Name	Race	Age	Sex	Census	Md	Remarks
2126 Russel, Mary	N cher	3	F	Dead	No	
2127 Russel, Jack	N cher	1	M	9059	No	
2128 Robin, Big	N cher	70	M	Dead	No	
2129 Robin, Nancy	N cher	30	F	9068	No	
2130 Robin, Loam	N cher	7	M	9041	No	
2131 Robin, Allsah	N cher	4	F	Dead	No	
2132 Ratling Goard, Jim	N cher	6	M	5974	No	
2133 Ratling Goard, Sis	N cher	6m	F	6751	No	
2134 Runabout,	N cher	40	M	Dead	Yes	Farmer
2135 Runabout, Wahnenah	N cher	40	F	4191	Yes	
2136 Runabout, Ailsy	N cher	4	F	Dead	No	
2137 Ratter,	N cher	80	M	Dead	Yes	
2138 Ratter, Tahney	N cher	75	F	Dead	Yes	
2139 Ratter, Nancy	N cher	28	F	7475	No	
2140 Round, James	N cher	51	M	Dead	Yes	
2141 Round, Louisa	N cher	32	F	Dead	Yes	
2142 Riley, Lucy	N cher	19	F	4753	Yes	
2143 Riley, Minnie V	N cher	4m	F	4745	No	
2144 Reed, Joseph	N cher	25	M	D468	No	
2145 Reed, Mollie	N cher	3	F	Dead	No	
2146 Rinson, Tredwell	AWhite	36	M	2841	Yes	
2147 Rinson, Ester	N cher	20	F	2841	No	
2148 Rogers, Thomas	N cher	33	M	2963	Yes	Mr Thomas Rogers is guardian for these two little girls (Nettie & Cynthia BLB) who are his brothers (John Howard Rogers BLB) children
2149 Rogers, Nancy	AWhite	24	F	2963	Yes	
2150 Rogers, Laura	N cher	4	F	3020	No	
2151 Rogers, Thos	N cher	2	M	2885	No	
2152 Rogers, Nettie	N cher	10	F	Dead	No	
2153 Rogers, Cynthia	N cher	8	F	2899	No	
2154 Rogers, W N	N cher	28	M	Dead	No	
2155 Rogers, Sarah D	N cher	2	F	Dead	No	
2156 Rogers, John L	N cher	33	M	5240	Yes	
2157 Rogers, Berilla	N cher	37	F	2827	Yes	
2158 Rogers, Robert	N cher	6	M	2829	No	
2159 Rogers, Wm O	N cher	5	M	4655	No	
2160 Rogers, Geo W	N cher	2	M	189	No	
2161 Rogers, Martha	N cher	50	F	Dead	No	
2162 Ratcliffe, Winnie	A col	80	F	Dead	No	
2163 Ratcliffe, Ruth	A col	19	F	Dead	No	
2164 Ratcliffe, Frank	A col	15	M	F829	No	

Name	Race	Age	Sex	Census	Md	Remarks
2165 Ratcliffe, Sarah	N Col	13	M?	F835	No	
2166 Ratcliffe, Edah	N Col	16	F	F**4	No	
2167 Ratcliffe, Neely	N Col	7	M	F715	No	
2168 Rogers, Rachel	A shaw	21	F	3760	No	
2169 Rogers, Joseph	N cher	22	M	4367	No	
2170 Riley, Thos J	N cher	18	M	164	Yes	On Dawes as James T Riley (BLB)
2171 Rabbit, Thos	N cher	18	M	7483	No	Farmer
2172 Rogers, Polly	A shaw	50	F	Dead	No	
2173 Rogers, Sallie	A shaw	29	F	Dead	No	
2174 Rodman, Thos	A White	36	M	D1666	Yes	Carpenter
2175 Rodman, Ninnia	A shaw	26	F	3862	Yes	
2176 Rodman, Antoine	N cher	7	M	D1662	No	Osage P O Pawhuska
2177 Rodman, Geo W	N Shaw	5	M	4122	No	
2178 Rodman, Virginia	N Shaw	1m	F	3861	No	
2179 Ross, Jinanna	N cher	18	F	D1663	No	
2180 Redbird,	N cher	40	M	8365	Yes	Farmer
2181 Redbird, Sarah	N cher	30	F	8365	Yes	
2182 Redbird, Lydia	N cher	50	F	Dead	No	
2183 Rogers, Betsy or Beckey			F	4893		
2184 Rogers, Joseph			M	D1664		
2185 Rising Fawn, Jennie			F	Dead		
2186 Rising Fawn, Child				D1665		Name of children not known
2187 Rising Fawn, Child				D1666		
2188 Randle, Jas	A del	17	M	Del 255	No	
2189 Ridge, Ahleecher	N cher	36	M	Dead	Yes	
2190 Ridge, Sarah	N cher	40	F	6655	Yes	
2191 Ridge, Nancy	N cher	15	F	2541	No	
2192 Runaway,	N cher	25	M	Dead	Yes	Daughters give his first name as Jim (BLB)
2193 Runaway, Watty	N cher	24	F	Dead	Yes	
2194 Runaway, Socking	N cher	8	F	8489	No	On Dawes as Sokiny James (BLB)
2195 Runaway, Kahhawker	N cher	4	F	Dead	No	
2196 Runaway, Soyugeesky	N cher	2	M	Dead	No	
2197 Runaway, Chewan	N cher	1m	F	8520	No	On Dawes as Lena James (BLB)
2198 Russel, Aaron	N cher	37	M	Dead	Yes	
2199 Russel, Quatsy	N cher	40	F	Dead	Yes	
2200 Russel, Watt	N cher	2	M	402	No	
2201 Raburn, James	A White	65	M	Dead	Yes	
2202 Raburn, Ceily	N cher	43	F	3344	Yes	
2203 Sixkiller, Henry	N cher	21	M	Dead	No	
2204 Starr, E Jane	N cher	1	M	Dead	No	

The Delaware District

Name	Race	Age	Sex	Census	Md	Remarks
2205 Seven, Nelly	N cher	50	F	Dead	No	
2206 Six, Wahhlany	N cher	40	F	Dead	No	
2207 Six, Teelaneteeskee	N cher	10	M	Dead	No	Married Jennie Summerfield (BLB)
2208 Six, Johnaky	N cher	10	M	Dead	No	
2209 Smith, Betsy	N cher	70	F	D1667	No	
2210 Smith, William	AWhite	28	M	3144	Yes	
2211 Smith, Lucy	A shaw	20	F	3144	Yes	
2212 Smith, Hattie	N Shaw	2	F	4946	No	
2213 Smith, Mary	N cher	54	F	Dead	No	Formerly Mrs Clark used to live at Grand Saline
2214 Smith, Billy	N cher	21	M	3888	No	
2215 Stephens, Spencer	N cher	45	M	2220	Yes	School Teacher
2216 Stephens, Sarah	N cher	47	F	2220	Yes	
2217 Stephens, Ida	N cher	15	F	3404	No	
2218 Stephens, Indianola	N cher	13	F	3902	No	
2219 Stephens, Spencer Jr.	N cher	11	M	5212	No	
2220 Stephens, Florence	N cher	9	F	10308	No	
2221 Stephens, Ernest	N cher	8	M	5260	No	
2222 Stephens, Jessie	N cher	4	F	2223	No	
2223 Stephens, Ann B	N cher	30	F	3747	No	School Teacher
2224 Shelton, M E	N cher	24	F	2761	No	Music Teacher, Dup 993 Saline Dist
2225 Shelton, Norman	N cher	22	M	9850	No	Dup 995 Sal Dist
2226 Shelton, Claud	N cher	20	M	3601	No	
2227 Shelton, H R	N cher	17	M	6819	No	
2228 Sloan, E E	N cher	28	M	3972	Yes	Farmer
2229 Sloan, N W	AWhite	25	F	3972	Yes	
2231 Sloan, J D	N cher	2	F	3995	No	
2232 Sloan, Wm A	N cher	1	M	5680	No	
2233 Squirrel, Daniel	N cher	40	M	Dead	No	
2234 Starr, Johnaky	N cher	37	M	Dead	No	
2235 Seven, Jessee	N cher	24	M	7472	No	
2236 Silversmith, Johnson	N cher	60	M	Dead	No	
2237 Stover, W R	N cher	25	M	5966	No	
2238 Starr, Susan	N cher	30	F	Dead	No	
2239 Sam,	N cher	22	M	8376	No	
2240 Shotpouch, John	N cher	53	M	Dead	No	
2241 Sutton, Wm H	N cher	24	M	2843	Yes	Stone mason, WH Sutton is a Cherokee and has lived in Missouri for several years and has never been readmitted according to law
2242 Sutton, Harriet R	AWhite	22	F	2843	Yes	

Name	Race	Age	Sex	Census	Md	Remarks
2243 Sutton, Wm D	N cher	3	M	Dead	No	
2244 Sutton, Mary C	N cher	1	F	2894	No	Dup 2273
2245 Sutton, Geo	N cher	26	M	Dead	Yes	Farmer
2246 Sutton, Mary	N cher	30	F	3066	Yes	
2247 Smith, Walter	N cher	24	M	2988	Yes	
2248 Smith, Julia	AWhite	18	F	2988	Yes	
2249 Suaky, David	N cher	29	M	Dead	Yes	
2250 Suaky, Louisa	N cher	27	F	3027	Yes	
2251 Suaky, Joel	N cher	10	M	4072	No	
2252 Suaky, Laura	N cher	6	F	3905	No	
2253 Suaky, Sarah	N cher	3	F	4701	No	
2254 Suaky, Nellie May	N cher	9m	F	5655	No	
2255 Starr, James	N cher	47	M	149	Yes	
2256 Starr, Emma	N cher	38	F	149	Yes	
2257 Starr, Caleb	N cher	9	M	3801	No	
2258 Starr, Luvena	N cher	6	F	Dead	No	
2259 Starr, Jesse	N cher	3	M	Dead	No	
2260 Starr, Emma	N cher	1	F	2844	No	
2261 Sheldon, Wm	N cher	5	M	3624	No	
2262 Sheldon, Mary	N cher	3	F	4193	No	
2263 Summers, A C				R738		
2264 Summers, Elizabeth			F	4147		
2265 Sixkiller, Henry			M	Dead		
2266 Stephens, Carrie			F	Dead		
2267 Stephens, Wm			M	6090		
2268 Stephens, Flora			F	D1669		
2269 Sutton, W H			M	2843		Dup 2241
2270 Sutton, Harriet O			F	2843		Dup 2242
2271 Sutton, Wm D			M	Dead		Dup 2243
2272 Sutton, Mary C			F	2894		Dup 2244
2273 Steen, Thos			M	7492		
2274 Starr, Ceetatah				Dead		
2275 Salkinnic,			M	8374		
2276 Starr, James			M	Dead		
2277 Stokes, J Y			M	5543	Yes	
2278 Stokes, Mary	AWhite	29	F	5543	Yes	
2279 Stokes, Ewing	N cher	19	M	5543	Yes	
2280 Stokes,	N cher	2w	M		No	No name given on the roll but probably a child by Stokes (BL:B)
2281 Suagee, Stand	N cher	30	M	2993	Yes	
2282 Suagee, Nancy	N cher	24	F	Dead	Yes	
2283 Suagee, Peter	N cher	7	M	5617	No	

Name	Race	Age	Sex	Census	Md	Remarks
2284 Suagee, Nora	N cher	2	F	6775	No	
2285 Suagee, Darcus	N cher	67	F	Dead	No	
2286 Smith, L B	A White	35	M	204	Yes	
2287 Smith, Florence C	N cher	30	F	204	Yes	
2288 Smith, Othie A	N cher	12	M	106	No	
2289 Smith, Ada	N cher	10	F	205	No	
2290 Smith, Walter E	N cher	6	M	176	No	
2291 Smith, Emmitt	N cher	4	M	204	No	
2292 Suwatt, Stein	N cher	35	M	Dead	Yes	
2293 Suwatt, Ester	N cher	30	F	7493	Yes	
2294 Suwatt, Louisa	N cher	11	F	6737	No	
2295 Suwatt, Mary Ann	N cher	9	F	Dead	No	
2296 Suwatt, Wm	N cher	7	M	7491	No	
2297 Suwatt, Scott	N cher	2	M	Dead	No	
2298 Six,				Dead	No	
2299 Six, Runabout	N cher	40	M	Dead	Yes	
2300 Six, Nancy	N cher	36	F	Dead	Yes	
2301 Six, Enoch	N cher	13	M	7509	No	
2302 Six, John	N cher	8	M	Dead	No	
2303 Six, Kate	N cher	10	F	Dead	No	
2304 Six, Nelly	N cher	50	F	Dead	No	
2304 Starr, William	N cher	21m	M	1593	No	
2305 Squirrel, Auwsy	N cher	46	M	Dead	No	Farmer
2306 Squirrel, Charley	N cher	20	M	Dead	No	
2307 Squirrel, Wutty	N cher	30	F	Dead	No	
2308 Squirrel, Ahlez	N cher	25	M	Dead	No	
2309 Squirrel, Sarah	N cher	9	F	7490	No	
2310 Squirrel, Mary	N cher	3	F	8057	No	
2311 Sixkiller, Luke	N cher	27	M	2966	Yes	
2312 Sixkiller, Emma	N cher	22	F	2966	Yes	
2313 Sixkiller, Mary	N cher	8	F	2896	No	
2314 Sixkiller, Mattie	N cher	7	F	2937	No	
2315 Sixkiller, Lewis	N cher	5	M	Dead	No	
2316 Sixkiller, Myrtle	N cher	9m	F	Dead	No	
2317 Smith, J M	A White	49	M	Dead	Yes	
2318 Smith, Jane	N cher	30	F	Dead	Yes	
2319 Smith, F P	N cher	10	M	161	No	
2320 Smith, Amos	A White	42	M	153	Yes	Machinist
2321 Smith, Ann E	A Shaw	24	F	Dead	Yes	
2322 Silverheel, John	A Shaw	45	M	Dead	Yes	Farmer
2323 Silverheel, Mary	A Shaw	22	F	Dead	Yes	Mary Silverheel and her twin babies have since died Charley

Name	Race	Age	Sex	Census	Md	Remarks
						and Eliza
2324 Silverheel, Joseph	A Shaw	14	M	Dead	No	
2325 Silverheel, Johny	N cher	7	M	8238	No	
2326 Silverheel, Charley	N cher	1	M	Dead	No	
2327 Silverheel, Eliza	N cher	1	F	Dead	No	
2328 Silverheel, Betsy	N cher	80	F	Dead	No	
2329 Silverheel, George	A Shaw	22	M	Dead	No	George Silverheel has died since
2330 Silverheel, Rachel	AWhite	22	F	3703	Yes	
2331 Silverheel, Geo	N cher	5	M	3703	No	
2332 Summers, Mary	A Shaw	35	F	3977	No	
2333 Summers, Geo	A Shaw	19	M	4883	No	
2334 Summers, Alonzo	A Shaw	17	M	Dead	No	
2335 Summers, Rhoda	A Shaw	11	F	4197	No	
2336 Summers, Emma	A Shaw	10	F	3975	No	
2337 Summers, Andrew	N cher	6	M	3976	No	
2338 Summers, Rose	N cher	2	M	3978	No	
2339 Stamp, Jula	A Shaw	17	F		No	No census card number given, nor is she listed as dead (BLB)
2340 Scott, John	AWhite	40	M	3495	Yes	Farmer
2341 Scott, Cherokee	N cher	25	F	3495	Yes	
2342 Scott, John B Jr.	N cher	8	M	3489	No	
2343 Scott, Susan	N cher	6	F	3819	No	On Dawes as Susan Kerr (BLB)
2344 Scott, Mary	N cher	5m	F	3918	No	On Dawes as Lillie M Jackson (BLB)
2345 Smith, J B	AWhite	21	M	3483	Yes	
2346 Smith, Emma	N cher	18	F	3483	Yes	
2347 Smith, J D	AWhite	48	M	Dead	Yes	
2348 Smith, Eliza	N cher	24	F	2910	Yes	
2349 Smith, Elizabeth	N cher	5	F	2922	No	
2350 Smith, Wm L	N cher	2	M	3003	No	
2351 Smith, Dennis	N cher	2m	M	2910	No	
2352 Smith, Josephine	N cher	19	F	2835	No	
2353 Snell, Eva	N cher	40	F	Dead	No	
2354 Suakee, Samuel	N cher	10	M	7000	No	
2355 Smith, Louiza	N cher	45	F	Dead	No	
2356 Smith, Fred	N cher	11	M	3667	No	
2357 Smith, Eliza	N cher	9	F	2905	No	
2358 Snell, Betsy	N cher	30	F	2858	No	
2359 Snell, David	N cher	3	M	2858	No	
2360 Snell, Joseph	N cher	1	M	Dead	No	
2361 Starr, Wm	N cher	29	M	8065	Yes	Farmer
2362 Starr, Lydia	N cher	26	F	Dead	Yes	
2363 Starr, Quahlayeke	N cher	5	F	Dead	No	

Name	Race	Age	Sex	Census	Md	Remarks
2364 Sharp, Darkie	N cher	40	F	Dead	No	
2365 Snell, Johnaky	N cher	59	M	7504	Yes	
2366 Snell, Kate	N cher	30	F	7504	Yes	
2367 Snell, Jane	N cher	13	F	7472	No	
2368 Snell, Ida	N cher	11	F	7509	No	
2369 Snell, Lou	N cher	8	F	2884	No	
2370 Snell, Coon	N cher	3	M	7508	No	
2371 Snell, Mary	N cher	5m	F	Dead	No	
2372 Seven, Lum	N cher	30	M	Dead	Yes	
2373 Seven, Mary Jane	N cher	29	F	Dead	Yes	
2374 Snell, John	N cher	36	M	Dead	Yes	
2375 Snell, Nellie	N cher	22	F	7000	Yes	
2376 Snell, Peter	N cher	2	M	Dead	No	
2377 Snell, Lucy	N cher	1	F	Dead	No	
2378 Snell, Seky	N cher	1	F	Dead	No	
2379 Snell, Annie	N cher	46	F	3303	No	
2380 Snell, Charley	N cher	13	M	Dead	No	
2381 Silversmith, Aggie	N cher	50	F	Dead	No	
2382 Silversmith, John	N cher	23	M	2856	No	
2383 Snell, Eli	N cher	25	M	8061	Yes	Farmer
2384 Snell, Kate	N cher	29	F	8061	Yes	
2385 Snell, Lucy	N cher	3	F	8062	No	
2386 Snell, Lewis	N cher	1	M	Dead	No	
2387 Snell, Jim	N cher	30	M	Dead	Yes	
2388 Snell, Sallie	N cher	45	F	Dead	Yes	
2389 Seltzer, Sparrow	N cher	27	M	8063	Yes	
2390 Seltzer, Whitegirl	N cher	26	F	8063	Yes	
2391 Seltzer, Danna	N cher	3	F	7476	No	
2392 Snell, Rider	N cher	7	M	Dead	No	
2393 Shaw, Cora Alice	N Shaw	7	F	3558	No	
2394 Seven, Joseph	N cher	5	M	6600	No	
2395 Seven, Rufus	N cher	3	M	D1670	No	Lives in Idaho, scouting
2396 Silversmith, Rebecca	N cher	20	F	4064	No	
2397 Silversmith, Adolphus	N cher	3	M	4118	No	
2398 Stephens, Andrew	AWhite	36	M	Dead	Yes	Farmer
2399 Stephens, Mary C	A Del	30	F	Del 6	Yes	
2400 Stephens, Rosanna	A Del	14	F	Del 9	No	
2401 Stephens, Mary Ann	A Del	11	F	Del 12	No	
2402 Stephens, John Henry	A Del	7	M	Del 27	No	
2403 Stephens, Fannie	A Del	3	F	Del 10	No	
2404 Sweetwater,	N cher	40	M	8330	Yes	
2405 Sweetwater, Anna	N cher	38	F	Dead	Yes	

Name	Race	Age	Sex	Census	Md	Remarks
2406 Smoke, Alex	N cher	24	M	Dead	Yes	
2407 Smoke, Bettie	N cher	30	F	7910	Yes	
2408 Smoke, Lewis	N cher	3	M	7909	No	
2409 Summerfield, Joseph	N cher	27	M	Dead	Yes	
2410 Summerfield, Wahleah	N cher	20	F	Dead	Yes	
2411 Summerfield, Jennie	N cher	8	F	8375	No	On Dawes as Jennie Leaf (Constitution) (BLB)
2412 Summerfield, Benj	N cher	7	M	Dead	No	
2413 Summerfield, Laywhat	N cher	6	M	8531	No	
2414 Summerfield, Kahsunny	N cher	2	M	8530	No	
2415 Summerfield, Kate	N cher	3m	F	8500	No	
2416 Smoke, Aley	N cher	50	F	Dead	No	
2417 Summerfield, Isaac	N cher	30	M	3605	No	
2418 Seenoster,	N cher	4	F	9117	No	
2419 Scuggin, Lacy	N cher	19	M	3648	Yes	
2420 Scuggin, Lizzie	N cher	22	F	3648	Yes	
2421 Scuggin, Sallie	N cher	3	F	Dead	No	
2422 Scuggin, Scott	N cher	2	M	3655	No	
2423 Solkin,	N cher	14	M	8529	No	
2424 Sawluntossky,	N cher	20	M	Dead	Yes	Farmer
2425 Sawluntossky, Kahwka	N cher	48	F	Dead	Yes	
2426 Sawluntossky, Nelly	N cher	9	F	D1671	No	
2427 Sawluntossky, Stahly	N cher	8	M	D1672	No	
2428 Sawluntossky, Tieeke	N cher	1	M	D1673	No	
2429 Sawluntossky, Lem	N cher	7	M	Dead	No	
2430 Starr, Jessie	N cher	24	M	3128	Yes	
2431 Starr, Jennie	N cher	21	F	3128	Yes	
2432 Starr, Joe	N cher	10	M	Dead	No	
2433 Sucker, Thompson	N cher	35	M	8976	Yes	
2434 Sucker, Aggy	N cher	20	F	8976	Yes	
2435 Starr, Zeke	N cher	45	M	Dead	Yes	
2436 Starr, Nancy	N cher	30	F	8543	Yes	
2437 Starr, Sallie	N cher	18	F	Dead	No	
2438 Starr, Sahkeah	N cher	7	M	Dead	No	
2439 Starr, Lines	N cher	5	F	7575	No	On Dawes as Linnie Sixkiller (BLB)
2440 Starr, Cotahny	N cher	3	F	Dead	No	
2441 Sharp, Frog	N cher	45	M	8356	Yes	
2442 Sharp, Lucy	N cher	20	F	Dead	Yes	
2443 Sharp, Awa	N cher	8	F	8335	No	
2444 Sharp, Rather	N cher	7	M	8361	No	
2445 Sharp, Ross	N cher	1	M	Dead	No	
2446 Sapsucker, Levi	N cher	28	M	8344	Yes	Mill man

Name	Race	Age	Sex	Census	Md	Remarks
2447 Sapsucker, Sartie	N cher	25	F	Dead	Yes	
2448 Sequaleese,	N cher	60	M	Dead	Yes	Sequaleese is blind (surname means Squirrell, he is the father of Peter Squirrell census 8491BLB)
2449 Sager, A C	AWhite	45	M	79	Yes	
2450 Sager, Amelia	N cher	28	F	79	Yes	
2451 Sager, Elnora	N cher	9	F	80	No	
2452 Sager, Mary Ennina	N cher	8	F	5034	No	
2453 Sager, Laura Anna	N cher	5	F	3869	No	
2454 Sager, Deborah	N cher	3	F	3624	No	
2455 Sager, Elizabeth	N cher	6m	F	5331	No	
2456 Sowini,	N cher	38	M	Dead	Yes	Farmer (aka Woodchopper Simon BLB)
2457 Sowini, Nancy	N cher	24	F	Dead	Yes	
2458 Sowini, Sarah	N cher	5	F	2396	No	
2459 Sowini, Raven	N cher	2	M	2995	No	David Simon (BLB)
2460 Sapsucker, Luke	N cher	35	M	7378	Yes	
2461 Sapsucker, Anna	N cher	25	F	Dead	Yes	
2462 Sapsucker, Mary	N cher	7	F	Dead	No	
2463 Sapsucker, Jack	N cher	6	M	Dead	No	
2464 Sapsucker, Nip	N cher	1	M	Dead	No	
2465 Snake, Wolfe	N cher	42	M	Dead	Yes	
2466 Snake, Eve	N cher	28	F	6982	Yes	
2467 Snake, Peter	N cher	9	M	6982	No	
2468 Snake, Oolaheate	N cher	5	M	7577	No	
2469 Snake, Wahnena W	N cher	9m	F	Dead	No	
2470 Snake, Rootiee	N cher	70	F	Dead	No	
2471 Squirrel, Moses	N cher	35	M	8818	Yes	
2472 Squirrel, Nancy	N cher	50	F	Dead	Yes	
2473 Squirrel, Mary	N cher	10	F	Dead	No	
2474 Squirrel, Sampson	N cher	6	M	Dead	No	
2475 Squirrel, Seny	N cher	5	M	Dead	No	
2476 Squirrel, Jessie	N cher	4	M	8799	No	
2477 Squirrel, Linnie	N cher	2	F	8819	No	
2478 Snail, Youngbird	N cher	40	M	Dead	Yes	Farmer
2479 Snail, Lucinda	N cher	30	M	8773	Yes	
2480 Snail, Tom	N cher	15	M	Dead	No	
2481 Snail, John	N cher	12	M	8980	No	
2482 Snail, Sallie	N cher	10	F	9047	No	
2483 Snail, Betsy	N cher	8	F	Dead	No	
2484 Snail, Ned	N cher	6	M	Dead	No	
2485 Snail, Chinannell	N cher	3	F	8927	No	

Name	Race	Age	Sex	Census	Md	Remarks
2486 Snail, Hunter	N cher	6m	M	8744	No	
2487 Snail, Wm	N cher	49	M	Dead	Yes	Surname also spelled Snell (BLB)
2488 Snail, Robeestu	N cher	28	F	Dead	Yes	
2489 Snail, Lucy	N cher	15	F	8912	No	
2490 Snail, Eli	N cher	13	M	8764	No	
2491 Snail, Joshua	N cher	10	M	8514	No	
2492 Snail, Carrie	N cher	8	F	8793	No	On Dawes as Carrie Fields (BLB)
2493 Snail, Jinnie	N cher	6	F	7737	No	On Dawes as Jennie Blossom (BLB)
2494 Snail, Gilbert	N cher	4	M	9033	No	
2495 Snail, Celia	N cher	2	F	Dead	No	
2496 Snail, Peggy	N cher	1m	F	7875	No	On Dawes as Fannie Glory (BLB)
2497 Squirrel, Daniel	N cher	26	M	8800	Yes	
2498 Squirrel, Alkinney	N cher	20	F	Dead	Yes	
2499 Simlin, Wilson	N cher	40	M	6690	Yes	
2500 Simlin, Rachel	N cher	30	F	6690	Yes	
2501 Simlin, Charlotte	N cher	6	F	6659	No	
2502 Simlin, Darcus	N cher	3	F	6662	No	
2503 Simons, Nancy Ann	N cher	46	F	3207	No	
2504 Simons, J R	N cher	45	M	Dead	Yes	
2505 Simons, Martha	N cher	35	F	3054	Yes	
2506 Shotpouch, Charley	N cher	31	M	Dead	Yes	Farmer
2507 Shotpouch, Sarah	N cher	31	F	Dead	Yes	
2508 Shotpouch, Frank	N cher	10	M	Dead	No	
2509 Shotpouch, Billy	N cher	1	M	Dead	No	
2510 Smoke, Buck	N cher	26	M	Dead	Yes	
2511 Smoke, Oosquinna	N cher	27	F	8361	Yes	
2512 Smoke, Charley	N cher	8	M	Dead	No	
2513 Smoke, Bettie	N cher	5	F	Dead	No	
2514 Smoke, Dick	N cher	3m	M	8518	No	
2515 Stover, Elisher	N cher	18	M	Dead	No	
2516 Sanders, Watson	N cher	55	M	8343	Yes	Mill hand
2517 Sanders, Ahnenakee	N cher	38	F	7949	Yes	On Dawes as Annie Round (BLB)
2518 Sanders, Nancy	N cher	8	F	414	No	
2519 Sam,	N cher	38	M	6666	Yes	Farmer
2520 Sam, Kate	N cher	34	F	6666	Yes	
2521 Sam, John	N cher	12	M	Dead	No	
2522 Sam, Charlie	N cher	8	M	Dead	No	
2523 Sam, Kate	N cher	5	F	3025	No	
2524 Sam, Jane	N cher	3	F	8980	No	Dead, (on Dawes as Annie Snail BLB)
2525 Sam, Johnaky	N cher	1	M	Dead	No	
2526 Smith, John	N cher	26	M	8524	Yes	

Name	Race	Age	Sex	Census	Md	Remarks
2527 Smith, Quate	N cher	23	F	Dead	Yes	
2528 Smith, Henry	N cher	3	M	Dead	No	
2529 Sturdevan, John	N cher	42	M	6445	Yes	
2530 Sturdevan, Elizabeth	N cher	37	F	6445	Yes	
2531 Selvidge, John	N cher	?	M	6002	No	
2532 Still, Geo	N cher	33	M	5995	Yes	Farmer
2533 Still, Mary	N cher	34	F	5995	Yes	
2534 Still, Samuel	N cher	15	M	Dead	No	
2535 Still, Green	N cher	10	M	5989	No	
2536 Still, John N	N cher	8	M	6985	No	
2537 Still, James L	N cher	6	M	5990	No	
2538 Still, Acey	N cher	4	M	2907	No	
2539 Sanders, Margaret	N cher	18	F	3519	No	
2540 Smith, Rachel	N cher	60	F	Dead	No	
2541 Smith, Frank	N cher	13	M	Dead	No	
2542 Smith, Suanna	N cher	45	F	Dead	No	
2543 Smith, John D	AWhite	45	M	344	Yes	
2544 Smith, Sarah	N cher	28	F	344	Yes	
2545 Smith, Lemock	N cher	6	F	6016	No	
2546 Smith, Deliliah	N cher	4	F	6721	No	
2547 Smith, Walter D	N cher	2	M	344	No	
2548 Scott, B E	N cher	27	M	5831	Yes	
2549 Scott, Sabina	N cher	20	F	5831	Yes	
2550 Smith, Henry J	N cher	25	M	206	Yes	
2551 Smith, Ella F	AWhite	25	F	Dead	Yes	
2552 Smith, Mirtie J	N cher	3	F	206	No	
2553 Smith, Margaret	N cher	41	F	207	No	
2554 Starr, George	N cher	65	M	Dead	Yes	
2555 Starr, Nakey	N cher	44	F	Dead	Yes	
2556 Starr, Winnie	N cher	11	F	Dead	No	
2557 Starr, Lizzie	N cher	9	F	7477	No	
2558 Starr, Tahskeekeetee	N cher	7	M	7470	No	
2559 Smith, John J	AWhite	40	M	195	Yes	Farmer
2560 Smith, Sarah E	N cher	36	F	195	Yes	Farmer
2561 Smith, Jefferson	N cher	17	M	Dead	No	
2562 Smith, Wm D	N cher	14	M	5145	No	
2563 Smith, Walter S	N cher	9	M	195	No	
2564 Smith, Maggie J	N cher	7	F	5357	No	
2565 Smith, Nathaniel D	N cher	3	M	195	No	
2566 Smith, Homer L	N cher	7m	M	195	No	
2567 Smith, Tom	N cher	36	M	5839	Yes	
2568 Smith, Wahlise	N cher	40	F	5839	Yes	

Name	Race	Age	Sex	Census	Md	Remarks
2569 Starr, James	N cher	33	M	Dead	Yes	
2570 Starr, Nannie	N cher	29	F	7529	Yes	On Dawes as Nancy Hilderbrand (BLB)
2571 Starr, Fallingblossom	N cher	7	M	7576	No	
2572 Starr, Lynnell	N cher	5	F	7575	No	Dup 2440 Del Dist (on Dawes as Linnie Sixkiller BLB)
2573 Starr, Geo	N cher	3	M	Dead	No	
2574 Starr, Maggie	N cher	6m	F	7530	No	On Dawes as Maggie Feather (BLB)
2575 Scraper, Henry	N cher	27	M	6742	Yes	
2576 Scraper, Lydia	N cher	30	F	6742	Yes	
2577 Scraper, Lyna	N cher	9m	F	4033	No	
2578 Sallie,	N cher	40	F	8967	No	
2579 Sagar, Wm	N cher	30	M	Dead	No	
2580 Smith, Elizabeth	N cher	18	F	2754	No	
2581 Smith, John	N cher	20	M	3358	No	
2582 Secrest, Olly	N cher	5	F	2269	No	
2583 Scraper, Thomas	N cher	24	M	6740	No	Farmer
2584 Shalers, Clemintine	N cher	6	F	5561	No	
2585 Thompson, Sadie L	N cher	9	F	D1674	No	
2586 Telookee, Jack	A Col	35	M	F825	Yes	Farmer
2587 Telookee, Nancy	A Shaw	20	F	Dead	Yes	
2588 Telookee, Lou	N cher	4	F	F697	No	Dup of 391
2589 Telookee, Sindy	N cher	1	F	Dead	No	
2590 Tiblo, Henry	N cher	60	M	Dead	Yes	
2591 Tiblo, Mary A	N cher	58	F	Del 8	Yes	
2592 Tekahnuhsky,	N cher	30	M	Dead	Yes	
2593 Tekahnuhsky, Nuhche	N cher	20	F	Dead	Yes	
2594 Tekahnuhsky, Cahlahchee	N cher	4	M	8546	No	
2595 Topper, Harry	N cher	68	M	Dead	Yes	
2596 Topper, Nelly	N cher	29	F	Dead	Yes	
2597 Topper, Nuhahnawawtia	N cher	19	M	Dead	No	
2598 Topper, Chunekelunt	N cher	10	M	Dead	No	
2599 Toolate,	N cher	26	M	8511	Yes	
2600 Toolate, Tehche	N cher	25	F	Dead	Yes	
2601 Toolate, Stand	N cher	8	M	Dead	No	
2602 Toolate, Teehahnachutt	N cher	2	M	Dead	No	
2603 Toolate, John Winn	N cher	3m	M	Dead	No	
2604 Toynete,	N cher	29	M	3651	Yes	Farmer
2605 Toynete, Charlotte	N cher	30	F	Dead	Yes	
2606 Toynete, Adam	N cher	9	M	3654	No	
2607 Teelenteske,	N cher	16	M	Dead	No	
2608 Thomas,	N cher	1m	M	D1675	No	

Name	Race	Age	Sex	Census	Md	Remarks
2609 Thompson, Charles	N cher	70	M	Dead	Yes	Chief Oochalata Thompson (BLB)
2610 Thompson, Rachel	N cher	30	F	3922	Yes	She is listed as being 65 years old on the Dawes roll (BLB)
2611 Tesquanee,	N cher	30	M	Dead	Yes	
2612 Tesquanee, Rachel	N cher	25	F	8350	Yes	
2613 Teekanassky,	N cher	60	M	Dead	Yes	
2614 Teekanassky, Tonsin	N cher	40	F	8350	Yes	
2614 Teekanassky, Josiah	N cher	12	M	Dead	No	
2614 Teekanassky, Kahucha	N cher	2	F	Dead	No	
2615 Tittle, Robert	N cher	30	M	3829	Yes	
2616 Tittle, Mary S	AWhite	29	F	3829	Yes	
2617 Tittle, Dora Alice	N cher	7	F	3808	No	
2618 Tittle, Daniel E	N cher	5	M	R23	No	
2619 Tittle, H C	N cher	2	M	3825	No	
2620 Toter, Bear	N cher	20	M	8378	Yes	
2621 Toter, Toonia	N cher	30	F	Dead	Yes	
2622 Toter, Come	N cher	5	F	D1676	No	
2623 Torbit, John T	AWhite	29	M	Dead	Yes	
2624 Torbit, Mary Jane	N cher	30	F	Dead	Yes	
2625 Torbit, Wm J	N cher	15m	M	4112	No	
2626 Tincup, Jas	N cher	34	M	2438	Yes	Farmer
2627 Tincup, Lucinda	AWhite	28	M	2438	Yes	
2628 Tincup, Alice	N cher	8	M	Dead	No	
2629 Tincup, Emma	N cher	6	M	202	No	
2630 Tincup, Laura	N cher	4	M	2646	No	
2631 Tincup, Wm W	N cher	3	M	2516	No	
2632 Tincup, Dora	N cher	8m	M	2576	No	
2633 Tincup, Lucy	N cher	53	M	Dead	No	
2634 Tekaloogeesky,	N cher	41	M	8367	Yes	Parents of Ike Cheater (census 8371 BLB)
2635 Tekaloogeesky, Ainsey	N cher	41	M	8367	Yes	
2636 Tekaloogeesky, Lizzie	N cher	8	M	8360	No	
2637 Tekaloogeesky, Ooshina	N cher	6	M	8384	No	
2638 Tekaloogeesky, Lucy	N cher	4	M	8372	No	
2639 Tamer, Aaron	N cher	46	M	Dead	Yes	
2640 Tamer, Mary	N cher	32	M	Dead	Yes	
2641 Tamer, Jinnie	N cher	16	M	3650	No	
2642 Tamer, Jas	N cher	10	M	3656	No	
2643 Tamer, John	N cher	8	M	Dead	No	
2644 Tamer, Charley	N cher	7	M	7498	No	
2645 Tamer, Sallie	N cher	6	M	Dead	No	
2646 Tamer, Senost	N cher	5	M	7950	No	

Name	Race	Age	Sex	Census	Md	Remarks
2647 Tamer, Lizzie	N cher	3	M	Dead	No	
2648 Tamer, Jalum	N cher	2m	M	Dead	No	See 2627
2649 Tanner, Jinnie	N cher	25	M	6665	Yes	
2650 Tanner, Lucy	N cher	20	M	Dead	Yes	
2651 Thompson,	N cher	56	M	7505	Yes	On Dawes as Thompson Muskrat (BLB)
2652 Thompson, Wahnenaw	N cher	47	M	Dead	Yes	
2653 Thompson, Chick	N cher	19	M	Dead	No	
2654 Thompson, Coffee	N cher	11	M	Dead	No	
2655 Tanner, Pheasant	N cher	31	M	6238	Yes	Farmer
2656 Tanner, Sallie	N cher	28	M	Dead	Yes	
2657 Tanner, Tom	N cher	8	M	3925	No	
2658 Tanner, Chewsa	N cher	3	M	Dead	No	
2659 Tanner, Tookah	N cher	1m	M	7663	No	
2660 Tee, Charley	N cher	60	M	9423	Yes	Surname should be Tehee (BLB)
2661 Tee, Nancy	N cher	28	F	9423	Yes	""
2662 Tee, Charley	N cher	12	M	8803	No	""
2663 Tee, Elowie	N cher	7	M	8523	No	""
2664 Tee, Susie	N cher	5	F	8971	No	"" (on Dawes as Susie Parchmeal BLB)
2665 Tee, John	N cher	2m	M	9075	No	Surname should be Tehee (BLB)
2666 Turner, Isaac	N cher	44	M	Dead	No	
2667 Turner, Wm	N cher	8	M	6665	No	
2668 Tekahnawheel,	N cher	60	M	Dead	Yes	
2669 Tekahnawheel, Awlser	N cher	40	F	8981	Yes	
2670 Tekahnawheel, Chulayna	N cher	11	M	Dead	No	
2671 Tekahnawheel, Sampson	N cher	4	M	Dead	No	
2672 Taylor, Wm	A White	24	M	6761	Yes	
2673 Taylor, Nancy	N cher	16	F	6761	Yes	
2674 Thompson, Willie P	N cher	12	M	3366	No	
2675 Tittle, Rosanna	N cher	56	F	Dead	No	
2676 Tittle, Susan	N cher	22	F	3486	No	
2677 Thompson, Elijah	N cher	14	M	Dead	No	
2678 Thompson, Rebecca	N cher	8	F	Dead	No	
2679 Thompson, Anna	N cher	56	F	Dead	No	
2680 Tassel, Corn	N cher	30	M	3206	Yes	Farmer
2681 Tassel, Rutha	N cher	25	F	Dead	No	
2682 Tassel, Lizzie	N cher	24	F	Dead	No	
2683 Tassel, Wahlanee	N cher	3	F	Dead	No	
2684 Tassel, Enawlee	N cher	3w	M	Dead	No	
2685 Trout, George	N cher	33	M	3813	Yes	
2686 Trout, Mary	A White	33	F	Dead	Yes	
2687 Trout, Sarah	N cher	10	F	3141	No	

The Delaware District

Name	Race	Age	Sex	Census	Md	Remarks
2688 Trout, Elizabeth	N cher	6	F	3441	No	
2689 Trout, Logan	N cher	5	M	3425	No	
2690 Trout, Troofinnie	N cher	6	F	Dead	No	
2691 Teekahnawchult,	N cher	7	F	Dead	No	
2692 Tabler, Peter	A White	55	M	Dead	Yes	Doctor
2693 Tabler, Rebecca	N cher	47	F	Dead	Yes	
2694 Thornton, Wm J	N cher	33	M	145	Yes	Farmer
2695 Thornton, Amanda M	N cher	31	F	145	Yes	
2696 Thornton, Elizabeth S	N cher	11	F	Dead	No	
2697 Thornton, Sadie L	N cher	9	F	2847	No	
2698 Thornton, Minnie E	N cher	6	F	147	No	
2699 Thornton, Eva V	N cher	3	F	4031	No	
2700 Thornton, Alice	N cher	8m	F	145	No	
2700 Thornton, D D	A White	60	M	77	Yes	
2701 Thornton, Susan A	N cher	54	F	Dead	Yes	
2702 Thornton, Mary L	N cher	9	F	2824	No	
2703 Thornton, Thos J	N cher	23	M	146	Yes	
2704 Thornton, Mary E	A White	19	F	D1383	No	
2705 Tacket, Wm	A White	63	M	Dead	Yes	Farmer
2706 Tacket, Sarah	N cher	46	F	6402	Yes	
2707 Taylor, Robert R	A White	37	M	3170	Yes	
2708 Taylor, Cynthia J	N cher	32	F	3140	Yes	
2709 Taylor, John N	N cher	8	M	3791	No	
2710 Taylor, Maggie	N cher	6	F	3700	No	
2711 Taylor, Chester	N cher	5	M	3376	No	
2712 Taylor, Thos	N cher	3	M	3745	No	
2713 Taylor, Vinnie	N cher	1	F	3847	No	
2714 Tucker, Daniel	N cher	31	M	4364	Yes	
2715 Tucker, Eliza	A White	19	F	F1123	Yes	
2716 Tucker, Bennie	N cher	4	M	Dead	No	
2717 Tucker, Spencer	N cher	1	M	Dead	No	
2718 Tucker, U S Grant	N cher	5m	M	Dead	No	
2719 Toyunesy,	N cher	52	M	Dead	Yes	
2720 Toyunesy, Jinnie	N cher	32	F	7481	Yes	
2721 Toyunesy, Rutha	N cher	13	F	Dead	No	
2722 Toyunesy, Susan	N cher	10	F	7480	No	
2723 Toyunesy, Daniel	N cher	8	M	3809	No	
2724 Toyunesy, Lewis	N cher	4	M	Dead	No	
2725 Trout, Andrew	N cher	25	M	3058	Yes	
2726 Trout, Sarah	A White	18	F	3058	Yes	
2727 Trout, Samuel	N cher	2	M	3290	No	
2728 Trout, Walter	N cher	4m	M	Dead	No	

Name	Race	Age	Sex	Census	Md	Remarks
2729 Tucker, Chas	A Shaw	64	M	Dead	No	
2730 Tucker, Joshua	A Shaw	25	M	3562	No	
2731 Tucker, John	A Shaw	23	M	4316	No	
2732 Tucker, Charley	A Shaw	21	M	Dead	No	
2733 Tucker, Samuel	A Shaw	14	M	3498	No	
2734 Thompson, Joseph L	N cher	41	M	3357	Yes	Farmer
2735 Thompson, Alice B	A Shaw	37	F	Dead	Yes	
2736 Thompson, Joella	N cher	18	F	3421	No	
2737 Thompson, Louis	N cher	5	M	3517	No	
2738 Thomas, Nicholas	N cher	40	M	3565	No	
2739 Trott, H H	N cher	28	M	Dead	No	
2740 Thomas, C Thos	N cher	18	M	109	No	
2741 Tiger, Lena	N cher	40	M	Dead	Yes	Roustabout
2742 Tiger, Rebecca	AWhite	25	F	Dead	Yes	
2743 Tiger, Emma	N cher	7	F	3494	No	
2744 Tiger, Willie	N cher	5	M	3643	No	
2745 Tiger, Thos	N cher	3	M	3894	No	
2746 Tiger, Eugene	N cher	3m	M	3493	No	
2747 Thompson, Jas A	N cher	35	M	3309	Yes	Stockman
2748 Thompson, Belle	N cher	25	F	Dead	Yes	
2749 Thompson, Jane Anna	N cher		F	4081	No	
2750 Trott, Eddie	N cher	3	M	3536	No	
2751 Trott, Jas C	N cher	42	M	2942	Yes	Carpenter
2752 Trott, Dora	N cher	25	F	2942	Yes	
2753 Trott, Eugene H	N cher	7	M	3412	No	
2754 Trott, Ada	N cher	9	F	4087	No	
2755 Trott, W L	N cher	36	M	3475	Yes	
2756 Trott, J L	AWhite	31	F	3475	Yes	
2757 Trott, W H	N cher	2	M	3831	No	
2758 Tyner, Andrew	AWhite	38	M	3589	Yes	Farmer
2759 Tyner, Ary	N cher	21	F	3589	Yes	
2760 Tyner, Kate	N cher	2	F	Dead	No	
2761 Tyner, Wm	N cher	2m	M	3589	No	
2762 Tooey, Peter	AWhite	36	M	3450	Yes	
2763 Tooey, Anna M	N cher	20	F	3450	Yes	
2764 Thompson, T F	N cher	38	M	3520	Yes	
2765 Thompson, S C	N cher	34	F	3520	Yes	
2766 Tucker, Dudley H	A Shaw	39	M	Dead	Yes	
2767 Tucker, Ella	A Shaw	38	F	3392	Yes	
2768 Tucker, Dudley H	N Shaw	12	M	2391	No	
2769 Tucker, John Melton	N Shaw	7	M	3497	No	
2770 Tucker, Ada	N Shaw	3	F	3270	No	

Name	Race	Age	Sex	Census	Md	Remarks
2771 Tucker, Logan	A Shaw	18m	M	3588	No	
2772 Tooley, Wm	N cher	25	M	3334	No	
2773 Thirsty, Sallie	N cher	21	F	Dead	No	
2774 Thirsty, Adam	N cher	2m	M	Dead	No	
2775 Tayahnet,	N cher	11	M	8528	No	
2776 Thirsty, Chrislaquahta				7477		
2777 Teechanoocowhescher,				Dead		
2778 Tap, Betsy	N cher	26	F	D1678	No	
2779 Tahneuhtah,	N cher	70	F	Dead	No	
2780 Tallow, John				8386		
2781 Vann, Jas D	N cher	33	M	Dead	Yes	
2782 Vann, Rosonna	A White	32	F	183	Yes	
2783 Vann, David W	N cher	23	M	181	No	
2784 Vann, Sarah A	N cher	18	F	3007	No	
2785 Vann, Emma	N cher	16	F	138	No	
2786 Vann, Jas	N cher	13	M	182	No	
2787 Vann, John J V	N cher	30	M	R743	Yes	Mill hand
2788 Vann, Valza	N cher	21	F	R743	Yes	
2789 Vann, Morton	N cher	4	M	Dead	No	
2790 Vann, Sam'l D	N cher	5m	M	Dead	No	
2791 Vann, Samuel	A Col	19	M	F740	No	
2792 Vann, Mary	N cher	28	F	3263	No	
2793 Vann, Minta	A Col	35	F	F789	No	Daughter of Johnson Vann of Saline (Col)
2794 Vann, Georgia	N Col	8	F	F755	No	
2795 Vann, Emma	N Col	7	F	Dead	No	
2796 Vann, Chas	N cher	8m	M	D1679	No	
2797 Vann, Emina	N cher	23	F	2734	No	
2798 Vann, Ellen	A Col	15	F	Dead	No	
2799 Vann, Kate	A Col	10	F	F756	No	
2800 Vann or Boot, Wm				Dead		
2801 Vann or Boot, Rachel				Dead		
2802 Vann or Boot, Mary				F713		
2803 Vann or Boot, Stanford				F806		
2804 Vann or Boot, Lucy				F773		
2805 Ward, Jas	N cher	33	M	3085	Yes	
2806 Ward, Mary Ann	N cher	25	F	3085	Yes	
2807 Ward, John L	N cher	4	M	3355	No	
2808 Ward, Sarah E J	N cher	1	F	3316	No	
2809 Williams, Arthur	A Col	44	M	Dead	Yes	Farmer
2810 Williams, Eliza	N Col	20	F	Dead	Yes	
2811 Williams, Eley	N Col	9m	F	Dead	No	

Name	Race	Age	Sex	Census	Md	Remarks
2812 Williams, Florence	N cher	24	F	Dead	No	School Teacher
2813 Williams, Herbert	N cher	6	M	Dead	No	
2814 Williams, Manda	N cher	4	F	10712?	No	
2815 Williams, Geo	A White	36	M	2832	Yes	Farmer
2816 Williams, Malinda	N cher	24	F	2832	Yes	
2817 Williams, Samuel C	N cher	5	M	2984	No	
2818 Williams, Geo Ann L	N cher	8	F	2949	No	
2819 Williams, Willie A	N cher	3	M	3338	No	
2820 Williams, Zack T	N cher	8m	M	Dead	No	
2821 Williams, W G	A Shaw	26	M	3182	No	Dup of 3398 Coo
2822 Williams, Charley	N cher	5	M	D1680	No	
2823 Williams, Francis	A Col	21	F	FD194	No	Granddaughter of Johnson Vann deceased A citizen
2824 Williams, Thursday	N Col	6m	F	Dead	No	
2825 Wiley, Worcester	N cher	22	M	7298	No	
2826 Wutty	N cher	70	F	Dead	No	
2827 Writer, John	N cher	20	M	Dead	No	
2828 White, Becky	A Del	30	F	DelD41	No	
2829 Woodard, Ann E	N cher	39	F	7582	No	
2830 Wicked, Webster	N cher	24	M	2840	No	Farmer
2831 Walker, Hester Ann	A White	55	F	8510	No	
2832 Walker, Sarah	N cher	16	F	2840	No	
2833 Wolfe, Austin	N cher	20	M	Dead	No	
2834 Ward, Mack	N cher	23	M	5088	No	
2835 Ward, Geo M	N cher	38	M	70	Yes	
2836 Ward, Martha J	N cher	22	F	70	Yes	
2837 Ward, Josaphine	N cher	16	F	Dead	No	
2838 Ward, Laura J	N cher	15	F	Dead	No	
2839 Ward, Nancy	N cher	10?	F	2893	No	
2840 Ward, John M	N cher	7	M	2851	No	
2841 Ward, Wm H	N cher	5	M	Dead	No	
2842 Ward, Vann V	N cher	40	M	3078	Yes	
2843 Ward, Mary M	A White	18	F	D1681	Yes	
2844 Ward, Mary	A White	70	F	Dead	No	
2845 Whipper, Joseph	N cher	1	M	D1682	No	
2846 Work, Charley	N cher	28	M	3147	Yes	
2847 Work, Chowweuke	N cher	26	F	3147	Yes	
2848 Work, Ailsey	N cher	4	F	7513	No	
2849 Work, Wahley	N cher	1	F	7377	No	
2850 Wells, Washington	A Shaw	45	M	2836	No	
2851 Woodall, W C	N cher	44	M	148	Yes	Farmer
2852 Woodall, M A	N cher	41	F	Dead	Yes	

Name	Race	Age	Sex	Census	Md	Remarks
2853 Woodall, T V	N cher	20	M	3136	No	
2854 Woodall, Lucy J	N cher	17	F	49	No	
2855 Woodall, Wm H	N cher	8	M	3398	No	
2856 Woodall, Wattie	N cher	6	M	3375	No	
2857 Woodall, Susan E	N cher	3	F	7092	No	
2858 Woodall, Geo C	A White	76	M	Dead	No	
2859 Wooten, Elias	A White	46	M	Dead	Yes	
2860 Wooten, Amanda	N cher	28	F	Dead	Yes	
2861 Wooten, Geo W	N cher	9	M	Dead	No	
2862 Wooten, Ettie	N cher	4	F	3987	No	
2863 Wooten, James M	N cher	21m	M	D1684	No	
2864 Woodall, Lucien	N cher	24	M	3214	Yes	
2865 Woodall, Mary Jane	N cher	20	F	Dead	Yes	
2866 Woodall, Wm C	N cher	3	M	4126	No	
2867 Woodard, Francis	N cher	20	F	Dead	No	
2868 Woodard, Wm	N cher	4	M	9364	No	
2869 Washington, Franklin	A Del	34	M	Dead	Yes	
2870 Washington, Whitewoman	A Del	40	F	Dead	Yes	
2871 Washington, Joseph	N cher	6	M	Dead	No	
2872 Wheeler, Alice	N cher	24	F	3098	No	
2873 Wheeler, Rosella	N cher	2	F	3088	No	
2874 Wheeler, Anna F	N cher	19	F	Dead	No	
2875 Willis, Mollie	N cher	14	F	173	No	
2876 Washington, Geo	A Del	61	M	Dead	No	Farmer
2877 Washington, Edson	A Del	23	M	Del 53	No	
2878 Washington, Albert	A Del	23	M	Dead	No	
2879 Washington, Jas	A Del	14	M	Del 1	No	
2880 Washington, Eliza	A Del	30	F	Dead	No	
2881 Washington, Lily	N cher	5	F	Del 88	No	
2882 Washington, Cyrus	N cher	16	M	Del 349	No	
2883 Washington, John	A Del	23	M	Dead	Yes	
2884 Washington, Harriet	A White	21	F	Dead	Yes	
2885 Washington, John Richard	N cher	1	M	Dead	No	
2886 Washington, Richard	A Del	15m	M	Dead	No	
2887 Walker, P L	A White	30	M	3874	Yes	
2888 Walker, Mary M	N cher	23	F	3874	Yes	
2889 Walker, M R	N cher	5	M	3867	No	
2890 Walker, J A	N cher	3	M	3864	No	
2891 Walker, N O	N cher	4m	F	3874	No	
2892 Williams, RM	A White	50	M	Dead	Yes	
2893 Williams, Margaret	A Shaw	41	F	Dead	Yes	
2894 Williams, Charles P	A Shaw	21	M	3886	No	

	Name	Race	Age	Sex	Census	Md	Remarks
2895	Williams, Eliza J	A Shaw	18	F	174	No	
2896	Williams, Alonzo	A Shaw	15	M	4152	No	
2897	Williams, Malisa	A Shaw	15	F	4135	No	
2898	Williams, Pricilia	A Shaw	13	F	191	No	
2899	Williams, Mary	A Shaw	6	F	Dead	No	
2900	Williams, Authan	A Shaw	18	M	Dead	No	
2901	Williams, J C	N cher	32	M	2838	Yes	
2902	Williamson, Margaret	N cher	26	F	Dead	Yes	
2903	Williamson, Jas C	N cher	4	M	D1686	No	
2904	Williamson, Leon	N cher	2	M	3951	No	
2905	Williams, Warren	AWhite	35	M	D1687	Yes	Farmer
2906	Williams, Mary	A Shaw	26	F	Dead	Yes	
2907	Williams, G B	N cher	5	M	3816	No	
2908	Williams, Mattie	N cher	3	F	3719	No	
2909	Williams, Lewis	N cher	1	M	3678	No	
2910	Williams, Ira	AWhite	37	M	Dead	Yes	
2911	Williams, Mary A	N cher	38	F	Dead	Yes	
2912	Williams, Vinnie M	N cher	6	F	4023	No	
2913	Williams, Elgin M	N cher	4	M	3916	No	
2914	Walker, Nancy J	N cher	13	F	6594	No	
2915	Weir, Webster W	N cher	35	M	3093	Yes	
2916	Weir, Sabra	N cher	30	F	3093	Yes	
2917	Weir, Samuel K	N cher	10	M	3015	No	
2918	Weir, John W	N cher	8	M	3804	No	
2919	Weir, Daniel Webster	N cher	6	M	3249	No	
2920	Weir, Wm A	N cher	2	M	3627	No	
2921	Wheeler, Samuel	AWhite	44	M	D1688	Yes	
2922	Wheeler, Mary Ann	A Shaw	37	F	Dead	Yes	
2923	Wheeler, Julia	A Shaw	17	F	3966	No	
2924	Wheeler, Louisa	A Shaw	16	F	3639	No	
2925	Wheeler, Tolbert	A Shaw	12	M	4058	No	
2926	Whetstone, Susan	A Shaw	50	F	Dead	No	
2927	Whiteday, Wm A	A Shaw	30	M	3295	Yes	
2928	Whiteday, Martha	A Shaw	25	F	3295	Yes	
2929	Whiteday, Mary	N cher	6	F	3240	No	
2930	Whiteday, Charley	N cher	4	M	3021	No	
2931	Whiteday, Torry	N cher	4m	F	3295	No	
2932	Whiteday, Henry	N cher	40	M	7507	Yes	Farmer
2933	White, Lucy	N cher	39	F	Dead	Yes	
2934	White, Worcherster	N cher	14	M	Dead	No	
2935	White, Snell	N cher	13	M	Dead	No	
2936	White, Hill	N cher	12	M	3201	No	

Name	Race	Age	Sex	Census	Md	Remarks
2937 White, Lizzie	N cher	8	F	3607	No	
2938 White, Mary Ellie	N cher	1	F	7507	No	
2939 White, Samantha	N cher	4	F	3608	No	
2940 Wolfe, Young	N cher	69	M	Dead	Yes	
2941 Wolfe, Betsy	N cher	40	F	Dead	Yes	
2942 Welch, John Cobb	N cher	30	M	3610	Yes	
2943 Welch, Ailsey	N cher	25	F	3610	Yes	
2944 Welch, Mollie	N cher	6	F	2851	No	
2945 Welch, Betsy	N cher	2	F	Dead	No	
2946 Welch, Johnathan	N cher	1m	M	Dead	No	
2947 Welch, Jas	N cher	37	M	Dead	Yes	
2948 Welch, Lucinda	AWhite	55	F	D455	Yes	
2949 Welch, David	N cher	39	M	2944	Yes	
2950 Welch, Hester	N cher	35	F	2944	Yes	
2951 Welch, John	N cher	14	M	2384	No	
2952 Welch, Jas	N cher	13	M	6044	No	
2953 Welch, Edward	N cher	5	M	7036	No	
2954 Waterback, John	N cher	44	M	Dead	No	
2955 Weaver, John	AWhite	34	M	3159	Yes	
2956 Weaver, Mary	A Del	24	F	Del 11	No	
2957 Weaver, Mary F	A Del	3	F	Del 13	No	
2958 Weaver, David M	A Del	3m	M	Del 11	No	
2959 Wright, Jas	N cher	28	M	7482	Yes	Farmer
2960 Wright, Hattie	AWhite	19	F	7482	Yes	
2961 Wright, Ailcy	N cher	2	F	7484	No	
2962 Williard, Nancy	A Shaw	30	F	3690	No	
2963 Wingfield, Geo W	AWhite	36	M	Dead	Yes	Trader
2964 Wingfield, Lucinda	N cher	35	F	3554	Yes	
2965 Wingfield, Robt O	N cher	14	M	3903	No	
2966 Wingfield, Cora E	N cher	11	F	5683	No	
2967 Wingfield, Francis V	N cher	8	F	3854	No	
2968 Wingfield, Henry E	N cher	6	M	3860	No	
2969 Wingfield, Flora B	N cher	2	F	3291	No	
2970 Woods, James F	N cher	20	M	2921	Yes	Farmer
2971 Woods, Malinda J	AWhite	17	F	2921	Yes	
2972 Woods, W H C	N cher	5m	M	3429	No	
2973 Woods, Jessee	AWhite	50	M	Dead	Yes	Blacksmith
2974 Woods, Manda M	N cher	24	F	3018	Yes	
2975 Woods, Henry	N cher	16	M	54	No	
2976 Woods, Mary F	N cher	15	F	2971	No	
2977 Woods, Joseph	N cher	12	M	Dead	No	
2978 Woods, Marcella	N cher	7	F	2903	No	

Name	Race	Age	Sex	Census	Md	Remarks
2979 Woods, Francis M	N cher	6m	M	3105	No	
2980 Woods, Wm	N cher	26	M	42	Yes	Farmer
2981 Woods, Arcenthia	A Shaw	23	F	42	Yes	
2982 Woods, Charlie	N cher	10	M	4093	No	
2983 Woods, Martin	N cher	4	M	6436	No	
2984 Woods, Anna	N cher	6m	F	76	No	
2985 Washington,	N cher	2	M	Dead	No	
2986 Waterback,	N cher	30	M	Dead	Yes	Farmer
2987 Waterback, Betsy	N cher	30	F	Dead	Yes	
2988 Wahnenaw	N cher	12	F	8354	No	
2989 Wahley,	N cher	20	F	Dead	Yes	
2990 Woodall, J T	N cher	42	M	3415	Yes	
2991 Woodall, Bettie	N cher	26	F	3415	Yes	
2992 Woodall, Lizzie	N cher	8	F	3591	No	
2993 Woodall, Walter	N cher	6	M	3445	No	
2994 Woodall, Leander	N cher	4	M	3399	No	
2995 Woodall, Lewis	N cher	2	M	3409	No	
2996 Woodall, Ira	N cher	1m	M	3415	No	
2997 Williams, Ton	N cher	20	M	6995	No	
2998 Watie, Oo	N cher	30	M	8387	Yes	
2999 Watie, Nancy	N cher	30	F	Dead	Yes	
3000 Watie, Philipe	N cher	13	M	8332	No	
3001 Watie, Kahlaneeskey	N cher	9	M	Dead	No	
3002 Watie, Ridge	N cher	5	M	Dead	No	
3003 Wahleuke,	N cher	30	M	Dead	Yes	
3004 Wahleuke, Wutty	N cher	39	F	Dead	Yes	
3005 Wahleuke, Stacy	N cher	18	F	Dead	No	
3006 Washburn, Percy H	N cher	31	M	6072	Yes	
3007 Washburn, Alice C	AWhite	26	F	6072	Yes	
3008 Washburn, James W	N cher	7	M	Dead	No	
3009 Washburn, Alva B	N cher	5	M	5825	No	
3010 Washburn, Washington	N cher	3	M	3873	No	
3011 Washburn, Claud L	N cher	19m	M	6072	No	
3012 Welch, John	N cher	18	M	Dead	Yes	
3013 Welch, Wahleake	N cher	21	F	Dead	Yes	
3014 Wolfe, Wm	N cher	39	M	6668	Yes	
3015 Wolfe, Susanna	N cher	28	F	Dead	Yes	
3016 Wolfe, Olsey	N cher	2	F	Dead	No	
3017 Washingboy, Dick	N cher	14	M	D1689	No	
3018 Wahlasky,	N cher	50	M	Dead	Yes	
3019 Wahlasky, Hester	N cher	35	F	8496	Yes	
3020 Wahlasky, Willy	N cher	19	M	8346	No	

Name	Race	Age	Sex	Census	Md	Remarks
3021 Washburn, G L	N cher	23	M	2939	No	Mill man
3022 Washburn, Mary F	N cher	15	F	3339	No	
3023 Washburn, Edward	N cher	10	M	5803	No	
3024 Wolfe, Rider	N cher	23	M	Dead	Yes	Farmer
3025 Wolfe, Lydia	N cher	20	F	8524	Yes	
3026 Wolfe, Nelly	N cher	1	F	8521	No	
3027 Wafford, Wm	N cher	35	M	8504	Yes	
3028 Wafford, Ahna	N cher	25	F	8504	Yes	
3029 Wafford, Charley	N cher	7	M	8926	No	
3030 Wafford, Nelly	N cher	5	F	Dead	No	
3031 Wafford, Arch	N cher	9m	M	Dead	No	
3032 Wafford, Jas D	N cher	35	M	Dead	No	
3033 Wafford, Nancy	N cher	33	F	374	No	
3034 Wolfe, Daniel	N cher	60	M	Dead	Yes	
3035 Wolfe, Anna	A White	70	F	8915	Yes	
3036 Whist, Tenhla				8493		Dup of 3091 Del
3037 Whist, Peggy			F	Dead		
3038 Whist, Jennie			F			No census card number given, not listed as dead (BLB)
3039 Whist, Driver						" "
3040 Wiley, R F	A White	52	M	5788	Yes	Farmer
3041 Wiley, Mary J	N cher	40	F	5788	Yes	
3042 Wiley, Percy H	N cher	19	M	5781	No	
3043 Wiley, R L	N cher	17	M	5739	No	
3044 Wiley, Julia	N cher	14	F	6959	No	
3045 Wiley, Capitola D	N cher	12	F	6811	No	
3046 Wiley, Albert Sidney	N cher	9	M	6863	No	
3047 Ward, W B	N cher	6	M	1330	No	
3048 Ward, Zoe	N cher	9	F	5788	No	
3049 Ward, John L	N cher	28	M	68	Yes	
3050 Ward, Laura	A White	20	F	68	Yes	
3051 Ward, Dora	N cher	4m	F	6473	No	
3052 Ward, Louisa	N cher	53	F	Dead	Yes	
3053 Ward, Jane	A White	36	F	4665	No	
3054 Ward, Wm	N cher	24	M	69	No	
3055 Ward, Oliver	N cher	17	M	Dead	No	
3056 Ward, Moolie	N cher	16	F	4661	No	
3057 Ward, Moses	N cher	64	M	4749	Yes	
3058 Ward, Elizabeth	A White	50	F	Dead	Yes	
3059 Ward, Joel	N cher	15	M	4800	No	
3060 Ward, Helen	N cher	18	F	5066	No	
3061 Ward, Joseph L	N cher	35	M	2512	Yes	

Name	Race	Age	Sex	Census	Md	Remarks
3062 Ward, Alice N	A White	25	F	2512	Yes	
3063 Ward, Lilliam Alma	N cher	4	F	5832	No	
3064 Ward, Etta Estla	N cher	2	F	7494	No	
3065 Ward, Willie May	N cher	1	F	2512	No	
3066 Ward, G D	N cher	32	M	3060	Yes	
3067 Ward, Eliza F	A White	29	F	3030	Yes	
3068 Ward, Lelia Alma	N cher	8	F	4653	No	
3069 Ward, James O	N cher	7	M	7134	No	
3070 Ward, John E	N cher	3	M	2958	No	
3071 Ward, Samuel	N cher	55	M	Dead	Yes	
3072 Ward, Eliza	N cher	28	F	2860	Yes	
3073 Ward, Jennette	N cher	9	F	4202	No	
3074 Ward, Minnie	N cher	7	F	2829	No	
3075 Ward, Ninnie	N cher	4	F	4200	No	
3076 Ward, Joseph	N cher	2	M	2860	No	
3077 Wilson, Zona	N cher	2m	F	86	No	
3078 Wilson, Thos	N cher	27	M	Dead	Yes	Farmer
3079 Wilson, Ruth	N cher	22	F	Dead	Yes	
3080 Wilson, Lodia	N cher	3	F	3858	No	
3081 Wilson, Adam	N cher	1	M	Dead	No	
3082 Woodall, Washington	N cher	27	M	4103	Yes	
3083 Woodall, Susanna	N cher	23	F	4103	Yes	
3084 Woodall, Martha F	N cher	5	F	4134	No	
3085 Woodall, Lucy Ann	N cher	2	F	5841	No	
3086 Woodall, Louisa	N cher	2m	F	4110	No	
3087 Wilkerson, Eleanore	N cher	13	F	107	No	
3088 Wicket, John	N cher	21	M	Dead	Yes	
3089 Wicket, Alice	N cher	17	F	Dead	Yes	
3090 Williams, Emma	N cher	1m	F	5488	No	
3091 Wheat, Tenala	N cher	20	F	8493	No	On Dawes as Charley Watermellon (BLB)
3092 Wheat, Aggy	N cher	18	M		No	Dup of 3037
3093 Wheat, Jennie	N cher	2	M	8526	No	
3094 Wheat, Driver	N cher	1m	M	8982	No	On Dawes as John Watermellon (BLB)
3095 Woodall, G D				D1691		
3096 Warcola, Nancy			F	D1691		
3097 Walton, Wm			M	Dead		
3098 Walton, Sarah			F	3931		
3099 Walton, Minnie Viola			F	D1692		Married out see W E Rogers
3100 Walton, Geo			M	Dead		
3101 Walton, Meranda			F	Dead		
3102 Walton, Joseph			M	Dead		

The Delaware District

Name	Race	Age	Sex	Census	Md	Remarks
3103 Willie, Lewis			M	D1693		Dead
3104 Willie, Bellows				D1694		Dead
3105 Youngbeaver, Lucy	N cher	30	F	8966	No	
3106 Youngbeaver, Dave	N cher	18	M	8917	No	Farmer
3107 Youngbeaver, Charley	N cher	15	M	8495	No	On Dawes as Charley Owens (BLB)
3108 Youngbeaver, Seladin	N cher	12	M	8503	No	On Dawes as Saledin Owens (BLB)
3109 Yeargin, Jas	AWhite	38	M	171	Yes	
3110 Yeargin, Mary J	N cher	32	F	171	Yes	
3111 Yeargin, Joseph D	N cher	11	M	10234	No	
3112 Yeargin, Scott A	N cher	9	M	10233	No	
3113 Yeargin, Mary E	N cher	4	F	2644	No	
3114 Yeargin, Kate E	N cher	2	F	198	No	
3115 Yearger, Jacob	AWhite	68	M	Dead	Yes	
3116 Yearger, Laura V	N cher	36	F	170	Yes	
3117 Yearger, George W	N cher	2	M	Dead	No	
3118 Young, Christophus C	N cher	29	M	3883	Yes	
3119 Young, Eva	A Shaw	20	F	3883	Yes	
3120 Yost, James D	AWhite	41	M	3552	Yes	
3121 Yost, Virginia A	A Del	27	F	Dead	Yes	
3122 Yost, Mary Bell	N Del	5	F	Del 65	No	
3123 Yost, Ida May	N Del	6m	F	Del 33	No	
3124 Yonah,	N cher	19	M	Dead	No	
3125 Yonah, Akin	N cher	25	F		No	No census card number given, nor is she listed as dead (BLB)
3126 Youngbird,	N cher	30	M	Dead	No	
3127 Yowlsuch,	N cher	60	M	Dead		Farmer
3128 Yowlsuch, Tarne	N cher	50	F	Dead		
3129 Yowlsuch, Teacher	N cher	2	M	Dead		

Name	Race	Age	Sex	Census	Md	Remarks
1 Augerhole, Wat	NCher	55	M	Dead	Yes	Immigrant admitted A W, Mechanic
1a Augerhole, Annie	NCher	54	F	Dead	Yes	
2 Augerhole, Alexander	NCher	21	M	Dead	No	
3 Ahleach, Thompson	NCher	24	M	8710	No	Farmer
4 Adair, Martha	NCher	18	F	5825	No	
5 Ahkilahnigi, Alice	NCher	24	F	8110	No	
6 Adair, Y B	NCher	31	M	Dead	No	Farmer
7 Adair, Washington	NCher	27	M	Dead	No	Stone Mason
8 Adair, William	NCher	25	M	Dead	No	
9 Adair, J Caroline	NCher	19	F	Dead	No	
10 Augerhole, Austin	NCher	31	F	Dead	No	
11 Adair, Ben	A Col	72	M	Dead	No	Admitted under the treaty of 1866, Farmer
12 Acorn, Eliza	NCher	22	F	785	No	
13 Acorn, Dick	NCher	24	M	795	No	
14 Adair, N B	NCher	26	F	838	No	
15 Abbott, John	AWhite	27	M	6028	Yes	Farmer
16 Abbott, E T	NCher	24	F	Dead	Yes	Admitted with R W Walker
17 Abbott, E L	NCher	4	F	5748	No	
18 Abbott, N E	NCher	2	M	5001	No	
19 Abbott, John W	NCher	5m	M	6043	No	
20 Adair, Nancy	NCher	50	F	650	Yes	
21 Adair, Sam	NCher	13	M	8150	No	
22 Adair, Joe	NCher	9	M	Dead	No	
23 Adair, Jennie	NCher	7	F	Dead	No	
24 Adair, Louis	NCher	4	M	6497	No	
25 Adair, Squirrel	NCher	70	M	Dead	Yes	Farmer
26 Adair, Sallie	NCher	60	F	634	Yes	
27 Adair, R B	NCher	17	M	Dead	No	
28 Adair, Betsy	NCher	12	F	769	No	
29 Adair, J M	NCher	12	M	Dead	No	
30 Adair, Candy	NCher	30	M	627	Yes	Farmer
31 Adair, Tom	NCher	7	M	6495	No	
32 Adair, Choowoeluky	NCher	50	M	Dead	Yes	
33 Adair, Rebbecca	NCher	60	F	Dead	Yes	
34 Adair, Mary	NCher	15	F	3273	No	
35 Adair, Wm	NCher	13	M	1005	No	
36 Adair, Lucy	NCher	10	F	Dead	No	
37 Adair, Peter	NCher	29	M	592	Yes	
38 Adair, Charlotte	NCher	22	F	592	Yes	
39 Adair, Betty	NCher	6	F	605	No	
40 Adair, Quaty	NCher	5	F	773	No	

The Flint District

Name	Race	Age	Sex	Census	Md	Remarks
41 Adair, Ailsy	NCher	2	F	Dead	No	
42 Ahleach, Nelson	NCher	21	M	Dead	Yes	Farmer
43 Ahleach, Eliza	NCher	31	F	628	Yes	Lives with Charles Smith
44 Adair, Nancy	NCher	79	F	Dead	No	
45 Allen, W A	NCher	20	M	580	No	Farmer
46 Adair, Caty	NCher	43	F	Dead	No	
47 Adair, Herry	NCher	16	M	4636	No	
48 Adair, Lucy	NCher	7	F	Dead	No	
49 Adair, Tookah	NCher	70	F	Dead	Yes	
50 Adair, Jenny	NCher	23	F	D1697	Yes	
51 Adair, Unte	NCher	5	M	930	No	
52 Adair, J B	NCher	36	M	897	Yes	Farmer
53 Adair, Betty	NCher	36	F	897	Yes	
54 Adair, Jackoline	NCher	13	M	797	No	
55 Adair, T W	NCher	11	M	932	No	
56 Adair, Sammie	NCher	9	M	896	No	
57 Adair, Joe	NCher	7	M	874	No	
58 Adair, John	NCher	5	M	860	No	
59 Adair, Stand W	NCher	2	M	894	No	
60 Adair, Lizzie Bell	NCher	19	F	9330	Yes	
61 Adair, Wuttie	NCher	3	F	892	No	
62 Adair, Mary	NCher	1m	F	Dead	No	
63 Acorn, Ned	NCher	50	M	687	Yes	
64 Acorn, Caty	NCher	50	F	687	No	
65 Acorn, Ezekiel	NCher	16	M	709	No	
66 Acorn, Cyntha	NCher	11	F	D1699	No	Dead
67 Acorn, John	NCher	6	M	689	No	
68 Adair, H M	NCher	40	M	582	Yes	
69 Adair, E M	NCher	9	M	546	No	
70 Adair, J W	NCher	7	M	2491	No	
71 Adair, M L	NCher	5	F	Dead	No	
72 Aikin, Aner	NCher	15	F	820	No	
73 Aikin, W T	NCher	18	M	Dead	No	Farmer
74 Adair, Deborah	NCher	51	F	644	No	
75 Adair, J W	NCher	20	M	6452	No	
76 Adair, M E	NCher	13	F	187	No	
77 Adair, M C	NCher	11	M	Dead	No	
78 Adair, G S	NCher	8	M	594	No	
79 Adair, L J	NCher	60	F	6423	No	
80 Aikin, Rad	NCher	16	M	2138	No	Farmer
81 Aikin, M M	NCher	13	F	861	No	
82 Aikin, Ras	NCher	16	M	2138	No	Farmer

Name	Race	Age	Sex	Census	Md	Remarks
83 Adair, E W	NCher	43	M	Dead	Yes	Farmer
84 Adair, L J	AWhite	28	F	5891	Yes	
85 Adair, L M	NCher	20	M	6424	No	
86 Adair, C L	NCher	5	M	4020	No	
87 Adair, M L	NCher	3	F	362	No	
88 Adams, Charlotte	NCher	50	F	Dead	Yes	
89 Adams, Jack	NCher	10	M	756	No	
90 Alic, Long	NCher	21	M	8897	No	Dup #841, Farmer
91 Adair, Samuel	NCher	13	M	6420	No	
92 Adair, Lucinda	NCher	11	F	792	No	
93 Byas, Lucy J	NCher	32	F	7512	Yes	
94 Bryson, William	NCher	13	M	Dead	Yes	
95 Buffington, Ellis	NCher	32	M	6892	Yes	Farmer
96 Buffington, M C	AWhite	31	M	Dead	Yes	
97 Buffington, T C	NCher	7	M	6552	No	
98 Buffington, O P	NCher	4	F	6553	No	
99 Byars, Rachel	NCher	3	F	2651	No	Dup of 242 Illinois
100 Beaver, Susie	ACreek	30	F	8897	No	
101 Beaver, Annie	ACreek	26	F	8900	No	
102 Beaver, Lem	ACreek	22	M	Dead	No	Mechanic
103 Bird, Peter	NCher	25	M	843	No	Farmer
104 Boon, Ezekiel	NCher	25	M	Dead	No	
105 Brady, Vance	NCher	21	M	5134	No	Admitted 1867
106 Buzzard, James	NCher	22	M	936	No	
107 Bowlin, Rachel	NCher	18	F	Dead	No	
108 Bowlin, Wily	NCher	28	M	Dead	No	Farmer
109 Bat, Harry	NCher	50?	M	Dead	No	
110 Beanstick, Cyntha	NCher	20	F	Dead	No	
111 Bunch, Alexander	NCher	20	M	7633	Yes	Farmer
112 Bunch, Nancy Nelly	NCher	25	F	Dead	Yes	
113 Bunch, Jug	NCher	23	M	8703	Yes	Farmer
114 Bunch, Aniwaki	NCher	20	F	8703	Yes	
115 Bunch, Jenny	NCher	5m	F	Dead	No	
116 Bat, John	NCher	27	M	625	Yes	Farmer
117 Bat, Mary	NCher	25	F	625	Yes	
118 Bat, Ike	NCher	12	M	614	No	
119 Bat, William	NCher	33	M	Dead	No	
120 Bowlin, Martin	NCher	25	M	8308	Yes	Farmer
121 Bowlin, Ann	NCher	24	M	8308	Yes	
122 Bowlin, Dian	NCher	4	F	1222	No	
123 Bowlin, Chas	NCher	3	M	Dead	No	
124 Bowlin, Jesse	NCher	1	M	Dead	No	

The Flint District

Name	Race	Age	Sex	Census	Md	Remarks
125 Bazzard, Dian	NCher	70	F	Dead	No	Emigrant Widow
126 Bendabout, Moses	NCher	40	M	8714	Yes	
127 Bendabout, Betsy	NCher	23	F	Dead	Yes	
128 Bendabout, James	NCher	7	M	8114	No	enrolled at Stilwell
129 Bendabout, Oolawhuli	NCher	2	M	Dead	No	
130 Bat, Jack	NCher	40	M	620	Yes	Farmer
131 Bat, Lucy	NCher	31	F	620	Yes	
132 Bat, Luie	NCher	14	F	690	No	
133 Bat, Ahki	NCher	12	F	8100	No	
134 Bat, Blue	NCher	11	M	Dead	No	
135 Bat, Ani	NCher	9	F	Dead	No	
136 Bat, Peace	NCher	7	M	Dead	No	
137 Bat, Samuel	NCher	5	M	Dead	No	
138 Bat, Bettie	NCher	2	F	Dead	No	
139 Bat, Moses	NCher	5m	M	620	No	
140 Barepaw, Anie	NCher	35	F	948	Yes	
141 Barepaw, Carlarah	NCher	5	F	947	No	
142 Bowlin, Johnson	NCher	56	M	Dead	Yes	Farmer
143 Bowlin, Tooki	NCher	45	M	8694	Yes	
144 Bowlin, Chas	NCher	12	M	8705	No	
145 Bowlin, Nelly	NCher	10	F	Dead	No	
146 Bowlin, Lucy	NCher	30	F	8714	Yes	Widow
147 Bowlin, Chulcoh	NCher	9	M	Dead	No	
148 Bowlin, Oniwaki	NCher	7	F	8710	No	
149 Bowlin, Cahitah	NCher	5	F	Dead	No	
150 Bowlin, Bettie	NCher	3	F	8715	No	
151 Bowlin, Runied	NCher	1mo	F	Dead	No	
152 Bowlin, Lucy	NCher	26	F	8696	Yes	Widow
153 Bowlin, Anie	NCher	8	F	Dead	No	
154 Barepaw, Polly	NCher	32	F	8724	No	Widow
155 Barepaw, James	NCher	11	M	8575	No	
156 Barepaw, Susan	NCher	9	F	8200	No	She married Jake Mankiller (BLB)
157 Barepaw, Chas	NCher	6	M	8558	No	
158 Barepaw, Lucie	NCher	3	F	Dead	No	
159 Beanstick, Sut	NCher	29	M	8217	Yes	Farmer
160 Beanstick, Tise	NCher	25	F	8217	Yes	at Stilwell
161 Beanstick, Chas	NCher	3	M	8244	No	
162 Bill, John	NCher	26	M	D1701	Yes	Farmer
163 Bill, Lizzie	NCher	21	F	D1701	Yes	
164 Beaver, Creek	A Creek	55	M	8898	Yes	
165 Beaver, Casawyarki	NCher	55	F	8898	Yes	

	Name	Race	Age	Sex	Census	Md	Remarks
166	Beaver, Liddy	NCher	13	F	8899	No	
167	Beaver, Lewis	NCher	8	M	8024	No	
168	Beaver, Clem	NCher	6	M	8596	No	
169	Beaver, Willie	NCher	5	M	8964	No	
170	Beaver, Carolina	NCher	5	F	8551	No	enrolled at Stilwell
171	Bird, Juqui	NCher	60	F	Dead	Yes	
172	Bowlin, Nancy	NCher	28	F	1467	Yes	Emigrant Widow (commission made and error correct number should be 8305 BLB)
173	Bowlin, Wakee	NCher	2m	F	7541	No	
174	Bigby, Samuel	NCher	46	M	Dead	Yes	Farmer
175	Bigby, Margaret	NCher	18	F	6457	No	
176	Bigfoot, Arch	NCher	53	M	Dead	Yes	Farmer
177	Bigfoot, Annie	NCher	54	F	Dead	Yes	
178	Bigfoot, Miller	NCher	10	M	8161	No	
179	Beanstick, James	NCher	41	M	Dead	Yes	Farmer
180	Beanstick, Cinda	NCher	30	F	Dead	Yes	
181	Beanstick, Hester	NCher	11	F	Dead	No	
182	Beanstick, Easter	NCher	9	F	Dead	No	
183	Beanstick, Bettie	NCher	6	F	7833	No	
184	Beanstick, Toni	NCher	63	F	Dead	Yes	
185	Beaver, Mohawk	NCher	34	M	8729	Yes	Farmer
186	Beaver, Martha	NCher	30	F	8729	Yes	
187	Beaver, Cyntha	NCher	8	F	8550	No	
188	Beaver, Washington	NCher	7	M	8422	No	
189	Beaver, James	NCher	30	M	8429	Yes	Farmer
190	Beaver, Catie	NCher	30	F	Dead	Yes	
191	Bunch, Rabbit	NCher	37	M	Dead	Yes	Farmer
192	Bunch, Jinny	NCher	20	F	8702	Yes	
193	Bunch, Carlot	NCher	17	F	4636	No	
194	Bunch, Rebecca	NCher	30	F	8106	Yes	
195	Bunch, Charles	NCher	11	M	8156	No	
196	Bunch, Ollie	NCher	7	F	Dead	No	
197	Bunch, Sanders	NCher	6	M	7833	No	
198	Bunch, Bettie	NCher	2	F	7595	No	
199	Bigfeather, Cloud	NCher	46	M	Dead	Yes	Farmer
200	Bigfeather, Charlotte	NCher	48	F	Dead	Yes	
201	Bigfeather, Soole	NCher	15	F	911	No	
202	Beanstick, Alexander	NCher	55	M	Dead	Yes	Farmer
203	Beanstick, Wuttie	NCher	43	F	8872	Yes	
204	Beanstick, John	NCher	16	M	8736	No	
205	Beanstick, Gegle	NCher	12	M	9873	No	

Name	Race	Age	Sex	Census	Md	Remarks
206 Beanstick, Nannie	NCher	10	F	689	No	
207 Beanstick, Mary	NCher	8	F	Dead	No	
208 Bird, Young	NCher	60	M	Dead	Yes	
209 Bird, Alle	NCher	30	F	7801	Yes	
210 Bearpaw, Nancy	NCher	42	F	8869	Yes	
211 Bearpaw, John	NCher	42	M	Dead	Yes	Farmer
212 Bearpaw, James	NCher	12	M	Dead	No	
213 Bearpaw, Isaac	NCher	10	M	8986	No	
214 Bearpaw, John	NCher	38	M	Dead	Yes	Farmer
215 Byers, William	NCher	21	M	1098	Yes	Farmer
216 Byers, E E	NCher	22	F	1098	Yes	
217 Byers, Henry	NCher	2m	M	1098	No	
218 Byers, Chas	NCher	43	M	1022	Yes	Farmer
219 Byers, Ann	NCher	28	F	1022	Yes	
220 Byers, Wilson	NCher	9	M	1166	No	
221 Byers, Kasie	NCher	7	F	1021	No	
222 Byers, Elinor	NCher	3	F	8392	No	
223 Byers, James	NCher	1	M	1114	No	
224 Beale, Lucy	A cher	78	F	Dead	Yes	Admitted 1867
225 Brown, J W	NCher	31	M	323	Yes	Admitted with James Brown & family, Farmer
226 Brown, E L	AWhite	33	F	323	Yes	
227 Brown, O E	NCher	8	F	6003	No	
228 Brown, J B	NCher	5	F	373	No	
229 Brown, M	NCher	3	F	333	No	
230 Brown, M J	NCher	3m	F	323	No	
231 Bean, Alvira	NCher	54	F	812	Yes	
232 Bean, Chas	NCher	17	M	570	No	
233 Byers, Nick	NCher	45	M	743	Yes	
234 Byers, Mary	NCher	31	F	743	Yes	
235 Byers, Joseph	NCher	7	M	837	No	
236 Bunch, John	NCher	24	M	8202	Yes	
237 Bunch, Ollie	NCher	25	F	8202	Yes	
238 Bunch, Eliza	NCher	6	F	8021	No	
239 Bunch, Christie	NCher	1	M	Dead	No	
240 Billy, George	NCher	23	M	D1702	No	
241 Byers, Rachel	NCher	3	F	2651	No	Dup of 1131 as Rachel Starr
242 Canoo, Tieska	NCher	22	M		Yes	Farmer
243 Canoo, Jinsy	NCher	19	F	Dead	Yes	
244 Canoo, William	NCher	3	M	Dead	No	
245 Canoo, Tookah	NCher	1	F	8162	No	
246 Cloud, J M	AWhite	42	M	523	Yes	Husband claims admission under Act of Nov 15, 1870

Name	Race	Age	Sex	Census	Md	Remarks
247 Cloud, M C	A cher	40	F	523	Yes	
248 Cloud, R L	A cher	15	M	839	No	
249 Cloud, J L	A cher	13	M	613	No	
250 Cloud, M or H E	A cher	10	F	Dead	No	
251 Cloud, J E	NCher	8	M	2526	No	
252 Cloud, J H	NCher	6	M	652	No	
253 Cloud, J or G S	NCher	3	M	601	No	
254 Christie, William	NCher	30	M	Dead	Yes	Farmer
255 Christie, Nelly	NCher	26	F	8136	Yes	
256 Christie, Mariah	NCher	7	F	7341	No	
257 Christie, Polly	NCher	3	F	Dead	No	
258 Christie, Jack	NCher	1	M	Dead	No	
260 Christie, O-ki-ni	NCher	50	F	622	Yes	Emigrant Widow
261 Christie, Nancy	NCher	25	F	Dead	Yes	
262 Christie, Calot	NCher	3m	F	7540	No	
262 Christie, William	NCher	27	M	9360	Yes	Farmer
263 Christie, Susie	NCher	28	F	8652	Yes	
264 Christie, Lucy	NCher	5	F	8449	No	On Dawes as Lucy Fields (BLB)
265 Christie, Watie	NCher	3	M	9155	No	
266 Christie, Spring Frog	NCher	1	M	9360	No	
267 Christie, James	NCher	40	M	D1703	Yes	Trans. to census card 10894
268 Christie, Nancy	NCher	39	F	D1703	Yes	Trans. to census card 10894
269 Christie, Stand	NCher	15	M	Dead	No	
270 Christie, Richard	NCher	13	M	946	No	
280 Christie, Taker	NCher	10	F	8048	No	
281 Christie, Stephen	NCher	8	M	D1704	No	
282 Christie, Tooki	NCher	5	F	9422	No	
283 Christie, Alice	NCher	2	F	9028	No	
284 Coody, Scott	NCher	15	M	Dead	No	
285 Christie, Bettie	NCher	50	F	Dead	Yes	
286 Christie, Nancy	NCher	9	F	9184	No	
287 Christie, Bettie	NCher	5	F	605	No	
288 Christie, Caty	NCher	50	F	Dead	Yes	Weaver
289 Christie, James	NCher	15	M	Dead	No	
290 Christie, Buffalow	NCher	22	M	931	Yes	
291 Christie, Aki	NCher	20	F	931	Yes	
292 Christie, William	NCher	1	M	929	No	
293 Christie, Jackson	NCher	43	M	Dead	Yes	Mechanic
294 Christie, Nelly	NCher	27	F	Dead	Yes	
295 Christie, French	NCher	22	M	Dead	Yes	Farmer
296 Christie, Lucinda	NCher	24	F	Dead	No	
297 Christie, Tooki	NCher	2	F	Dead	No	

Name	Race	Age	Sex	Census	Md	Remarks
298 Christie, Eeila	NCher	1	F	D1708	No	Lives in Ill Dist with Boon Chambers
299 Cheer, Martin	NCher	22	M	Dead	Yes	Farmer
300 Cheer, Emily	NCher	19	F	8155	Yes	
301 Chowenah,	NCher	39	M	8186	Yes	Farmer
302 Chowenah, Ootiye	NCher	35	F	8186	Yes	
303 Chowenah, Getup	NCher	4	M	8178	No	
304 Chowenah, Thomson	NCher	3	M	Dead	No	
305 Chucalate, Daniel	NCher	22	M	8286	Yes	Farmer
306 Chucalate, Cantake	NCher	20	F	8877	Yes	
307 Chucalate, Daka	NCher	7	F	8397	No	
308 Chucalate, Chucanil	NCher	2	F	7406	No	
309 Choate, Josh	NCher	23	M	886	Yes	
310 Choate, Jennie	NCher	21	F	8138	Yes	
311 Choate, Eliza	NCher	36	F	Dead	No	
312 Choate, Baxter	NCher	10	M	864	No	
313 Choate, Bell	NCher	8	F	1321	No	
314 Choate, Mary	NCher	6	F	893	No	
315 Choate, John	NCher	4	M	885	No	
316 Choate, George	NCher	36	M	1008	Yes	Farmer
317 Choate, Chas	NCher	10	M	1048	No	
318 Choate, Susie	NCher	8	F	1083	No	
319 Choate, Louie	NCher	6	F	Dead	No	
320 Choate, Lillian	NCher	4	F	1143	No	
321 Choate, George	NCher	1	M	1162	No	
322 Cocrum, Caneyah	NCher	30	M	Dead	Yes	
323 Cocrum, Susie	NCher	4	F	9235	No	
324 Cocrum, Annie	NCher	1	F	D1709	No	
325 Chucalate, Thomson	NCher	78	M	Dead	Yes	
326 Chucalate, Rachel	NCher	50	F	8102	Yes	
327 Chucalate, Jinny	NCher	7	F	Dead	No	
328 Chucalate, Walker	NCher	4	M	8554	No	
329 Chucalate, Welsey	NCher	30	M	8213	Yes	Farmer
330 Chucalate, Bettie	NCher	31	F	8213	Yes	
331 Chucalate, Smith	NCher	7	M	8193	No	
332 Chucalate, Fields	NCher	3	M	8173	No	
333 Chucalate, John	NCher	4m	M	8224	No	
334 Chucalate, Betty	NCher	26	F	8286	Yes	
335 Chucalate, Three Jacks	NCher	4	M	Dead	No	
336 Chucalate, Ice	NCher	1	M	8284	No	
337 Chulio, Hawk	NCher	45	M	Dead	Yes	Farmer
338 Chulio, Ahleki	NCher	50	F	Dead	Yes	

Name	Race	Age	Sex	Census	Md	Remarks
339 Chulio, Tooleist	NCher	16	M	8426	No	
340 Chulio, Jack	NCher	25	M	8199	Yes	
341 Chulio, Cayahye	NCher	20	F	Dead	Yes	
342 Chulio, Nickati	NCher	1	F	8224	No	
343 Cheer, Sundy	A cher	30	M	Dead	Yes	Mechanic
344 Cheer, Eliza	A cher	9	F	Dead	No	
345 Chandler, John W	AWhite	26	M	123	Yes	Mechanic
346 Chandler, C C	NCher	19	F	123	Yes	
347 Chandler, Claud	NCher	4m	M	123	No	
348 Canoe, Jack	NCher	44	M	Dead	Yes	Farmer
349 Canoe, Olie	NCher	46	F	Dead	Yes	
350 Canoe, Nicie	NCher	2	F	921	No	Census 921 belongs to Narcissa Taylor (BLB)
351 Chikilly, Nancy	NCher	40	F	8567	Yes	
352 Chikilly, Lucy	NCher	8	F	Dead	No	
353 Chambers, James	NCher	30	M	Dead	No	Farmer
354 Chaney, Elinor	A cher	34	F	Dead	Yes	
355 Chaney, L S	NCher	14	F	5150	No	
356 Chaney, W L	NCher	7	M	D1709	No	
357 Chaney, M E	NCher	4	F	D7710	No	
358 Chaney, M D	NCher	1	F	6465	No	
359 Cocrum, George	A cher	46	M	8154	Yes	Mechanic
360 Cockrum, Bettie	NCher	34	F	Dead	Yes	
361 Cockrum, George	NCher	19	M	8166	No	
362 Cockrum, Toonie,	NCher	11	F	Dead	No	
363 Cockrum, Alsie	NCher	12	F	2147	No	
364 Cockrum, Elsie	NCher	6	F	D1711	No	__ Ill Dist
365 Cockrum, Sanders	NCher	1	M	8251	No	
366 Cockrum, Louis	NCher	28	M	871	Yes	Farmer
367 Cockrum, Nancy	NCher	27	F	871	Yes	On Dawes as Betsy Cochran (BLB)
368 Cockrum, Cherokee	NCher	16	F	Dead	No	
369 Cockrum, John	NCher	6	M	888	No	
370 Cockrum, Cale Star	NCher	5	M	883	No	
371 Cockrum, Eve	NCher	6	F	871	No	On Dawes as Mary Cochran (BLB)
372 Catcher, Chas	NCher	36	M	726	Yes	Farmer
373 Catcher, Ann	NCher	23	F	726	Yes	
374 Catcher, Louis	NCher	6	M	875	No	
375 Catcher, Rebecca	NCher	4	F	8763	No	
376 Catcher, Johnson	NCher	1	M	6185	No	
377 Christie, William	NCher	25	M	Dead	Yes	
378 Christie, Martha	NCher	13	F	946	Yes	

Name	Race	Age	Sex	Census	Md	Remarks
379 Christie, Mary	NCher	3m	F	946	No	
380 Cockrum, James	NCher	37	M	Dead	Yes	Farmer
381 Cockrum, Annie	NCher	34	F	Dead	Yes	
382 Cockrum, Nancy	NCher	12	F	8260	No	
383 Cockrum, Cladia	NCher	9	F	905	No	
384 Cockrum, Ham	NCher	7	M	746	No	
385 Cockrum, Osi	NCher	6	M	888	No	
386 Cockrum, Susie	NCher	4	F	9143	No	
387 Cockrum, Bettie	NCher	2	F	9159	No	
388 Cockrum, Tom	NCher	1	M	Dead	No	
389 Cloud, C C	A cher	21	F	303	No	
390 Cloud, L J	A cher	10	M	555	No	
391 Collins, Robt.	NCher	24	M	995	No	
392 Collins, Ruth	NCher	18	F	912	No	
393 Cahnoniheski, David	NCher	26	M	Dead	No	Farmer
394 Christie, Walker	NCher	30	F	8566	No	
395 Christie, Ailsy	NCher	19	F	8552	No	
396 Christie, Taylor	NCher	21	M	8932	No	Farmer
397 Cockrum, John	NCher	22	M	Dead	No	
398 Cockrum, Sallie	NCher	20	F	651	No	
399 Cockrum, John	NCher	22	M	622	No	Farmer
400 Cornells, Polly	NCher	19	F	752	No	
401 Collins, Tim T	NCher	26	M	Dead	No	Farmer
402 Cowart, Wm L	NCher	17	M	555	No	
403 Coody, Scott	NCher	15	M	Dead	No	Dup of 285
404 Cockrum, Sut	NCher	22	M	8155		Farmer
405 Christie, Nelson				D1712		
406 Clemons, Wuttie	NCher	30	F	D1713	No	
407 Daughrity, Silk	NCher	29	M	791	Yes	Farmer
408 Daughrity, Polly	NCher	31	F	Dead	Yes	
409 Daughrity, Isaac	NCher	3	M	Dead	No	
410 Daughrity, Lucy	NCher	40	F	Dead	No	
411 Daughrity, Elk	NCher	20	M	879	No	
412 Daughrity, Moses	NCher	18	M	8242	No	
413 Daughrity, Jennie	NCher	48	F	Dead	No	Immigrant Admitted act of 70
414 Daughrity, Jack	NCher	30	M	Dead	Yes	Farmer
415 Daughrity, Susie	NCher	22	F	6147	Yes	
416 Daughrity, Culbril	NCher	4	M	Dead	No	
417 Daughrity, Nancy	NCher	2	F	Dead	No	
418 Daughrity, Cyntha	NCher	1	F	Dead	No	
419 Daughrity, Adam	NCher	24	M	Dead	Yes	Farmer
420 Daughrity, Nancy	NCher	22	F	7627	Yes	

Name	Race	Age	Sex	Census	Md	Remarks
421 Daughrity, Sam	NCher	2	M	8116	No	
422 Daughrity, Ake	NCher	4m	M	Dead	No	
423 Duck, Ake	NCher	66	M	Dead	No	Admitted Act of 70
424 Duck, Ollie	NCher	45	F	8837	Yes	
425 Duck, George	NCher	10	M	8241	No	
426 Dawson, Joseph	NCher	38	M	Dead	Yes	Farmer, Readmitted
427 Dawson, Mary	NCher	38	F	674	Yes	
428 Duncan, Martha	NCher	42	F	1747	Yes	Admitted Act of Council
429 Dannenberg, R M	NCher	28	M	7195	Yes	Enrolled in G Snake in 1883
430 Dannenberg, E B	AWhite	26	F	D1347	Yes	In state of Missouri, Insane
431 Dannenberg, J C	NCher	6	M	5924	No	
432 Dannenberg, Daniel	NCher	4	M	637	No	
433 Dannenberg, Joseph	NCher	2	M	7195	No	
434 Dannenberg, D B	NCher	3m	M	Dead	No	R875, born in Missouri and is there at this time
435 Daniels, Dick	NCher	25	M	Dead	No	Blind
436 Daniels, Jennie	NCher	22	F	8112	No	
437 Dryhead, Lucinda	NCher	22	F	873	No	
438 Duck, Blaford	NCher	22	M	Dead	No	Farmer
439 Daughrity, Okohimunt	NCher	21	M	8176?	No	
440 Dahlahsiniy, Awa	NCher	29	M	Dead	No	
441 Daughrit, Dick	NCher	25	M	Dead	No	
442 Downing, Mulberry	NCher	21	M	6422	No	
443 Duck, Lucy	NCher	26	F	8836	No	
444 Davis, George	NCher	42	M	Dead	No	Farmer
445 Dry, Peter	NCher	59	M	Dead	Yes	Claims admission under the act of 1870
446 Duval, John	NCher	10	M		No	No census card number given, nor is he listed as dead (BLB)
447 Davis, W H	NCher	42	M	683	Yes	Farmer
448 Davis, E L D	NCher	34	F	683	Yes	
449 Davis, Lowry	NCher	9	M	7206	No	
450 Davis, Peny	NCher	6	M	6794	No	
451 Davis, Kinney	NCher	6	M	6847	No	
452 Davis, Mary	NCher	5	F	5900	No	
453 Davis, Eugene	NCher	3	M	6794	No	
454 Doublehead, Charlotte	NCher	65	F	Dead	Yes	Immigrant
455 Doublehead, Black B	NCher	30	M	7835	Yes	Farmer
456 Doublehead, Annie	NCher	24	F	Dead		
457 Doublehead, Addie	NCher	1	F	8152	No	
458 Doublehead, Peter	NCher	32	M	8205	Yes	Farmer
459 Doublehead, Wuttie	NCher	35	F	Dead	Yes	
460 Doublehead, Charlotte	NCher	6	F	8204	No	

Name	Race	Age	Sex	Census	Md	Remarks
461 Doublehead, Aggie	NCher	6m	F	8185	No	
462 Daughrity, Peggy	NCher	45	F	8840	No	
463 Duncan, Taylor	NCher	26	M	713	Yes	Farmer
464 Duncan, Liddy	NCher	21	F	713	Yes	
465 Duncan, Joseph	NCher	1	M	719	No	
466 Diver, Rose	NCher	70	F	Dead	No	Admitted 1866 Treaty
467 Downing, Whotleberry	NCher	52	M	Dead	Yes	Farmer
468 Downing, Polly	NCher	35	F	Dead	Yes	
469 Downing, Stand	NCher	12	M	Dead	No	
470 Downing, Thomas	NCher	8	M	8763	No	
471 Dearinwater, Walanketan	NCher	30	M	8855	Yes	Farmer
472 Dearinwater, Lucinda	NCher	28	F	8855	Yes	
473 Dearinwater, Cherokee	NCher	5	F	8856	No	
474 Dearinwater, Dick	NCher	3	M	8857	No	
475 Dearinwater, Wuttie	NCher	1	F	8858	No	
476 Dearinwater, Betty	NCher	70	F	Dead	Yes	
477 Daughrity, Nancy	NCher	46	F	Dead	Yes	
478 Daughrity, George	NCher	15	M	Dead	No	
479 Daughrity, Caty	NCher	11	F	Dead	No	
480 Duck, Jesse	NCher	38	M	8854	Yes	Farmer
481 Duck, Cely	NCher	24	F	Dead	Yes	
482 Duck, Jennie	NCher	1	F	8868	No	
483 Dannenberg, L L	NCher	27	M	558	Yes	Farmer
484 Dannenberg, M J	AWhite	27	F	558	Yes	
485 Dannenberg, W H	NCher	4	F	551	No	
486 Daniels, Sallie	NCher	50	F	8896	Yes	
487 Daniels, Longarm	NCher	13	M		No	No census card number given, nor is he listed as dead (BLB)
488 Daniels, Daniel	NCher	4	M	8876	No	
489 Dannenberg, J M	NCher	37	M	534	Yes	Merchant
490 Dannenberg, A E	AWhite	27	F	534	Yes	
491 Dannenberg, J L	NCher	9	M	549	No	
492 Dannenberg, L B	NCher	6	M	534	No	
493 Dannenberg, R C	NCher	3	M	534	No	
494 Doherity, H B	NCher	13	M	Dead	No	
495 Elis or Henson Pos	A Cher	24	M	712	No	On Dawes as Poss Henson (BLB)
496 Eli, Buck	NCher	22	M	Dead	Yes	Claims admission under the act of Nov 18, 1870, Farmer
497 Eli, Alie	NCher	22	F	8148	Yes	
498 Eli, Eli	NCher	1	M	7635	No	On Dawes as Taylor Eli (BLB)
499 Eli, Alice	NCher	43	F	Dead	No	
500 Eli, Annie	NCher	3	F	Dead	No	
501 Finly, George	AWhite	32	M	Dead	Yes	

Name	Race	Age	Sex	Census	Md	Remarks
502 Finly, Emma	NCher	20	F	6804	Yes	
503 Finly, Jennie	NCher	6	F	6802	No	
504 Finly, Thomas	NCher	5	M	7297	No	
505 Finly, Campbell	NCher	1	M	5811	No	
506 Frisley, Peggy	NCher	23	F	8593	No	Married to William Eagle
507 French, Linie	NCher	22	F	D1719	No	Dead
508 Frog, Selloat	NCher	26	M	9026	Yes	Farmer
509 Frog, Polly	NCher	26	F	Dead	Yes	
510 Frog, Louis	NCher	9	M	Dead	No	
511 Frog, Peggy	NCher	2	F	8964	No	
512 Frog, Jinny	NCher	1	F	8168	No	
513 Frisley, George	NCher	43	M	Dead	Yes	Farmer
514 Frisley, Mary	NCher	42	F	Dead	Yes	
515 Frisley, Sarah Jane	NCher	9	F	Dead	No	
516 Frisley, Magnolia	NCher	1	F	Dead	No	
517 Foster, Aki	NCher	12	F	Dead	No	
518 Foster, Charlotte	NCher	2	F	691	No	
519 Frisley, Sallie	NCher	65	F	8730	No	Immigrant Widow
520 Fletcher, Benjamin	NCher	21	M	544	Yes	Farmer
521 Fletcher, Harriett	NCher	19	F	544	Yes	
522 Feather, Tundi	A Cher	73	M	Dead	Yes	Farmer
523 Feather, Nancy	NCher	9	F	Dead	No	
524 Feather, Huetiyah	NCher	7	F	896	No	
525 Feather, Spade	NCher	5	M	Dead	No	
526 Feather, Jessie	NCher	42	M	7834	Yes	
527 Feather, Sallie	NCher	39	F	7640	Yes	
528 Feather, Eliza	NCher	12	F	7633	No	On Dawes as Eliza Bunch (BLB)
529 Feather, White	NCher	9	M	7639	No	
530 Feather, Nannie	NCher	7	F	729	No	On Dawes as Nannie Bird (BLB)
531 Feather, Creek	NCher	5	M	7635	No	On Dawes as Jennie Eli (BLB)
532 Feather, James	NCher	3	F	8182	No	
533 Feather, Arch	NCher	15	M	9011	No	Lives in Tahlequah Dist (On Dawes Roll as Arch Rabbit BLB)
534 Feather, Seale	NCher	21	M	8109	Yes	Farmer
535 Feather, Jennie	NCher	27	F	8109	Yes	
536 Feather, Lucy	NCher	3	F	8107	No	
537 Feather, Joseph	NCher	1	M	8209	No	
538 Feather, Sellout	NCher	32	M	Dead	Yes	
539 Feather, Susie	NCher	25	F	8172	Yes	
540 Feather, Cultie	NCher	10	F	8241	No	
541 Feather, David	NCher	6	M	8030	No	
542 Feather, McKee	NCher	1	M	Dead	No	

Name	Race	Age	Sex	Census	Md	Remarks
543 French, Naked	NCher	21	M	8096	Yes	Farmer
544 French, Lizzie	NCher	20	F		Yes	No census card listed, nor is she listed as dead (BLB)
545 Frog, North	NCher	25	M	8172	Yes	
546 Frog, Charlotte	NCher	26	F	8096	Yes	
547 French, Polly	NCher	30	F	D1721	Yes	
548 French, Whiteman	NCher	7	M	D1722	No	
549 French, Scott	NCher	5	M	D1723	No	
550 French, Annie	NCher	3	F	D1724	No	
551 Fulsom, Mary	NCher	36	F	819	Yes	
552 Fulsom, John	NCher	15	M	7153	No	
553 Fulsom, Edward	NCher	12	M	926	No	
554 Fulsom, Thomas	NCher	10	M	Dead	No	
555 Fulsom, William	NCher	7	M	Dead	No	
556 Fulsom, George	NCher	3m	M	Dead	No	
557 Freeman, B H	NCher	29	M	Dead	Yes	Farmer
558 Freeman, N L	NCher	23	F	813	Yes	
559 Freeman, W P	NCher	1	M	624	No	
560 Fields, Eliza	NCher	8	F	7453	No	
561 Foster, James	NCher	8	M	9279	No	
562 Fievkiller, Joseph	NCher	21	M	837	No	Farmer
563 Foster, Peter	NCher	10	M	913	No	
564 Greice, George	NCher	24	M	9105	Yes	Farmer
565 Greice, Wuttie	NCher	21	F	9105	Yes	
566 Greice, Isaac	NCher	7	M	8034	No	
567 Greice, Ollie	NCher	5	F	Dead	No	
568 Greice, Annie	NCher	2	F	Dead	No	
569 Gritts, Nancy	NCher	25	F	7683	No	Weaver
570 Gritts, William	NCher	3	M	9028	No	
571 Gitingdown, Chas	NCher	44	M	8264	Yes	Farmer
572 Gitingdown, Lucy	NCher	44	F	8264	Yes	
573 Gitingdown, Chas	NCher	15	M	8931	No	
574 Gitingdown, Jesse	NCher	9	M	8211	No	
575 Gitingdown, Annie	NCher	7	F	8187	No	
576 George, Nancy	NCher	80	F	Dead	Yes	Imigrant Widow
577 Garvin, Edward Robt	NCher	25	M	Dead	Yes	Farmer
578 Garvin, Peggy	NCher	20	F	Dead	Yes	
579 Garvin, Wilks	NCher	3	M	Dead	Yes	
580 Gunsalis, Delia	NCher	39	F	Dead	Yes	Surname should be Gonzales (BLB)
581 Gunsalis, Levi	NCher	9	M	Dead	No	
582 Gunsalis, Spencer	NCher	7	M	8165	No	
583 Gunsalis, Rachel	NCher	35	F	Dead	No	

Name	Race	Age	Sex	Census	Md	Remarks
584 Gunsalis, Ninnie	NCher	11	F	Dead	No	
585 Gunsalis, Luella	NCher	9	F	7605	No	
586 Gunsalis, Frank	NCher	7	M	2327	No	
587 Gunsalis, Anderson	NCher	3	M	938	No	
588 Gunsalis, Cale	NCher	2	M	939	No	
589 Glass, Easter	A Col	49	M	Dead	Yes	
590 Glass, William	NCher	33	M	776	Yes	
591 Glass, Cattawyn	NCher	30	F	776	Yes	
592 Glass, Julie	NCher	13	F	723	No	
593 Glass, Annie	NCher	10	F	762	No	
594 Glass, Lucy	NCher	8	F	724	No	
595 Glass, Wuttie	NCher	5	F	719	No	
596 Glass, Stephen	NCher	2	M	775	No	
597 Gott, William	NCher	39	M	645	Yes	Teacher
598 Gott, M L	NCher	23	F	645	Yes	
599 Gott, J W	NCher	1	M	6868	No	
500a Glory, Dick	NCher	46	M	Dead	Yes	Farmer
501a Glory, Martha	NCher	36	F	Dead	Yes	
502a Glory, George	NCher	11	M	Dead	No	
503a Glory, Jane	NCher	8	F	Dead	No	
504a Glory, Sarah	NCher	5	F	Dead	No	
505a Glory, Chas	NCher	1m	M		No	No census card number given, nor is he listed as dead (BLB)
506a Goback, Liddy	NCher	46	F	779	Yes	
507a Goback, Naked	NCher	15	M	1756	No	
508a Goss, J W	AWhite	32	M	828	Yes	Farmer
509a Goss, J B	NCher	40	F	828	Yes	
510a Goss, J E	NCher	8	F	549	No	
511a Goss, G O	NCher	5	M	829	No	
512a Goss, H O	NCher	3	M	822	No	
513a Guthrie, C P	AWhite	50	M	747	Yes	Mechanic
514a Guthrie, S A	NCher	44	F	Dead	Yes	Immigrant admitted Act of _____
515a Guthric, L P	NCher	18	M	6917	No	
516a Guthrie, C P	NCher	16	M	912	No	
517a Guthrie, W P	NCher	14	F	390	No	
518a Guthrie, Sarah	NCher	13	F	786	No	
519a Guthrie, W D	NCher	10	M	6104	No	
520a Guthrie, Florence	NCher	5	F	584	No	
521a Guthrie, Oscar	NCher	3	M	8207	No	
522a Glass, James	NCher	28	M	Dead	Yes	
523a Glass, Lucy	NCher	20	F	D1725	Yes	Dead
524a Glass, Tom	NCher	1	M	784	No	

The Flint District

Name	Race	Age	Sex	Census	Md	Remarks
525a Gott, Wat	NCher	21	M	2304	Yes	
526a Gott, J W	NCher	23	M	577	Yes	
527a Gott, Nellie	NCher	19	F	Dead	No	
528a Gritts, Susie	NCher	20	F	Dead	No	
529a Gritts, John	NCher	23	M	Dead	No	
530a Gritts,				D1726	No	
531a Grimit, William	NCher	21	M	8110	No	Farmer
532a Glass, Charlotte	NCher	25	F	D1727	No	Dead
533a Glass, Joe	NCher	21	M	F606	No	
534a Glass, Louis	NCher	25	M	D1728	No	
535a Glass, Joe	A Col	50	M	Dead	No	
536a Glass, Josh	NCher	25	M	9280	No	
537a Glass, Lung	NCher	30	M	Dead	No	
538a Glass, Sam	NCher	30	M	Dead	No	
539a Griffin, Loo	NCher	17	F	Dead	No	
540a Glass, Susie	NCher	50	F	Dead	Yes	
541a Glass, John	NCher	20	M	Dead	No	
542a Glass, John	NCher	70	M	Dead	Yes	Farmer
543a Glass, Justis	NCher	6	M		No	No census card number given, nor is he listed as dead (BLB)
544a Glass, Aron	NCher	1	M	Dead	No	
545a Godrick, John	NCher	5	M	1986	No	
546a Glenn, Martha					No	No census card number given, nor is she listed as dead (BLB)
547a Hopper, Martin	NCher	26	M	8839	Yes	Farmer
548a Hopper, Polly	NCher	20	F	8577	Yes	
549a Hopper, Ollie	NCher	3m	F	8731	No	
550a Harp, Sam	AWhite		M	1556	Yes	Farmer
551a Harp, Sarah	NCher		F	Dead	Yes	
552a Harp, Mary	NCher		F	1070	Yes	
553a Harp, Ellis	NCher		M	1577	Yes	
554a Harp, Maggie	NCher		F	1556	No	
555a Harp, Catie or Bull	NCher		F	775	No	
556a Henson, William	NCher	49	M	Dead	No	
557a Henson, Martha	NCher	45	F	Dead	No	
558a Henson, Chas	NCher	20	M	Dead	No	
559a Henson, Scott	NCher	19	M	Dead	No	
560a Henson, Dick	NCher	15	M	4285	No	
561a Henson, Powhattan	NCher	7	M	7341	No	
562a Holland, M J	NCher	18	M	1971	Yes	Farmer
563a Holland, M M	AWhite	19	F	Dead	Yes	
564a Hog, Sallie	NCher	27	F	8121	Yes	
565a Home, James	NCher	21	M	8953	No	

Name	Race	Age	Sex	Census	Md	Remarks
566a Holland, A B	NCher	21	M	Dead	No	Claims admittance under the act of 70
567a Holland, M A	NCher	18	F	530	No	
568a Horn, George	NCher	25	M	Dead	No	Admitted 1873
569a Horn, James	NCher	23	M	863	No	
570a Houseburg, John	NCher	33	M	9330	No	
571a Hooper, Jarah	NCher	21	F	Dead	No	
572a Hardbarger, John	NCher	36	M	8585	No	
573a Hunter, Wm P	A Cher	21	M	D1729	No	Dead
574a Head, Nellie	NCher	48	F	D1730	No	Dead
575a Head, Lizzie	NCher	21	F	Dead	No	
576a Harris, Nancy	NCher	80	F	Dead	Yes	
577a Holland, J W	AWhite	40	M	4774	Yes	Admitted 1873, Farmer
578a Holland, M E	A Cher	43	F	4774	Yes	Claims admittance under the act of 70
579a Holland, J A	A Cher	15	M	4870	No	Farmer
580a Holland, N S	A Cher	13	M	855	No	
581a Holland, M E	A Cher	10	F	4797	No	
582a Holland, Malvinel	NCher	9	F	4287?	No	
583a Holland, J A	NCher	7	M	5132	No	
584a Holland, L B	NCher	4	F	4775	No	
585a Holland, I J	NCher	2	F	5535	No	
586a Halcomb, Rachel	NCher	48	F	Dead	Yes	Widow
587a Halcomb, Elizabeth	NCher	11	F	Dead	No	
588a Holland, Pleasant	A Cher	29	M	230	Yes	Admitted with James Holland of G Snake, Farmer
589a Holland, Nancy	A Cher	27	F	230	Yes	
590a Holland, Caladonia	A Cher	8	F	Dead	No	
591a Holland, John	A Cher	5	M	706	No	
592a Holland, Alie	A Cher	3	F	437	No	
593a Holland, Pleas	A Cher	1	M	6870	No	
594a Hooper, Diyahlana	NCher	30	M	Dead	Yes	Farmer
595a Hooper, Lucy	NCher	20	F	8933	Yes	
596a Hooper, Aheoowa	NCher	5	M	8954	No	
597a Hooper, Jack	NCher	3	M	8955	No	
598a Hooper, Addie	NCher	1m	F	8558	No	
599a Hunt, John	A Cher	47	M	R249	Yes	Enrollment Refused, Farmer
600 Henson, Joseph	A Cher	25	M	Dead	Yes	
601 Henson, Jane	NCher	26	F	876	Yes	
602 Henson, Pruellia	NCher	5	F	Dead	No	
603 Henson, Nula	NCher	3	M	927	No	
604 Henson, Wm Mac	NCher	1w	M	D1731	No	
605 Hooper, Young S	A Cher	36	M	8486	No	

Name	Race	Age	Sex	Census	Md	Remarks
606 Hooper, Alcie	NCher	42	M	Dead	Yes	
607 Hooper, Jennie	NCher	7	M?	Dead	No	
608 Hooper, Stand	NCher	4	M	8099	No	Dead
609 Hooper, Bushyhead	NCher	1	M	7807	No	
610 Hooper,	NCher	36	M	Dead	Yes	Farmer
611 Hooper, Lucy	NCher	42	F	Dead	Yes	
612 Hooper, Fall B	NCher	7	M	Dead	No	
613 Hooper, Stay H	NCher	4	M	Dead	No	
614 Hooper, Wasting	NCher	1	M	D1732	No	Dead
615 Hand, William	NCher	26	M	Dead	Yes	Farmer
616 Hand, Lily	NCher	38	F	Dead	Yes	
617 Hand, Alley	NCher	11	F	8099	No	
618 Hunter, Lecie	NCher	35	F	8865	Yes	
619 Hunter, Dobber	NCher	7	M	Dead	No	
620 Howard, George	A Cher	38	M	2388	Yes	Farmer
621 Howard, Luvena	NCher	20	F	Dead	Yes	
622 Howard, Cicero	NCher	1	M	6120	No	
623 Head, Naked	NCher	46	M	Dead	Yes	Farmer
624 Head, Polly	NCher	60	F	Dead	Yes	
625 Head, Holland	NCher	19	M	867	No	
626 Head, Tom	NCher	16	M	8866	No	
627 Hummenstriker, Jennie	NCher	27	F	8559	No	
628 Hummenstriker, Mary	NCher	4	F	8864	No	
629 Henson, Thomas	A Cher	35	M	Dead	Yes	Claims admittance under the Act of Nov 18, 1870, Farmer
630 Henson, Mary	AWhite	32	F	Dead	Yes	
631 Henson, Alleck	NCher	15	M	Dead	No	
632 Henson, James	NCher	12	M	6465	No	
633 Henson, Jackson	NCher	11	M	Dead	No	
634 Henson, Artie	NCher	9	F	5152	No	
635 Henson, Josie	NCher	7	F	3734	No	
636 Henson, Terrel	NCher	5	M	1500	No	
637 Henson, Muskogee	NCher	4	M	1658	No	
638 Henson, Tennessee	NCher	3	F	7556	No	
639 Henson, Bondinot	NCher	3m	M	D1733	No	Dead
640 Henson, Margaret	NCher	70	F	Dead	Yes	Claims Admittance under Act of Nov 18, 1870
641 Hummenstriker, Mulberry	NCher	24	M	8852	Yes	Farmer
642 Hummenstriker, Sakie	NCher	20	F	8852	No	
643 Henson, William	A Cher	22	M	Dead	No	Claims admittance under the Act of Nov 18, 1870, but not at home
644 Hummenstriker, Liddy	NCher	18	F	864	No	
645 Hummenstriker, George	NCher	24	M	Dead	No	

Name	Race	Age	Sex	Census	Md	Remarks
646 Harris, Nancy	NCher	80	F	Dead	Yes	Widow
647 Hilderbrand, David	NCher	21	M	D1734		Teacher, Dead
648 Heron, Laura				5464	No	Dup 940 G Snake
649 Heron, John				D3116	No	Dup 941 G Snake
650 Heron, Rachel				6793	No	Dup 942 G Snake
651 Henson, John	A Cher	13	M	D1735	No	Ill Dist
652 Henson, Downing	A Cher	10	M	Dead	No	
653 Henson, George	A Cher	8	M	D1218	No	
654 Henson, Cale	NCher	7	M	Dead	No	
655 Henson, Alice	NCher	5	F	8	No	
656 Henson, Mary	NCher	1	F	D1221	No	
657 Ice, John	NCher	10	M	D1736	No	Dead
658 Jones, Reader	NCher	20	M	8201	Yes	Farmer
659 Jones, Rose	NCher	18	F	8201	Yes	
660 Jones, Sam	NCher	1	M	8734	No	
661 Johnson, S L	AWhite	32	M	522	Yes	Farmer
662 Johnson, M A	A Cher	26	F	522	Yes	Admitted with James Holland and Family Goingsnake Dist
663 Johnson, A R	NCher	4	M	669	No	
664 Johnson, W O	NCher	2	M	623	No	
665 Johnson, James	NCher	3m	M	522	No	
666 Johnson, Adaline	A Col	34	F	Dead	Yes	
667 Johnson, Nicie	A Col	17	F	F461	No	
668 Johnson, Andrew	A Col	4	M	F461	No	
669 Johnson, Walter	A Col	2	M	F403	No	
670 Jones, Polly	A Cher	25	F	Dead	Yes	Claims under the Act of Nov 18, 1870
671 Jones, Peggy	NCher	8	F	Dead	No	
672 Jones, Bettie	NCher	6	F	Dead	No	
673 Jones, Johnson	NCher	2	M	8148	No	
674 Jones, Stand A	NCher	1	M	Dead	No	
675 Jones, Allie	A Cher	55	F	Dead	No	
676 Jones, Mary	A Cher	16	F	Dead	No	
677 Jackson, Ancie	NCher	55	F	Dead	Yes	Immigrant, Widow
678 Jackson, Annie	NCher	8	F	8423	No	
679 Jones, Celia	A Cher	60	F	Dead	No	
680 Jones, Sallie	A Cher	14	F	8031	No	
681 Jones, Jinny	A Cher	11	F	8704	No	
682 Jones, Stout	A Cher	30	M	7592	Yes	Farmer
683 Jones, Margaret	NCher	22	F	7592	Yes	This family goes by Chair on the Dawes Roll (BLB)
684 Jones, Sammie	NCher	5	M	8157	No	
685 Jones, Johnson	NCher	3	M	7595	No	

Name	Race	Age	Sex	Census	Md	Remarks
686 Jones, Mandard	NCher	3m	M	Dead	No	
687 Johnson, Wm	NCher	24	M	6502	Yes	Farmer
688 Johnson, Lucy	NCher	20	F	6502	Yes	
689 Johnson, Chas	NCher	1w	M	6502	No	
690 Johnson, Lucy J	NCher	42	F	Dead	Yes	Teacher, Widow
700 Johnson, George	NCher	17	M	5557	No	
701 Johnson, Nannie	NCher	12	F	675*?	No	
702 Johnson, Susan	NCher	32	F	Dead	Yes	Weaver
703 Johnson, White	NCher	10		Dead	No	
704 Johnson, Annie	NCher	8	F	6494	No	
705 Johnson, Jane	NCher	7	F	899	No	
706 Johnson, John	NCher	2	M	697	No	
707 Justis, John	NCher	42	M	Dead	Yes	Farmer
708 Justis, Betsy	NCher	33	F	8936	Yes	
709 Justis, Arch	NCher	13	M	Dead	No	
710 Justis, John	NCher	9	M	8944	No	
711 Justis, Sally	NCher	7	F	Dead	No	
712 Justis, Lucy	NCher	2w	F	Dead	No	
713 Johnson, John W	AWhite	46	M	825	Yes	Farmer
714 Johnson, A A	A Cher	37	F	825	Yes	Admitted in 1873
715 Johnson, J T	A Cher	14	M	827	No	
716 Johnson, V E	A Cher	12	F	632	No	
717 Johnson, L A	A Cher	10	F	833	No	
718 Johnson, J A	A Cher	9	F	875	No	Blind
719 Johnson, J M	NCher	7	M	824	No	
720 John, John Long	NCher	60	M	Dead	Yes	Immigrant Act of _____, Farmer
721 Jones, Newton	A Cher	24	M	Dead	No	Claims under the Act of Nov 18, 1870
722 Jones, Coark	A Cher	21	M	Dead	No	
723 Johnson, John	A Col	23	M	FD1169	No	
724 Killwoman, John	NCher	23	M	8185	No	
725 Killwoman, Fog	NCher	70	M	Dead	Yes	
726 Killwoman, Bettie	NCher	50	F	Dead	Yes	
727 Killwoman, Layingby F	NCher	20	M	Dead	No	
728 Killwoman, Bigold	NCher	15	M	8260	No	
729 Killwoman, Bird	NCher	14	M	8240	No	
730 Killwoman, Young Bird	NCher	4	M	949	No	
731 Killwoman, Joanna	NCher	32	F	D1741	Yes	
732 Killwoman, Watlyah	NCher	3	F	8214?	No	Wife of Zeke Acorn
733 Killwoman, Mistress	NCher	1	F	D1743	No	
734 Keith, Polly	NCher	70	F	Dead	Yes	
735 Keith, Welanhite	NCher	53	M	Dead	Yes	Mechanic

Name	Race	Age	Sex	Census	Md	Remarks
736 Keith, Catie	NCher	42	F	707	Yes	
737 Keith, Jinny	NCher	8	F	Dead	No	
738 Keith, Sally	NCher	7	F	702	No	
739 Keith, Annie	NCher	5	F	708	No	
740 Keith, James	NCher	1	M	695	No	
741 Killer, Jackson	NCher	47	M	Dead	Yes	Farmer
742 Killer, Sallie	NCher	43	F	Dead	Yes	
743 Killer, Larin	NCher	12	M	9245	No	
744 Killer, Allis	NCher	11	F	8416	No	
745 Killer, Susie	NCher	8	F	Dead	No	
746 Killer, Lillie	NCher	6	F	Dead	No	
747 Killer, Bettie	NCher	4	F	8120	No	
748 Killahnigl, Peter	NCher	26	M	Dead	No	Farmer
749 Keys, Wm C	A Cher	20	M	Dead	Yes	Admitted in 1872
750 Keys, Fanny	AWhite	17	F	Dead	No	
751 Locus, Charles	NCher	23	M	Dead	Yes	Claims admittance under Act Nov 18, 1870, Farmer
752 Locust, Eli	NCher	24	F	Dead	Yes	
753 Locust, Sinagooyah	A Cher	52	M	Dead	Yes	Claims admittance under Act Nov 18, 1870, Farmer
754 Locust, Lucy	A Cher	43	F	Dead	Yes	
755 Locust, Molly	A Cher	17	F	Dead	No	
756 Locust, William	A Cher	15	M	Dead	No	
757 Locust, Getmoney	A Cher	13	M	Dead	No	
758 Locust, Walsie	A Cher	11	F	Dead	No	
759 Locust, Polly	A Cher	9	F	Dead	No	
760 Locust, Young Butcher	NCher	6	M	D1744	No	
761 Locust, Nah-hool	NCher	33	M	Dead	Yes	Farmer
762 Locust, Stand	NCher	9	M	881	No	
763 Locust, Jesse	A Cher	29	M	2171	Yes	Claims admittance under Act Nov 18, 1870, Farmer
764 Locust, Annie	NCher	28	F	Dead	Yes	
765 Locust, Wright	NCher	6	M	Dead	No	
766 Locust, Nancy	NCher	4	F	7624	No	
767 Locust, Aki	NCher	1	F	2175	No	
768 Locust, Maggie	NCher	36	F	Dead	Yes	Claims admittance under Act Nov 18, 1870
769 Locust, Lizi	NCher	7	F	8594	No	
770 Locust, Nancy	NCher	1	F	Dead	No	
780 Liver, Dorcas	NCher	70	F	Dead	Yes	
781 Liver, Chulo	NCher	39	M	7832	Yes	Farmer
782 Liver, Eliza	NCher	38	F	7832	Yes	
783 Liver, Susie	NCher	14	F	8159	No	
784 Liver, Tomson	NCher	13	M	1220	No	

The Flint District

Name	Race	Age	Sex	Census	Md	Remarks
785 Liver, Nancy	NCher	9	F	8156	No	
786 Liver, George	NCher	8	M	8835	No	
787 Liver, Jackson	NCher	6	M	8153	No	
788 Liver, Charlotte	NCher	5	F	8101	No	
789 Liver, Peggy	NCher	3	F	8157	No	
790 Liver, Jinny	NCher	1	F	8103	No	
791 Littlejohn, W N	AWhite	34	M	1017	Yes	Farmer
792 Littlejohn, Catherine	NCher	23	F	1017	Yes	
793 Littlejohn, J W	NCher	10	F	1158	No	
794 Littlejohns, C P	NCher	8	M	7255	No	
795 Littlejohns, N E	NCher	6	F	1069	No	
796 Littlejohns, M B	NCher	2	F	Dead	No	
797 Liver, John	NCher	20	M	485	Yes	Farmer
798 Liver, Lidda	NCher	20	F	485	Yes	
799 Locus, John	NCher	42	M	Dead	Yes	Mechanic, Claims admittance under Act Nov 18, 1870
800 Locus, Bettie	NCher	25	F	Dead	Yes	
801 Locus, Julia	NCher	13	F	Dead	No	
802 Locus, Seven Starr	NCher	21	M	10268	No	
803 Lemaster, John	AWhite	31	M	119	Yes	Farmer
804 Lemaster, Narcissa	NCher	24	F	119	Yes	
805 Lemaster, Joseph	NCher	8	M	92	No	
806 Lemaster, Edward	NCher	3	M	188	No	
807 Lemaster, William	NCher	6m	M	95	No	
808 Liver, Going Sleep	NCher	23	M	Dead	Yes	Farmer
809 Liver, Cohenah	NCher	28	F	Dead	Yes	
810 Liver, Dirt	NCher	10	M	Dead	No	
811 Liver, Luny	NCher	7	M	9301	No	On Dawes as Looney Goingtosleep (BLB)
812 Liver, Luly	NCher	2	M	Dead	No	Dead
813 Leach, Mary	NCher	31	F	8427	Yes	Widow
814 Leach, Lucy	NCher	8	F	Dead	No	
815 Leach, Ellen	NCher	5	F	8428	No	
816 Leach, Tookah	NCher	1	F	8236	No	Dead (her cousin, Sarah Leach claimed to he her she is at 885 Flint BLB)
817 Lynch, C L	NCher	36	M	760	Yes	Farmer
818 Lynch, N E	NCher	35	F	760	Yes	
819 Lynch, John B	NCher	11	M	858	No	
820 Lynch, Lizzie	NCher	9	F	808	No	
821 Lynch, Arley	NCher	6	F	576	No	
822 Lynch, Tonanie	NCher	4	M	Dead	No	
823 Lynch, Mary	NCher	1	F	Dead	No	

Name	Race	Age	Sex	Census	Md	Remarks
824 Locust, Martha	A Cher	24	F	1963	Yes	
825 Littlejohn, N B	AWhite	39	M	553	Yes	Merchant, Claims admittance under Act Nov 18, 1870
826 Littlejohn, N A	A Cher	28	F	553	Yes	
827 Littlejohn, S A	NCher	6	F	679	No	
828 Littlejohn, G M	NCher	4	F	818	No	
829 Littlejohn, E L	NCher	2	F	741	No	
830 Linn, Alexander	AWhite	38	M	Dead	Yes	Claims admittance under Act Nov 18, 1870
831 Linn, M W	A Cher	42	F	Dead		
832 Linn, Thomas	A Cher	20	M	6194		
833 Linn, C G W	A Cher	10	M	9203		
834 Linn, William	NCher	1	M	D1746		In Coo Dist
835 Locut, Fish	NCher	25	M	8307	No	Farmer
836 Love, William	NCher	12	M	Dead	No	
837 Liver, John	NCher	21	M	485		Duplicate 798
838 Liver, Lidda	NCher	20	F	485		Duplicate 799
839 Locus, Cla-yu-ki						Dup #11 Flint Dist (#12 Eliza Acorn? BLB)
840 Long, Allea	NCher	21	M	8897		
841 Muskrat, Dorcus	NCher	50	F	716	Yes	
842 Morris, G C	A Cher	21	M	Dead	No	Admitted 1867, Farmer
843 Mankiller, Arch	NCher	22	M	8229	No	
844 Morris, W E	A Cher	23	M	752	No	Admitted 1867
845 Morris, J H	A Cher	21	F	740	No	
846 Martin, Ham	AWhite	58	M	Dead	Yes	
847 Martin, Rebecca	A Cher	61	F	Dead	Yes	
848 Martin, Dille	A Cher	17	F	6260	No	
849 McKee, Wm J	A Cher	38	M	6390	Yes	Admitted 1867, Farmer
850 McKee, Addie E	A Cher	33	F	Dead	Yes	Admitted 1867
851 McKee, Molly M	A Cher	13	F	6704	No	Admitted 1867
852 McKee, Willie R	NCher	10	M	6706	No	
853 McKee, Florence	NCher	7	F	6628	No	
854 McKee, Joe Rasmus	NCher	4	M	6709	No	
855 McKee, Alfred	NCher	2	M	6908	No	
856 McClure, Ruth	NCher	19	F	640	No	Seamstress
857 McClure, Alice	NCher	14	F	537	No	
858 Miller, Wm H	NCher	33	M	5496	No	Farmer
859 Murphy, Arch	NCher	24	M	Dead	No	
860 McLemore, William	NCher	30	M	688	Yes	
861 McLemore, Eliza	NCher	25	F	688	No	
862 McLemore, Mary	NCher	4m	F	Dead	No	
863 Morris, Gideon	A Cher	88	M	Dead	Yes	Admitted 1867, Farmer

Name	Race	Age	Sex	Census	Md	Remarks
864 Morris, Rebecca	NCher	87	F	Dead	Yes	Admitted 1867
865 Morris, Pheobe	AWhite	45	F	582	No	Admitted 1867
866 Mankiller, Wm	NCher	22	M	8228	Yes	Farmer
867 Mankiller, Nancy	NCher	20	F	8228	Yes	
868 Mankiller, Wart	NCher	1	M	Dead	No	
869 Mankiller, Addie E	NCher	1w	F	Dead	No	
870 Mankiller, Lucy	NCher	60	F	Dead	Yes	Old Settler, Widow, Farmer
871 Mankiller, Eli	NCher	15	N	Dead	No	
872 Miller, M J	AWhite	41	F	Dead	Yes	
873 Morris, G W	A Cher	14	M	D1747	No	
873a Morris, E J	A Cher	17	F	Dead	No	
874 Morris, H N	A Cher	1w	M	4961	No	
875 Morris, T M	A Cher	22	M	5137	Yes	Admitted 1867, Farmer
876 Mankiller, Jake	A Cher	26	M	8200	Yes	Farmer
877 Mankiller, Polly	NCher	23	F	8229	Yes	
878 Murphy, Bigbullet	NCher	60	M	Dead	Yes	Mechanic
879 Murphy, Sallie	NCher	60	F	8561	Yes	Immigrant
880 Murphy, Betsy	NCher	15	F	8587	No	
881 Murphy, Lilie	NCher	13	F	Dead	No	
882 Murphy, Nietidahnl	NCher	6	M	8578	No	
883 Murphy, Nancy	NCher	30	F	Dead	No	Immigrant Widow
884 Murphy, Meducenial	NCher	7	M	Dead	No	
885 Murphy, Wattiyah	NCher	4	F	8236	No	
886 Mankiller, Anie	NCher	60	F	Dead	No	Old Settler, Widow,
887 Murphy, Lord	NCher	26	M	Dead	Yes	Mechanic
888 Murphy, Catie	NCher	24	F	928	Yes	
889 Murphy, Jennie	NCher	1	F	955	No	
890 McLemore, French	NCher	33	M	Dead	Yes	Farmer
891 McLemore, Julie	NCher	30	F	902	Yes	
892 McLemore, George	NCher	11	M	903	No	
893 McLemore, Mary	NCher	9	F	Dead	No	
894 McLemore, Samuel	NCher	6	M	8726	No	
895 McLemore, Tom	NCher	3	M	957	No	
896 McLemore, Sarah	NCher	1	F	8193	No	
897 McLemore, Robert	NCher	63	M	Dead	Yes	Immigrant, Farmer
898 McLemore, Polly	NCher	64	F	Dead	Yes	
899 Marshall, Sallie	NCher	31	F	8566	Yes	Weaver
900 Miller, Alfred	NCher	54	M	749	Yes	Old Settler, Farmer
901 Miller, Cornelious	NCher	20	M	878	No	
902 Miller, Silus	NCher	16	M	1373	No	On Dawes as Slias Miller (BLB)
903 Musrat, Nancy	NCher	25	F	8676	No	
904 Muskrat, Ellis	NCher	6	M	Dead	No	

Name	Race	Age	Sex	Census	Md	Remarks
905 Muskrat, William	NCher	1	M	Dead	No	
906 Muskrat, Chuckalele	NCher	21	M	8232	Yes	Farmer
907 Muskrat, Peggie	NCher	19	F	8232	Yes	
908 Muskrat, Catie	NCher	2	F	8287	No	
909 Muskrat, James	NCher	9m	M	1129	No	
910 Morris, Wilson	A Cher	59	M	Dead	Yes	
911 Morris, E E	AWhite	53	F	531	Yes	
912 Morris, L C	A Cher	13	M	753	No	
913 Morris, A C	NCher	9	F	Dead	No	
914 Morris, John	A Cher	30	M	7537	Yes	Admitted 1867, Farmer
915 Morris, Anie	NCher	30	F	Dead	Yes	
916 Morris, Gideon	NCher	7	M	1063	No	
917 Morris, Mary A	NCher	5	F	791	No	
918 Morris, Sallie	NCher	2	F	7537	No	
919 Mixwater, Mink	NCher	67	M	Dead	Yes	Immigrant readmitted with his family 1867, Farmer
920 Mixwater, Bettie	A Cher	38	F	Dead	Yes	
921 Mixwater, Sarah	A Cher	16	F	Dead	No	
922 Mixwater, Stand	A Cher	13	M	Dead	No	
923 Mixwater, Laura	A Cher	10	F	Dead	No	
924 Mixwater, George	NCher	8	M	8989	No	
925 Muskrat, David	NCher	33	M	7826	Yes	Farmer
926 Muskrat, Polly	NCher	33	F	7826	Yes	
927 Muskrat, Emie	NCher	12	F	Dead	No	
928 Muskrat, Peggy	NCher	8	F	8867	No	
929 Muskrat, John	NCher	6	M	8853	No	
930 Muskrat, Lecie	NCher	3	F	8253	No	
931 Mars, Ben	NCher	26	M	Dead	Yes	Farmer
932 Mars, Anie	NCher	22	F	Dead	Yes	
933 Mars, Charles	NCher	5	M	7465	No	
934 Mars, Polly	NCher	1	F	Dead	No	
935 Muskrat, Jennie	NCher	50	F	Dead		
936 Muskrat, Ross	NCher	19	M	Dead		
937 Merrell, Friday	NCher	24	M	Dead	Yes	Farmer
938 Merrell, Anie	NCher	23	F	Dead	Yes	
939 Miller, John	NCher	23	M	901	Yes	Farmer
940 Miller, Looreni	NCher	17	F	901	Yes	
941 Miller, Ida M	NCher	1m	F	561	No	
942 Newton, D R	AWhite	26	M	D1750	Yes	Dead, Farmer
943 Newton, Martha	NCher	21	F	D1751	Yes	Lives in G Snake, admitted, date forgotten. James Brown's daughter who had a terrible time getting time getting his claim

Name	Race	Age	Sex	Census	Md	Remarks
						through courts and council
944 Nofire, Charles	NCher	21	M	Dead	No	
945 Nakedhead, Gray	NCher	21	M	D1752	No	
946 Nelson, Wesley	NCher	22	M	1457	No	
947 Nofire, Jessie	NCher	24	M	Dead	Yes	
948 Nofire, Jane	NCher	22	F	8935	Yes	
949 Nofire, John	NCher	3	M	9023	No	
950 Nofire, Anie	NCher	5m	F	8932	No	
951 Nofire, Huetiyah	NCher	50	F	Dead	Yes	Immigrant Widow
952 Nofire, Stephen	NCher	5	M	Dead	No	
953 Nofire, Lucy	NCher	3	F	Dead	No	
954 Nofire, Robert	NCher	35	M	Dead	Yes	Farmer
955 Nofire, Anie	NCher	25	F	8294	Yes	Dead
956 Nofire, John	NCher	15	M	Dead	No	
957 Nofire, Cootiye	NCher	11	F	8583	No	
958 Nofire, Mary	NCher	6	F	Dead	No	
959 Nofire, Ground Squirrel	NCher	4	M	D1753	No	
960 Nofire, Josh	NCher	1	M	8027	No	
961 Nakedhead, Olie	NCher	48	F	Dead	Yes	Immigrant Widow
962 Nakedhead, Akire	NCher	12	F	Dead	No	
963 Nakedhead, Dennis	NCher	10	M	1325	No	
964 Nakedhead, Sallie	NCher	7	F	7805	No	
965 Nakedhead, Blair	NCher	3	M	Dead	No	
966 Nakedhead, James	NCher	25	M	7804	Yes	Farmer
967 Nakedhead, Anie	NCher	20	F	Dead	Yes	
968 Nely, Sallie	NCher	43	F	Dead	Yes	
969 Nely, Smith	NCher	18	M	768	No	
970 Neyahittah, John	NCher	30	M	Dead	Yes	Farmer
971 Neyahittah, Cotiye	NCher	30	F	8690	Yes	
972 Neyahittah, Standabout	NCher	12	M	Dead	No	
973 Neyahittah, Caniyah	NCher	6	F	8198	No	
974 Neyahittah, Clerk	NCher	1	M	8204	No	
975 Nakedhead, Jinie	NCher	21	F	D1754	No	In Del Dist
976 Nakedhead, Agie	NCher	2m	F	Dead	No	
977 Oatrun, Nancy	NCher	44	F	Dead	Yes	
978 Orterlifter, Andrew	NCher	25	M	8733	Yes	Mechanic
979 Orterlifter, Sisie	NCher	25	F	8733	No	Surname, Otterlifter (BLB)
980 Orterlifter, John	NCher	27	M	Dead	No	
981 Pettit, Mary	NCher	26	F	Dead	Yes	
982 Pettit, Malvinie	NCher	3	F	Dead	No	
983 Price, Annie	NCher	24	F	577	Yes	Her mother was admitted by Cher Council and she (Ann Price) is not

Name	Race	Age	Sex	Census	Md	Remarks
						reported _____ (Unable to read the last sentence BLB)
984 Price, M A	NCher	3	F	767	No	
985 Paden, B F	NCher	44	M	873	Yes	Farmer
986 Paden, T J	A Cher	25	M	5826	No	
987 Pheasant, Celia	NCher	23	F	8842	No	Seamstress
988 Pheasant, Phoebe	NCher	18	F	8844	No	Weaver
989 Price, M C	A Cher	22	F	6005	No	
990 Poorbear, Chas	NCher	58	M	Dead	Yes	Farmer
991 Poorbear, Lucy	NCher	40	F	D1757	Yes	Widow
992 Poorbear, Betsy	NCher	50	F	Dead	Yes	Widow, Farmer
993 Pheasant, Lecie	NCher	70	F	8841	Yes	Widow
994 Pritchet, Hiyan	NCher	39	F	8569	Yes	
995 Pritchet, Wuttie	NCher	15	F	8194	No	
996 Pritchet, Nellie	NCher	13	F	8570	No	
997 Pritchet, Sallie	NCher	41	F	Dead	Yes	Widow
998 Pritchet, Diana	NCher	15	F	Dead	No	
999 Pritchet, Wm	NCher	12	M	8593	No	Surname Eagle (BLB)
1000 Pritchet, Tom	NCher	9	M	691	No	Surname Ghorley (BLB)
1001 Petet, Nancy	NCher	46	F	*843?	Yes	Immigrant Widow (Can't read first census number BLB)
1002 Price, Joseph	A Cher	43	M	Dead	Yes	Admitted 1851 and claims ____, Farmer
1003 Price, S L	NCher	42	F	811	Yes	Admitted date forgotten
1004 Price, S F E	NCher	17	F	Dead	No	
1005 Price, J S	NCher	13	M	965	No	
1006 Price, J H	NCher	11	M	862	No	
1007 Price, M A	NCher	8	F	7331	No	
1008 Price, N E	NCher	1	F	966	No	
1009 Paden, A F T	NCher	33	M	542	Yes	Admitted 1857, Farmer
1010 Paden, M J	NCher	37	F	542	Yes	
1011 Paden, C E	NCher	13	F	502		
1012 Paden, J H	NCher	10	M	3970		
1013 Paden, Z T	NCher	8	M	676		
1014 Paden, G W	NCher	5	M	717		
1015 Paden, R E L	NCher	3	M	643		
1016 Paden, M E	NCher	3m	F	641		
1017 Patterson, Chas	AWhite	33	M	6531	Yes	Farmer
1018 Patterson, Caroline	NCher	33	F	Dead	Yes	
1019 Patterson, Anne	NCher	8	F	665		
1020 Patterson, Wm	NCher	6	M	856		
1021 Patterson, Lenard	NCher	4	M	7174		
1022 Patterson, John A	NCher	2	M	804		

Name	Race	Age	Sex	Census	Md	Remarks
1023 Patterson, Chas W	NCher	1	M	5564		
1024 Paden, Almira	NCher	62	F	Dead	Yes	Old Settler Readmitted 1857
1025 Paden, Louis	NCher	10	M	3963	No	
1026 Paden, Tommie	NCher	2	M	6987	No	
1027 Procter, Nelson	NCher	25	M	1123	Yes	Farmer
1028 Procter, Liddy	NCher	29	F	1123	Yes	
1029 Procter, Addie	NCher	1	F	8178	No	
1030 Procter, Jennie	NCher	54	F	Dead	Yes	
1031 Payne, I J	AWhite	27	M	Dead	Yes	Admitted with John Holland's family, 1872, Farmer
1032 Payne, S L	NCher	19	F	Dead	Yes	
1033 Payne, W P	NCher	1	M	5282	No	
1034 Poorbear, Hunter	NCher	31	M	8895	Yes	Farmer, on Dawes as Aggie Buffalofish (BLB)
1035 Poorbear, Agie	NCher	40	F	8895	Yes	Farmer, on Dawes as Hunter Buffalofish (BLB)
1036 Powell, Joseph	A Cher	26	M	1158		Admitted act of (Nov 18, 1870? BLB)
1036a Quinton, Louis	NCher	48	M	1142	Yes	Farmer
1037 Quinton, Lethie	NCher	35	F	1142	Yes	
1038 Quinton, Jeff	NCher	13	M	8271	No	
1039 Quinton, Mack	NCher	10	M	6116	No	
1040 Quinton, George	NCher	8	M	911	No	
1041 Quinton, David	NCher	6	M	1142	No	
1042 Quinton, Frank	NCher	4	M	8874	No	
1043 Quinton, Whealer	NCher	1m	M	Dead	No	
1044 Rinkle, John	NCher	50	M	Dead	Yes	Farmer
1045 Rat, Jinnie	NCher	24	F	D1758	Yes	Immigrant Widow, Lives in Tah Dist
1046 Rat, Ground Hog	NCher	32	M	Dead	Yes	Immigrant, Widower, Farmer
1047 Rat, John	NCher	50	M	Dead	Yes	Farmer
1048 Rat, Sallie	NCher	40	F	8707	Yes	
1049 Rat, John	NCher	12	M	Dead	No	
1050 Rat, Wart	NCher	6	M	Dead	No	
1051 Rat, White	NCher	4	M	9154	No	On Dawes as James Rat (BLB)
1052 Rat, Tobacco	NCher	4	M	8704	No	On Dawes as White Johnson (BLB)
1053 Rat, Addie	NCher	1m	F	7618	No	
1054 Rat, David	NCher	22	M	Dead	Yes	Farmer
1055 Rat, William	NCher	30	M	8699	Yes	On Dawes as Sallie (BLB)
1056 Rat, Chicoo	NCher	2	M	Dead	No	
1057 Rat, Wilie	NCher	4	F	898	No	On Dawes as William French (BLB)
1058 Rat, Ned	NCher	2w	M	Dead	No	
1059 Rainwater, Catherine	NCher	26	F	D1760	Yes	In Del Dist

Name	Race	Age	Sex	Census	Md	Remarks
1060 Rainwater, Lulie	NCher	4	F	D1761	No	
1061 Rainwater, Ned	NCher	2w	M	D1762	No	
1062 Rooster, Thomas	NCher	34	M	Dead	Yes	Farmer
1063 Rooster, Peggie	NCher	30	F	Dead	Yes	
1064 Rooster, James	NCher	12	M	8604	No	
1065 Rattler, Allen	A Cher	50	M	Dead	Yes	Claims admission under act of Nov 18, 1870, Farmer
1066 Rattler, Nicie	A Cher	25	F	Dead	Yes	
1067 Rattler, Wm T	NCher	6	M	Dead	No	
1068 Rattler, Jeff	NCher	2	M	9143	No	
1069 Rabbit, Peggy	NCher	18	F	D1763	Yes	
1070 Rabbit, White girl	NCher	3m	F	D1764	No	Now in Saline
1071 Rooster, Polly	NCher	30	F	Dead	Yes	
1072 Rooster, Julia	NCher	6	F	D1765	No	
1073 Rooster, Salie	NCher	4	F	2615	No	
1074 Rooster, Caroline	NCher	60	F	Dead	No	
1075 Rooster, Taylor	NCher	22	M	Dead	Yes	Farmer
1076 Rooster, Detaskaski	NCher	30	F	Dead		
1077 Rooster, Cayahe	NCher	4	F	8024	No	
1078 Rogers, Andrew	NCher	14	M	7542	No	Farmer
1079 Ross, Lucinda	NCher	32	F	816	No	
1080 Ross, Sam	NCher	9	M	6437	No	
1081 Ross, Rufus	NCher	8	M	5996	No	
1082 Ross, Elizabeth	NCher	7	F	903	No	
1083 Ross, John	NCher	5	M	6187	No	
1084 Ross, Penelope	NCher	3	F	815	No	
1085 Ross, William	NCher	1	M	8122	No	
1086 Ross, Albert	NCher	1	M	865	No	
1087 Rider, Leroy	NCher	24	M	Dead	Yes	Farmer
1088 Rider, Sallie	A Cher	18	F	D1766	No	Non citizen does not apply
1089 Russell, Wm	NCher	30	M	790	Yes	Farmer
1090 Russell, Lucy	NCher	40	F	790	Yes	
1091 Russell, Ethylin	NCher	6	F	6352	No	
1092 Russell, May	NCher	5	F	1353	No	
1093 Russell, James	NCher	3	M	6553	No	
1094 Russell, George	NCher	1	M	6489	No	
1095 Redbird, Lucinda	NCher	44	F	8846	No	Widow
1096 Ragsdale, Isaac	NCher	29	M	1253	Yes	Farmer
1097 Ragsdale, Jennie	NCher	25	F	1253	Yes	
1098 Ragsdale, George	NCher	5	M	1311	No	
1099 Ragsdale, E J	NCher	6m	F	6101	No	
1100 Ross, Lucy	NCher	60	F	Dead	Yes	Widow

Name	Race	Age	Sex	Census	Md	Remarks
1101 Roe, Liddy	NCher	46	F	8845	Yes	
1102 Roe, French	NCher	50	M	Dead	Yes	Farmer
1103 Roe, Waki	NCher	46	F	Dead	Yes	
1104 Roe, Eliza	NCher	6	F	D1767	No	
1105 Rily, George	NCher	23	M	D1268	No	Lives in G Snake Dist
1106 Redbird, Dollar	NCher	48	M	Dead		Ad A(ct) of C(ouncil)
1107 Step, Chas	NCher	21	M	778		Farmer
1108 Sanders, Burn	NCher	25	M	Dead		Mechanic
1109 Sanders, Naki	NCher	31	F	8568		
1110 Sanders, Lecie	NCher	23	F	8300		
1111 Sanders, Jane	NCher	21	F	8571		
1112 Sanders, Aki	NCher	20	F	8725		
1113 Soap, Caroline	NCher	21	F	8161		
1114 Shell, John	A Cher	61	M	Dead	Yes	Admitted 1867 by Act of Council
1115 Shell, Jiney	NCher	35	F	809	Yes	
1116 Shell, Rebecca	NCher	10	F	Dead	No	
1117 Shell, Sallie	NCher	7	F	817	No	
1118 Shell, Sand	NCher	4	M	8098	No	
1119 Shell, Stand	A Cher	39	M	Dead	Yes	Admitted 1867 by Act of Council, Mechanic
1120 Shell, Rachel	A Cher	38	F	Dead	Yes	
1121 Shell, Jay	NCher	7	F	8030	No	
1122 Stephens, Elijia	A Cher	30	M?	6135	Yes	Farmer
1123 Stephens, Mary	A Cher	22	F	Dead	Yes	
1124 Stephens, Loo	NCher	4	F	R876	No	Dead, Tah Dist
1125 Stephens, Levi	NCher	2	M	6454	No	
1126 Stephens, Elizabeth	NCher	7m	F	6709	No	
1127 Starr, Caleb	NCher	58	M	Dead	Yes	Old Settler Admitted A(ct) of C(ouncil), Farmer
1128 Starr, Lucinda	NCher	56	F	Dead	Yes	Immigrant
1129 Starr, Callie	NCher	11	F	Dead	No	
1130 Starr, Rachel	NCher	8	F	2651		Dup of #241 Rachel Byers
1131 Starr, Washington	NCher	18	M	1185	Yes	
1132 Starr, Nancy	NCher	19	F	Dead	Yes	
1133 Sawney, Columbus	NCher	23	M	694	Yes	Farmer
1134 Sawney, Callie	NCher	21	F	781	Yes	
1135 Sawney, Allen	NCher	2	M	925	No	On Dawes as Samuel Sawney (BLB)
1136 Sawney, Johnson	NCher	6m	M	8253	No	On Dawes As Wm Johnson Sawney (BLB)
1137 Sawney, Noname	NCher	45	M	560	Yes	Immigrant, Admitted A(ct) of C(ouncil), Farmer
1138 Sawney, Sallie	NCher	45	F	560	Yes	""
1139 Sawney, Jack	NCher	18	M	8159		Farmer

Name	Race	Age	Sex	Census	Md	Remarks
1140 Sawney, Nancy	NCher	11	F	Dead		
1141 Sawney, Alleck	NCher	10	M	699		
1142 Spears, Mattie	NCher	22	F	D1772	Yes	Lives in Tah Dist
1143 Spears, Bettie	NCher	1	F	D1773	No	
1144 Stand, Cahawk	NCher	28	F	D1774	No	
1145 Smith, Rose	NCher	21	F	693	No	
1146 Sanders, Tom	NCher	21	M	Dead	No	Farmer
1147 Scott, Cherokee	NCher	21	M	Dead	No	
1148 Stealer, Chas	NCher	21	M	Dead	No	
1149 Swimmer, Wm	NCher	21	M	8950	No	
1150 Sanders, Frank	NCher	21	M	1657	No	
1151 Sanders, Alcie	NCher	30	F	1023	No	
1152 Sanders, Lizzie	NCher	23	F	1008	No	Teacher
1153 Sanders, Chas	NCher	33	M	Dead	No	Farmer
1154 Skitt, Nicie	NCher	19	F	Dead	No	
1155 Sawney, Squirl	NCher	23	M	Dead	No	Farmer
1156 Sawney, Annie	NCher	19	F	Dead	no	
1157 Starr, S J	A Cher	22	M	640	No	Farmer
1158 Starr, Fannie	NCher	22	F	8124	No	
1159 Sharp, Fannie E	A Cher	24	F	143	No	
1160 Sam, Sallie	A Cher	21	F	8838	No	
1161 Saunders, L S	AWhite	50	M	518	Yes	
1162 Saunders, J F M	A Cher	15	M	Dead	No	
1163 Saunders, C L	A Cher	13	M	5059	No	
1164 Saunders, S L	NCher	10	M	6567	No	
1165 Simons, Alley	NCher	30	F	9095	No	
1166 Simons, Joe	NCher	10	M	Dead	No	
1167 Simons, Avie	NCher	8	F	8208	No	
1168 Simons, John	NCher	6	M	D1175	No	
1169 Simons, Bloom	NCher	4	M	Dead	No	
1170 Simons, Olie	NCher	1	F	789	No	
1171 Simons, Mattie	NCher	30	F		No	Timmon Wuttie not Mattie Simmons dup pg 360
1172 Scruggs, Samuel B	AWhite	27	M	Dead	Yes	Farmer
1173 Scruggs, R E	A Cher	24	F	4660	Yes	
1174 Scruggs, R F	NCher	7	F	Dead	No	
1175 Scruggs, M J	NCher	5	M	Dead	No	
1176 Scruggs, Red Cloud	NCher	2	M	4060	No	
1177 Scraper, Ollie	NCher	70	F	Dead	Yes	Admitted 1867, Farmer
1178 Scraper, Annie	NCher	8	F	Dead	No	
1179 Skitt, John	NCher	38	M	Dead	Yes	Farmer
1180 Skitt, Betsey	NCher	30	F	Dead	Yes	

Name	Race	Age	Sex	Census	Md	Remarks
1181 Skitt, Ike	NCher	10	M	8698	No	
1182 Skitt, Mary	NCher	8	F	Dead	No	
1183 Skitt, Annie	NCher	6	F	8575	No	
1184 Skitt, Arch	NCher	3	M	Dead	No	
1185 Skitt, Bushyhead	NCher	1	M	Dead	No	
1186 Simons, Johnson	NCher	35	M	467	Yes	Farmer
1187 Smith, Chas	NCher	35	M	628	Yes	
1188 Smith, Wuttie	NCher	26	F	Dead	Yes	
1189 Smith, Lucy	NCher	11	F	628	No	
1190 Smith, Wm	NCher	9	M	685	No	
1191 Smith, James	NCher	7	M	Dead	No	
1192 Smith, Daniel	NCher	4	M	626	No	
1193 Smith, Samuel	NCher	2	M	638	No	
1194 Smith, Lahtiye	NCher	70	F	Dead	Yes	
1195 Smith, Callet	NCher	14	F	692	No	On Dawes as Caroline Scott original surname Skitt (BLB)
1196 Stops, Pess	NCher	80	M	Dead	Yes	
1197 Stop, Tahki	NCher	30	F	8264	Yes	
1198 Stop, Raniyahah	NCher	3	F	8264	No	
1199 Stop, Vat	NCher	2w	M	Dead	No	
1200 Stephens, Henderson	AWhite	35	M	6606	Yes	
1201 Stephens, Elmira	NCher	23	F	6606	Yes	
1202 Stephens, Nancy	NCher	5	F	6609	No	
1203 Stephens, Henry	NCher	3	M	6771	No	
1204 Swimmer, Lidda	NCher	60	F	Dead	Yes	Immigrant
1205 Swimmer, Jinne	NCher	1	F	Dead	No	
1206 Sunday, Rachel	NCher	1	F	8318	No	
1207 Sanders, Jane	NCher	49	F	Dead	Yes	Old Settler Widow
1208 Sanders, Martha	NCher	28	F	7317	Yes	
1209 Sanders, Naki	NCher	1m	F	D1777	No	
1210 Sanders, Rachel	NCher	60	F	Dead	Yes	
1211 Sanders, Huly	NCher	33	M	8563	Yes	
1212 Sanders, Mary	NCher	31	F	8563	Yes	
1213 Sanders, George	NCher	8	M	8299	No	
1214 Sanders, John	NCher	6	M	8695	No	
1215 Sanders, Alexandrew	NCher	2	M	8582	No	
1216 Swimmer, Lizzie	NCher	19	F	D1776	Yes	
1217 Swimmer, Addie	NCher	1	F	10317	No	
1218 Sanders, Fields	NCher	22	M	8164	Yes	Farmer
1219 Sanders, Susie	NCher	26	F	Dead	Yes	
1220 Sanders, Ned	NCher	4	M	8183	No	
1221 Sanders, Dick	NCher	2	M	8579	No	

Name	Race	Age	Sex	Census	Md	Remarks
1222 Sanders, Nanie	NCher	2w	F	8573	No	
1223 Scott, Hianie	NCher	68	F	Dead	Yes	
1224 Scott, George	NCher	27	M	8728	Yes	
1225 Scott, Ellen	NCher	23	F	Dead	Yes	
1226 Scott, John	NCher	39	M	8727	Yes	Farmer
1227 Scott, Laura	NCher	31	F	8727	Yes	
1228 Scott, Caroline	NCher	12	F	Dead	No	
1229 Scott, Nanie	NCher	10	F	Dead	No	
1230 Scott, Bean	NCher	8	M	Dead	No	
1231 Sanders, Isaac	NCher	37	M	877	Yes	Farmer
1232 Sanders, Isabel	NCher	35	F	877	Yes	
1233 Sanders, Delila J	NCher	7	M?	Dead		
1234 Sanders, David	NCher	5	M	891		
1235 Sanders, Susie	NCher	3	F	895		
1236 Sanders, William	NCher	1m	M	877		On Dawes as Charles W Sanders (BLB)
1237 Stewart, Wm N	AWhite	35	M	7308	Yes	
1238 Stewart, Celina K	NCher	33	F	7308	Yes	
1239 Stewart, John H	NCher	7	M	5358	No	
1240 Stewart, Wm N	NCher	5	M	5359	No	
1241 Sixkiller, Sam	NCher	28	M	847	Yes	Farmer
1242 Sixkiller, Nancy	NCher	30	F	847	Yes	
1243 Sixkiller, Gafford	NCher	6	M	8249	No	
1244 Sixkiller, Arch	NCher	3	M	887	No	
1245 Sixkiller, Lynch	NCher	5m	M	847	No	
1246 Sixkiller, Walter	NCher	24	M	848	Yes	Farmer
1247 Sixkiller, Julia	NCher	22	F	848	Yes	
1248 Sixkiller, Josaphene	NCher	3	F	2838	No	
1249 Sixkiller, Charlotte	NCher	3	F	757	No	
1250 Sixkiller, Cherokee	NCher	2	F	Dead	No	
1251 Stealer, Jealous	NCher	70	M	Dead	Yes	Farmer
1252 Stealer, Bettie	NCher	52	F	8104	Yes	
1253 Sunshine, Peter	NCher	25	M	Dead	Yes	Farmer
1254 Sunshine, Ollie	NCher	20	F	8237	Yes	
1255 Sunshine, Bloom	NCher	2	M	Dead	No	
1256 Sunshine, Henry	NCher	2m	M	Dead	No	
1257 Sanders, Samuel	NCher	35	M	Dead	Yes	Farmer
1258 Sanders, Mary	NCher	30	F	1191	Yes	
1259 Sanders, Chas	NCher	5	M	Dead	No	
1260 Sanders, Sam	NCher	3	M	Dead	No	
1261 Sanders, Sidia B	NCher	1	F	1191	No	Sadie B Sanders on Dawes (BLB)
1262 Smith, Jack	NCher	30	M	Dead	Yes	Farmer

Name	Race	Age	Sex	Census	Md	Remarks
1263 Smith, Polly	NCher	30	F	Dead	Yes	
1264 Smith, John	NCher	16	M	8315	No	
1265 Smith, Susie	NCher	50	F	8314	No	
1266 Smith, Loo	NCher	8	F	8316	No	
1267 Sixkiller, Charlotte	NCher	53	F	Dead	Yes	
1268 Secoadi, Salie	NCher	34	F	Dead	Yes	
1269 Secoadi, Lucy	NCher	10	F	Dead		
1270 Secoadi, Cornellus	NCher	6	M	8281		
1271 Secoadi, Wm M	NCher	3m	M	Dead		
1272 Starr, C E	A Cher	25	M	846	Yes	Admitted 1868, Farmer
1273 Starr, Mayrine	NCher	26	F	Dead	Yes	
1274 Starr, George Ann	NCher	2	F	1242	No	
1275 Starr, Nat F	NCher	1m	M	846	Yes	Admitted 1867, Farmer
1276 Sharp, John	AWhite	27	M	3600	Yes	
1277 Sharp, Susie	NCher	22	F	8939	No	
1278 Sharp, Lilie C	NCher	5	F	1184	No	
1279 Sharp, Edward L	NCher	3	M	4025	No	
1280 Sharp, Richard	NCher	1	M	3600	No	
1281 Sam, Ezekiel	A Cher	50	M	Dead	Yes	Claims admission under Act of Council 1870
1282 Sam, Lucinda	A Cher	40	F	Dead	Yes	
1283 Sam, Alexandrew	A Cher	18	M	7623	No	
1284 Sam, Sulti-ki	A Cher	14	M	715	No	
1285 Sam, Martha	A Cher	12	F	Dead	No	
1286 Sam, Olie	A Cher	10	F	8611	No	
1287 Sam, Pheba	A Cher		F		No	Census card number, appears to be 746 (BLB)
1288 Soap, Betsy	NCher	55	F	Dead	Yes	
1289 Soap, Runabout	NCher	18	M	7605		Farmer
1290 Soap, Cawhena	NCher	13	F	8847	No	
1291 Soap, Nannie	NCher	20	F	8273	Yes	
1292 Soap, Addie	NCher	1	F	9285	No	
1293 Soap, Nick	NCher	42	M	8850	Yes	
1294 Soap, Nelie	NCher	41	F	8850	Yes	
1295 Soap, Johnson	NCher	1	M	8849	No	
1296 Soap, Jenie	NCher	59	F	943	Yes	Dead
1297 Soap, Cahtahna	NCher	10	F	8242	No	
1298 Soap, Bushyhead	NCher	2w	M	Dead	No	
1299 Sanders, Thomas	NCher	28	M	841	Yes	Farmer
1300 Sanders, Bettie	NCher	21	F	841	Yes	
1301 Sanders, Thomas	NCher	2	M	889	No	
1302 Sevenstarrs, Adam	NCher	25	M	Dead	Yes	Farmer
1303 Sevenstarrs, Cintha	NCher	20	F	7855	Yes	

Name	Race	Age	Sex	Census	Md	Remarks
1304 Starr, James	NCher	25	M	704	Yes	Mechanic
1305 Starr, Saphrony	NCher	19	F	704	Yes	
1306 Sartogah,	NCher	70	M	Dead	Yes	Mechanic
1307 Sartogah, Mrs.	NCher	70	F	Dead	No	
1308 Soap, Lom	NCher	9	M	8216	No	
1309 Skitt, Bird	NCher	32	M	Dead	Yes	Farmer
1310 Skitt, Taut	NCher	19	F	8697	Yes	
1311 Skitt, Lilie	NCher	5	F	Dead	No	
1312 Skitt, Lina	NCher	2	F	8149	No	
1313 Skitt, Sam	NCher	5m	M	8697	No	
1314 Starr, Leroy	NCher	57	M	725	Yes	Old Settler, Farmer
1315 Sawney, Eve	NCher	5	F	8256	No	
1316 Scott, Liver	NCher	50	M	Dead	Yes	Farmer
1317 Scott, Polly	NCher	48	F	586	Yes	
1318 Scott, Columbus	NCher	13	M	10388	No	
1319 Scott, Huck	NCher	10	M	507	No	
1320 Scott, Obediah	NCher	3	M	510	No	On Dawes as Daniel Scott (BLB)
1321 Scott, Peggy	NCher	1	F	589	No	
1322 Smith, Andrew	AWhite	72	M	Dead	Yes	Admitted 1850, Farmer
1323 Smith, Sallie	A Cher	56	F	532	Yes	
1324 Sanders, David	NCher	26	M	8215	Yes	Farmer
1325 Sanders, Eliza	NCher	22	F	8215	Yes	
1326 Sanders, Sallie	NCher	1	F	7809	No	
1327 Sawney, Bettey	NCher	20	F	780	Yes	Immigrant Widow
1328 Sawney, Lucy	NCher	1	F	8118	No	
1329 Starr, E E	A Cher	30	M	963	Yes	Admitted 1868
1330 Starr, M E	NCher	23	F	963	Yes	
1331 Starr, Chas M	NCher	23	M	6550	Yes	
1332 Starr, Mary	NCher	6	F	567	No	
1333 Starr, Peggy	NCher	3	F	1444	No	
1334 Starr, Sallie	NCher	1	F	963	No	On Dawes as Daisy Starr (BLB)
1335 Skitt, Hulsey	NCher	65	M	Dead	Yes	Old Setter, Widower Farmer
1336 Skitt, R B	NCher	10	M	Dead		At school
1337 Sevenstars, Adam	NCher	25	M	Dead		
1338 Sevenstars, Cintha	NCher	20	F	7855	No	
1339 Townsend, Mary	NCher	27	F	303	Yes	Widow
1340 Townsend, Sarah J	NCher	7	F	613	No	
1341 Townsend, Jerry	NCher	5	M	7001	No	
1342 Tulsy, John	NCher	48	M	Dead	Yes	Farmer
1343 Tulsy, Lecie	NCher	48	F	7547	Yes	
1344 Tulsy, Mary	NCher	7	F	Dead		
1345 Tulsy, Nancy	NCher	5	F	7455		

Name	Race	Age	Sex	Census	Md	Remarks
1346 Tulsy, John	NCher	1	M	7548		
1347 Teehee, James	NCher	28	M	2551	Yes	Admitted 1867, Farmer
1348 Teehee, Ela	A Cher	19	F	Dead	Yes	
1349 Teehee, Margra	NCher	63	F	2558	Yes	
1350 Thompson, R H F	AWhite	40	M	6571	Yes	Farmer
1351 Thompson, Narsissa	A Cher	33	F	6571	Yes	
1352 Thompson, J D	NCher	11	M	6022	No	
1353 Thompson, A M	NCher	7	M	Dead	No	
1354 Thompson, R H	NCher	6	M	6589	No	
1355 Thompson, H E	NCher	4	F	461	No	
1356 Thompson, J C	NCher	2	M	8814	No	
1357 Taylor, Richard	NCher	25	M	550	Yes	Farmer
1358 Taylor, M A	NCher	22	F	550	Yes	
1359 Tanksley, Eler	NCher	3	F	5285	No	
1360 Taylor, William	NCher	21	M	817	No	
1361 Teehee, Chas	NCher	21	M	6697	Yes	Farmer
1362 Teehee, Elizabeth	NCher	30	F	2549	No	
1363 Tulsy, Dicie	NCher	28	F	7546	No	
1364 Tulsy, Sallie	NCher	26	F	7628	No	
1365 Taylor, Peggy	NCher	64	F	554	Yes	
1366 Vann, Jessy	NCher	46	M	Dead	Yes	Immigrant admitted A o C, Mechanic
1367 Vann, Alice	NCher	30	F	777	Yes	
1368 Vann, Jinie	NCher	12	F	694		
1369 Vann, Minie	NCher	9	F	8259		lives in G Snake Dist
1370 Vann, Elis	NCher	6	M	8233		
1371 Vann, Dickey	NCher	5	M	D1781		
1372 Vann, Cency	NCher	3	M	D2972		On census card 1470 (BLB)
1373 Vann, Nancy	NCher	2	F	1470		
1374 Vann, Jessey	NCher	28	M	8431		Farmer
1375 Vann, Turtle	NCher	30	M	Dead		Farmer
1376 Vann, Chas	NCher	30	M	8548		
1377 Vann, Lucinda	NCher	60	F	Dead	Yes	Old Settler Widow
1378 Vann, Young W	NCher	23	M	8717	Yes	Farmer
1379 Vann, Nancy	NCher	29	F	8572	Yes	lives in G Snake Dist
1380 Vann, Kay	NCher	5m	M	8983	No	
1381 Vann, Allen	NCher	26	M	8719	Yes	Farmer
1382 Vann, Lucy	NCher	3	F	Dead		____, both claim the child
1383 Vann, Che-kah-nae	NCher	27	F	8431	Yes	
1384 Vann, Dirt T	NCher	29	M	8549	Yes	Farmer
1385 Vann, Sallie	NCher	26	F	8549	Yes	
1386 Vann, Mack	NCher	6	M	8709	No	

Name	Race	Age	Sex	Census	Md	Remarks
1387 Vann, White	NCher	6	M			No Dup #1387
1388 Vann, Catie	NCher	3	F	8560	No	
1389 Vann, Bushyhead	NCher	5m	M	8723	No	
1390 Vann, Loon	NCher	21	M	8149	Yes	Farmer
1391 Vann, Nanie	NCher	20	F	D1783	Yes	
1392 Vann, Julie	NCher	1	F	D1784	No	
1393 Ward, Mart	NCher	67	M	Dead	Yes	Old Settler, Farmer, claims to be guardian for Sarah and Alice McClure, they live back and forth with ____ (George W McClure? BLB) and Mart Ward____
1394 Ward, Sallie	NCher	62	F	Dead	Yes	Claims admission under the Act of Nov 18, 1870
1395 Water, Rain	NCher	30	M	Dead	No	Farmer
1396 Wayner, Rachel	A Cher	20	F	D1785	No	Dead
1397 Wolf, Polly	NCher	21	F	778		
1398 Walker, R W	AWhite	55	M	Dead	Yes	Farmer
1399 Walker, M J	A Cher	50	F	Dead	Yes	
1400 Walker, J L	NCher	15	M	833	No	
1401 Walker, W H	NCher	13	M	6758	No	
1402 Walker, C A	NCher	10	F	Dead	No	
1403 Walker, C C	NCher	8	F	5859	No	
1404 Welch, John E	A Cher	33	M	6879	Yes	Admitted 1867, Farmer
1405 Welch, E A	A Cher	26	M	D1786	No	Non citizen, does not apply married a man named Wright
1406 Welch, J D	NCher	6	M	6846	No	
1407 Welch, T G	NCher	5	M	2633	No	
1408 Welch, R L	NCher	3	M	5669	No	
1409 Welch, M E	NCher	6m	M	5667	No	
1410 Welch, Emly	AWhite	57	F	Dead	Yes	
1411 Welch, George	A Cher	20	M	797	No	
1412 Welch, A G	A Cher	30	M	796	Yes	Farmer
1413 Welch, Mira	NCher	29	F	Dead	Yes	
1414 Welch, Laura	NCher	6	F	932	No	
1415 Wayn, John	NCher	25	M	Dead	Yes	Farmer
1416 Wayn, Olie	NCher	21	F	Dead	Yes	
1417 Walker, Ground S	NCher	25	M	8713	Yes	Farmer
1418 Walker, Mary	NCher	22	F	8713	Yes	
1419 Walker, Eli	NCher	2	M	9021	No	
1420 Walker, Spring Frog	NCher	80	M	Dead	Yes	Mechanic
1421 Wicket, Susan	NCher	42	F	Dead	Yes	
1422 Wicket, Chas	NCher	9	M	8425	No	
1423 Wolf, Hawk	NCher	46	M	Dead	Yes	
1424 Wolf, Catey	NCher	40	F	459	Yes	

Name	Race	Age	Sex	Census	Md	Remarks
1425 Wolf, Lidie	NCher	14	F	8657	No	
1426 Wolf, William	NCher	12	M	Dead		
1427 Wolf, Louisie	NCher	3	F	456		
1428 Waterdown, Moses	NCher	65	M	Dead	Yes	Farmer
1429 Waterdown, Dian	NCher	65	F	Dead	Yes	Widow
1430 Waterdown, Leach	NCher	25	M	Dead	Yes	
1431 Waterdown, Mary	NCher	20	F	8595	Yes	
1432 Waterdown, Lynch	NCher	5	M	8594		
1433 Waterdown, Dry	NCher	3	M	Dead		
1434 Waterdown, Jinie	NCher	1	F	8574		
1435 Weaver, Betty	NCher	48	F	Dead	Yes	
1436 Weaver, Catayah	NCher	16	F	7834		
1437 Weaver, Wade	NCher	13	M	Dead	No	
1438 Weaver, Chiamorge	NCher	5	M		No	
1439 Weaver, Mary	NCher	2	F	Dead	No	
1440 Welch, Loo	NCher	18	F	D1787		
1441 Walker, Aki	NCher	33	F	8119	Yes	
1442 Walker, Ahyunki	NCher	11	M	D1789		
1443 Walker, Jinnie	NCher	9	F	D1790		Transferred to census Card #8028 (BLB)
1444 Walker, Nancy	NCher	6	F	8210		Transferred to census Card #8210 (BLB)
1445 Walker, Jackson	NCher	3	M	D1792		Transferred to census Card #6273 (BLB)
1446 Ward, Samuel	NCher	40	M	Dead	Yes	Farmer
1447 Ward, Sina E	NCher	30	F	Dead	Yes	
1448 Ward, Annie S	NCher	12	F	Dead	No	
1449 Ward, George M	NCher	5	M	Dead	No	
1450 Ward, Samuel H	NCher	1m	M	640	No	
1451 Williams, T A	AWhite	39	M	D1793	Yes	
1452 Williams, S J	NCher	2	F	7242		
1453 Washington, Geo	NCher	13	M	Dead		
1454 Ward, George	A Cher	36	M	D1794	Yes	
1455 Ward, Rachel L	AWhite	23	F	D1795	Yes	From 1455 to and including 1470 have left the Nation and live in Tennessee
1456 Ward, C E	A Cher	10	F	D1796		
1457 Ward, Loo	A Cher	8	F	D1797		
1458 Ward, Mat S	A Cher	7	F	D1798		
1459 Ward, Cordelia	A Cher	4	F	D1799		
1460 Ward, George	A Cher	1	M	D1800		
1461 Ward, Matilda	A Cher	46	F	D1801	Yes	
1462 Ward, Chas R	A Cher	33	M	D1802	Yes	Admitted by ___ courts, Farmer
1463 Ward, E J	A Cher	31	F	D1803	Yes	

Name	Race	Age	Sex	Census	Md	Remarks
1464 Ward, Mary E	A Cher	11	F	D1804		
1465 Ward, Martha E	A Cher	10	F	D1805		
1466 Ward, Loo A	A Cher	7	F	D1806		
1467 Ward, Mat C	A Cher	5	F	D1807		
1468 Ward, Eler J	A Cher	4	F	D1808		
1469 Ward, Chas	A Cher	3	M	D1809		
1470 White, Thomas	NCher	45	M	619	Yes	Emigrant
1471 White, Agie	NCher	35	F	619	Yes	
1472 Wicked, Maria	NCher	50	F	923		
1473 Young, Anie	NCher	50	F	Dead	Yes	Emigrant Widow
1474 Young, William	NCher	46	M	1055	Yes	Immigrant
1475 Young, Bettie	NCher	22	F	Dead		
1476 Young, Minnie	NCher	6	F	1898		
1477 Young, Ester	NCher	1	F	1055		

www.ingramcontent.com/pod-product-compliance
Ingram Content Group UK Ltd.
Pitfield, Milton Keynes, MK11 3LW, UK
UKHW051300180426
11947UKWH00020B/1828